Introduction to
LITERATURE
pearson custom library

PEARSON

Cover Art: Photography by Chris Beaudoin. "Arches," courtesy of Sharon Meredith/iStockphoto; "Garden," courtesy of Benne Ochs/Getty Images; "Classic Arch" courtesy of Photodisc/Getty Images.

Printed in the United States of America.

V092

Please visit our website at *www.pearsonlearningsolutions.com.*

Attention bookstores: For permission to return any unsold stock, contact us at *pe-uscustomreturns@pearson.com.*

Pearson Learning Solutions, 501 Boylston Street, Suite 900, Boston, MA 02116
A Pearson Education Company
www.pearsoned.com

ISBN 10: 1-269-04920-8
ISBN 13: 978-1-269-04920-7

Introduction to
LITERATURE
pearson custom library

Acknowledgements

A project as broad, far-reaching, challenging, and path-breaking as *The Pearson Custom Library: Introduction to Literature* could not be undertaken or accomplished without the support and participation of many colleagues. For their contributions, research, ideas, and suggestions, the editors particularly wish to thank David L.G. Arnold, University of Wisconsin, Stevens Point; Lydia M. Barovero, Providence College; Lisa Bickmore, Salt Lake City Community College; Claire Connolly, University of Wales–Cardiff; Allison Fernley, Salt Lake City Community College; Lisa Fluet, Boston College; Clint Gardner, Salt Lake City Community College; Curtis Gruenler, Hope College; Hilary Justice, Illinois State University; Martin Kevorkian, University of Texas, Austin; Lynn Kilpatrick, University of Utah; Susanne Liaw; Mark Lovely, Merrimack College; James J. Lu, California Baptist University; Sarah McKibben, University of Notre Dame; Cristanne Miller, University of Buffalo, The State University of New York; Jim Miracky, College of the Holy Cross; Bill Morgan, Illinois State University; Mark Morrison, Pennsylvania State University; John Mulrooney, College of the Holy Cross; Jamil Mustafa, Lewis University; Lisa Perdigao, Florida Institute of Technology; Jason Pickavance, Salt Lake City Community College; Robin Schulze, Pennsylvania State University; Mary Trotter, University of Wisconsin–Madison; Steve Vineberg, College of the Holy Cross; Helen Whall, College of the Holy Cross; Mario Pereira, Brown University; and Janice Wiggins.

Your *Introduction to Literature* purchase includes access to online resources designed to complement your readings. This Companion Website is located at the following URL:

http://www.pearsoncustom.com/dbintrolit/introlit/student

When prompted, enter the User Name: **ilstudent** and Password: **illearn**

(*Note:* The User Name and Password are case-sensitive, so be sure to use upper and lower case characters exactly as shown above.)

Once logged in, you will have access to the following resources:

Link Library. A collection of vetted web links organized by key terms and literary figures which offer you background and context for many of the selections you'll be reading.

The Writing Process. Advice that can aid you during the writing process. Included are guidelines and suggestions for each phase of writing, from start to finish.

Plagiarism. Suggestions to help you maintain academic honesty, with illustrative examples.

Grammar Guide. Spells out some of the rules and conventions of standard written English.

MLA Style. A brief guide to help you follow MLA style in citing your sources. The Modern Language Association style is widely used for papers in English composition, literature, and foreign languages.

We invite you to explore!

Table of Contents

Ernest Hemingway
[1899–1961]

ERNEST HEMINGWAY *was born in Oak Park, Illinois. His father was a devoted naturalist who shared his outdoor pursuits with his family during summers spent in rural Michigan. His mother was a professional-level musician, who followed the Victorian practice of dressing all toddlers in feminine clothing. This has fueled speculation regarding Hemingway's hatred of her; their problems stemmed more directly from their similar strong, artistic personalities. Although he is often accused of misogyny, most critics now say that he was questioning gender roles, and subtly critiquing their artificiality. In his writing, Hemingway displaced his sympathy for his female characters and his awe at their innate power onto the natural world.*

Hemingway first worked as a reporter for the Kansas City Star. *At the outbreak of World War I he volunteered for the ambulance service (he never served as a combatant with any army), was stationed in Italy, and was wounded at the front. During convalescence, he fell in love with his nurse, on whom he later modeled Catherine in* A Farewell to Arms *(1929). He returned to the United States a celebrity—the first American wounded in the war. After the war, he lived briefly in Chicago, where he met his first wife, Hadley Richardson, and the writer Sherwood Anderson, on whose advice the couple moved to Paris. There he met Gertrude Stein, who strongly influenced his early style, and F. Scott Fitzgerald. Still a journalist, he strove for literary publication, but a suitcase containing almost all of his work was randomly stolen. He overcame subsequent writer's block by deliberately crafting single sentences and paragraphs. Critics cite these efforts as the formation of his concise early style. These paragraphs became the "chapters" between short stories in his first major work,* In Our Time *(1925). He achieved early critical success with* The Sun Also Rises *(1926). Critics were stymied by his 1930s work, especially* Death in the Afternoon *(1931), an allegory for the conflict between aesthetics and capitalism, but disguised as a bullfighting encyclopedia. Critics celebrated his return to a form they understood with* For Whom the Bell Tolls *(1940), his greatest mature novel, set during the Spanish Civil War, (which he had covered in the 1930s, predicting the spread of fascism and the advent of World War II). After covering the war in Europe, he began several ambitious projects that occupied the rest of his life. Dismissed as a has-been in the reviews for* Across the River and Into the Trees *(1950), he stunned the world with* The Old Man and the Sea *(1952). This novel drew on his fear instilled by two near-fatal plane crashes, and it earned the Nobel Prize in 1954. He published no more literature in his lifetime; much work appeared posthumously, including* A Moveable Feast *(1964) and* The Garden of Eden *(1986).*

In the two plane crashes, Hemingway suffered severe internal injuries and a skull fracture, but it was weeks before he received adequate medical care. He sought interim pain management through alcohol; his drinking, which had never had any impact on his writing, became a spiraling problem. He came under government scrutiny for his uncanny perception of political and ideological trends, especially in Cuba, where he had lived since 1939. Always prone to depression, and finally unable to write due to memory loss exacerbated by electro-shock therapy, Hemingway ended his life with a shotgun in Idaho on July 2, 1961.

—Hillary Justice, *Illinois State University*

Hills Like White Elephants

ERNEST HEMINGWAY

THE HILLS ACROSS THE valley of the Ebro[1] were long and white. On this side there was no shade and no trees and the station was between two lines of rails in the sun. Close against the side of the station there was the warm shadow of the building and a curtain, made of strings of bamboo beads, hung across the open door into the bar, to keep out flies. The American and the girl with him sat at a table in the shade, outside the building. It was very hot and the express from Barcelona would come in forty minutes. It stopped at this junction for two minutes and went on to Madrid.

"What should we drink?" the girl asked. She had taken off her hat and put it on the table.

"It's pretty hot," the man said.

"Let's drink beer."

"Dos cervezas," the man said into the curtain.

"Big ones?" a woman asked from the doorway.

"Yes. Two big ones."

The woman brought two glasses of beer and two felt pads. She put the felt pads and the beer glasses on the table and looked at the man and the girl. The girl was looking off at the line of hills. They were white in the sun and the country was brown and dry.

"They look like white elephants," she said.

"I've never seen one," the man drank his beer.

"No, you wouldn't have."

"I might have," the man said. "Just because you say I wouldn't have doesn't prove anything."

The girl looked at the bead curtain. "They've painted something on it," she said. "What does it say?"

"Anis del Toro. It's a drink."

"Could we try it?"

---

[1] River in northern Spain.

Reprinted from *Men Without Women*, by permission of Simon & Schuster. Electronic permission courtesy of Simon & Schuster.

The man called "Listen" through the curtain. The woman came out from the bar.

"Four reales."[2]

"We want two Anis del Toro."

"With water?"

"Do you want it with water?"

"I don't know," the girl said. "Is it good with water?"

"It's all right."

"You want them with water?" asked the woman.

"Yes, with water."

"It tastes like licorice," the girl said and put the glass down.

"That's the way with everything."

"Yes," said the girl. "Everything tastes of licorice. Especially all the things you've waited so long for, like absinthe."

"Oh, cut it out."

"You started it," the girl said. "I was being amused. I was having a fine time."

"Well, let's try and have a fine time."

"All right. I was trying. I said the mountains looked like white elephants. Wasn't that bright?"

"That was bright."

"I wanted to try this new drink. That's all we do, isn't it—look at things and try new drinks?"

"I guess so."

The girl looked across at the hills.

"They're lovely hills," she said. "They don't really look like white elephants. I just meant the coloring of their skin through the trees."

"Should we have another drink?"

"All right."

The warm wind blew the bead curtain against the table.

"The beer's nice and cool," the man said.

"It's lovely," the girl said.

"It's really an awfully simple operation, Jig," the man said. "It's not really an operation at all."

The girl looked at the ground the table legs rested on.

"I know you wouldn't mind it, Jig. It's really not anything. It's just to let the air in."

The girl did not say anything.

------

[2]Spanish coins

"I'll go with you and I'll stay with you all the time. They just let the air in and then it's all perfectly natural."

"Then what will we do afterward?"

"We'll be fine afterward. Just like we were before."

"What makes you think so?"

"That's the only thing that bothers us. It's the only thing that's made us unhappy."

The girl looked at the bead curtain, put her hand out and took hold of two of the strings of beads.

"And you think then we'll be all right and be happy."

"I know we will. You don't have to be afraid. I've known lots of people that have done it."

"So have I," said the girl. "And afterward they were all so happy."

"Well," the man said, "if you don't want to you don't have to. I wouldn't have you do it if you didn't want to. But I know it's perfectly simple."

"And you really want to?"

"I think it's the best thing to do. But I don't want you to do it if you don't really want to."

"And if I do it you'll be happy and things will be like they were and you'll love me?"

"I love you now. You know I love you."

"I know. But if I do it, then it will be nice again if I say things are like white elephants, and you'll like it?"

"I'll love it. I love it now but I just can't think about it. You know how I get when I worry."

"If I do it you won't ever worry?"

"I won't worry about that because it's perfectly simple."

"Then I'll do it. Because I don't care about me."

"What do you mean?"

"I don't care about me."

"Well, I care about you."

"Oh, yes. But I don't care about me. And I'll do it and then everything will be fine."

"I don't want you to do it if you feel that way."

The girl stood up and walked to the end of the station. Across, on the other side, were fields of grain and trees along the banks of the Ebro. Far away, beyond the river, were mountains. The shadow of a cloud moved across the field of grain and she saw the river through the trees.

"And we could have all this," she said. "And we could have everything and every day we make it more impossible."

"What did you say?"

"I said we could have everything."

"We can have everything."

"No, we can't."

"We can have the whole world."

"No, we can't."

"We can go everywhere."

"No, we can't. It isn't ours any more."

"It's ours."

"No, it isn't. And once they take it away, you never get it back."

"But they haven't taken it away."

"We'll wait and see."

"Come on back in the shade," he said. "You mustn't feel that way."

"I don't feel any way," the girl said. "I just know things."

"I don't want you to do anything that you don't want to do—"

"Nor that isn't good for me," she said. "I know. Could we have another beer?"

"All right. But you've got to realize—"

"I realize," the girl said. "Can't we maybe stop talking?"

They sat down at the table and the girl looked across at the hills on the dry side of the valley and the man looked at her and at the table.

"You've got to realize," he said, "that I don't want you to do it if you don't want to. I'm perfectly willing to go through with it if it means anything to you."

"Doesn't it mean anything to you? We could get along."

"Of course it does. But I don't want anybody but you. I don't want any one else. And I know it's perfectly simple."

"Yes, you know it's perfectly simple."

"It's all right for you to say that, but I do know it."

"Would you do something for me now?"

"I'd do anything for you."

"Would you please please please please please please please stop talking?"

He did not say anything but looked at the bags against the wall of the station.

There were labels on them from all the hotels where they had spent nights.

"But I don't want you to," he said, "I don't care anything about it."

"I'll scream," the girl said.

The woman came out through the curtains with two glasses of beer and put them down on the damp felt pads. "The train comes in five minutes," she said.

"What did she say?" asked the girl.

"That the train is coming in five minutes."

The girl smiled brightly at the woman, to thank her.

"I'd better take the bags over to the other side of the station," the man said. She smiled at him.

"All right. Then come back and we'll finish the beer."

He picked up the two heavy bags and carried them around the station to the other tracks. He looked up the tracks but could not see the train. Coming back, he walked through the barroom, where people waiting for the train were drinking. He drank an Anis at the bar and looked at the people. They were all waiting reasonably for the train. He went out through the bead curtain. She was sitting at the table and smiled at him.

"Do you feel better?" he asked.

"I feel fine," she said. "There's nothing wrong with me. I feel fine."

[1927]

QUESTIONS

ERNEST HEMINGWAY, *Hills Like White Elephants*

1. What is the couple arguing about in the story? What specific lines best illustrate their positions in this argument in the first half of the story? In the second half?

2. Toward the beginning of the story, the narrator notes that, "the express from Barcelona was coming in forty minutes." Near the end of the story, the man translates the barmaid's announcement that "the train is coming in five minutes." The couple does not have thirty-five minutes' worth of conversation between these lines. Where, specifically, in the story, does time pass in silence? What must each character be thinking, privately, during each silence in order for the next dialogue to make sense?

3. Compare the description of the Ebro valley that begins the story with the one that occurs halfway through (when Jig moves to the end of the station). Draw a map of the story's setting, including as many details as you can find. How does Hemingway use setting to symbolize the couple's problem and to illustrate possible "solutions"?

4. Consider that this story was written in the 1920s and set in Spain, a Catholic country. How do those details complicate the balance of power in this relationship, especially given the specifics of the couple's current circumstances?

5. Hemingway is often considered a misogynist—a woman hater. What evidence can you find for this in the story? What evidence can you find in the story that contradicts it?

6. If there is no character change in a story, it is not a very good story. Consider Jig's attitude toward their situation throughout the story, and her attitude toward the American man. Identify any moments of change, however subtle. Then do the same for the American man's attitudes toward their situation and toward Jig. Who changes? When? How? Why?

7. The story follows the musical pattern of a "theme and variation." Everything that happens in the first half of the story also happens in the second half, but with slight alterations. Locate where in the story the "variation" half begins, list as many points of similarity as you can, and then describe the differences.

8. Many Hemingway stories involve a sporting conflict set in an arena—a matador engaging a bull in a bullring; a fisherman's epic battle with an

enormous fish encircled by the ocean's horizon. How does this story—which has nothing to do with sport—fit this pattern? What does this say about the larger stakes in the story? Does it elevate them to a universal, epic grandeur, or diminish them to the point of triviality? Or does the story support both readings?

9. What does the couple decide, either individually or together, to do at the end of the story?

11. Research the various options that have been historically available to women and couples who find themselves in similar situations to the one discussed in the story. Discuss how these options have evolved over the last hundred years, and then assess what elements of the couple's predicament remain unchanged despite changes in culture and technology.

12. Write about gender relations as you see them in your town, school, or social groups. How do men and women communicate, and how do they miscommunicate? Decide what, if anything, has changed since the 1920s.

13. Hemingway wrote this story on his honeymoon in 1927 and dedicated the manuscript to his Catholic bride, Pauline, who had just moved across the Atlantic to live with him in France. Write about how this biographical detail contributes to your understanding of the moment at which the man moves the suitcases in the story, and about how it might affect your conclusion regarding what the couple's final decision might be.

William Faulkner

[1897–1962]

Born in New Albany, Mississippi, WILLIAM CUTHBERT FALKNER *(The writer added the "u" to his name as a young man) moved with his family to Oxford, Mississippi in 1902, where his father worked as a livery stable owner, a hardware store owner, and finally as a business manager at the University of Mississippi. Although the presence of the university in this otherwise small, nondescript southern town likely influenced Faulkner's decision to become a writer, it is more probable that he looked to his paternal grandfather, William Clark Falkner (1825–1889), as a source of inspiration. A writer and a figure out of antebellum mythology, the Old Colonel, as the family referred to him, lead a life of almost cartoonish violence and bravado, stories of which filled the young Faulkner with wonder. With some modifications, this larger-than-life figure made his way into Faulkner's fiction as Colonel John Sartoris, a recurrent character in Faulkner's fiction.*

Faulkner's relationships with both his parents also enhanced and complicated his literary aspirations. While his mother was devoted to reading and culture, his father was immersed in the masculine world of horses, whisky, and physical violence. These parental influences are evident in a body of fiction that is both dizzyingly intellectual and insistently physical. Though he demonstrated early precociousness at school, he was drifting away by the eighth grade, and he never managed to take a degree at the local university. In 1918 he volunteered for and was rejected by the Army Air Corps because of his diminutive size. Not to be cheated out of the opportunity to relive the martial grandeur of his grandfather, he traveled to Toronto and enlisted in the RAF in July 1918, only to have World War I end before he could complete his training. He returned to Oxford in December of that year sporting an RAF captain's uniform, a phony limp, and a story about being shot down over enemy lines in France. Though no one in Oxford much believed him, he carried an obsession with World War I that stayed with him from his first novel, Soldier's Pay *(1926), through the late work* A Fable *(1954), both of which focus on the hollowness and hypocrisy that sometimes overshadow the heroics of war.*

Faulkner's literary career can be considered in terms of three phases. Throughout the early 1920s, Faulkner wrote a series of unsuccessful works—a collection of poetry titled the The Marble Faun *(1924) and the early novels* Soldier's Pay, Mosquitoes *(1927), and* Flags in the Dust *(published in 1929 as* Sartoris*). This period is also marked by transience and uncertainty, as Faulkner moved to New York, New Orleans, and back to Oxford. He studied briefly at the University of Mississippi, served for a time as the university's postmaster, and* *worked at odd jobs about the town of Oxford. Despite its flaws,* Flags in the Dust *represents Faulkner's first attempt to use the history of his family and his region as a source for his art. The novel therefore heralds the second, mature phase of his career. Faulkner gained critical acclaim with* The Sound and the Fury *(1929), the story of a disintegrating Southern family told through the modernist techniques of stream-of-consciousness narration and multiple, fragmented points of view. In 1930, the noteworthy Faulkner then became somewhat notorious with the publication of* Sanctuary, *a lurid potboiler about bootlegging, prostitution, and rape. In the same year, Faulkner completed yet another important novel,* As I Lay Dying. *Here again presented through the distracted comments of several narrators (including a purported lunatic, a traumatized young boy, and a delusional religious zealot), this harrowing tale treats a poor rural family who struggle to carry their dead mother to a cemetery many miles away. In this story, the language of the rural South becomes a kind of mythological poetry. This burst of creative activity launched the major period of Faulkner's career, eleven or twelve years that saw the publication of* Light in August *(1932),* Absalom, Absalom! *(1935),* The Unvanquished *(1938),* The Wild Palms *(1939), and* Go Down, Moses *(1942). During this time Faulkner also wrote short stories and worked in Hollywood as a screenwriter, an occupation he loathed. His near destitution would only begin to abate in 1948, when he was paid $50,000 by MGM for the film rights to his 1948 novel* Intruder in the Dust *and when, in 1949, he received the Nobel Prize for Literature. The third and final phase of Faulkner's career is characterized by a mellowing of his artistic vision, as is evident in his final novel,* The Rievers *(1962). In his later years, Faulkner assumed the role of "elder man of letters." He traveled to Japan as a kind of literary ambassador, served as a writer-in-residence at the University of Virginia, and addressed cadets at West Point, where his son-in-law had gone to school. He also weighed in on the racial controversies of the time, but his comments seemed to anger equally those on all sides of the debate. As he aged, Faulkner's health suffered from his heavy drinking and from several falls sustained while riding horses. It is suspected that one of these falls landed him in the hospital on July 5, 1962, where he died of a heart attack the next day.*

Critical reception of Faulkner's work ranged from prudish dismissal to adulation, but today he is widely regarded as the best American writer of the twentieth century. During the eighties and nineties many critics began to question this status, given the apparent racism and misogyny that color Faulkner's canon. This debate is ongoing, but what remains unimpeachable, besides the explosive beauty of his experiments with language and style, and with the form of the novel itself, is his quiet confidence in the perseverance of the human soul.

—David L. G. Arnold, *University of Wisconsin, Stevens Point*

A Rose for Emily

WILLIAM FAULKNER

I

WHEN MISS EMILY GRIERSON DIED, our whole town went to her funeral: the men through a sort of respectful affection for a fallen monument, the women mostly out of curiosity to see the inside of her house, which no one save an old manservant—a combined gardener and cook—had seen in at least ten years.

It was a big, squarish frame house that had once been white, decorated with cupolas and spires and scrolled balconies in the heavily lightsome style of the seventies, set on what had once been our most select street. But garages and cotton gins had encroached and obliterated even the august names of that neighborhood; only Miss Emily's house was left, lifting its stubborn and coquettish decay above the cotton wagons and the gasoline pumps—an eyesore among eyesores. And now Miss Emily had gone to join the representatives of those august names where they lay in the cedar-bemused cemetery among the ranked and anonymous graves of Union and Confederate soldiers who fell at the battle of Jefferson.

Alive, Miss Emily had been a tradition, a duty, and a care; a sort of hereditary obligation upon the town, dating from that day in 1894 when Colonel Sartoris, the mayor—he who fathered the edict that no Negro woman should appear on the streets without an apron—remitted her taxes, the dispensation dating from the death of her father on into perpetuity. Not that Miss Emily would have accepted charity. Colonel Sartoris invented an involved tale to the effect that Miss Emily's father had loaned money to the town, which the town, as a matter of business, preferred this way of repaying. Only a man of Colonel Sartoris' generation and thought could have invented it, and only a woman could have believed it.

When the next generation, with its more modern ideas, became mayors and aldermen, this arrangement created some little dissatisfaction. On the first of the year they mailed her a tax notice. February came, and there was no

---

Reprinted from *The Collected Short Stories of William Faulkner*, by permission of Lee Caplin.

reply. They wrote her a formal letter, asking her to call at the sheriff's office at her convenience. A week later the mayor wrote her himself, offering to call or to send his car for her, and received in reply a note on paper of an archaic shape, in a thin, flowing calligraphy in faded ink, to the effect that she no longer went out at all. The tax notice was also enclosed, without comment.

They called a special meeting of the Board of Aldermen. A deputation waited upon her, knocked at the door through which no visitor had passed since she ceased giving china-painting lessons eight or ten years earlier. They were admitted by the old Negro into a dim hall from which a staircase mounted into still more shadow. It smelled of dust and disuse—a close, dank smell. The Negro led them into the parlor. It was furnished in heavy, leather-covered furniture. When the Negro opened the blinds of one window, a faint dust rose sluggishly about their thighs, spinning with slow motes in the single sun-ray. On a tarnished gilt easel before the fireplace stood a crayon portrait of Miss Emily's father.

They rose when she entered—a small, fat woman in black, with a thin gold chain descending to her waist and vanishing into her belt, leaning on an ebony cane with a tarnished gold head. Her skeleton was small and spare; perhaps that was why what would have been merely plumpness in another was obesity in her. She looked bloated, like a body long submerged in motionless water, and of that pallid hue. Her eyes, lost in the fatty ridges of her face, looked like two small pieces of coal pressed into a lump of dough as they moved from one face to another while the visitors stated their errand.

She did not ask them to sit. She just stood in the door and listened quietly until the spokesman came to a stumbling halt. Then they could hear the invisible watch ticking at the end of the gold chain.

Her voice was dry and cold. "I have no taxes in Jefferson. Colonel Sartoris explained it to me. Perhaps one of you can gain access to the city records and satisfy yourselves."

"But we have. We are the city authorities, Miss Emily. Didn't you get a notice from the sheriff, signed by him?"

"I received a paper, yes," Miss Emily said. "Perhaps he considers himself the sheriff. . . . I have no taxes in Jefferson."

"But there is nothing on the books to show that, you see. We must go by the—"

"See Colonel Sartoris. I have no taxes in Jefferson."

"But, Miss Emily—"

"See Colonel Sartoris." (Colonel Sartoris had been dead almost ten years.) "I have no taxes in Jefferson. Tobe!" The Negro appeared. "Show these gentlemen out."

II

So she vanquished them, horse and foot, just as she had vanquished their fathers thirty years before about the smell. That was two years after her father's death and a short time after her sweetheart—the one we believed would marry her—had deserted her. After her father's death she went out very little; after her sweetheart went away, people hardly saw her at all. A few of the ladies had the temerity to call, but were not received, and the only sign of life about the place was the Negro man—a young man then—going in and out with a market basket.

"Just as if a man—any man—could keep a kitchen properly," the ladies said, so they were not surprised when the smell developed. It was another link between the gross, teeming world and the high and mighty Griersons.

A neighbor, a woman, complained to the mayor, Judge Stevens, eighty years old.

"But what will you have me do about it, madam?" he said.

"Why, send her word to stop it," the woman said. "Isn't there a law?"

"I'm sure that won't be necessary," Judge Stevens said. "It's probably just a snake or a rat that nigger of hers killed in the yard. I'll speak to him about it."

The next day he received two more complaints, one from a man who came in diffident deprecation. "We really must do something about it, Judge. I'd be the last one in the world to bother Miss Emily, but we've got to do something." That night the Board of Aldermen met—three graybeards and one younger man, a member of the rising generation.

"It's simple enough," he said. "Send her word to have her place cleaned up. Give her a certain time to do it in, and if she don't . . ."

"Dammit, sir," Judge Stevens said, "will you accuse a lady to her face of smelling bad?"

So the next night, after midnight, four men crossed Miss Emily's lawn and slunk about the house like burglars, sniffing along the base of the brickwork and at the cellar openings while one of them performed a regular sowing motion with his hand out of a sack slung from his shoulder. They broke open the cellar door and sprinkled lime there, and in all the outbuildings. As they recrossed the lawn, a window that had been dark was lighted and Miss Emily sat in it, the light behind her, and her upright torso motionless as that of an idol. They crept quietly across the lawn and into the shadow of the locusts that lined the street. After a week or two the smell went away.

That was when people had begun to feel sorry for her. People in our town remembering how old lady Wyatt, her great-aunt, had gone completely crazy at last, believed that the Griersons held themselves a little too high for what they really were. None of the young men were quite good enough for Miss Emily and such. We had long thought of them as a tableau: Miss Emily a slender figure in white in the background, her father a spraddled silhouette in the foreground, his back to her and clutching a horsewhip, the two of them framed by the backflung front door. So when she got to be thirty and was still single, we were not pleased exactly, but vindicated; even with insanity in the family she wouldn't have turned down all of her chances if they had really materialized.

When her father died, it got about that the house was all that was left to her; and in a way, people were glad. At last they could pity Miss Emily. Being left alone, and a pauper, she had become humanized. Now she too would know the old thrill and the old despair of a penny more or less.

The day after his death all the ladies prepared to call at the house and offer condolence and aid, as is our custom. Miss Emily met them at the door, dressed as usual and with no trace of grief on her face. She told them that her father was not dead. She did that for three days, with the ministers calling on her, and the doctors trying to persuade her to let them dispose of the body. Just as they were about to resort to law and force, she broke down, and they buried her father quickly.

We did not say she was crazy then. We believed she had to do that. We remembered all the young men her father had driven away, and we knew that with nothing left, she would have to cling to that which had robbed her, as people will.

III

She was sick for a long time. When we saw her again, her hair was cut short, making her look like a girl, with a vague resemblance to those angels in colored church windows—sort of tragic and serene.

The town had just let the contracts for paving the sidewalks, and in the summer after her father's death they began to work. The construction company came with niggers and mules and machinery, and a foreman named Homer Barron, a Yankee—a big, dark, ready man, with a big voice and eyes lighter than his face. The little boys would follow in groups to hear him cuss the niggers, and the niggers singing in time to the rise and fall of picks. Pretty soon he knew everybody in town. Whenever you heard a lot of laughing anywhere about the square, Homer Barron would be in the center of the group. Presently we began to see him and Miss Emily on Sunday afternoons driving in the yellow-wheeled buggy and the matched team of bays from the livery stable.

At first we were glad that Miss Emily would have an interest, because the ladies all said, "Of course a Grierson would not think seriously of a Northerner, a day laborer." But there were still others, older people, who said that even grief could not cause a real lady to forget *noblesse oblige*—without calling it *noblesse oblige*. They just said, "Poor Emily. Her kinsfolk should come to her." She had some kin in Alabama; but years ago her father had fallen out with them over the estate of old lady Wyatt, the crazy woman, and there was no communication between the two families. They had not even been represented at the funeral.

And as soon as the old people said, "Poor Emily," the whispering began. "Do you suppose it's really so?" they said to one another. "Of course it is. What else could . . ." This behind their hands; rustling of craned silk and satin behind jalousies closed upon the sun of Sunday afternoon as the thin, swift clop-clop-clop of the matched team passed: "Poor Emily."

She carried her head high enough—even when we believed that she was fallen. It was as if she demanded more than ever the recognition of her dignity as the last Grierson; as if it had wanted that touch of earthliness to reaffirm her imperviousness. Like when she bought the rat poison, the arsenic. That was over a year after they had begun to say "Poor Emily," and while the two female cousins were visiting her.

"I want some poison," she said to the druggist. She was over thirty then, still a slight woman, though thinner than usual, with cold, haughty black eyes in a face the flesh of which was strained across the temples and about the eye-sockets as you imagine a lighthouse-keeper's face ought to look. "I want some poison," she said.

"Yes, Miss Emily. What kind? For rats and such? I'd recom—"

"I want the best you have. I don't care what kind."

The druggist named several. "They'll kill anything up to an elephant. But what you want is—"

"Arsenic," Miss Emily said. "Is that a good one?"

"Is . . . arsenic? Yes ma'am. But what you want—"

"I want arsenic."

The druggist looked down at her. She looked back at him, erect, her face like a strained flag. "Why, of course," the druggist said. "If that's what you want. But the law requires you to tell what you are going to use it for."

Miss Emily just stared at him, her head tilted back in order to look him eye for eye, until he looked away and went and got the arsenic and wrapped it up. The Negro delivery boy brought her the package; the druggist didn't come back. When she opened the package at home there was written on the box, under the skull and bones: "For rats."

IV

So the next day we all said, "She will kill herself"; and we said it would be the best thing. When she had first begun to be seen with Homer Barron, we had said, "She will marry him." Then we said, "She will persuade him yet," because Homer himself had remarked—he liked men, and it was known that he drank with the younger men in the Elk's Club—that he was not a marrying man. Later we said, "Poor Emily," behind the jalousies as they passed on Sunday afternoon in the glittering buggy, Miss Emily with her head high and Homer Barron with his hat cocked and a cigar in his teeth, reins and whip in a yellow glove.

Then some of the ladies began to say that it was a disgrace to the town and a bad example to the young people. The men did not want to interfere, but at last the ladies forced the Baptist minister—Miss Emily's people were Episcopal—to call upon her. He would never divulge what happened during that interview, but he refused to go back again. The next Sunday they again drove about the streets and the following day the minister's wife wrote to Miss Emily's relations in Alabama.

So she had blood-kin under her roof again and we sat back to watch developments. At first nothing happened. Then we were sure that they had to be married. We learned that Miss Emily had been to the jeweler's and ordered a man's toilet set in silver, with the letters H.B. on each piece. Two days later we learned that she had bought a complete outfit of men's clothing, including a nightshirt, and we said "They are married." We were really glad. We were glad because the two female cousins were even more Grierson than Miss Emily had ever been.

So we were surprised when Homer Barron—the streets had been finished some time since—was gone. We were a little disappointed that there was not a public blowing-off, but we believed that he had gone on to prepare for Miss Emily's coming, or to give a chance to get rid of the cousins. (By that time it was a cabal, and we were all Miss Emily's allies to help circumvent the cousins.) Sure enough, after another week they departed. And, as we had expected all along, within three days Homer Barron was back in town. A neighbor saw the Negro man admit him at the kitchen door at dusk one evening.

And that was the last we saw of Homer Barron. And of Miss Emily for some time. The Negro man went in and out with the market basket, but the front door remained closed. Now and then we would see her at a window for a moment, as the men did that night when they sprinkled the lime, but for almost six months she did not appear on the streets. Then we knew that this was to be expected too; as if that quality of her father which had thwarted her woman's life so many times had been too virulent and too furious to die.

When we next saw Miss Emily, she had grown fat and her hair was turning gray. During the next few years it grew grayer and grayer until it attained an even pepper-and-salt iron-gray, when it ceased turning. Up to the day of her death at seventy-four it was still that vigorous iron-gray, like the hair of an active man.

From that time on her front door remained closed, save for a period of six or seven years, when she was about forty, during which she gave lessons in china-painting. She fitted up a studio in one of the downstairs rooms, where the daughters and granddaughters of Colonel Sartoris' contemporaries were sent to her with the same regularity and in the same spirit that they were sent on Sundays with a twenty-five cent piece for the collection plate. Meanwhile her taxes had been remitted.

Then the newer generation became the backbone and the spirit of the town, and the painting pupils grew up and fell away and did not send their children to her with boxes of color and tedious brushes and pictures cut from the ladies' magazines. The front door closed upon the last one and remained closed for good. When the town got free postal delivery Miss Emily alone refused to let them fasten the metal numbers above her door and attach a mailbox to it. She would not listen to them.

Daily, monthly, yearly we watched the Negro grow grayer and more stooped, going in and out with the market basket. Each December we sent her a tax notice, which would be returned by the post office a week later, unclaimed. Now and then we would see her in one of the downstairs windows—she had evidently shut up the top floor of the house—like the carven torso of an idol in a niche, looking or not looking at us, we could never tell which. Thus she passed from generation to generation—dear, inescapable, impervious, tranquil, and perverse.

And so she died. Fell ill in the house filled with dust and shadows, with only a doddering Negro man to wait on her. We did not even know she was sick; we had long since given up trying to get any information from the Negro. He talked to no one, probably not even to her, for his voice had grown harsh and rusty, as if from disuse.

She died in one of the downstairs rooms, in a heavy walnut bed with a curtain, her gray head propped on a pillow yellow and moldy with age and lack of sunlight.

V

The Negro met the first of the ladies at the front door and let them in, with their hushed, sibilant voices and their quick, curious glances, and then he disappeared. He walked right through the house and out the back and was not seen again.

The two female cousins came at once. They held the funeral on the second day, with the town coming to look at Miss Emily beneath a mass of bought flowers, with the crayon face of her father musing profoundly above the bier and the ladies sibilant and macabre; and the very old men—some in their brushed Confederate uniforms—on the porch and the lawn, talking of Miss Emily as if she had been a contemporary of theirs, believing that they had danced with her and courted her perhaps, confusing time with its mathematical progression, as the old do, to whom all the past is not a diminishing road, but, instead, a huge meadow which no winter ever quite touches, divided from them now by the narrow bottleneck of the most recent decade of years.

Already we knew that there was one room in the region above the stairs which no one had seen in forty years, and which would have to be forced. They waited until Miss Emily was decently in the ground before they opened it.

The violence of breaking down the door seemed to fill this room with pervading dust. A thin, acrid pall as of the tomb seemed to lie everywhere upon this room decked and furnished as for a bridal: upon the valance curtains of faded rose color, upon the rose-shaded lights, upon the dressing table, upon the delicate array of crystal and the man's toilet things backed with tarnished silver, silver so tarnished that the monogram was obscured. Among them lay a collar and tie, as if they had just been removed, which, lifted, left upon the surface a pale crescent in the dust. Upon a chair hung the suit, carefully folded; beneath it the two mute shoes and the discarded socks.

The man himself lay in the bed.

For a long while we just stood there, looking down at the profound and fleshless grin. The body had aparently once lain in the attitude of an embrace, but now the long sleep that outlasts love, that conquers even the grimace of love, had cuckolded him. What was left of him, rotted beneath what was left of the nightshirt, had become inextricable from the bed in which he lay; and upon him and upon the pillow beside him lay that even coating of the patient and biding dust.

Then we noticed that in the second pillow was the indentation of a head. One of us lifted something from it, and leaning forward, that faint and invisible dust dry and acrid in the nostrils, we saw a long strand of iron-gray hair.

[1930]

19

QUESTIONS

1. Describe your experience of reading "A Rose for Emily." What portions of the story do you find intriguing, surprising, or unsettling?

2. How does Faulkner use the tactic of suspense and surprise to captivate the reader?

3. Who narrates this story? Why is this figure's perspective important in the understanding we gain of Emily Grierson?

4. Describe Emily's relationship with her father. How is this important in our attempt to understand Emily's character?

5. How does the narrator describe Emily's house and neighborhood? How is this description important in our attempt to understand Emily's character?

6. Describe Homer Barron. How does his character and the relationship he develops with Emily help us understand Emily's character?

7. In what sense does the notion that Emily has been sleeping beside a corpse suggest a critique of the South on Faulkner's part?

8. Research and compose an interpretive essay about Faulkner's participation in the literary Gothic. What are the basic conventions of Gothic literature? What are some of its cultural, philosophical, and even political implications? How does Faulkner interpret Gothic traditions in "A Rose for Emily"?

Flannery O'Connor
[1925–1964]

Born an only child in Savannah, Georgia, FLANNERY O'CONNOR moved with her parents to a farm near Milledgeville, Georgia, at age twelve. Her father died of lupus, a disease of the immune system, when O'Connor was fifteen; O'Connor herself succumbed to the disease at age thirty-nine. An intellectual in a rural environment, she quickly began to see the world as sometimes annoying, but often amusing. O'Connor graduated from Georgia State College of Women in 1945, where she was a cartoonist for the student newspaper. Many of her stories draw characters in cartoonish ways, a whimsical, and sometimes slightly cruel, way of seeing humanity. O'Connor went on to the University of Iowa, where she received her Masters of Fine Arts in 1947. It was at the University of Iowa where she published her first short story, "The Geranium," in Accent (1946). She went on to an artist's residency at Yaddo in Saratoga Springs, New York, where she developed the professional friendships that were to sustain her throughout her artistic life. Though she returned to the family farm permanently due to her health, she continued to correspond with her artistic colleagues. Her correspondence was collected and published in 1979 as Letters of Flannery O'Connor: The Habit of Being.

O'Connor wrote constantly throughout her short life, producing two novels and numerous short stories that have amused readers for the last forty years. Her novels, Wise Blood (1952) and The Violent Bear It Away (1960), present a world where grotesque characters search for meaning, almost without awareness of their own searches. Critics found the novels somewhat perplexing and gave mixed reviews, but the critical reaction to O'Connor's short stories, collected in A Good Man Is Hard to Find (1955) and Everything That Rises Must Converge (1965), has been consistent and positive throughout the years. There are two important things to know about O'Connor, without which none of her work can be adequately understood: she was a devout Catholic and a southerner. The stories portray the southern qualities much more obviously than they do the Catholicism, but the human search for grace and forgiveness is an important theme throughout her writing. O'Connor depicted the rural south in comic strokes that sometimes bordered on cruel, such as in her description of the idiot blue-eyed cooing daughter of the old farm woman in "A Good Man Is Hard to Find," and the young Bible salesman in "Good Country People" with hair like brown gravy rolling down his head. In a later story, "Revelation," a young college-educated woman hits a pious farm woman with a large human psychology book *for mouthing meaningless platitudes. The scene is one of O'Connor's best, but it also demonstrates why some readers find her offensive. Her characters may seem to be on the road to destruction, but O'Connor presents them through her own particular aesthetic, revealing their humanity, and their search for wholeness.*

A Good Man Is Hard to Find

FLANNERY O'CONNOR

THE GRANDMOTHER DIDN'T WANT to go to Florida. She wanted to visit some of her connections in east Tennessee and she was seizing every chance to change Bailey's mind. Bailey was the son she lived with, her only boy. He was sitting on the edge of his chair at the table, bent over the orange sports section of the *Journal*. "Now look here, Bailey," she said, "see here, read this," and she stood with one hand on her thin hip and the other rattling the newspaper at his bald head. "Here this fellow that calls himself The Misfit is aloose from the Federal Pen and headed toward Florida and you read here what it says he did to these people. Just you read it. I wouldn't take my children in any direction with the criminal like that aloose in it. I couldn't answer to my conscience if I did."

Bailey didn't look up from his reading so she wheeled around then and faced the children's mother; a young woman in slacks, whose face was as broad and innocent as a cabbage and was tied around with a green headkerchief that had two points on the top like rabbit's ears. She was sitting on the sofa, feeding the baby his apricots out of a jar. "The children have been to Florida before," the old lady said. "You all ought to take them somewhere else for a change so they would see different parts of the world and be broad. They never have been to east Tennessee."

The children's mother didn't seem to hear her, but the eight-year-old boy, John Wesley, a stocky child with glasses, said, "If you don't want to go to Florida, why dontcha stay at home?" He and the little girl, June Star, were reading the funny papers on the floor.

"She wouldn't stay at home to be queen for a day," June Star said without raising her yellow head.

"Yes, and what would you do if this fellow, The Misfit, caught you?" the grandmother asked.

"I'd smack his face," John Wesley said.

"She wouldn't stay at home for a million bucks," June Star said. "Afraid she'd miss something. She has to go everywhere we go."

"All right, Miss," the grandmother said. "Just remember that the next time you want me to curl your hair."

June Star said her hair was naturally curly.

The next morning the grandmother was the first one in the car, ready to go. She had her big black valise that looked like the head of a hippopotamus in one corner, and underneath it she was hiding a basket with Pitty Sing, the cat, in it. She didn't intend for the cat to be left alone in the house for three days because he would miss her too much and she was afraid he might brush against one of the gas burners and accidentally asphyxiate himself. Her son Bailey didn't like to arrive at a motel with a cat.

She sat in the middle of the back seat with John Wesley and June Star on either side of her. Bailey and the children's mother and the baby sat in the front and they left Atlanta at eight forty-five with the mileage on the car at 55890. The grandmother wrote this down because she thought it would be interesting to say how many miles they had been when they got back. It took them twenty minutes to reach the outskirts of the city.

The old lady settled herself comfortably, removing her white cotton gloves and putting them up with her purse on the shelf in front of the back window. The children's mother still had on slacks and still had her head tied up in a green kerchief, but the grandmother had on a navy blue straw sailor hat with a bunch of white violets on the brim and a navy blue dress with a small white dot in the print. Her collar and cuffs were white organdy trimmed with lace and at her neckline she had pinned a purple spray of cloth violets containing a sachet. In case of an accident, anyone seeing her dead on the highway would know at once that she was a lady.

She said she thought it was going to be a good day for driving, neither too hot nor too cold, and she cautioned Bailey that the speed limit was fifty-five miles an hour and that the patrolmen hid themselves behind billboards and small clumps of trees and sped out after you before you had a chance to slow down. She pointed out interesting details of the scenery: Stone Mountain; the blue granite that in some places came up to both sides of the highway; the brilliant red clay banks slightly streaked with purple; and the various crops that made rows of green lace-work on the ground. The trees were full of silverwhite sunlights and the meanest of them sparkled. The children were reading comic magazines and their mother had gone back to sleep.

"Let's go through Georgia fast so we don't have to look at it much," John Wesley said.

"If I were a little boy," said the grandmother, "I wouldn't talk about my native state that way. Tennessee has the mountains and Georgia has the hills."

"Tennessee is just a hillbilly dumping ground," John Wesley said, "and Georgia is a lousy state too."

"You said it," June Star said.

"In my time," said the grandmother, folding her thin veined fingers, "children were more respectful of their native states and their parents and everything else. People did right then. Oh look at the cute little pickaninny!" she said and pointed to a Negro child standing in the door of a shack. "Wouldn't that make a picture now?" she asked and they all turned and looked at the little Negro out of the back window. He waved.

"He didn't have any britches on," June Star said.

"He probably didn't have any," the grandmother explained. "Little niggers in the country don't have things like we do. If I could paint, I'd paint that picture," she said.

The children exchanged comic books.

The grandmother offered to hold the baby and the children's mother passed him over the front seat to her. She set him on her knee and bounced him and told him about the things they were passing. She rolled her eyes and screwed up her mouth and stuck her leathery thin face into his smooth bland one. Occasionally he gave her a faraway smile. They passed a large cotton field with five or six graves fenced in the middle of it, like a small island. "Look at the graveyard!" the grandmother said, pointing it out. "That was the old family burying ground. That belonged to the plantation."

"Where's the plantation?" John Wesley asked.

"Gone With the Wind," said the grandmother. "Ha. Ha."

When the children finished all the comic books they had brought, they opened the lunch and ate it. The grandmother ate a peanut butter sandwich and an olive and would not let the children throw the box and the paper napkins out the window. When there was nothing else to do they played a game by choosing a cloud and making the other two guess what shape it suggested. John Wesley took one the shape of a cow and June Star guessed a cow and John Wesley said, no, an automobile, and June Star said he didn't play fair, and they began to slap each other over the grandmother.

The grandmother said she would tell them a story if they would keep quiet. When she told a story, she rolled her eyes and waved her head and was very dramatic. She said once when she was a maiden lady she had been courted by a Mr. Edgar Atkins Teagarden from Jasper, Georgia. She said he was a very good-looking man and a gentleman and that he brought her a watermelon every Saturday afternoon with his initials cut in it, E.A.T. Well, one Saturday, she said, Mr. Teagarden brought the watermelon and there was nobody at home and he left it on the front porch and returned in his buggy to Jasper, but she never got the watermelon, she said, because a nigger boy ate it when he saw the initials, E.A.T.! This story tickled John Wesley's funny bone and he giggled and giggled but June Star didn't think it was any good. She said she wouldn't marry a man that just brought her a watermelon on Saturday.

The grandmother said she would have done well to marry Mr. Teagarden because he was a gentleman and had bought Coca-Cola stock when it first came out and that he had died only a few years ago, a very wealthy man.

They stopped at The Tower for barbecued sandwiches. The Tower was a part-stucco and part-wood filling station and dance hall set in a clearing outside of Timothy. A fat man named Red Sammy Butts ran it and there were signs stuck here and there on the building and for miles up and down the highway saying, TRY RED SAMMY'S FAMOUS BARBECUE. NONE LIKE FAMOUS RED SAMMY'S! RED SAM! THE FAT BOY WITH THE HAPPY LAUGH. A VETERAN! RED SAMMY'S YOUR MAN!

Red Sammy was lying on the bare ground outside The Tower with his head under a truck while a gray monkey about a foot high, chained to a small chinaberry tree, chattered nearby. The monkey sprang back into the tree and got on the highest limb as soon as he saw the children jump out of the car and run toward him.

Inside, The Tower was a long dark room with a counter at one end and tables at the other and dancing space in the middle. They all sat down at a broad table next to the nickelodeon and Red Sam's wife, a tall burnt-brown woman with hair and eyes lighter than her skin, came and took their order. The children's mother put a dime in the machine and played "The Tennessee Waltz," and the grandmother said that tune always made her want to dance. She asked Bailey if he would like to dance but he only glared at her. He didn't have a naturally sunny disposition like she did and trips made him nervous. The grandmother's brown eyes were very bright. She swayed her head from side to side and pretended she was dancing in her chair. June Star said play something she could tap to so the children's mother put in another dime and played a fast number and June Star stepped out onto the dance floor and did her tap routine.

"Ain't she cute?" Red Sam's wife said, leaning over the counter. "Would you like to come be my little girl?"

"No, I certainly wouldn't," June Star said. "I wouldn't live in a broken-down place like this for a million bucks!" and she ran back to the table.

"Ain't she cute?" the woman repeated, stretching her mouth politely.

"Aren't you ashamed?" hissed the grandmother.

Red Sam came in and told his wife to quit lounging on the counter and hurry up with these people's order. His khaki trousers reached just to his hip bones and his stomach hung over them like a sack of meal swaying under his shirt. He came over and sat down at a table nearby and let out a combination sigh and yodel. "You can't win," he said. "You can't win," and he wiped his sweating red face off with a gray handkerchief. "These days you don't know who to trust," he said. "Ain't that the truth?"

"People are certainly not nice like they used to be," said the grandmother.

"Two fellers come in here last week," Red Sammy said, "driving a Chrysler. It was an old beat-up car but it was a good one and these boys looked all right to me. Said they worked at the mill and you know I let them fellers charge the gas they bought? Now why did I do that?"

"Because you're a good man!" the grandmother said at once.

"Yes'm, I suppose so," Red Sam said as if he were struck with this answer.

His wife brought the orders, carrying the five plates all at once without a tray, two in each hand and one balanced on her arm. "It isn't a soul in this green world of God's that you can trust," she said. "And I don't count nobody out of that, not nobody," she repeated, looking at Red Sammy.

"Did you read about that criminal, The Misfit, that's escaped?" asked the grandmother.

"I wouldn't be a bit surprised if he didn't attack this place right here," said the woman. "If he hears about it being here, I wouldn't be none surprised to see him. If he hears it's two cent in the cash register, I wouldn't be a tall surprised if he . . ."

"That'll do," Red Sam said. "Go bring these people their Co'-Colas," and the woman went off to get the rest of the order.

"A good man is hard to find," Red Sammy said. "Everything is getting terrible. I remember the day you could go off and leave your screen door unlatched. Not no more."

He and the grandmother discussed better times. The old lady said that in her opinion Europe was entirely to blame for the way things were now. She said the way Europe acted you would think we were made of money and Red Sam said it was no use talking about it, she was exactly right. The children ran outside into the white sunlight and looked at the monkey in the lacy chinaberry tree. He was busy catching fleas on himself and biting each one carefully between his teeth as if it were a delicacy.

They drove off again into the hot afternoon. The grandmother took cat naps and woke up every few minutes with her own snoring. Outside of Toombsboro she woke up and recalled an old plantation that she had visited in this neighborhood once when she was a young lady. She said the house had six white columns across the front and that there was an avenue of oaks leading up to it and two little wooden trellis arbors on either side in front where you sat down with your suitor after a stroll in the garden. She recalled exactly which road to turn off to get to it. She knew that Bailey would not be willing to lose any time looking at an old house, but the more she talked about it, the more she wanted to see it once again and find out if the little twin arbors were still standing. "There was a secret panel in this house," she said craftily, not telling the truth but wishing that she were, "and the story went that all the family silver was hidden in it when Sherman came through but it was never found. . . ."

"Hey!" John Wesley said. "Let's go see it! We'll find it! We'll poke at the wood work and find it! Who lives there? Where do you turn off at? Hey Pop, can't we turn off there?"

"We never have seen a house with a secret panel!" June Star shrieked. "Let's go to the house with the secret panel! Hey, Pop, can't we go see the house with the secret panel!"

"It's not far from here, I know," the grandmother said. "It wouldn't take over twenty minutes."

Bailey was looking straight ahead. His jaw was as rigid as a horseshoe. "No," he said.

The children began to yell and scream that they wanted to see the house with the secret panel. John Wesley kicked the back of the front seat and June Star hung over her mother's shoulder and whined desperately into her ear that they never had any fun even on their vacation, that they could never do what THEY wanted to do. The baby began to scream and John Wesley kicked the back of the seat so hard that his father could feel the blows in his kidney.

"All right!" he shouted and drew the car to a stop at the side of the road. "Will you all shut up? Will you all just shut up for one second? If you don't shut up, we won't go anywhere."

"It would be very educational for them," the grandmother murmured.

"All right," Bailey said, "but get this. This is the only time we're going to stop for anything like this. This is the one and only time."

"The dirt road that you have to turn down is about a mile back," the grandmother directed. "I marked it when we passed."

"A dirt road," Bailey groaned.

After they had turned around and were headed toward the dirt road, the grandmother recalled other points about the house, the beautiful glass over the front doorway and the candle lamp in the hall. John Wesley said that the secret panel was probably in the fireplace.

"You can't go inside the house," Bailey said. "You don't know who lives there."

"While you all talk to the people in front, I'll run around behind and get in a window," John Wesley suggested.

"We'll all stay in the car," his mother said.

They turned onto the dirt road and the car raced roughly along in a swirl of pink dust. The grandmother recalled the times when there were no paved roads and thirty miles was a day's journey. The dirt road was hilly and there were sudden washes in it and sharp curves on dangerous embankments. All at once they would be on a hill, looking down over the blue tops of trees for miles around, then the next minute, they would be in a red depression with the dust-coated trees looking down on them.

"This place had better turn up in a minute," Bailey said, "or I'm going to turn around."

The road looked as if no one had traveled on it in months.

"It's not much further," the grandmother said and just as she said it, a horrible thought came to her. The thought was so embarrassing that she turned red in the face and her eyes dilated and her feet jumped up, upsetting her valise in the corner. The instant the valise moved, the newspaper top she had over the basket under it rose with a snarl and Pitty Sing, the cat, sprang onto Bailey's shoulder.

The children were thrown to the floor and their mother, clutching the baby, was thrown out the door onto the ground; the old lady was thrown into the front seat. The car turned over once and landed right-side-up in a gulch on the side of the road. Bailey remained in the driver's seat with the cat—gray-striped with a broad white face and an orange nose—clinging to his neck like a caterpillar.

As soon as the children saw they could move their arms and legs, they scrambled out of the car shouting, "We've had an ACCIDENT!" The grandmother was curled up under the dashboard, hoping she was injured so that Bailey's wrath would not come down on her all at once. The horrible thought she had had before the accident was that the house she had remembered so vividly was not in Georgia but in Tennessee.

Bailey removed the cat from his neck with both hands and flung it out the window against the side of a pine tree. Then he got out of the car and started looking for the children's mother. She was sitting against the side of the red gutted ditch, holding the screaming baby, but she only had a cut down her face and a broken shoulder. "We've had an ACCIDENT!" the children screamed in a frenzy of delight.

"But nobody's killed," June Star said with disappointment as the grandmother limped out of the car, her hat still pinned to her head but the broken front brim standing up at a jaunty angle and the violet spray hanging off the side. They all sat down in the ditch, except the children, to recover from the shock. They were all shaking.

"Maybe a car will come along," said the children's mother hoarsely.

"I believe I have injured an organ," said the grandmother, pressing her side, but no one answered her. Bailey's teeth were clattering. He had on a yellow sport shirt with bright parrots designed in it and his face was as yellow as the shirt. The grandmother decided that she would not mention that the house was in Tennessee.

The road was about ten feet above and they could see only the tops of the trees on the other side of it. Behind the ditch they were sitting in there were more woods, tall and dark and deep. In a few minutes they saw a car some distance away on top of a hill, coming slowly as if the occupants were watching them. The grandmother stood up and waved both arms dramatically to attract their attention. The car continued to come on slowly, disappeared around a bend and appeared again, moving even slower, on top of the hill they had gone over. It was a big black battered hearselike automobile. There were three men in it.

It came to a stop just over them and for some minutes, the driver looked down with a steady expressionless gaze to where they were sitting, and didn't speak. Then he turned his head and muttered something to the other two and they got out. One was a fat boy in black trousers and a red sweat shirt with a silver stallion embossed on the front of it. He moved around on the right side of them and stood staring, his mouth partly open in a kind of loose grin. The other had on khaki pants and a blue striped coat and a gray hat pulled down very low, hiding most of his face. He came around slowly on the left side. Neither spoke.

The driver got out of the car and stood by the side of it, looking down at them. He was an older man than the other two. His hair was just beginning to gray and he wore silver-rimmed spectacles that gave him a scholarly look. He had a long creased face and didn't have on any shirt or undershirt. He had on blue jeans that were too tight for him and he was holding a black hat and a gun. The two boys also had guns.

"We've had an ACCIDENT!" the children screamed.

The grandmother had the peculiar feeling that the bespectacled man was someone she knew. His face was as familiar to her as if she had known him all her life but she could not recall who he was. He moved away from the car and began to come down the embankment, placing his feet carefully so that he wouldn't slip. He had on tan and white shoes and no socks, and his ankles were red and thin. "Good afternoon," he said, "I see you all had you a little spill."

"We turned over twice!" said the grandmother.

"Oncet," he corrected. "We see it happen. Try their car and see will it run, Hiram," he said quietly to the boy with the gray hat.

"What you got that gun for?" John Wesley asked. "Whatcha gonna do with that gun?"

"Lady," the man said to the children's mother, "would you mind calling them children to sit down by you? Children make me nervous. I want all you all to sit down right together there where you're at."

"What are you telling us what to do for?" June Star asked.

Behind them the line of woods gaped like a dark open mouth. "Come here," said their mother.

"Look here now," Bailey began suddenly, "we're in a predicament! We're in . . ."

The grandmother shrieked. She scrambled to her feet and stood staring. "You're The Misfit!" she said. "I recognized you at once!"

"Yes'm," the man said, smiling slightly as if he were pleased in spite of himself to be known. "But it would have been better for all of you, lady, if you hadn't of reckernized me."

Bailey turned his head sharply and said something to his mother that shocked the children. The old lady began to cry and The Misfit reddened.

"Lady," he said, "don't you get upset. Sometimes a man says things he don't mean. I don't reckon he meant to talk to you thataway."

"You wouldn't shoot a lady, would you?" the grandmother said and removed a clean handkerchief from her cuff and began to slap at her eyes with it.

The Misfit pointed the toe of his shoe into the ground and made a little hole and then covered it up again. "I would hate to have to," he said.

"Listen," the grandmother almost screamed, "I know you're a good man. You don't look a bit like you have common blood. I know you must come from nice people!"

"Yes mam," he said, "finest people in the world." When he smiled he showed a row of strong white teeth. "God never made a finer woman than my mother and my daddy's heart was pure gold," he said. The boy with the red sweat shirt had come around behind them and was standing with his gun at his hip. The Misfit squatted down on the ground. "Watch them children, Bobby Lee," he said. "You know they make me nervous." He looked at the six of them huddled together in front of him and he seemed to be embarrassed as if he couldn't think of anything to say. "Ain't a cloud in the sky," he remarked, looking up at it. "Don't see no sun but don't see no cloud neither."

"Yes, it's a beautiful day," said the grandmother. "Listen," she said, "you shouldn't call yourself The Misfit because I know you're a good man at heart. I can just look at you and tell."

"Hush!" Bailey yelled. "Hush! Everybody shut up and let me handle this!" He was squatting in the position of a runner about to spring forward but he didn't move.

"I pre-chate that, lady," The Misfit said and drew a little circle in the ground with the butt of his gun.

"It'll take a half a hour to fix this here car," Hiram called, looking over the raised hood of it.

"Well, first you and Bobby Lee get him and that little boy to step over yonder with you," The Misfit said, pointing to Bailey and John Wesley. "The boys want to ask you something," he said to Bailey. "Would you mind stepping back in them woods there with them?"

"Listen," Bailey began, "we're in a terrible predicament! Nobody realizes what this is," and his voice cracked. His eyes were as blue and intense as the parrots in his shirt and he remained perfectly still.

The grandmother reached up to adjust her hat brim as if she were going to the woods with him but it came off in her hand. She stood staring at it and after a second she let it fall on the ground. Hiram pulled Bailey up by the arm as if he were assisting an old man. John Wesley caught hold of his father's hand and Bobby Lee followed. They went off toward the woods and just as they reached the dark edge, Bailey turned and supporting himself against a gray naked pine trunk, he shouted, "I'll be back in a minute, Mamma, wait on me!"

"Come back this instant!" his mother shrilled but they all disappeared into the woods.

"Bailey Boy!" the grandmother called in tragic voice but she found she was looking at The Misfit squatting on the ground in front of her. "I just know you're a good man," she said desperately. "You're not a bit common!"

"Nome, I ain't a good man," The Misfit said after a second as if he had considered her statement carefully, "but I ain't the worst in the world neither. My daddy said I was a different breed of dog from my brothers and sisters. 'You know,' Daddy said, 'it's some that can live their whole life out without asking about it and it's others has to know why it is, and this boy is one of the latters. He's going to be into everything!' " He put on his black hat and looked up suddenly and then away deep into the woods as if he were embarrassed again. "I'm sorry, I don't have on a shirt before you ladies," he said, hunching his shoulders slightly. "We buried our clothes that we had on when we escaped and we're just making do until we can get better. We borrowed these from some folks we met," he explained.

"That's perfectly all right," the grandmother said. "Maybe Bailey has an extra shirt in his suitcase."

"I'll look and see terrectly," The Misfit said.

"Where are they taking him?" the children's mother screamed.

"Daddy was a card himself," The Misfit said. "You couldn't put anything over on him. He never got in trouble with the Authorities though. Just had the knack of handling them."

"You could be honest too if you'd only try," said the grandmother. "Think how wonderful it would be to settle down and live a comfortable life and not have to think about somebody chasing you all the time."

The Misfit kept scratching in the ground with the butt of his gun as if he were thinking about it. "Yes'm, somebody is always after you," he murmured.

The grandmother noticed how thin his shoulder blades were just behind his hat because she was standing up looking down on him. "Do you ever pray?" she asked.

He shook his head. All she saw was the black hat wiggle between his shoulder blades. "Nome," he said.

There was a pistol shot from the woods, followed closely by another. Then silence. The old lady's head jerked around. She could hear the wind move through the tree tops like a long satisfied insuck of breath. "Bailey Boy!," she called.

"I was a gospel singer for a while," The Misfit said. "I been most everything. Been in the arm service, both land and sea, at home and abroad, been twict married, been an undertaker, been with the railroads, plowed Mother Earth, been in a tornado, seen a man burnt alive oncet," and he looked up at the children's mother and the little girl who were sitting close together, their faces white and their eyes glassy; "I even seen a woman flogged," he said.

"Pray, pray," the grandmother began, "pray, pray . . ."

"I never was a bad boy that I remember of," The Misfit said in an almost dreamy voice, "but somewheres along the line I done something wrong and got sent to the penitentiary. I was buried alive," and he looked up and held her attention to him by a steady stare.

"That's when you should have started to pray," she said. "What did you do to get sent to the penitentiary that first time?"

"Turn to the right, it was a wall," The Misfit said, looking up again at the cloudless sky. "Turn to the left, it was a wall. Look up it was a ceiling, look down it was a floor. I forgot what I done, lady. I set there and set there, trying to remember what it was I done and I ain't recalled it to this day. Oncet in a while, I would think it was coming to me, but it never come."

"Maybe they put you in by mistake," the old lady said vaguely.

"Nome," he said. "It wasn't no mistake. They had the papers on me."

"You must have stolen something," she said.

The Misfit sneered slightly. "Nobody had nothing I wanted," he said. "It was a head-doctor at the penitentiary said what I had done was kill my daddy but I known that for a lie. My daddy died in nineteen ought nineteen of the epidemic flu and I never had a thing to do with it. He was buried in the Mount Hopewell Baptist churchyard and you can go there and see for yourself."

"If you would pray," the old lady said, "Jesus would help you."

"That's right," The Misfit said.

"Well then, why don't you pray?" she asked trembling with delight suddenly.

"I don't want no hep," he said, "I'm doing all right by myself."

Bobby Lee and Hiram came ambling back from the woods. Bobby Lee was dragging a yellow shirt with bright blue parrots in it.

"Throw me that shirt, Bobby Lee," The Misfit said. The shirt came flying at him and landed on his shoulder and he put it on. The grandmother couldn't name what the shirt reminded her of. "No, lady," The Misfit said while he was buttoning it up, "I found out the crime don't matter. You can do one thing or you can do another, kill a man or take a tire off his car, because sooner or later you're going to forget what it was you done and just be punished for it."

The children's mother had begun to make heaving noises as if she couldn't get her breath. "Lady," he asked, "would you and that little girl like to step off yonder with Bobby Lee and Hiram and join your husband?"

"Yes, thank you," the mother said faintly. Her left arm dangled helplessly and she was holding the baby, who had gone to sleep, in the other. "Hep that lady up, Hiram," The Misfit said as she struggled to climb out of the ditch, "and Bobby Lee, you hold onto that little girl's hand."

"I don't want to hold hands with him," June Star said. "He reminds me of a pig."

The fat boy blushed and laughed and caught her by the arm and pulled her off into the woods after Hiram and her mother.

Alone with The Misfit, the grandmother found that she had lost her voice. There was not a cloud in the sky nor any sun. There was nothing around her but woods. She wanted to tell him that he must pray. She opened and closed her mouth several times before anything came out. Finally she found herself saying, "Jesus. Jesus," meaning, Jesus will help you, but the way she was saying it, it sounded as if she might be cursing.

"Yes'm," The Misfit said as if he agreed. "Jesus thown everything off balance. It was the same case with Him as with me except He hadn't committed any crime and they could prove I had committed one because they had the papers on me. Of course," he said, "they never shown me any papers. That's why I sign myself now, I said long ago, you get you a signature and sign everything you do and keep a copy of it. Then you'll know what you done and you can hold up the crime to the punishment and see do they match and in the end you'll have something to prove you ain't been treated right. I call myself The Misfit," he said, "because I can't make what all I done wrong fit with all I gone through in punishment."

There was a piercing scream from the woods, followed closely by a pistol report. "Does it seem right to you, lady, that one is punished a heap and another ain't punished at all?"

"Jesus!" the old lady cried. "You've got good blood! I know you wouldn't shoot a lady! I know you come from nice people! Pray! Jesus, you ought not to shoot a lady. I'll give you all the money I've got!"

"Lady," The Misfit said, looking beyond her far into the woods, "there was never a body that give the undertaker a tip."

There were two more pistol reports and the grandmother raised her head like a parched old turkey hen crying for water and called, "Bailey Boy, Bailey Boy!" as if her heart would break.

"Jesus was the only One that ever raised the dead," The Misfit continued, "and He shouldn't have done it. He thown everything off balance. If He did what He said, then it's nothing for you to do but thow away everything and follow Him, and if He didn't then it's nothing for you to do but enjoy the few minutes you got left the best way you can—by killing somebody or burning down his house or doing some other meanness to him. No pleasure but meanness," he said and his voice had become almost a snarl.

"Maybe He didn't raise the dead," the old lady mumbled, not knowing what she was saying and feeling so dizzy that she sank down in the ditch with her legs twisted under her.

"I wasn't there so I can't say He didn't," The Misfit said. "I wisht I had of been there," he said, hitting the ground with his fist. "It ain't right I wasn't there because if I had of been there I would of known. Listen lady," he said in a high voice, "if I had of been there I would of known and I wouldn't be like I am now." His voice seemed about to crack and the grandmother's head cleared for an instant. She saw the man's face twisted close to her own as if he were going to cry and she murmured, "Why, you're one of my babies. You're one of my own children!" She reached out and touched him on the shoulder. The Misfit sprang back as if a snake had bitten him and shot her three times through the chest. Then he put his gun down on the ground and took off his glasses and began to clean them.

Hiram and Bobby Lee returned from the woods and stood over the ditch, looking down at the grandmother who half sat and half lay in a puddle of blood with her legs crossed under her like a child's and her face smiling up at the cloudless sky.

Without his glasses, The Misfit's eyes were red-rimmed and pale and defenseless-looking. "Take her off and thow her where you thown the others," he said, picking up the cat that was rubbing itself against his leg.

"She was a talker, wasn't she?" Bobby Lee said, sliding down the ditch with a yodel.

"She would of been a good woman," The Misfit said, "if it had been somebody there to shoot her every minute of her life."

"Some fun!" Bobby Lee said.

"Shut up, Bobby Lee," The Misfit said. "It's no real pleasure in life."

[1953]

QUESTIONS

FLANNERY O'CONNOR, *A Good Man Is Hard to Find*

1. What does the grandmother do that causes the accident? What mistake about place does she make? How does her mistake fit with her personality?

2. The conversation with Red Sammy reveals many of the issues of the story. What does Red Sammy have to say about the nature of human beings?

3. The Misfit has been jailed for crimes he does not remember. How do we know that he really is a criminal? What should readers make of his claims about himself?

4. Is it true that no one can be trusted, as Red Sammy and the Grandmother say? What can be said about people who do not trust other people?

5. O'Connor took the idea of this story from a newspaper article about a criminal called The Misfit. What does society do with its misfits? How are they generally treated, and what does this treatment do to them?

6. O'Connor believed that people needed something to wake them up from their complacency. What do the grandmother's last words say about our need to recognize the needs of others?

7. O'Connor uses imagery and color to bring her ideas vividly to life. How does she use color in place, dress, and figure in this story? Note the descriptions of the monkey, the cat, Bailey's shirt.

8. The story centers around the moment of the accident. What is the irony of the children's response to the accident? What clues tell the reader that someone will, indeed, be killed?

9. Sammy uses the words "a good man is hard to find," after his wife has said that she trusts no one, including him. Why are these words put in the mouth of a man like Sammy?

10. Find a newspaper article that interests you and write a story that includes the information in the article.

11. Read about the South of the past that the grandmother remembers. Write about life in that time and place. Consider race and class issues as you write.

12. What causes cruelty? What is the mind set of people who have lost their ability to identify with others? Write about this issue, using a particular event in past or current history (World War II, The Civil war, etc.).

Passages from Essays and Letters

FLANNEY O'CONNOR

On Reality

To "A."

2 August 55

THANK YOU FOR WRITING me again. I feel I should apologize for answering so promptly because I may seem to force on you a correspondence that you don't have time for or that will become a burden. I myself am afflicted with time, as I do not work out on account of an energy-depriving ailment and my work in, being creative, can go on only a few hours a day. I live on a farm and don't see many people. My avocation is raising peacocks, something that requires everything of the peacock and nothing of me, so time is always at hand.

I believe too that there is only one Reality and that that is the end of it, but the term, "Christian Realism," has become necessary for me, perhaps in a purely academic way, because I find myself in a world where everybody has his compartment, puts you in yours, shuts the door and departs. One of the awful things about writing when you are a Christian is that for you the ultimate reality is the Incarnation, the present reality is the Incarnation, and nobody believes in the Incarnation; that is, nobody in your audience. My audience are the people who think God is dead. At least these are the people I am conscious of writing for.

As for Jesus' being a realist: if He was not God, He was no realist, only a liar, and the crucifixtion an act of justice.

Dogma can in no way limit a limitless God. The person outside the Church attaches a different meaning to it than the person in. For me a dogma is only a gateway to contemplation and is an instrument of freedom and not of restriction. It preserves mystery for the human mind. Henry James said the young woman of the future would know nothing of mystery or manners. He had no business to limit it to one sex.

You are right that I won't ever be able entirely to understand my own work or even my own motivations. It is first of all a gift, but the direction it has taken has been because of the Church in me or the effect of the Church's teaching, not because of a personal perception or love of God. For you to think this would be possible because of your ignorance of me; for me to think it would be sinful in a high degree. I am not a mystic and I do not lead a holy life. Not that I can claim any interesting or pleasurable sins (my sense of the devil is strong) but I know all about the garden variety, pride, gluttony, envy and sloth, and what is more to the point, my virtues are as timid as my vices. I think sin occasionally brings one closer to God, but not habitual sin and not this petty kind that blocks every small good. A working knowledge of the devil can be very well had from resisting him.

However, the individual in the Church is, no matter how worthless himself, a part of the Body of Christ and a participator in the Redemption. There is no blueprint that the Church gives for understanding this. It is a matter of faith and the Church can force no one to believe it. When I ask myself how I know I believe, I have no satisfactory answer at all, no assurance at all, no feeling at all. I can only say with Peter, Lord I believe, help my unbelief. And all I can say about my love of God, is, Lord help me in my lack of it. I distrust pious phrases, particularly when they issue from my mouth. I try militantly never to be affected by the pious language of the faithful but it is always coming out when you least expect it. In contrast to the pious language of the faithful, the liturgy is beautifully flat.

I am wondering if you have read Simone Weil. I never have and doubt if I would understand her if I did; but from what I have read about her, I think she must have been a very great person. She and Edith Stein are the two 20th-century women who interest me most.

Whether you are a Christian or not, we both worship the God Who Is. St. Thomas on his death bed said of the *Summa*, "It's all straw,"—this was in the vision of that God.

On Reading

9 August 55

I have thought of Simone Weil in connection with you almost from the first and I got out this piece I enclose and reread it and the impression was not lessened. In the face of anyone's experience, someone like myself who has had almost no experience, must be humble. I will never have the experience of the convert, or of the one who fails to be converted, or even in all probability of the formidable sinner; but your effort not to be seduced by the Church moves me greatly. God permits it for some reason though it is the devil's greatest work of hallucination. Fr. [Jean] de Menasce told somebody not to come into the Church until he felt it would be an enlargement of his freedom. This is what you are doing and you are right, but do not make your feeling of the voluptuous seductive powers of the Church into a hard shell to protect yourself from her. I suppose it is like marriage, that when you get into it, you find it is the beginning, not the end, of the struggle to make love work.

I think most people come to the Church by means the Church does not allow, else there would be no need their getting to her at all. However, this is true inside as well, as the operation of the Church is entirely set up for the sinner; which creates much misunderstanding among the smug.

I suppose I read Aristotle in college but not to know I was doing it; the same with Plato. I don't have the kind of mind that can carry such beyond the actual reading, i.e., total non-retention has kept my education from being a burden to me. So I couldn't make any judgment on the *Summa*, except to say this: I read it for about twenty minutes every night before I go to bed. If my mother were to come in during this process and say, "Turn off that light. It's late," I with lifted finger and broad bland beatific expression, would reply, "On the contrary, I answer that the light, being eternal and limitless, cannot be turned off. Shut your eyes," or some such thing. In any case, I feel I can personally guarantee that St. Thomas loved God because for the life of me I cannot help loving St. Thomas. His brothers didn't want him to waste himself being a Dominican and so locked him up in a tower and introduced a prostitute into his apartment; her he ran out with a red-hot poker. It would be fashionable today to be in sympathy with the woman, but I am in sympathy with St. Thomas.

I don't know B.R. well, but he came out here one evening and had dessert with us. I have a friend who is very fond of him and so I hear a lot about him and his troubles, of which he seems to be so well supplied that it's a miracle he's still alive. My impression was that he was a very fine and a very proud man. When he was sick about a year ago, I sent him a copy of St. Bernard's letters and in thanking me, he said he was an agnostic. You are right that he's an anachronism, I guess, strangely cut-off anyway. I wrote to my friend who is so fond of him that perhaps he might be sent something to read that would at least set him thinking in a wider direction, but I am afraid this filled the poor girl with apprehension, she thinking I would probably produce Cardinal Newman or somebody. I had had in mind Gabriel Marcel whose Gifford Lectures I had just read. This girl is a staunch and excellent Presbyterian with a polite horror of anything Romish. . . .

I have some long and tall thoughts on the subject of God's working through nature, but I will not inflict them on you now. I find I have a habit of announcing the obvious in pompous and dogmatic periods. I like to forget that I'm only a storyteller. Right now I am trying to write a lecture that I have been invited to deliver next spring in Lansing, Mich. to a wholesale gathering of the AAUW. I am trying to write this thing on the justification of distortion in fiction, call it something like "The Freak in Modern Fiction." Anyway, I have it borne in on me that my business is to write and not talk about it. I have ten months to write the lecture in and it is going to take every bit of it. I don't read much modern fiction. I have never read Nelson Algren that you mention. I feel lumpish.

The South & Catholicism

To Cecil Dawkins

16 July 57

You certainly are nice to want to give me that dog but I'll have to take the thought for the dog. I didn't tell you what I raise: I raise peacocks—and you can't keep dogs and peacocks on the same place. When people come to see us with a dog, we have to ask them to keep the dog in the car—else the peachickens will take to the trees and have nervous prostrations. I have 27 right now. This place sounds like the jungle at night as they yell and scream at the slightest atmospheric disturbance or mechanical noise. In addition to the peafowl I have ducks and geese and several different kinds of chickens but the peafowl are the main interest. I spend a good deal of my time sitting on the back steps with them. They have no proper sense of place; we have a very nice lawn that they could decorate to advantage but they prefer to sit on the tractors or the top of the chicken house or the garbage-can lid. So I adjust myself to their tastes, including being anti-dog. But I do appreciate your wanting to give it to me.

I am always vastly irritated by these people (I guess like [Wallace] Stegner) who know as much about the South as I do about lower Hobokin and on the strength of it advise Southern writers to leave it and forget the myth. Which myth? If you're a writer and the South is what you know, then it's what you'll write about and how you judge it will depend on how you judge yourself. It's perhaps good and necessary to get away from it physically for a while, but this is by no means to escape it. I stayed away from the time I was 20 until I was 25 with the notion that the life of my writing depended on my staying away. I would certainly have persisted in that delusion had I not got very ill and had to come home. The best of my writing has been done here.

This is not to say that what the South gives is enough, or that it is even significant in any but a practical way—as in providing the texture and the idiom and so forth. But these things have to be provided. So much depends on what you have an ear for. And I don't think you can have much of an ear for what you hear when you're over 20—that is, for a new kind of talk and life. The advantages and disadvantages of being a Southern writer can be endlessly debated but the fact remains that if you are, you are.

Catholicity has given me my perspective on the South and probably gives you yours. I know what you mean about being repulsed by the Church when you have only the Jansenist-Mechanical Catholic to judge it by. I think that the reason such Catholics are so repulsive is that they don't really have faith but a kind of false certainty. They operate by the slide rule and the Church for them is not the body of Christ but the poor man's insurance system. It's never hard for them to believe because actually they never think about it. Faith has to take in all the other possibilities it can. Anyhow, I don't think it's a matter of wanting miracles. The miracles seem in fact to be the great embarrassment for the modern man, a kind of scandal. If the miracles could be argued away and Christ reduced to the status of a teacher, domesticated and fallible, then there'd be no problem. Anyway, to discover the Church you have to set out by yourself. The French Catholic novelists were a help to me in this—Bloy, Bernanos, Mauriac. In philosophy, Gilson, Maritain and Gabriel Marcel, an Existentialist. They all seemed to be French for a while and then I discovered the Germans—Max Picard, Romano Guardini and Karl Adam. The Americans seem just to be producing pamphlets for the back of the Church (to be avoided at all costs) and installing heating systems—though there are a few good sources like *Thought*, a quarterly published at Fordham. This spring I went to lecture at Notre Dame and met some very intelligent people. In any case, discovering the Church is apt to be a slow procedure but it can only take place if you have a free mind and no vested interest in disbelief . . .

Since you hadn't read Caroline Gordon, I'm sending you a copy of a quarterly that came out last year and was entirely devoted to her. You might find something in it that would be of use.

The Devil

To John Hawkes

26 December 59

I certainly do mean Tarwater's friend to be the Devil. If I could have treated Rayber in the same way I treat Tarwater, then it would have been possible to show to what extent Rayber, like Tarw., accepts and resists the Devil; but I couldn't do this because the Devil who prompts Rayber speaks a language I can't get down, an idiom I just can't reproduce—maybe because it's so dull I can't sustain any interest in it. The Devil that prompts Rayber would never say, "How about all those drowned at sea that the fish have et . . .?" etc.

Several years ago a friend of mine in a writing class at Iowa wrote me that his workshop had read and discussed the first chapter of this novel (it was in *New World Writing*) and the discussion revolved around who the voice was. Only one thought it was the Devil. The rest of them thought it was a voice of light, there to liberate Tarwater from that "horrible old man . . ."

Meeks is one of those comic characters but, like Mr. Shiftlet [in "The Life You Save May Be Your Own"] of the Devil because nothing in him resists the Devil. There's not much use to distinguish between them. In general the Devil can always be a subject for my kind of comedy one way or another. I suppose this is because he is always accomplishing ends other than his own. More than in the Devil I am interested in the indication of Grace, the moment when you know that Grace has been offered and accepted—such as the moment when the Grandmother realizes the Misfit is one of her own children. These moments are prepared for (by me anyway) by the intensity of the evil circumstances. It is the violation in the woods that brings home to Tarwater the real nature of his rejection. I couldn't have brought off the final vision without it.

This is too much talk about my own book. You should be getting an advance copy shortly as I think they are to be sent out some time after Jan. 1 and I hope you will see some improvement in the prose of the middle section, thanks to your advice. I'll be waiting on those chapters of yours with real anticipation and a feeling of kinship. And my best to you and Sophie for the new year.

[1979]

Joyce Carol Oates
[1938–   ]

JOYCE CAROL OATES *numbers among the most prolific authors in U.S. literary history; since the 1968 publication of her first volume of short stories,* By the North Gate, *Oates has published at least one book or has had at least one play produced every single year—and frequently more than one. All told, in just over forty years, she has published forty novels under her own name, another eight novels under the pseudonym Rosamund Smith, twenty-six volumes of short fiction, fifteen volumes of poetry, eleven volumes of essays and other nonfiction, five books for children and young adults, and somewhere around twenty plays. The tremendous quantity of her writing alone is worth noting, but what makes Oates a remarkable writer is the range of her interests and styles; she is equally successful at domestic novels and at horror fiction, at crime stories and at the gothic romance. Much of her writing bears a thread of subterranean, and at times overt, violence; as she has told an interviewer, "I am a chronicler of the American experience. We have been historically a nation prone to violence, and it would be unreal to ignore this fact. What intrigues me is the response to violence: its aftermath in the private lives of women and children in particular."*

Joyce Carol Oates was born in rural Lockport, New York, and spent much of her time growing up on her grandparents' farm. She began writing at an extremely early age, completing her first novel at age fifteen; the publisher she submitted it too, however, felt that it was too dark for young adult readers. Oates attended Syracuse University, from which she graduated in 1960, and received a master's degree from University of Wisconsin in 1961. She married that same year, and she and her husband, Raymond Joseph Smith, moved to Detroit, where Oates taught at the University of Detroit from 1961 to 1967. She was a member of the faculty of the University of Windsor, in Ontario, Canada, from 1967 to 1978, and became a writer-in-residence at Princeton University in 1978, where she remains today as the Roger S. Berlind Distinguished Professor in the Humanities. That she has combined teaching with writing, and done each so successfully, is a stunning accomplishment, one that few writers can claim. Oates has, in addition, won a plethora of prizes, including three O. Henry Awards; the Rosenthal Award of the National Institute of Arts and Letters; the National Book Award; the O. Henry Special Award for Continuing Achievement, twice; the Elmer Holmed Bobst Award for Lifetime Achievement in Fiction; the Bram Stoker Lifetime Achievement Award for horror fiction; and too many others to enumerate.

Among her many novels, to name only a few, are them *(1969), a story of racial tension, political violence, and urban upheaval set in Detroit in the middle decades of the twentieth century;* Because It Is Bitter, and Because It Is My Heart

(1990), which explores racial segregation and violence in the late 1950s; Black Water *(1992), a fictionalized updating of the story of Senator Ted Kennedy's car accident at Chappaquiddick that left the young woman he was with dead;* Foxfire *(1993), which traces the bonds among members of a girl gang, and the damage such bonds cause;* We Were the Mulvaneys *(1996), the story of a family's downfall in the wake of sexual violence; and* Blonde *(2000), a fictional retelling of the life of Marilyn Monroe. Oates's most recent publications include* Black Girl/White Girl *(2006) and* The Gravedigger's Daughter *(2007). What links these disparate texts is their similar concern, as Oates has pointed out, with "the moral and social conditions of my generation." Her explorations of these conditions resonate with millions of readers, and continue to draw more readers in each year, with each new publication.*

Where Are You Going, Where Have You Been?

JOYCE CAROL OATES

HER NAME WAS CONNIE. She was fifteen and she had a quick nervous giggling habit of craning her neck to glance into mirrors, or checking other people's faces to make sure her own was all right. Her mother, who noticed everything and knew everything and who hadn't much reason any longer to look at her own face, always scolded Connie about it. "Stop gawking at yourself, who are you? You think you're so pretty?" she would say. Connie would raise her eyebrows at these familiar complaints and look right through her mother, into a shadowy vision of herself as she was right at that moment: she knew she was pretty and that was everything. Her mother had been pretty once too, if you could believe those old snapshots in the album, but now her looks were gone and that was why she was always after Connie.

"Why don't you keep your room clean like your sister? How've you got your hair fixed—what the hell stinks? Hair spray? You don't see your sister using that junk."

Her sister June was twenty-four and still lived at home. She was a secretary in the high school Connie attended, and if that wasn't bad enough—with her in the same building—she was so plain and chunky and steady that Connie had to hear her praised all the time by her mother and her mother's sisters. June did this, June did that, she saved money and helped clean the house and cooked and Connie couldn't do a thing, her mind was all filled with trashy daydreams. Their father was away at work most of the time and when he came home he wanted supper and he read the newspaper at supper and after supper he went to bed. He didn't bother talking much to them, but around his bent head Connie's mother kept picking at her until Connie wished her mother was dead and she herself was dead and it was all over. "She makes me want to throw up sometimes," she complained to her friends. She had a high, breathless, amused voice which made everything she said sound a little forced, whether it was sincere or not.

There was one good thing: June went places with girl friends of hers, girls who were just as plain and steady as she, and so when Connie wanted to do that her mother had no objections. The father of Connie's best girl friend drove the girls the three miles to town and left them off at a shopping plaza, so that they could walk through the stores or go to a movie, and when he came to pick them up again at eleven he never bothered to ask what they had done.

They must have been familiar sights, walking around that shopping plaza in their shorts and flat ballerina slippers that always scuffed the sidewalk, with charm bracelets jingling on their thin wrists; they would lean together to whisper and laugh secretly if someone passed by who amused or interested them. Connie had long dark blond hair that drew anyone's eye to it, and she wore part of it pulled up on her head and puffed out and the rest of it she let fall down her back. She wore a pullover jersey blouse that looked one way when she was at home and another way when she was away from home. Everything about her had two sides to it, one for home and one for anywhere that was not home: her walk that could be childlike and bobbing, or languid enough to make anyone think she was hearing music in her head, her mouth which was pale and smirking most of the time, but bright and pink on these evenings out, her laugh which was cynical and drawling at home—"Ha, ha, very funny"—but high-pitched and nervous anywhere else, like the jingling of the charms on her bracelet.

Sometimes they did go shopping or to a movie, but sometimes they went across the highway, ducking fast across the busy road, to a drive-in restaurant where older kids hung out. The restaurant was shaped like a big bottle, though squatter than a real bottle, and on its cap was a revolving figure of a grinning boy who held a hamburger aloft. One night in mid-summer they ran across, breathless with daring, and right away someone leaned out a car window and invited them over, but it was just a boy from high school they didn't like. It made them feel good to be able to ignore him. They went up through the maze of parked and cruising cars to the bright-lit, fly-infested restaurant, their faces pleased and expectant as if they were entering a sacred building that loomed out of the night to give them what haven and what blessing they yearned for. They sat at the counter and crossed their legs at the ankles, their thin shoulders rigid with excitement, and listened to the music that made everything so good: the music was always in the background like music at a church service, it was something to depend upon.

A boy named Eddie came in to talk with them. He sat backwards on his stool, turning himself jerkily around in semi-circles and then stopping and turning again, and after a while he asked Connie if she would like something to eat. She said she did and so she tapped her friend's arm on her way out— her friend pulled her face up into a brave droll look—and Connie said she would meet her at eleven, across the way. "I just hate to leave her like that," Connie said earnestly, but the boy said that she wouldn't be alone for long. So they went out to his car and on the way Connie couldn't help but let her eyes wander over the windshields and faces all around her, her face gleaming with a joy that had nothing to do with Eddie or even this place; it might have been the music. She drew her shoulders up and sucked in her breath with the pure pleasure of being alive, and just at that moment she happened to glance at a face just a few feet from hers. It was a boy with shaggy black hair, in a convertible jalopy painted gold. He stared at her and then his lips widened into a grin. Connie slit her eyes at him and turned away, but she couldn't help glancing back and there he was still watching her. He wagged a finger and laughed and said, "Gonna get you, baby," and Connie turned away again without Eddie noticing anything.

She spent three hours with him, at the restaurant where they ate hamburgers and drank Cokes in wax cups that were always sweating, and then down an alley a mile or so away, and when he left her off at five to eleven only the movie house was still open at the plaza. Her girl friend was there, talking with a boy. When Connie came up the two girls smiled at each other and Connie said, "How was the movie?" and the girl said, "You should know." They rode off with the girl's father, sleepy and pleased, and Connie couldn't help but look at the darkened shopping plaza with its big empty parking lot and its signs that were faded and ghostly now, and over at the drive-in restaurant where cars were still circling tirelessly. She couldn't hear the music at this distance.

Next morning June asked her how the movie was and Connie said, "Soso."

She and that girl and occasionally another girl went out several times a week that way, and the rest of the time Connie spent around the house—it was summer vacation—getting in her mother's way and thinking, dreaming, about the boys she met. But all the boys fell back and dissolved into a single face that was not even a face, but an idea, a feeling, mixed up with the urgent insistent pounding of the music and the humid night air of July. Connie's mother kept dragging her back to the daylight by finding things for her to do or saying, suddenly, "What's this about the Pettinger girl?"

And Connie would say nervously, "Oh, her. That dope." She always drew thick clear lines between herself and such girls, and her mother was simple and kindly enough to believe her. Her mother was so simple, Connie thought, that it was maybe cruel to fool her so much. Her mother went scuffling around the house in old bedroom slippers and complained over the telephone to one sister about the other, then the other called up and the two of them complained about the third one. If June's name was mentioned her mother's tone was approving, and if Connie's name was mentioned it was disapproving. This did not really mean she disliked Connie and actually Connie thought that her mother preferred her to June because she was prettier, but the two of them kept up a pretense of exasperation, a sense that they were tugging and struggling over something of little value to either of them. Sometimes, over coffee, they were almost friends, but something would come up—some vexation that was like a fly buzzing suddenly around their heads—and their faces went hard with contempt.

One Sunday Connie got up at eleven—none of them bothered with church—and washed her hair so that it could dry all day long, in the sun. Her parents and sister were going to a barbecue at an aunt's house and Connie said no, she wasn't interested, rolling her eyes to let her mother know just what she thought of it. "Stay home alone then," her mother said sharply. Connie sat out back in a lawn chair and watched them drive away, her father quiet and bald, hunched around so that he could back the car out, her mother with a look that was still angry and not at all softened through the windshield, and in the back seat poor old June all dressed up as if she didn't know what a barbecue was, with all the running yelling kids and the flies. Connie sat with her eyes closed in the sun, dreaming and dazed with the warmth about her as if this were a kind of love, the caresses of love, and her mind slipped over onto thoughts of the boy she had been with the night before and how nice he had been, how sweet it always was, not the way someone like June would suppose but sweet, gentle, the way it was in movies and promised in songs; and when she opened her eyes she hardly knew where she was, the back yard ran off into weeds and a fence-line of trees and behind it the sky was perfectly blue and still. The asbestos "ranch house" that was now three years old startled her—it looked small. She shook her head as if to get awake.

It was too hot. She went inside the house and turned on the radio to drown out the quiet. She sat on the edge of her bed, barefoot, and listened for an hour and a half to a program called XYZ Sunday Jamboree, record after record of hard, fast, shrieking songs she sang along with, interspersed by exclamations from "Bobby King": "An' look here you girls at Napoleon's—Son and Charley want you to pay real close attention to this song coming up!"

And Connie paid close attention herself, bathed in a glow of slowpulsed joy that seemed to rise mysteriously out of the music itself and lay languidly about the airless little room, breathed in and breathed out with each gentle rise and fall of her chest.

After a while she heard a car coming up the drive. She sat up at once, startled, because it couldn't be her father so soon. The gravel kept crunching all the way in from the road—the driveway was long—and Connie ran to the window. It was a car she didn't know. It was an open jalopy, painted a bright gold that caught the sunlight opaquely. Her heart began to pound and her fingers snatched at her hair, checking it, and she whispered "Christ. Christ," wondering how bad she looked. The car came to a stop at the side door and the horn sounded four short taps as if this were a signal Connie knew.

She went into the kitchen and approached the door slowly, then hung out the screen door, her bare toes curling down off the step. There were two boys in the car and now she recognized the driver: he had shaggy, shabby black hair that looked crazy as a wig and he was grinning at her.

"I ain't late, am I?" he said.

"Who the hell do you think you are?" Connie said.

"Toldja I'd be out, didn't I?"

"I don't even know who you are."

She spoke sullenly, careful to show no interest or pleasure, and he spoke in a fast bright monotone. Connie looked past him to the other boy, taking her time. He had fair brown hair, with a lock that fell onto his forehead. His sideburns gave him a fierce, embarrassed look, but so far he hadn't even bothered to glance at her. Both boys wore sunglasses. The driver's glasses were metallic and mirrored everything in miniature.

"You wanta come for a ride?" he said.

Connie smirked and let her hair fall loose over one shoulder.

"Don'tcha like my car? New paint job," he said. "Hey."

"What?"

"You're cute."

She pretended to fidget, chasing flies away from the door.

"Don'tcha believe me, or what?" he said.

"Look, I don't even know who you are," Connie said in disgust.

"Hey, Ellie's got a radio, see. Mine's broke down." He lifted his friend's arm and showed her the little transistor the boy was holding, and now Connie began to hear the music. It was the same program that was playing inside the house.

"Bobby King?" she said.

"I listen to him all the time. I think he's great."

"He's kind of great," Connie said reluctantly.

"Listen, that guy's great. He knows where the action is."

Connie blushed a little, because the glasses made it impossible for her to see just what this boy was looking at. She couldn't decide if she liked him or if he was just a jerk, and so she dawdled in the doorway and wouldn't come down or go back inside. She said, "What's all that stuff painted on your car?"

"Can'tcha read it?" He opened the door very carefully, as if he was afraid it might fall off. He slid out just as carefully, planting his feet firmly on the ground, the tiny metallic world in his glasses slowing down like gelatine hardening and in the midst of it Connie's bright green blouse. "This here is my name, to begin with," he said. ARNOLD FRIEND was written in tarlike black letters on the side, with a drawing of a round grinning face that reminded Connie of a pumpkin, except it wore sunglasses. "I wanta introduce myself, I'm Arnold Friend and that's my real name and I'm gonna be your friend, honey, and inside the car's Ellie Oscar, he's kinda shy." Ellie brought his transistor radio up to his shoulder and balanced it there. "Now these numbers are a secret code, honey," Arnold Friend explained. He read off the numbers 33, 19, 17 and raised his eyebrows at her to see what she thought of that, but she didn't think much of it. The left rear fender had been smashed and around it was written, on the gleaming gold background: DONE BY CRAZY WOMAN DRIVER. Connie had to laugh at that. Arnold Friend was pleased at her laughter and looked up at her. "Around the other side's a lot more—you wanta come and see them?"

"No."

"Why not?"

"Why should I?"

"Don'tcha wanta see what's on the car? Don'tcha wanta go for a ride?"

"I don't know."

"Why not?"

"I got things to do."

"Like what?"

"Things."

He laughed as if she had said something funny. He slapped his thighs. He was standing in a strange way, leaning back against the car as if he were balancing himself. He wasn't tall, only an inch or so taller than she would be if she came down to him. Connie liked the way he was dressed, which was the way all of them dressed: tight faded jeans stuffed into black, scuffed boots, a belt that pulled his waist in and showed how lean he was, and a white pullover shirt that was a little soiled and showed the hard small muscles of his arms and shoulders. He looked as if he probably did hard work, lifting and carrying things. Even his neck looked muscular. And his face was a familiar face, somehow: the jaw and chin and cheeks slightly darkened, because he hadn't shaved for a day or two, and the nose long and hawklike, sniffing as if she were a treat he was going to gobble up and it was all a joke.

"Connie, you ain't telling the truth. This is your day set aside for a ride with me and you know it," he said, still laughing. The way he straightened and recovered from his fit of laughing showed that it had been all fake.

"How do you know what my name is?" she said suspiciously.

"It's Connie."

"Maybe and maybe not."

"I know my Connie," he said, wagging his finger. Now she remembered him even better, back at the restaurant, and her cheeks warmed at the thought of how she sucked in her breath just at the moment she passed him—how she must have looked to him. And he had remembered her. "Ellie and I come out here especially for you," he said. "Ellie can sit in back. How about it?"

"Where?"

"Where what?"

"Where're we going?"

He looked at her. He took off the sunglasses and she saw how pale the skin around his eyes was, like holes that were not in shadow but instead in light. His eyes were chips of broken glass that catch the light in an amiable way. He smiled. It was as if the idea of going for a ride somewhere, to some place, was a new idea to him.

"Just for a ride, Connie sweetheart."

"I never said my name was Connie," she said.

"But I know what it is. I know your name and all about you, lots of things," Arnold Friend said. He had not moved yet but stood still leaning back against the side of his jalopy. "I took a special interest in you, such a pretty girl, and found out all about you like I know your parents and sister are gone somewheres and I know where and how long they're going to be gone, and I know who you were with last night, and your best girl friend's name is Betty. Right?"

He spoke in a simple lilting voice, exactly as if he were reciting the words to a song. His smile assured her that everything was fine. In the car Ellie turned up the volume on his radio and did not bother to look around at them.

"Ellie can sit in the back seat," Arnold Friend said. He indicated his friend with a casual jerk of his chin, as if Ellie did not count and she should not bother with him.

"How'd you find out all that stuff?" Connie said.

"Listen: Betty Schultz and Tony Fitch and Jimmy Pettinger and Nancy Pettinger," he said, in a chant. "Raymond Stanely and Bob Hutter—"

"Do you know all those kids?"

"I know everybody."

"Look, you're kidding. You're not from around here."

"Sure."

"But—how come we never saw you before?"

"Sure you saw me before," he said. He looked down at his boots, as if he were a little offended. "You just don't remember."

"I guess I'd remember you," Connie said.

"Yeah?" He looked up at this, beaming. He was pleased. He began to mark time with the music from Ellie's radio, tapping his fists lightly together. Connie looked away from his smile to the car, which was painted so bright it almost hurt her eyes to look at it. She looked at that name, ARNOLD FRIEND. And up at the front fender was an expression that was familiar—MAN THE FLYING SAUCERS. It was an expression kids had used the year before, but didn't use this year. She looked at it for a while as if the words meant something to her that she did not yet know.

"What're you thinking about? Huh?" Arnold Friend demanded. "Not worried about your hair blowing around in the car, are you?"

"No.

"Think I maybe can't drive good?"

"How do I know?"

"You're a hard girl to handle. How come?" he said. "Don't you know I'm your friend? Didn't you see me put my sign in the air when you walked by?"

"What sign?"

"My sign." And he drew an X in the air, leaning out toward her. They were maybe ten feet apart. After his hand fell back to his side the X was still in the air, almost visible. Connie let the screen door close and stood perfectly still inside it, listening to the music from her radio and the boy's blend together. She stared at Arnold Friend. He stood there so stiffly relaxed, pretending to be relaxed, with one hand idly on the door handle as if he were keeping himself up that way and had no intention of ever moving again. She recognized most things about him, the tight jeans that showed his thighs and buttocks and the greasy leather boots and the tight shirt, and even that slippery friendly smile of his, that sleepy dreamy smile that all the boys used to get across ideas they didn't want to put into words. She recognized all this and also the singsong way he talked, slightly mocking, kidding, but serious and a little melancholy, and she recognized the way he tapped one fist against the other in homage to the perpetual music behind him. But all these things did not come together.

She said suddenly, "Hey, how old are you?"

His smile faded. She could see then that he wasn't a kid, he was much older—thirty, maybe more. At this knowledge her heart began to pound faster.

"That's a crazy thing to ask. Can'tcha see I'm your own age?"

"Like hell you are."

"Or maybe a coupla years older, I'm eighteen."

"Eighteen?" she said doubtfully.

He grinned to reassure her and lines appeared at the corners of his mouth. His teeth were big and white. He grinned so broadly his eyes became slits and she saw how thick the lashes were, thick and black as if painted with a black tarlike material. Then he seemed to become embarrassed abruptly, and looked over his shoulder at Ellie. "*Him*, he's crazy," he said. "Ain't he a riot, he's a nut, a real character." Ellie was still listening to the music. His sunglasses told nothing about what he was thinking. He wore a bright orange shirt unbuttoned halfway to show his chest, which was a pale, bluish chest and not muscular like Arnold Friend's. His shirt collar was turned up all around and the very tips of the collar pointed out past his chin as if they were protecting him.

He was pressing the transistor radio up against his ear and sat there in a kind of daze, right in the sun.

"He's kinda strange," Connie said.

"Hey, she says you're kinda strange! Kinda strange!" Arnold Friend cried. He pounded on the car to get Ellie's attention. Ellie turned for the first time and Connie saw with shock that he wasn't a kid either—he had a fair, hairless face, cheeks reddened slightly as if the veins grew too close to the surface of his skin, the face of a forty-year-old baby. Connie felt a wave of dizziness rise in her at this sight and she stared at him as if waiting for something to change the shock of the moment, make it all right again. Ellie's lips kept shaping words, mumbling along with the words blasting in his ear.

"Maybe you two better go away," Connie said faintly.

"What? How come?" Arnold Friend cried. "We come out here to take you for a ride. It's Sunday." He had the voice of the man on the radio now. It was the same voice, Connie thought. "Don'tcha know it's Sunday all day and honey, no matter who you were with last night today you're with Arnold Friend and don't you forget it!—Maybe you better step out here," he said, and this last was in a different voice. It was a little flatter, as if the heat was finally getting to him.

"No. I got things to do."

"Hey."

"You two better leave."

"We ain't leaving until you come with us."

"Like hell I am—"

"Connie, don't fool around with me. I mean, I mean, don't fool *around*," he said, shaking his head. He laughed incredulously. He placed his sunglasses on top of his head, carefully, as if he were indeed wearing a wig, and brought the stems down behind his ears. Connie stared at him, another wave of dizziness and fear rising in her so that for a moment he wasn't even in focus but was just a blur, standing there against his gold car, and she had the idea that he had driven up the driveway all right but had come from nowhere before that and belonged nowhere and that everything about him and even about the music that was so familiar to her was only half real.

"If my father comes and sees you—"

"He ain't coming. He's at a barbecue."

"How do you know that?"

"Aunt Tillie's. Right now they're—uh—they're drinking. Sitting around," he said vaguely, squinting as if he were staring all the way to town and over to Aunt Tillie's backyard. Then the vision seemed to get clear and he nodded energetically. "Yeah. Sitting around. There's your sister in a blue dress, huh? And high heels, the poor sad bitch—nothing like you, sweetheart! And your mother's helping some fat woman with the corn, they're cleaning the corn—husking the corn—"

"What fat woman?" Connie cried.

"How do I know what fat woman. I don't know every goddam fat woman in the world!" Arnold Friend laughed.

"Oh, that's Mrs. Hornby. . . . Who invited her?" Connie said. She felt a little light-headed. Her breath was coming quickly.

"She's too fat. I don't like them fat. I like them the way you are, honey," he said, smiling sleepily at her. They stared at each other for a while, through the screen door. He said softly, "Now what you're going to do is this: you're going to come out that door. You're going to sit up front with me and Ellie's going to sit in the back, the hell with Ellie, right? This isn't Ellie's date. You're my date. I'm your lover, honey."

"What? You're crazy—"

"Yes, I'm your lover. You don't know what that is but you will," he said. "I know that too. I know all about you. But look: it's real nice and you couldn't ask for nobody better than me, or more polite. I always keep my word. I'll tell you how it is, I'm always nice at first, the first time. I'll hold you so tight you won't think you have to try to get away or pretend anything because you'll know you can't. And I'll come inside you where it's all secret and you'll give in to me and you'll love me—"

"Shut up! You're crazy!" Connie said. She backed away from the door. She put her hands against her ears as if she'd heard something terrible, something not meant for her. "People don't talk like that, you're crazy," she muttered. Her heart was almost too big now for her chest and its pumping made sweat break out all over her. She looked out to see Arnold Friend pause and then take a step toward the porch lurching. He almost fell. But, like a clever drunken man, he managed to catch his balance. He wobbled in his high boots and grabbed hold of one of the porch posts.

"Honey?" he said. "You still listening?"

"Get the hell out of here!"

"Be nice, honey. Listen."

"I'm going to call the police—"

He wobbled again and out of the side of his mouth came a fast spat curse, an aside not meant for her to hear. But even this "Christ!" sounded forced. Then he began to smile again. She watched this smile come, awkward as if he were smiling from inside a mask. His whole face was a mask, she thought wildly, tanned down onto his throat but then running out as if he had plastered make-up on his face but had forgotten about his throat.

"Honey—? Listen, here's how it is. I always tell the truth and I promise you this: I ain't coming in that house after you."

"You better not! I'm going to call the police if you—if you don't—"

"Honey," he said, talking right through her voice, "honey, I'm not coming in there but you are coming out here. You know why?"

She was panting. The kitchen looked like a place she had never seen before, some room she had run inside but which wasn't good enough, wasn't going to help her. The kitchen window had never had a curtain, after three years, and there were dishes in the sink for her to do—probably—and if you ran your hand across the table you'd probably feel something sticky there.

"You listening, honey? Hey?"

"—going to call the police—"

"Soon as you touch the phone I don't need to keep my promise and can come inside. You won't want that."

She rushed forward and tried to lock the door. Her fingers were shaking. "But why lock it," Arnold Friend said gently, talking right into her face. "It's just a screen door. It's just nothing." One of his boots was at a strange angle, as if his foot wasn't in it. It pointed out to the left, bent at the ankle. "I mean, anybody can break through a screen door and glass and wood and iron or anything else if he needs to, anybody at all and specially Arnold Friend. If the place got lit up with a fire honey you'd come running out into my arms, right into my arms and safe at home—like you knew I was your lover and'd stopped fooling around. I don't mind a nice shy girl but I don't like no fooling around." Part of those words were spoken with a slight rhythmic lilt, and Connie somehow recognized them—the echo of a song from last year, about a girl rushing into her boy friend's arms and coming home again—

Connie stood barefoot on the linoleum floor, staring at him. "What do you want?" she whispered.

"I want you," he said.

"What?"

"Seen you that night and thought, that's the one, yes sir. I never needed to look any more."

"But my father's coming back. He's coming to get me. I had to wash my hair first—" She spoke in a dry, rapid voice, hardly raising it for him to hear.

"No, your daddy is not coming and yes, you had to wash your hair and you washed it for me. It's nice and shining and all for me, I thank you, sweetheart," he said, with a mock bow, but again he almost lost his balance. He had to bend and adjust his boots. Evidently his feet did not go all the way down; the boots must have been stuffed with something so that he would seem taller. Connie stared out at him and behind him Ellie in the car, who seemed to be looking off toward Connie's right, into nothing. This Ellie said, pulling the words out of the air one after another as if he were just discovering them, "You want me to pull out the phone?"

"Shut your mouth and keep it shut," Arnold Friend said, his face red from bending over or maybe from embarrassment because Connie had seen his boots. "This ain't none of your business."

"What—what are you doing? What do you want?" Connie said. "If I call the police they'll get you, they'll arrest you—"

"Promise was not to come in unless you touch that phone, and I'll keep that promise," he said. He resumed his erect position and tried to force his shoulders back. He sounded like a hero in a movie, declaring something important. He spoke too loudly and it was as if he were speaking to someone behind Connie. "I ain't made plans for coming in that house where I don't belong but just for you to come out to me, the way you should. Don't you know who I am?"

"You're crazy," she whispered. She backed away from the door but did not want to go into another part of the house, as if this would give him permission to come through the door. "What do you. . . . You're crazy, you . . ."

"Huh? What're you saying, honey?"

Her eyes darted everywhere in the kitchen. She could not remember what it was, this room.

"This is how it is, honey: you come out and we'll drive away, have a nice ride. But if you don't come out we're gonna wait till your people come home and then they're all going to get it."

"You want that telephone pulled out?" Ellie said. He held the radio away from his ear and grimaced, as if without the radio the air was too much for him.

"I toldja shut up, Ellie," Arnold Friend said, "you're deaf, get a hearing aid, right? Fix yourself up. This little girl's no trouble and's gonna be nice to me, so Ellie keep to yourself, this ain't your date—right? Don't hem in on me. Don't hog. Don't crush. Don't bird dog. Don't trail me," he said in a rapid meaningless voice, as if he were running through all the expressions he'd learned but was no longer sure which one of them was in style, then rushing on to new ones, making them up with his eyes closed, "Don't crawl under my fence, don't squeeze in my chipmunk hole, don't sniff my glue, suck my popsicle, keep your own greasy fingers on yourself!" He shaded his eyes and peered in at Connie, who was backed against the kitchen table. "Don't mind him honey he's just a creep. He's a dope. Right? I'm the boy for you and like I said you come out here nice like a lady and give me your hand, and nobody else gets hurt, I mean, your nice old bald-headed daddy and your mummy and your sister in her high heels. Because listen: why bring them in this?"

"Leave me alone," Connie whispered.

"Hey, you know that old woman down the road, the one with the chickens and stuff—you know her?"

"She's dead!"

"Dead? What? You know her?" Arnold Friend said.

"She's dead—"

"Don't you like her?"

"She's dead—she's—she isn't here any more—"

"But don't you like her, I mean, you got something against her? Some grudge or something?" Then his voice dipped as if he were conscious of a rudeness. He touched the sunglasses perched on top of his head as if to make sure they were still there. "Now you be a good girl."

"What are you going to do?"

"Just two things, or maybe three," Arnold Friend said. "But I promise it won't last long and you'll like me that way you get to like people you're close to. You will. It's all over for you here, so come on out. You don't want your people in any trouble, do you?"

She turned and bumped against a chair or something, hurting her leg, but she ran into the back room and picked up the telephone. Something roared in her ear, a tiny roaring, and she was so sick with fear that she could do nothing but listen to it—the telephone was clammy and very heavy and her fingers groped down to the dial but were too weak to touch it. She began to scream into the phone, into the roaring. She cried out, she cried for her mother, she felt her breath start jerking back and forth in her lungs as if it were something Arnold Friend were stabbing her with again and again with no tenderness. A noisy sorrowful wailing rose all about her and she was locked inside it the way she was locked inside the house.

After a while she could hear again. She was sitting on the floor with her wet back against the wall.

Arnold Friend was saying from the door, "That's a good girl. Put the phone back."

She kicked the phone away from her.

"No, honey. Pick it up. Put it back right."

She picked it up and put it back. The dial tone stopped.

"That's a good girl. Now you come outside."

She was hollow with what had been fear, but what was now just an emptiness. All that screaming had blasted it out of her. She sat, one leg cramped under her, and deep inside her brain was something like a pinpoint of light that kept going and would not let her relax. She thought, I'm not going to see my mother again. She thought, I'm not going to sleep in my bed again. Her bright green blouse was all wet.

Arnold Friend said, in a gentle-loud voice that was like a stage voice, "The place where you came from ain't there any more, and where you had in mind to go is cancelled out. This place you are now—inside your daddy's house—is nothing but a cardboard box I can knock down any time. You know that and always did know it. You hear me?"

She thought, I have got to think. I have to know what to do.

"We'll go out to a nice field, out in the country here where it smells so nice and it's sunny," Arnold Friend said. "I'll have my arms around you so you won't need to try to get away and I'll show you what love is like, what it does. The hell with this house! It looks solid all right," he said. He ran a fingernail down the screen and the noise did not make Connie shiver, as it would have the day before. "Now put your hand on your heart, honey. Feel that? That feels solid too but we know better, be nice to me, be sweet like you can because what else is there for a girl like you but to be sweet and pretty and give in?— and get away before her people come back?"

She felt her pounding heart. Her hand seemed to enclose it. She thought for the first time in her life that it was nothing that was hers, that belonged to her, but just a pounding, living thing inside this body that wasn't really hers either.

"You don't want them to get hurt," Arnold Friend went on. "Now get up, honey. Get up all by yourself."

She stood.

"Now turn this way. That's right. Come over here to me—Ellie, put that away, didn't I tell you? You dope. You miserable creepy dope," Arnold Friend said. His words were not angry but only part of an incantation. The incantation was kindly. "Now come out through the kitchen to me honey and let's see a smile, try it, you're a brave sweet little girl and now they're eating corn and hotdogs cooked to bursting over an outdoor fire, and they don't know one thing about you and never did and honey you're better than them because not a one of them would have done this for you."

Connie felt the linoleum under her feet; it was cool. She brushed her hair back out of her eyes. Arnold Friend let go of the post tentatively and opened his arms for her, his elbows pointing in toward each other and his wrists limp, to show that this was an embarrassed embrace and a little mocking, he didn't want to make her self-conscious.

She put out her hand against the screen. She watched herself push the door slowly open as if she were safe back somewhere in the other doorway, watching this body and this head of long hair moving out into the sunlight where Arnold Friend waited.

"My sweet little blue-eyed girl," he said, in a half-sung sigh that had nothing to do with her brown eyes but was taken up just the same by the vast sun-lit reaches of the land behind him and on all sides of him, so much land that Connie had never seen before and did not recognize except to know that she was going to it.

[1970]

QUESTIONS

JOYCE CAROL OATES, *Where Are You Going, Where Have You Been?*

1. How does the story portray Connie's relationship with her family? With her friends?

2. What details does the story use to create Connie's character? Are there particular details that foreshadow the dangerous situation she finds herself in at the story's end?

3. Who is Arnold Friend? How do his car, his clothes, his hair, and the other details of his description contribute to his character?

4. Why does Connie leave the house at the story's end? What is the significance of her choice? What does Arnold Friend offer her? Where is she going?

5. Joyce Carol Oates is known for her ability to create terror out of the mundane facts of everyday life. How does this story evoke terror in the reader?

6. Oates dedicates the story to Bob Dylan, a singer/songwriter and key figure of late 1960s youth culture. How does that dedication affect your reading of the story? Why do you think Oates chose to dedicate the story to Dylan?

7. What significance does music hold in the story? How is the music of the time used to set the scene, to create characters, and to deepen your understanding of the events here unfolding?

Gabriel García Márquez
[1928–   ]

GABRIEL GARCÍA MÁRQUEZ *was born in 1928 in Aracataca, Colombia. Born into poverty, he was raised by his grandparents who greatly influenced García Márquez's life and work. His grandfather was a veteran of the civil war that occurred in Colombia in the late 1920s in response to the so-called "banana massacres." His grandmother was a natural storyteller, influencing García Márquez's writing style—magical realism—with ghost stories and other superstitions. In 1954 he began working as a journalist for* El Espectador *until the government shut down the paper. By this time, García Márquez had already settled in Paris after having traveled through Switzerland, Italy, Poland, and Hungary. In 1955 he published his first collection of stories, titled* Leaf Storm and Other Stories, *stories heavily influenced by the American writer William Faulkner. Soon after, he published* No One Writes to the Colonel *(1961) and* An Evil Hour *(1962). However, he was not yet satisfied with his writing and suffered great disappointment about his output until he finally experienced the inspiration that would lead to his masterwork,* One Hundred Years of Solitude *(1967), which was written in a creative burst that lasted eighteen months. In this novel, which brought him great fame, García Márquez felt he had achieved mythic expression and a way of storytelling akin to the stories told him by his grandmother. In 1975 he published* Autumn of the Patriarch, *followed by* Operacion Carlotta *(1977), a collection of essays about Cuba. In 1981 he was given the French Legion of Honor medal, and in 1982 he was awarded the Nobel Prize for Literature.* Love in a Time of Cholera *appeared in 1986 to rave reviews and served to enhance García Márquez's ability to take the world stage against political oppression and dictatorship.* News of a Kidnapping *(1996), a journalistic work, dealt with the subject of the Colombian drug trade. In 1999, García Márquez bought the Colombian news magazine,* Cambio, *which continues to advance progressive political themes.*

A Very Old Man with Enormous Wings

GABRIEL GARCÍA MÁRQUEZ

ON THE THIRD day of rain they had killed so many crabs inside the house that Pelayo had to cross his drenched courtyard and throw them into the sea, because the newborn child had a temperature all night and they thought it was due to the stench. The world had been sad since Tuesday. Sea and sky were a single ash-gray thing and the sands of the beach, which on March nights glimmered like powdered light, had become a stew of mud and rotten shellfish. The light was so weak at noon that when Pelayo was coming back to the house after throwing away the crabs, it was hard for him to see what it was that was moving and groaning in the rear of the courtyard. He had to go very close to see that it was an old man, a very old man, lying face down in the mud, who, in spite of his tremendous efforts, couldn't get up, impeded by his enormous wings.

Frightened by that nightmare, Pelayo ran to get Elisenda, his wife, who was putting compresses on the sick child, and he took her to the rear of the courtyard. They both looked at the fallen body with mute stupor. He was dressed like a ragpicker. There were only a few faded hairs left on his bald skull and very few teeth in his mouth, and his pitiful condition of a drenched, great-grandfather had taken away any sense of grandeur he might have had. His huge buzzard wings, dirty and half-plucked, were forever entangled in the mud. They looked at him so long and so closely that Pelayo and Elisenda very soon overcame their surprise and in the end found him familiar. Then they dared speak to him, and he answered in an incomprehensible dialect with a strong sailor's voice. That was how they skipped over the inconvenience of the wings and quite intelligently concluded that he was a lonely castaway from some foreign ship wrecked by the storm. And yet, they called in a neighbor woman who knew everything about life and death to see him, and all she needed was one look to show them their mistake.

"He's an angel," she told them. "He must have been coming for the child, but the poor fellow is so old that the rain knocked him down."

On the following day everyone knew that a flesh-and-blood angel was held captive in Pelayo's house. Against the judgment of the wise neighbor woman, for whom angels in those times were the fugitive survivors of a celestial conspiracy, they did not have the heart to club him to death. Pelayo watched over him all afternoon from the kitchen, armed with his bailiff's club, and before going to bed he dragged him out of the mud and locked him up with the hens in the wire chicken coop. In the middle of the night, when the rain stopped, Pelayo and Elisenda were still killing crabs. A short time afterward the child woke up without a fever and with a desire to eat. Then they felt magnanimous and decided to put the angel on a raft with fresh water and provisions for three days and leave him to his fate on the high seas. But when they went out into the courtyard with the first light of dawn, they found the whole neighborhood in front of the chicken coop having fun with the angel, without the slightest reverence, tossing him things to eat through the openings in the wire as if he weren't a supernatural creature but a circus animal.

Father Gonzaga arrived before seven o'clock, alarmed at the strange news. By that time onlookers less frivolous than those at dawn had already arrived and they were making all kinds of conjectures concerning the captive's future. The simplest among them thought that he should be named mayor of the world. Others of sterner mind felt that he should be promoted to the rank of five-star general in order to win all wars. Some visionaries hoped that he could be put to stud in order to implant on earth a race of winged wise men who could take charge of the universe. But Father Gonzaga, before becoming a priest, had been a robust woodcutter. Standing by the wire, he reviewed his catechism in an instant and asked them to open the door so that he could take a close look at that pitiful man who looked more like a huge decrepit hen among the fascinated chickens. He was lying in a corner drying his open wings in the sunlight among the fruit peels and breakfast leftovers that the early risers had thrown him. Alien to the impertinences of the world, he only lifted his antiquarian eyes and murmured something in his dialect when Father Gonzaga went into the chicken coop and said good morning to him in Latin. The parish priest had his first suspicion of an impostor when he saw that he did not understand the language of God or know how to greet His ministers. Then he noticed that seen close up he was much too human: he had an unbearable smell of the outdoors, the back side of his wings was strewn with parasites and his main feathers had been mistreated by terrestrial winds, and nothing about him measured up to the proud dignity of angels. Then he came out of the chicken coop and in a brief sermon warned the curious against the risks of being ingenuous. He reminded them that the devil had the bad habit of making use of carnival tricks in order to confuse the unwary. He argued that if wings were not the essential element in determining the difference between hawk and an airplane, they were even less so in the recognition of angels. Nevertheless, he promised to write a letter to his bishop so that the latter would write to his primate so that the latter would write to the Supreme Pontiff in order to get the final verdict from the highest courts.

His prudence fell on sterile hearts. The news of the captive angel spread with such rapidity that after a few hours the courtyard had the bustle of a marketplace and they had to call in troops with fixed bayonets to disperse the mob that was about to knock the house down. Elisenda, her spine all twisted from sweeping up so much marketplace trash, then got the idea of fencing in the yard and charging five cents admission to see the angel.

The curious came from far away. A traveling carnival arrived with a flying acrobat who buzzed over the crowd several times, but no one paid any attention to him because his wings were not those of an angel but, rather, those of a sidereal bat. The most unfortunate invalids on earth came in search of health: a poor woman who since childhood had been counting her heartbeats and had run out of numbers; a Portuguese man who couldn't sleep because the noise of the stars disturbed him; a sleepwalker who got up at night to undo the things he had done while awake; and many others with less serious ailments. In the midst of that shipwreck disorder that made the earth tremble, Pelayo and Elisenda were happy with fatigue, for in less than a week they had crammed their rooms with money and the line of pilgrims waiting their turn to enter still reached beyond the horizon.

The angel was the only one who took no part in his own act. He spent his time trying to get comfortable in his borrowed nest, befuddled by the hellish heat of the oil lamps and sacramental candles that had been placed along the wire. At first they tried to make him eat some mothballs, which, according to the wisdom of the wise neighbor woman, were the food prescribed for angels. But he turned them down, just as he turned down the papal lunches that the penitents brought him, and they never found out whether it was because he was an angel or because he was an old man that in the end he ate nothing but eggplant mush. His only supernatural virtue seemed to be patience. Especially during the first days, when the hens pecked at him, searching for the stellar parasites that proliferated in his wings, and the cripples pulled out feathers to touch their defective parts with, and even the most merciful threw stones at him, trying to get him to rise so they could see him standing. The only time they succeeded in arousing him was when they burned his side with an iron for branding steers, for he had been motionless for so many hours that they thought he was dead. He awoke with a start, ranting in his hermetic language and with tears in his eyes, and he flapped his wings a couple of times, which brought on a whirlwind of chicken dung and lunar dust and a gale of panic that did not seem to be of this world. Although many thought that his reaction had been one not of rage but of pain, from then on they were careful not to annoy him, because the majority understood that his passivity was not that of a hero taking his ease but that of a cataclysm in repose.

Father Gonzaga held back the crowd's frivolity with formulas of maidservant inspiration while awaiting the arrival of a final judgment on the nature of the captive. But the mail from Rome showed no sense of urgency. They spent their time finding out if the prisoner had a navel, if his dialect had any connection with Aramaic, how many times he could fit on the head of a pin, or whether he wasn't just a Norwegian with wings. Those meager letters might have come and gone until the end of time if a providential event had not put an end to the priest's tribulations.

It so happened that during those days, among so many other carnival attractions, there arrived in town the traveling show of the woman who had been changed into a spider for having disobeyed her parents. The admission to see her was not only less than the admission to see the angel, but people were permitted to ask her all manner of questions about her absurd state and to examine her up and down so that no one would ever doubt the truth of her horror. She was a frightful tarantula the size of a ram and with the head of a sad maiden. What was most heartrending, however, was not her outlandish shape but the sincere affliction with which she recounted the details of her misfortune. While still practically a child she had sneaked out of her parents' house to go to a dance, and while she was coming back through the woods after having danced all night without permission, a fearful thunderclap rent the sky in two and through the crack came the lightning bolt of brimstone that changed her into a spider. Her only nourishment came from the meatballs that charitable souls chose to toss into her mouth. A spectacle like that, full of so much human truth and with such a fearful lesson, was bound to defeat without even trying that of a haughty angel who scarcely deigned to look at mortals. Besides, the few miracles attributed to the angel showed a certain mental disorder, like the blind man who didn't recover his sight but grew three new teeth, or the paralytic who didn't get to walk but almost won the lottery, and the leper whose sores sprouted sunflowers. Those consolation miracles, which were more like mocking fun, had already ruined the angel's reputation when the woman who had been changed into a spider finally crushed him completely. That was how Father Gonzaga was cured forever of his insomnia and Pelayo's courtyard went back to being as empty as during the time it had rained for three days and crabs walked through the bedrooms.

The owners of the house had no reason to lament. With the money they saved they built a two-story mansion with balconies and gardens and high netting so that crabs wouldn't get in during the winter, and with iron bars on the windows so that angels wouldn't get in. Pelayo also set up a rabbit warren close to town and gave up his job as bailiff for good, and Elisenda bought some satin pumps with high heels and many dresses of iridescent silk, the kind worn on Sunday by the most desirable women in those times. The chicken coop was the only thing that didn't receive any attention. If they washed it down with creolin and burned tears of myrrh inside it every so often, it was not in homage to the angel but to drive away the dungheap stench that still hung everywhere like a ghost and was turning the new house into an old one. At first, when the child learned to walk, they were careful that he not get too close to the chicken coop. But then they began to lose their fears and got used to the smell, and before the child got his second teeth he'd gone inside the chicken coop to play, where the wires were falling apart. The angel was no less standoffish with him than with other mortals, but he tolerated the most ingenious infamies with the patience of a dog who had no illusions. They both came down with chicken pox at the same time. The doctor who took care of the child couldn't resist the temptation to listen to the angel's heart, and he found so much whistling in the heart and so many sounds in his kidneys that it seemed impossible for him to be alive. What surprised him most, however, was the logic of his wings. They seemed so natural on that completely human organism that he couldn't understand why other men didn't have them too.

When the child began school it had been some time since the sun and rain had caused the collapse of the chicken coop. The angel went dragging himself about here and there like a stray dying man. They would drive him out of the bedroom with a broom and a moment later find him in the kitchen. He seemed to be in so many places at the same time that they grew to think that he'd been duplicated, that he was reproducing himself all through the house, and the exasperated and unhinged Elisenda shouted that it was awful living in that hell full of angels. He could scarcely eat and his antiquarian eyes had also become so foggy that he went about bumping into posts. All he had left were the bare cannulae of his last feathers. Pelayo threw a blanket over him and extended him the charity of letting him sleep in the shed, and only then did they notice that he had a temperature at night, and was delirious with the tongue twisters of an old Norwegian. That was one of the few times they became alarmed, for they thought he was going to die and not even the wise neighbor woman had been able to tell them what to do with dead angels.

And yet he not only survived his worst winter, but seemed improved with the first sunny days. He remained motionless for several days in the farthest corner of the courtyard, where no one would see him, and at the beginning of December some large, stiff feathers began to grow on his wings, the feathers of a scarecrow, which looked more like another misfortune of decrepitude. But he must have known the reason for those changes, for he was quite careful that no one should notice them, that no one should hear the sea chanteys that he sometimes sang under the stars. One morning Elisenda was cutting some bunches of onions for lunch when a wind that seemed to come from the high seas blew into the kitchen. Then she went to the window and caught the angel in his first attempts at flight. They were so clumsy that his fingernails opened a furrow in the vegetable patch and he was on the point of knocking the shed down with the ungainly flapping that slipped on the light and couldn't get a grip on the air. But he did manage to gain altitude. Elisenda let out a sigh of relief, for herself and for him, when she saw him pass over the last houses, holding himself up in some way with the risky flapping of a senile vulture. She kept watching him even when she was through cutting the onions and she kept on watching until it was no longer possible for her to see him, because then he was no longer an annoyance in her life but an imaginary dot on the horizon of the sea.

[1968]

QUESTIONS

GABRIEL GARCÍA MÁRQUEZ, *A Very Old Man with Enormous Wings*

1. What is an allegory? How is the García Márquez story an example of an allegorical tale? What was your initial response to the story?

2. How does García Márquez combine realistic detail and plot line with the fantastical and surreal?

3. The point of view of the story is offered by a third-person omniscient narrator. How does the narrator's attitude towards the townspeople shift in the course of the plot?

4. What statement might García Márquez be making given the cruel treatment of the angel by the people in the village? Were you surprised by their response? Why or why not?

5. What is the role of the priest in the story? What happens when he seeks guidance as to the meaning of the angel?

6. Why does the plot shift—spin off really—to the account of the girl changed into a spider for disobeying her parents?

7. This story is an example of what is referred to as "magical realism." Research this literary movement and explain its significance in a brief report.

8. Some critics have asserted that the angel represents the artist and an impoverishment of the imagination. Are there any signs of such conditions in our culture today? Is there reason to be cynical about the state of the imagination? Explore possible justifications for this view in a short essay. Cite pertinent examples of social or moral disorder.

Sophocles

[c. 496–406 B.C.E.]

In ancient Greece, plays were performed annually at a religious festival for Dionysus, the god of wine. These performances were competitive, and the Athenian playwright SOPHOCLES remarkably earned approximately twenty first prizes in these drama contests. During his long lifetime, this master tragedian wrote an estimated one hundred plays, yet only seven remain: Oedipus the King, Electra, Antigone, Trachinian Women, Ajax, Philoctetes, and Oedipus at Colonus.

Ironically, the influential tragedy for which Sophocles is perhaps most famous—Oedipus Rex (Oedipus the King)—won only second prize. The three "Theban Plays"—Oedipus Rex, Oedipus at Colonus, and Antigone—depict the fate of Oedipus, king of Thebes, and his children. Sophocles drew Oedipus, a man who unwittingly killed his father and married his mother, from familiar Greek myth. Through his dramatic depictions of Oedipus's life, Sophocles addressed the question of destiny and fate. These tragedies ask if man is master of his own fate, or if he is merely a puppet directed by the will of higher power. During the twentieth century, the Oedipus myth was famously invoked by the psychologist Sigmund Freud in his theory of the Oedipus Complex. Here, Freud hypothesized that a crucial stage in childhood development was characterized by the male child's desire for sexual involvement with the mother and the attendant rivalry with the father.

Sophocles is credited with a number of important theatrical innovations. He introduced props and scenic backdrops, which established for the audience the location of the the story. He reduced the size of the chorus and instituted the practice of providing a third actor on the stage. Traditionally, two actors performed all of the roles in classical drama; with the addition of this third actor, plots became more complex. Sophocles also began to present the whole of dramatic action in one play, rather than offering it in a trilogy, as his predecessor and teacher Aeschylus had done. This new plot structure, which often centered on inevitability and doubt, increased psychological depth for dramatic characters. Sophocles also provided readers and audiences with rich and complex characterizations of tragic women, such as Electra and Antigone.

Throughout his life, Sophocles was involved in public issues as a statesman, general, and priest. He lived through the height of Athenian power during the fifth century B.C.E. and actively contributed to the rise of Athens following the Persian Wars. He died at age ninety, having witnessed the decline of Athens during the thirty-year Peloponnesian War waged among the Greek states.

Oedipus Rex

SOPHOCLES
TRANSLATED BY DUDLEY FITTS AND ROBERT FITZGERALD

CHARACTERS

OEDIPUS,	King of Thebes, supposed son of Polybos and Merope, King and Queen of Corinth
IOKASTE[1],	wife of Oedipus and widow of the late King Laios
KREON,	brother of Iokaste, a prince of Thebes
TEIRESIAS,	a blind seer who serves Apollo
PRIEST MESSENGER,	from Corinth
SHEPHERD,	former servant of Laios
SECOND MESSENGER,	from the palace
CHORUS OF THEBAN ELDERS CHORAGOS,	leader of the Chorus
ANTIGONE and ISMENE,	young daughters of Oedipus and Iokaste. They appear in the Exodos but do not speak.
SUPPLIANTS, GUARDS, SERVANTS	

THE SCENE

Before the palace of Oedipus, King of Thebes. A central door and two lateral doors open onto a platform which runs the length of the facade. On the platform, right and left, are altars; and three steps lead down into the orchestra, or chorus-ground. At the beginning of the action these steps are crowded by suppliants who have brought branches and chaplets of olive leaves and who sit in various attitudes of despair. Oedipus enters.

---

[1]Iokaste has been translated as Jocasta in other versions of the play.

PROLOGUE²

OEDIPUS. My children, generations of the living
In the line of Kadmos,³ nursed at his ancient hearth:
Why have you strewn yourselves before these altars
In supplication, with your boughs and garlands?
The breath of incense rises from the city   5
With a sound of prayer and lamentation.
                                        Children,
I would not have you speak through messengers,
And therefore I have come myself to hear you—
I, Oedipus, who bear the famous name.
(*To a Priest.*) You, there, since you are eldest in the company,   10
Speak for them all, tell me what preys upon you,
Whether you come in dread, or crave some blessing:
Tell me, and never doubt that I will help you
In every way I can; I should be heartless
Were I not moved to find you suppliant here.   15
PRIEST. Great Oedipus, O powerful king of Thebes!
You see how all the ages of our people
Cling to your altar steps: here are boys
Who can barely stand alone, and here are priests
By weight of age, as I am a priest of God,   20
And young men chosen from those yet unmarried;
As for the others, all that multitude,
They wait with olive chaplets in the squares,
At the two shrines of Pallas,⁴ and where Apollo⁵
Speaks in the glowing embers.
                              Your own eyes 25
Must tell you: Thebes is tossed on a murdering sea
And can not lift her head from the death surge.
A rust consumes the buds and fruits of the earth;
The herds are sick; children die unborn,
And labor is vain. The god of plague and pyre   30
Raids like detestable lightning through the city,

---

²Part of play that explains background and current action.

³Founder of Thebes.

⁴Pallas Athene, goddess of wisdom

⁵God of the sun.

And all the house of Kadmos is laid waste,
All emptied, and all darkened: Death alone
Battens upon the misery of Thebes.
You are not one of the immortal gods, we know;   *35*
Yet we have come to you to make our prayer
As to the man surest in mortal ways
And wisest in the ways of God. You saved us
From the Sphinx,⁶ that flinty singer, and the tribute
We paid to her so long; yet you were never   *40*
Better informed than we, nor could we teach you:
A god's touch, it seems, enabled you to help us.

Therefore, O mighty power, we turn to you:
Find us our safety, find us a remedy,
Whether by counsel of the gods or of men.   *45*
A king of wisdom tested in the past
Can act in a time of troubles, and act well.
Noblest of men, restore
Life to your city! Think how all men call you
Liberator for your boldness long ago;   *50*
Ah, when your years of kingship are remembered,
Let them not say *We rose, but later fell*—
Keep the State from going down in the storm!
Once, years ago, with happy augury,
You brought us fortune; be the same again!   *55*
No man questions your power to rule the land:
But rule over men, not over a dead city!
Ships are only hulls, high walls are nothing,
When no life moves in the empty passageways.
OEDIPUS. Poor children! You may be sure I know   *60*
All that you longed for in your coming here.
I know that you are deathly sick; and yet,
Sick as you are, not one is as sick as I.
Each of you suffers in himself alone
His anguish, not another's; but my spirit   . *65*
Groans for the city, for myself, for you.

---

⁶Mythological winged creature with lion's body and human head that tormented Thebes by demand-
ing the answer to this riddle: What has one voice and yet becomes four-footed and two-footed and
three-footed? When the riddle was answered incorrectly, she ate the respondent. Oedipus gives the
correct answer: A man crawls on all fours in infancy, walks on two feet when grown, and leans on a
staff in old age. After Oedipus answers correctly, the Sphinx kills herself.

I was not sleeping, you are not waking me.
No, I have been in tears for a long while
And in my restless thought walked many ways.
In all my search I found one remedy,   *70*
And I have adopted it: I have sent Kreon,
Son of Menoikeus, brother of the queen,
To Delphi,[7] Apollo's place of revelation,
To learn there, if he can,
What act or pledge of mine may save the city.   *75*
I have counted the days, and now, this very day,
I am troubled, for he has overstayed his time.
What is he doing? He has been gone too long.
Yet whenever he comes back, I should do ill
Not to take any action the god orders.   *80*

PRIEST. It is a timely promise. At this instant
    They tell me Kreon is here.

OEDIPUS. O Lord Apollo!
    May his news be fair as his face is radiant!

PRIEST. Good news, I gather! he is crowned with bay,
    The chaplet is thick with berries.

OEDIPUS. We shall soon know;   *85*
    He is near enough to hear us now. (*Enter Kreon.*) O prince:
    Brother: son of Menoikeus:
    What answer do you bring us from the god?

KREON. A strong one. I can tell you, great afflictions
    Will turn out well, if they are taken well.   *90*

OEDIPUS. What was the oracle? These vague words
    Leave me still hanging between hope and fear.

KREON. Is it your pleasure to hear me with all these
    Gathered around us? I am prepared to speak,
    But should we not go in?

OEDIPUS. Speak to them all,   *95*
    It is for them I suffer, more than for myself.

KREON. Then I will tell you what I heard at Delphi.
    In plain words
    The god commands us to expel from the land of Thebes
    An old defilement we are sheltering.   *100*
    It is a deathly thing, beyond cure;
    We must not let it feed upon us longer.

---

[7]Greek temple and oracle of Apollo.

OEDIPUS. What defilement? How shall we rid ourselves of it?
KREON. By exile or death, blood for blood. It was
    Murder that brought the plague-wind on the city.   *105*
OEDIPUS. Murder of whom? Surely the god has named him?
KREON. My Lord: Laios once ruled this land,
    Before you came to govern us.
OEDIPUS. I know;
    I learned of him from others; I never saw him.
KREON. He was murdered; and Apollo commands us now   *110*
    To take revenge upon whoever killed him.
OEDIPUS. Upon whom? Where are they? Where shall we find a clue
    To solve that crime, after so many years?
KREON. Here in this land, he said. Search reveals
    Things that escape an inattentive man.   *115*
OEDIPUS. Tell me: Was Laios murdered in his house,
    Or in the fields, or in some foreign country?
KREON. He said he planned to make a pilgrimage.
    He did not come home again.
OEDIPUS. And was there no one,
    No witness, no companion, to tell what happened?   *120*
KREON. They were all killed but one, and he got away
    So frightened that he could remember one thing only.
OEDIPUS. What was that one thing? One may be the key
    To everything, if we resolve to use it.
KREON. He said that a band of highwaymen attacked them,   *125*
    Outnumbered them, and overwhelmed the king.
OEDIPUS. Strange, that a highwayman should be so daring—
    Unless some faction here bribed him to do it.
KREON. We thought of that. But after Laios' death
    New troubles arose and we had no avenger.   *130*
OEDIPUS. What troubles could prevent your hunting down the killers?
KREON. The riddling Sphinx's song
    Made us deaf to all mysteries but her own.
OEDIPUS. Then once more I must bring what is dark to light.
    It is most fitting that Apollo shows,   *135*
    As you do, this compunction for the dead.
    You shall see how I stand by you, as I should,
    Avenging this country and the god as well,
    And not as though it were for some distant friend,
    But for my own sake, to be rid of evil.   *140*
    Whoever killed King Laios might—who knows?—

Lay violent hands even on me—and soon.
I act for the murdered king in my own interest.
Come, then, my children: leave the altar steps,
Lift up your olive boughs!

One of you go 145
And summon the people of Kadmos to gather here.
I will do all that I can; you may tell them that.

(Exit a Page.)

So, with the help of God,
We shall be saved—or else indeed we are lost.
PRIEST. Let us rise, children. It was for this we came,   150
And now the king has promised it.
Phoibos⁸ has sent us an oracle; may he descend
Himself to save us and drive out the plague.

(Exeunt⁹ Oedipus and Kreon into the palace by the central door. The Priest and the Suppliants disperse right and left. After a short pause the Chorus enters the orchestra.)

PARADOS¹⁰

Strophe¹¹ 1

CHORUS. What is God singing in his profound
    Delphi of gold and shadow?
    What oracle for Thebes, the Sunwhipped city?
    Fear unjoints me, the roots of my heart tremble.
    Now I remember, O Healer, your power, and wonder: 5
    Will you send doom like a sudden cloud, or weave it
    Like nightfall of the past?
    Speak to me, tell me, O
    Child of golden Hope, immortal Voice.

---

⁸Apollo

⁹They go out. (Latin)

¹⁰Song or ode the Chorus chants when they enter the stage.

¹¹Song the Chorus sings as they dance from stage right to stage left.

Antistrophe[12] 1

Let me pray to Athene, the immortal daughter of Zeus,   *10*
And to Artemis[13] her sister
Who keeps her famous throne in the market ring,
And to Apollo, archer from distant heaven—
O gods, descend! Like three streams leap against
The fires of our grief, the fires of darkness;   *15*
Be swift to bring us rest!
As in the old time from the brilliant house
Of air you stepped to save us, come again!

Strophe 2

Now our afflictions have no end,
Now all our stricken host lies down   *20*
And no man fights off death with his mind;
The noble plowland bears no grain,
And groaning mothers can not bear—
See, how our lives like birds take wing,
Like sparks that fly when a fire soars,   *25*
To the shore of the god of evening.

Antistrophe 2

The plague burns on, it is pitiless,
Though pallid children laden with death
Lie unwept in the stony ways,
And old gray women by every path   *30*
Flock to the strand about the altars
There to strike their breasts and cry
Worship of Phoibos in wailing prayers:
Be kind, God's golden child!

Strophe 3

There are no swords in this attack by fire,   *35*
No shields, but we are ringed with cries.
Send the besieger plunging from our homes

---

[12]Song the Chorus sings as they dance back from stage left to stage right.

[13]Goddess of wild animals and the hunt.

Into the vast sea-room of the Atlantic
Or into the waves that foam eastward of Thrace—
For the day ravages what the night spares—   40
Destroy our enemy, lord of the thunder!
Let him be riven by lightning from heaven!

Antistrophe 3

Phoibos Apollo, stretch the sun's bowstring,
That golden cord, until it sing for us,
Flashing arrows in heaven!
Artemis, Huntress,   45
Race with flaring lights upon our mountains!
O scarlet god,[14] O golden-banded brow,
O Theban Bacchos in a storm of Maenads,[15]

(*Enter Oedipus, center.*)

Whirl upon Death, that all the Undying hate!
Come with blinding torches, come in joy!   50

SCENE 1

OEDIPUS. Is this your prayer? It may be answered. Come,
Listen to me, act as the crisis demands,
And you shall have relief from all these evils.

Until now I was a stranger to this tale,
As I had been a stranger to the crime.   5
Could I track down the murderer without a clue?
But now, friends,
As one who became a citizen after the murder,
I make this proclamation to all Thebans:
If any man knows by whose hand Laios, son of Labdakos,   10
Met his death, I direct that man to tell me everything,
No matter what he fears for having so long withheld it.
Let it stand as promised that no further trouble
Will come to him, but he may leave the land in safety.
Moreover: If anyone knows the murderer to be foreign,   15
Let him not keep silent: he shall have his reward from me.

---

[14]Bacchus, god of wine, creative ecstasy, and dramatic poetry

[15]Women who worship Bacchus.

However, if he does conceal it; if any man
Fearing for his friend or for himself disobeys this edict,
Hear what I propose to do:
I solemnly forbid the people of this country,   20
Where power and throne are mine, ever to receive that man
Or speak to him, no matter who he is, or let him
Join in sacrifice, lustration, or in prayer.
I decree that he be driven from every house,
Being, as he is, corruption itself to us: the Delphic   25
Voice of Apollo has pronounced this revelation.
Thus I associate myself with the oracle
And take the side of the murdered king.

As for the criminal, I pray to God—
Whether it be a lurking thief, or one of a number—   30
I pray that that man's life be consumed in evil and wretchedness.
And as for me, this curse applies no less
If it should turn out that the culprit is my guest here,
Sharing my hearth.
                                    You have heard the penalty.
I lay it on you now to attend to this   35
For my sake, for Apollo's, for the sick
Sterile city that heaven has abandoned.
Suppose the oracle had given you no command:
Should this defilement go uncleansed for ever?
You should have found the murderer: your king,   40
A noble king, had been destroyed!
                                                Now I,

Having the power that he held before me,
Having his bed, begetting children there
Upon his wife, as he would have, had he lived—
Their son would have been my children's brother,   45
If Laios had had luck in fatherhood!
(And now his bad fortune has struck him down)—
I say I take the son's part, just as though
I were his son, to press the fight for him
And see it won! I'll find the hand that brought   50
Death to Labdakos' and Polydoros' child,
Heir of Kadmos' and Agenor's line.[16]

---

[16]Labdakos, Polydoros, Kadmos, Agenor, father, grandfather, great-grandfather, and great-great-grandfather of Laios.

And as for those who fail me,
May the gods deny them the fruit of the earth,
Fruit of the womb, and may they rot utterly!   55
Let them be wretched as we are wretched, and worse!

For you, for loyal Thebans, and for all
Who find my actions right, I pray the favor
Of justice, and of all the immortal gods.
CHORAGOS. Since I am under oath, my lord, I swear   60
    I did not do the murder, I can not name
    The murderer. Phoibos ordained the search;
    Why did he not say who the culprit was?
OEDIPUS. An honest question. But no man in the world
    Can make the gods do more than the gods will.   65
CHORAGOS. There is an alternative, I think—
OEDIPUS.   Tell me.
    Any or all, you must not fail to tell me.
CHORAGOS. A lord clairvoyant to the lord Apollo,
    As we all know, is the skilled Teiresias.
    One might learn much about this from him, Oedipus.   70
OEDIPUS. I am not wasting time:
    Kreon spoke of this, and I have sent for him—
    Twice, in fact; it is strange that he is not here.
CHORAGOS. The other matter—that old report—seems useless.
OEDIPUS. What was that? I am interested in all reports.   75
CHORAGOS. The king was said to have been killed by highwaymen.
OEDIPUS. I know. But we have no witnesses to that.
CHORAGOS. If the killer can feel a particle of dread,
    Your curse will bring him out of hiding!
OEDIPUS.   No.
    The man who dared that act will fear no curse.   80

(*Enter the blind seer Teiresias, led by a Page.*)

CHORAGOS. But there is one man who may detect the criminal.
    This is Teiresias, this is the holy prophet
    In whom, alone of all men, truth was born.
OEDIPUS. Teiresias: seer: student of mysteries,
    Of all that's taught and all that no man tells,   85
    Secrets of Heaven and secrets of the earth:
    Blind though you are, you know the city lies
    Sick with plague; and from this plague, my lord,
    We find that you alone can guard or save us.

Possibly you did not hear the messengers?   *90*
Apollo, when we sent to him,
Sent us back word that this great pestilence
Would lift, but only if we established clearly
The identity of those who murdered Laios.
They must be killed or exiled.
                                              Can you use   *95*
Birdflight[17] or any art of divination
To purify yourself, and Thebes, and me
From this contagion? We are in your hands.
There is no fairer duty
Than that of helping others in distress.   *100*
TEIRESIAS. How dreadful knowledge of the truth can be
  When there's no help in truth! I knew this well,
  But did not act on it; else I should not have come.
OEDIPUS. What is troubling you? Why are your eyes so cold?
TEIRESIAS. Let me go home. Bear your own fate, and I'll   *105*
  Bear mine. It is better so: trust what I say.
OEDIPUS. What you say is ungracious and unhelpful
  To your native country. Do not refuse to speak.
TEIRESIAS. When it comes to speech, your own is neither temperate
  Nor opportune. I wish to be more prudent.   *110*
OEDIPUS. In God's name, we all beg you—
TEIRESIAS.   You are all ignorant.
  No; I will never tell you what I know.
  Now it is my misery; then, it would be yours.
OEDIPUS. What! You do know something, and will not tell us?
  You would betray us all and wreck the State?   *115*
TEIRESIAS. I do not intend to torture myself, or you.
  Why persist in asking? You will not persuade me.
OEDIPUS. What a wicked old man you are! You'd try a stone's
  Patience! Out with it! Have you no feeling at all?
TEIRESIAS. You call me unfeeling. If you could only see   *120*
  The nature of your own feelings . . .
OEDIPUS.   Why,
  Who would not feel as I do? Who could endure
  Your arrogance toward the city?
TEIRESIAS.   What does it matter?
  Whether I speak or not, it is bound to come.

---

[17]Prophets predicted the future by observing the flight of birds.

OEDIPUS. Then, if "it" is bound to come, you are bound to tell me. 125
TEIRESIAS. No, I will not go on. Rage as you please.
OEDIPUS. Rage? Why not!

         And I'll tell you what I think:
  You planned it, you had it done, you all but
  Killed him with your own hands: if you had eyes,
  I'd say the crime was yours, and yours alone. 130
TEIRESIAS. So? I charge you, then,
  Abide by the proclamation you have made:
  From this day forth
  Never speak again to these men or to me;
  You yourself are the pollution of this country. 135
OEDIPUS. You dare say that! Can you possibly think you have
  Some way of going free, after such insolence?
TEIRESIAS. I have gone free. It is the truth sustains me.
OEDIPUS. Who taught you shamelessness? It was not your craft.
TEIRESIAS. You did. You made me speak. I did not want to. 140
OEDIPUS. Speak what? Let me hear it again more clearly.
TEIRESIAS. Was it not clear before? Are you tempting me?
OEDIPUS. I did not understand it. Say it again.
TEIRESIAS. I say that you are the murderer whom you seek.
OEDIPUS. Now twice you have spat out infamy.
  You'll pay for it! 145
TEIRESIAS. Would you care for more? Do you wish to be really angry?
OEDIPUS. Say what you will. Whatever you say is worthless.
TEIRESIAS. I say you live in hideous shame with those
  Most dear to you. You can not see the evil.
OEDIPUS. Can you go on babbling like this for ever? 150
TEIRESIAS. I can, if there is power in truth.
OEDIPUS.   There is:
  But not for you, not for you,
  You sightless, witless, senseless, mad old man!
TEIRESIAS. You are the madman. There is no one here
  Who will not curse you soon, as you curse me. 155
OEDIPUS. You child of total night! I would not touch you;
  Neither would any man who sees the sun.
TEIRESIAS. True: it is not from you my fate will come.
  That lies within Apollo's competence,
  As it is his concern.
OEDIPUS.   Tell me, who made 160
  These fine discoveries? Kreon? or someone else?

TEIRESIAS. Kreon is no threat. You weave your own doom.
OEDIPUS. Wealth, power, craft of statemanship!
 Kingly position, everywhere admired!
 What savage envy is stored up against these,   *165*
 If Kreon, whom I trusted, Kreon my friend,
 For this great office which the city once
 Put in my hands unsought—if for this power
 Kreon desires in secret to destroy me!

 He has bought this decrepit fortune-teller, this   *170*
 Collector of dirty pennies, this prophet fraud—
 Why, he is no more clairvoyant than I am!
                Tell us:
 Has your mystic mummery ever approached the truth?
 When that hellcat the Sphinx was performing here,
 What help were you to these people?   *175*
 Her magic was not for the first man who came along:
 It demanded a real exorcist. Your birds—
 What good were they? or the gods, for the matter of that?
 But I came by,
 Oedipus, the simple man, who knows nothing—   *180*
 I thought it out for myself, no birds helped me!
 And this is the man you think you can destroy,
 That you may be close to Kreon when he's king!
 Well, you and your friend Kreon, it seems to me,
 Will suffer most. If you were not an old man,   *185*
 You would have paid already for your plot.
CHORAGOS. We can not see that his words or yours
 Have been spoken except in anger, Oedipus,
 And of anger we have no need. How to accomplish
 The god's will best: that is what most concerns us.   *190*
TEIRESIAS. You are a king. But where argument's concerned
 I am your man, as much a king as you.
 I am not your servant, but Apollo's.
 I have no need of Kreon or Kreon's name.

 Listen to me. You mock my blindness, do you?   *195*
 But I say that you, with both your eyes, are blind:
 You can not see the wretchedness of your life,
 Nor in whose house you live, no, nor with whom.
 Who are your father and mother? Can you tell me?

You do not even know the blind wrongs 200
That you have done them, on earth and in the world below.
But the double lash of your parents' curse will whip you
Out of this land some day, with only night
Upon your precious eyes.
Your cries then—where will they not be heard? 205
What fastness of Kithairon[18] will not echo them?
And that bridal-descant of yours—you'll know it then,
The song they sang when you came here to Thebes
And found your misguided berthing.
All this, and more, that you can not guess at now, 210
Will bring you to yourself among your children.

Be angry, then. Curse Kreon. Curse my words.
I tell you, no man that walks upon the earth
Shall be rooted out more horribly than you. 215
OEDIPUS. Am I to bear this from him?—Damnation
Take you! Out of this place! Out of my sight!
TEIRESIAS. I would not have come at all if you had not asked me.
OEDIPUS. Could I have told that you'd talk nonsense, that
You'd come here to make a fool of yourself, and of me?
TEIRESIAS. A fool? Your parents thought me sane enough. 220
OEDIPUS. My parents again!—Wait: who were my parents?
TEIRESIAS. This day will give you a father, and break your heart.
OEDIPUS. Your infantile riddles! Your damned abracadabra!
TEIRESIAS. You were a great man once at solving riddles.
OEDIPUS. Mock me with that if you like; you will find it true. 225
TEIRESIAS. It was true enough. It brought about your ruin.
OEDIPUS. But if it saved this town?
TEIRESIAS (*to the Page*).   Boy, give me your hand.
OEDIPUS.   Yes, boy; lead him away.
    —While you are here
We can do nothing. Go; leave us in peace.
TEIRESIAS. I will go when I have said what I have to say. 230
How can you hurt me? And I tell you again:
The man you have been looking for all this time,
The damned man, the murderer of Laios,
That man is in Thebes. To your mind he is foreign-born, 235
But it will soon be shown that he is a Theban,

[18]As a baby, Oedipus was abandoned at this mountain.

A revelation that will fail to please.

                                A blind man,
Who has his eyes now; a penniless man, who is rich now;
And he will go tapping the strange earth with his staff.
To the children with whom he lives now he will be   240
Brother and father—the very same; to her
Who bore him, son and husband—the very same
Who came to his father's bed, wet with his father's blood.
Enough. Go think that over.
If later you find error in what I have said,   245
You may say that I have no skill in prophecy.

(*Exit Teiresias, led by his Page. Oedipus goes into the palace.*)

ODE[19] 1

Strophe 1

CHORUS. The Delphic stone of prophecies
        Remembers ancient regicide
        And a still bloody hand.
        That killer's hour of flight has come.
        He must be stronger than riderless   5
        Coursers of untiring wind,
        For the son of Zeus[20] armed with his father's thunder
        Leaps in lightning after him;
        And the Furies[21] hold his track, the sad Furies.

Antistrophe 1

        Holy Parnassos'[22] peak of snow   10
        Flashes and blinds that secret man,
        That all shall hunt him down:
        Though he may roam the forest shade
        Like a bull gone wild from pasture
        To rage through glooms of stone.   15

---

[19]Song sung by Chorus.

[20]Ruler of the Olympian gods.

[21]Goddesses of vengeance.

[22]Mountain sacred to Apollo.

Doom comes down on him; flight will not avail him;
For the world's heart calls him desolate,
And the immortal voices follow, for ever follow.

Strophe 2

But now a wilder thing is heard
From the old man skilled at hearing Fate in the wing-beat
    of a bird. 20
Bewildered as a blown bird, my soul hovers and can not find
Foothold in this debate, or any reason or rest of mind.
But no man ever brought—none can bring
Proof of strife between Thebes' royal house,
Labdakos' line, and the son of Polybos;[23] 25
And never until now has any man brought word
Of Laios' dark death staining Oedipus the King.

Antistrophe 2

Divine Zeus and Apollo hold
Perfect intelligence alone of all tales ever told;
And well though this diviner works, he works in his own night; 30
No man can judge that rough unknown or trust in second sight,
For wisdom changes hands among the wise.
Shall I believe my great lord criminal
At a raging word that a blind old man let fall?
I saw him, when the carrion woman[24] faced him of old, 35
Prove his heroic mind. These evil words are lies.

SCENE 2

KREON. Men of Thebes:
    I am told that heavy accusations
    Have been brought against me by King Oedipus.

    I am not the kind of man to bear this tamely.

    If in these present difficulties 5
    He holds me accountable for any harm to him

---

[23]King who adopted Oedipus.

[24]Sphinx

Through anything I have said or done—why, then,
I do not value life in this dishonor.
It is not as though this rumor touched upon
Some private indiscretion. The matter is grave. 10
The fact is that I am being called disloyal
To the State, to my fellow citizens, to my friends.
CHORAGOS. He may have spoken in anger, not from his mind.
KREON. But did you not hear him say I was the one
Who seduced the old prophet into lying? 15
CHORAGOS. The thing was said; I do not know how seriously.
KREON. But you were watching him! Were his eyes steady?
Did he look like a man in his right mind?
CHORAGOS.   I do not know.
I can not judge the behavior of great men.
But here is the king himself.

(*Enter Oedipus.*)

OEDIPUS.   So you dared come back. 20
Why? How brazen of you to come to my house,
You murderer!
                              Do you think I do not know
That you plotted to kill me, plotted to steal my throne?
Tell me, in God's name: am I coward, a fool,
That you should dream you could accomplish this? 25
A fool who could not see your slippery game?
A coward, not to fight back when I saw it?
You are the fool, Kreon, are you not? hoping
Without support or friends to get a throne?
Thrones may be won or bought: you could do neither. 30
KREON. Now listen to me. You have talked; let me talk, too.
You can not judge unless you know the facts.
OEDIPUS. You speak well: there is one fact; but I find it hard
To learn from the deadliest enemy I have.
KREON. That above all I must dispute with you. 35
OEDIPUS. That above all I will not hear you deny.
KREON. If you think there is anything good in being stubborn.
Against all reason, then I say you are wrong.
OEDIPUS. If you think a man can sin against his own kind
And not be punished for it, I say you are mad. 40
KREON. I agree. But tell me: what have I done to you?
OEDIPUS. You advised me to send for that wizard, did you not?
KREON. I did. I should do it again.

OEDIPUS.   Very well. Now tell me:
    How long has it been since Laios—
KREON.   What of Laios?
OEDIPUS. Since he vanished in that onset by the road?   45
KREON. It was long ago, a long time.
OEDIPUS.   And this prophet,
    Was he practicing here then?
KREON.   He was; and with honor, as now.
OEDIPUS. Did he speak of me at that time?
KREON.   He never did,
    At least, not when I was present.
OEDIPUS.   But . . . the enquiry?
    I suppose you held one?
KREON.   We did, but we learned nothing.   50
OEDIPUS. Why did the prophet not speak against me then?
KREON. I do not know; and I am the kind of man
    Who holds his tongue when he has no facts to go on.
OEDIPUS. There's one fact that you know, and you could tell it.
KREON. What fact is that? If I know it, you shall have it.   55
OEDIPUS. If he were not involved with you, he could not say
    That it was I who murdered Laios.
KREON. If he says that, you are the one that knows it!—
    But now it is my turn to question you.
OEDIPUS. Put your questions. I am no murderer.   60
KREON. First, then: You married my sister?
OEDIPUS.   I married your sister.
KREON. And you rule the kingdom equally with her?
OEDIPUS. Everything that she wants she has from me.
KREON. And I am the third, equal to both of you?
OEDIPUS. That is why I call you a bad friend.   65
KREON. No. Reason it out, as I have done.
    Think of this first: would any sane man prefer
    Power, with all a king's anxieties,
    To that same power and the grace of sleep?
    Certainly not I.   70
    I have never longed for the king's power—only his rights.
    Would any wise man differ from me in this?
    As matters stand, I have my way in everything
    With your consent, and no responsibilities.
    If I were king, I should be a slave to policy.   75
    How could I desire a scepter more
    Than what is now mine—untroubled influence?

No, I have not gone mad; I need no honors,
Except those with the perquisites I have now.
I am welcome everywhere; every man salutes me,   *80*
And those who want your favor seek my ear,
Since I know how to manage what they ask.
Should I exchange this ease for that anxiety?
Besides, no sober mind is treasonable.
I hate anarchy   *85*
And never would deal with any man who likes it.
Test what I have said. Go to the priestess
At Delphi, ask if I quoted her correctly.
And as for this other thing: if I am found
Guilty of treason with Teiresias,   *90*
Then sentence me to death. You have my word
It is a sentence I should cast my vote for—
But not without evidence!
You do wrong
When you take good men for bad, bad men for good.
A true friend thrown aside—why, life itself   *95*
Is not more precious!
In time you will know this well:
For time, and time alone, will show the just man,
Though scoundrels are discovered in a day.
CHORAGOS. This is well said, and a prudent man would ponder it.
Judgments too quickly formed are dangerous.   *100*
OEDIPUS. But is he not quick in his duplicity?
And shall I not be quick to parry him?
Would you have me stand still, hold my peace, and let
This man win everything, through my inaction?
KREON. And you want—what is it, then? To banish me?   *105*
OEDIPUS. No, not exile. It is your death I want,
So that all the world may see what treason means.
KREON. You will persist, then? You will not believe me?
OEDIPUS. How can I believe you?
KREON.   Then you are a fool.
OEDIPUS. To save myself?
KREON.   In justice, think of me. *110*
OEDIPUS. You are evil incarnate.
KREON.   But suppose that you are wrong?
OEDIPUS. Still I must rule.
KREON.   But not if you rule badly.
OEDIPUS. O city, city!

KREON.   It is my city, too!
CHORAGOS. Now, my lords, be still. I see the queen,
 Iokaste, coming from her palace chambers;   *115*
 And it is time she came, for the sake of you both.
 This dreadful quarrel can be resolved through her.

(*Enter Iokaste.*)

IOKASTE. Poor foolish men, what wicked din is this?
 With Thebes sick to death, is it not shameful
 That you should take some private quarrel up?   *120*
 (*To Oedipus.*) Come into the house.
         —And you, Kreon, go now:
 Let us have no more of this tumult over nothing.
KREON. Nothing? No, sister: what your husband plans for me
 Is one of two great evils: exile or death.
OEDIPUS. He is right.
      Why, woman I have caught him squarely *125*
 Plotting against my life.
KREON.   No! Let me die
 Accurst if ever I have wished you harm!
IOKASTE. Ah, believe it, Oedipus!
 In the name of the gods, respect this oath of his
 For my sake, for the sake of these people here!   *130*

Strophe 1

CHORAGOS. Open your mind to her, my lord. Be ruled by her, I beg you!
OEDIPUS. What would you have me do?
CHORAGOS. Respect Kreon's word. He has never spoken like a fool,
 And now he has sworn an oath.
OEDIPUS.   You know what you ask?
CHORAGOS.   I do.
OEDIPUS.   Speak on, then.
CHORAGOS. A friend so sworn should not be baited so,   *135*
 In blind malice, and without final proof.
OEDIPUS. You are aware, I hope, that what you say
 Means death for me, or exile at the least.

Strophe 2

CHORAGOS. No, I swear by Helios, first in heaven!
 May I die friendless and accurst,   *140*

The worst of deaths, if ever I meant that!
It is the withering fields
That hurt my sick heart:
Must we bear all these ills,
And now your bad blood as well?   145
OEDIPUS. Then let him go. And let me die, if I must,
Or be driven by him in shame from the land of Thebes.
It is your unhappiness, and not his talk,
That touches me.

                                        As for him—

Wherever he goes, hatred will follow him.   150
KREON. Ugly in yielding, as you were ugly in rage!
Natures like yours chiefly torment themselves.
OEDIPUS. Can you not go? Can you not leave me?
KREON.   I can.
You do not know me; but the city knows me,
And in its eyes I am just, if not in yours.   155

(*Exit Kreon.*)

Antistrophe 1

CHORAGOS. Lady Iokaste, did you not ask the King to go to his
    chambers?
IOKASTE. First tell me what has happened.
CHORAGOS. There was suspicion without evidence; yet it rankled
    As even false charges will.
IOKASTE. On both sides?
CHORAGOS.   On both.
IOKASTE.   But what was said? 160
CHORAGOS. Oh let it rest, let it be done with!
    Have we not suffered enough?
OEDIPUS. You see to what your decency has brought you:
    You have made difficulties where my heart saw none.

Antistrophe 2

CHORAGOS. Oedipus, it is not once only I have told you—   165
    You must know I should count myself unwise
    To the point of madness, should I now forsake you—
    You, under whose hand,
    In the storm of another time,
    Our dear land sailed out free.   170
    But now stand fast at the helm!

IOKASTE. In God's name, Oedipus, inform your wife as well:
  Why are you so set in this hard anger?
OEDIPUS. I will tell you, for none of these men deserves
  My confidence as you do. It is Kreon's work,   *175*
  His treachery, his plotting against me.
IOKASTE. Go on, if you can make this clear to me.
OEDIPUS. He charges me with the murder of Laios.
IOKASTE. Has he some knowledge? Or does he speak from hearsay?
OEDIPUS. He would not commit himself to such a charge,   *180*
  But he has brought in that damnable soothsayer
  To tell his story.
IOKASTE.   Set your mind at rest.
  If it is a question of soothsayers, I tell you
  That you will find no man whose craft gives knowledge
  Of the unknowable.
                                      Here is my proof: *185*
  An oracle was reported to Laios once
  (I will not say from Phoibos himself, but from
  His appointed ministers, at any rate)
  That his doom would be death at the hands of his own son—
  His son, born of his flesh and of mine!   *190*

  Now, you remember the story: Laios was killed
  By marauding strangers where three highways meet;
  But his child had not been three days in this world
  Before the king had pierced the baby's ankles
  And left him to die on a lonely mountainside.   *195*

  Thus, Apollo never caused that child
  To kill his father, and it was not Laios' fate
  To die at the hands of his son, as he had feared.
  This is what prophets and prophecies are worth!
  Have no dread of them.
                                      It is God himself *200*
  Who can show us what he wills, in his own way.
OEDIPUS. How strange a shadowy memory crossed my mind,
  Just now while you were speaking; it chilled my heart.
IOKASTE. What do you mean? What memory do you speak of?
OEDIPUS. If I understand you, Laios was killed   *205*
  At a place where three roads meet.

IOKASTE. So it was said;
  We have no later story.
OEDIPUS. Where did it happen?
IOKASTE. Phokis, it is called: at a place where the Theban Way
  Divides into the roads toward Delphi and Daulia.
OEDIPUS. When?
IOKASTE. We had the news not long before you came   210
  And proved the right to your succession here.
OEDIPUS. Ah, what net has God been weaving for me?
IOKASTE. Oedipus! Why does this trouble you?
OEDIPUS. Do not ask me yet.
  First, tell me how Laios looked, and tell me
  How old he was.
IOKASTE. He was tall, his hair just touched 215
  With white; his form was not unlike your own.
OEDIPUS. I think that I myself may be accurst
  By my own ignorant edict.
IOKASTE. You speak strangely.
  It makes me tremble to look at you, my king.
OEDIPUS. I am not sure that the blind man can not see.   220
  But I should know better if you were to tell me—
IOKASTE. Anything—though I dread to hear you ask it.
OEDIPUS. Was the king lightly escorted, or did he ride
  With a large company, as a ruler should?
IOKASTE. There were five men with him in all: one was a herald; 225
  And a single chariot, which he was driving.
OEDIPUS. Alas, that makes it plain enough!
                                         But who—
  Who told you how it happened?
IOKASTE. A household servant,
  The only one to escape.
OEDIPUS. And is he still
  A servant of ours?
IOKASTE. No; for when he came back at last 230
  And found you enthroned in the place of the dead king,
  He came to me, touched my hand with his, and begged
  That I would send him away to the frontier district
  Where only the shepherds go—
  As far away from the city as I could send him. 235
  I granted his prayer; for although the man was a slave,
  He had earned more than this favor at my hands.

OEDIPUS. Can he be called back quickly?
IOKASTE.   Easily.
　　But why?
OEDIPUS. I have taken too much upon myself
　　Without enquiry; therefore I wish to consult him.　　　　*240*
IOKASTE. Then he shall come.
　　　　　　　　　　　　But am I not one also
　　To whom you might confide these fears of yours?
OEDIPUS. That is your right; it will not be denied you,
　　Now least of all; for I have reached a pitch
　　Of wild foreboding. Is there anyone　　　　　　　　*245*
　　To whom I should sooner speak?

　　Polybos of Corinth is my father.
　　My mother is a Dorian: Merope.
　　I grew up chief among the men of Corinth
　　Until a strange thing happened—　　　　　　　　　*250*
　　Not worth my passion, it may be, but strange.
　　At a feast, a drunken man maundering in his cups
　　Cries out that I am not my father's son!
　　I contained myself that night, though I felt anger
　　And a sinking heart. The next day I visited　　　　　*255*
　　My father and mother, and questioned them. They stormed,
　　Calling it all the slanderous rant of a fool;
　　And this relieved me. Yet the suspicion
　　Remained always aching in my mind;
　　I knew there was talk; I could not rest;　　　　　　*260*
　　And finally, saying nothing to my parents,
　　I went to the shrine at Delphi.
　　The god dismissed my question without reply;
　　He spoke of other things.
　　　　　　　　　　　　　　Some were clear,
　　Full of wretchedness, dreadful, unbearable:　　　　*265*
　　As, that I should lie with my own mother, breed
　　Children from whom all men would turn their eyes;
　　And that I should be my father's murderer.

　　I heard all this, and fled. And from that day
　　Corinth to me was only in the stars　　　　　　　*270*

Descending in that quarter of the sky,
As I wandered farther and farther on my way
To a land where I should never see the evil
Sung by the oracle. And I came to this country
Where, so you say, King Laios was killed.   275

I will tell you all that happened there, my lady.
There were three highways
Coming together at a place I passed;
And there a herald came towards me, and a chariot
Drawn by horses, with a man such as you describe   280
Seated in it. The groom leading the horses
Forced me off the road at his lord's command;
But as this charioteer lurched over towards me
I struck him in my rage. The old man saw me
And brought his double goad down upon my head   285
As I came abreast.
                            He was paid back, and more!
Swinging my club in this right hand I knocked him
Out of his car, and he rolled on the ground.
                                I killed him.

I killed them all.
Now if that stranger and Laios were—kin,   290
Where is a man more miserable than I?
More hated by the gods? Citizen and alien alike
Must never shelter me or speak to me—
I must be shunned by all.
                           And I myself
Pronounced this malediction upon myself!   295

Think of it: I have touched you with these hands,
These hands that killed your husband. What defilement!

Am I all evil, then? It must be so,
Since I must flee from Thebes, yet never again
See my own countrymen, my own country,   300
For fear of joining my mother in marriage
And killing Polybos, my father.
                                Ah,

If I was created so, born to this fate,
Who could deny the savagery of God?

O holy majesty of heavenly powers!   *305*
May I never see that day! Never!
Rather let me vanish from the race of men
Than know the abomination destined me!
CHORAGOS. We too, my lord, have felt dismay at this.
    But there is hope: you have yet to hear the shepherd.   *310*
OEDIPUS. Indeed, I fear no other hope is left me.
IOKASTE. What do you hope from him when he comes?
OEDIPUS.   This much:
    If his account of the murder tallies with yours,
    Then I am cleared.
IOKASTE.   What was it that I said
    Of such importance?
OEDIPUS.   Why, "marauders," you said, *315*
    Killed the king, according to this man's story.
    If he maintains that still, if there were several,
    Clearly the guilt is not mine: I was alone.
    But if he says one man, singlehanded, did it,
    Then the evidence all points to me.   *320*
IOKASTE. You may be sure that he said there were several;
    And can he call back that story now? He can not.
    The whole city heard it as plainly as I.
    But suppose he alters some detail of it:
    He can not ever show that Laios' death   *325*
    Fulfilled the oracle: for Apollo said
    My child was doomed to kill him; and my child—
    Poor baby!—it was my child that died first.

    No. From now on, where oracles are concerned,
    I would not waste a second thought on any.   *330*
OEDIPUS. You may be right.
                                    But come: let someone go
    For the shepherd at once. This matter must be settled.
IOKASTE. I will send for him.
    I would not wish to cross you in anything,
    And surely not in this.—Let us go in.   *335*

(*Exeunt into the palace.*)

ODE 2

Strophe 1

CHORUS. Let me be reverent in the ways of right,
    Lowly the paths I journey on;
    Let all my words and actions keep
    The laws of the pure universe
    From highest Heaven handed down.   5
    For Heaven is their bright nurse,
    Those generations of the realms of light;
    Ah, never of mortal kind were they begot,
    Nor are they slaves of memory, lost in sleep:
    Their Father is greater than Time, and ages not.   10

Antistrophe 1

    The tyrant is a child of Pride
    Who drinks from his great sickening cup
    Recklessness and vanity,
    Until from his high crest headlong
    He plummets to the dust of hope.   15
    That strong man is not strong.
    But let no fair ambition be denied;
    May God protect the wrestler for the State
    In government, in comely policy,
    Who will fear God, and on his ordinance wait.   20

Strophe 2

    Haughtiness and the high hand of disdain
    Tempt and outrage God's holy law;
    And any mortal who dares hold
    No immortal Power in awe
    Will be caught up in a net of pain: 25
    The price for which his levity is sold.
    Let each man take due earnings, then,
    And keep his hands from holy things,
    And from blasphemy stand apart—
    Else the crackling blast of heaven   30
    Blows on his head, and on his desperate heart.
    Though fools will honor impious men,
    In their cities no tragic poet sings.

Antistrophe 2

Shall we lose faith in Delphi's obscurities,
We who have heard the world's core   35
Discredited, and the sacred wood
Of Zeus at Elis praised no more?
The deeds and the strange prophecies
Must make a pattern yet to be understood.
Zeus, if indeed you are lord of all,   40
Throned in light over night and day,
Mirror this in your endless mind:
Our masters call the oracle
Words on the wind, and the Delphic vision blind!
Their hearts no longer know Apollo,   45
And reverence for the gods has died away.

SCENE 3

Enter Iokaste.

IOKASTE. Princes of Thebes, it has occurred to me
   To visit the altars of the gods, bearing
   These branches as a suppliant, and this incense.
   Our king is not himself: his noble soul
   Is overwrought with fantasies of dread,   5
   Else he would consider
   The new prophecies in the light of the old.
   He will listen to any voice that speaks disaster,
   And my advice goes for nothing. (*She approaches the
      altar, right.*)
                              To you, then, Apollo,
   Lycean lord, since you are nearest, I turn in prayer   10
   Receive these offerings, and grant us deliverance
   From defilement. Our hearts are heavy with fear
   When we see our leader distracted, as helpless sailors
   Are terrified by the confusion of their helmsman.

(*Enter Messenger.*)

MESSENGER. Friends, no doubt you can direct me: 15
   Where shall I find the house of Oedipus,
   Or, better still, where is the king himself?
CHORAGOS. It is this very place, stranger; he is inside.
   This is his wife and mother of his children.

MESSENGER. I wish her happiness in a happy house,   20
    Blest in all the fulfillment of her marriage.
IOKASTE. I wish as much for you: your courtesy
    Deserves a like good fortune. But now, tell me:
    Why have you come? What have you to say to us?
MESSENGER. Good news, my lady, for your house and your husband.   25
IOKASTE. What news? Who sent you here?
MESSENGER.   I am from Corinth.
    The news I bring ought to mean joy for you,
    Though it may be you will find some grief in it.
IOKASTE. What is it? How can it touch us in both ways?
MESSENGER. The word is that the people of the Isthmus   30
    Intend to call Oedipus to be their king.
IOKASTE. But old King Polybos—is he not reigning still?
MESSENGER. No. Death holds him in his sepulchre.
IOKASTE. What are you saying? Polybos is dead?
MESSENGER. If I am not telling the truth, may I die myself.   35
IOKASTE (*to a Maidservant*). Go in, go quickly; tell this to your master.
    O riddlers of God's will, where are you now!
    This was the man whom Oedipus, long ago,
    Feared so, fled so, in dread of destroying him—
    But it was another fate by which he died.   40

(*Enter Oedipus, center.*)

OEDIPUS. Dearest Iokaste, why have you sent for me?
IOKASTE. Listen to what this man says, and then tell me
    What has become of the solemn prophecies.
OEDIPUS. Who is this man? What is his news for me?
IOKASTE. He has come from Corinth to announce your father's
    death!   45
OEDIPUS. Is it true, stranger? Tell me in your own words.
MESSENGER. I can not say it more clearly: the king is dead.
OEDIPUS. Was it by treason? Or by an attack of illness?
MESSENGER. A little thing brings old men to their rest.
OEDIPUS. It was sickness, then?
MESSENGER.   Yes, and his many years.   50
OEDIPUS. Ah!
    Why should a man respect the Pythian hearth,[25] or
    Give heed to the birds that jangle above his head?

─────────────

[25]Delphi

They prophesied that I should kill Polybos,
Kill my own father; but he is dead and buried,   55
And I am here—I never touched him, never,
Unless he died of grief for my departure,
And thus, in a sense, through me. No. Polybos
Has packed the oracles off with him underground.
They are empty words.
IOKASTE.   Had I not told you so?   60
OEDIPUS. You had; it was my faint heart that betrayed me.
IOKASTE. From now on never think of those things again.
OEDIPUS. And yet—must I not fear my mother's bed?
IOKASTE. Why should anyone in this world be afraid
       Since Fate rules us and nothing can be foreseen?   65
       A man should live only for the present day.

       Have no more fear of sleeping with your mother:
       How many men, in dreams, have lain with their mothers!
       No reasonable man is troubled by such things.
OEDIPUS. That is true, only—   70
       If only my mother were not still alive!
       But she is alive. I can not help my dread.
IOKASTE. Yet this news of your father's death is wonderful.
OEDIPUS. Wonderful. But I fear the living woman.
MESSENGER. Tell me, who is this woman that you fear?   75
OEDIPUS. It is Merope, man; the wife of King Polybos.
MESSENGER. Merope? Why should you be afraid of her?
OEDIPUS. An oracle of the gods, a dreadful saying.
MESSENGER. Can you tell me about it or are you sworn to silence?
OEDIPUS. I can tell you, and I will.   80
       Apollo said through his prophet that I was the man
       Who should marry his own mother, shed his father's blood
       With his own hands. And so, for all these years
       I have kept clear of Corinth, and no harm has come—
       Though it would have been sweet to see my parents again.   85
MESSENGER. And is this the fear that drove you out of Corinth?
OEDIPUS. Would you have me kill my father?
MESSENGER.   As for that
       You must be reassured by the news I gave you.
OEDIPUS. If you could reassure me, I would reward you.
MESSENGER. I had that in mind, I will confess: I thought   90
       I could count on you when you returned to Corinth.

OEDIPUS. No. I will never go near my parents again.
MESSENGER. Ah, son, you still do not know what you are doing—
OEDIPUS. What do you mean? In the name of God tell me!
MESSENGER. —If these are your reasons for not going home.   95
OEDIPUS. I tell you, I fear the oracle may come true.
MESSENGER. And guilt may come upon you through your parents?
OEDIPUS. That is the dread that is always in my heart.
MESSENGER. Can you not see that all your fears are groundless?
OEDIPUS. Groundless? Am I not my parents' son?   100
MESSENGER. Polybos was not your father.
OEDIPUS.   Not my father?
MESSENGER. No more your father than the man speaking to you.
OEDIPUS. But you are nothing to me!
MESSENGER.   Neither was he.
OEDIPUS. Then why did he call me son?
MESSENGER.   I will tell you:
     Long ago he had you from my hands, as a gift.   105
OEDIPUS. Then how could he love me so, if I was not his?
MESSENGER. He had no children, and his heart turned to you.
OEDIPUS. What of you? Did you buy me? Did you find me by chance?
MESSENGER. I came upon you in the woody vales of Kithairon.
OEDIPUS. And what were you doing there?
MESSENGER.   Tending my flocks. 110
OEDIPUS. A wandering shepherd?
MESSENGER.   But your savior, son, that day.
OEDIPUS. From what did you save me?
MESSENGER.   Your ankles should tell you that.
OEDIPUS. Ah, stranger, why do you speak of that childhood pain?
MESSENGER. I pulled the skewer that pinned your feet together.
OEDIPUS. I have had the mark as long as I can remember.   115
MESSENGER. That was why you were given the name[26] you bear.
OEDIPUS. God! Was it my father or my mother who did it?
     Tell me!
MESSENGER.   I do not know. The man who gave you to me
     Can tell you better than I.
OEDIPUS. It was not you that found me, but another?   120
MESSENGER. It was another shepherd gave you to me.
OEDIPUS. Who was he? Can you tell me who he was?
MESSENGER. I think he was said to be one of Laios' people.

---

[26]Oedipus means "swollen foot."

OEDIPUS. You mean the Laios who was king here years ago?
MESSENGER. Yes; King Laios; and the man was one of his herdsmen. 125
OEDIPUS. Is he still alive? Can I see him?
MESSENGER.   These men here
    Know best about such things.
OEDIPUS.   Does anyone here
    Know this shepherd that he is talking about?
    Have you seen him in the fields, or in the town?
    If you have, tell me. It is time things were made plain.   130
CHORAGOS. I think the man he means is that same shepherd
    You have already asked to see. Iokaste perhaps
    Could tell you something.
OEDIPUS.   Do you know anything
    About him, Lady? Is he the man we have summoned?
    Is that the man this shepherd means?
IOKASTE.   Why think of him? 135
    Forget this herdsman. Forget it all.
    This talk is a waste of time.
OEDIPUS.   How can you say that,
    When the clues to my true birth are in my hands?
IOKASTE. For God's love, let us have no more questioning!
    Is your life nothing to you?   140
    My own is pain enough for me to bear.
OEDIPUS. You need not worry. Suppose my mother a slave,
    And born of slaves: no baseness can touch you.
IOKASTE. Listen to me, I beg you: do not do this thing!
OEDIPUS. I will not listen; the truth must be made known.   145
IOKASTE. Everything that I say is for your own good!
OEDIPUS. My own good
    Snaps my patience, then; I want none of it.
IOKASTE. You are fatally wrong! May you never learn who you are!
OEDIPUS. Go, one of you, and bring the shepherd here.
    Let us leave this woman to brag of her royal name.   150
IOKASTE. Ah, miserable!
    That is the only word I have for you now.
    That is the only word I can ever have.

(*Exit into the palace.*)

CHORAGOS. Why has she left us, Oedipus? Why has she gone
    In such a passion of sorrow? I fear this silence: 155
    Something dreadful may come of it.

OEDIPUS.   Let it come!
   However base my birth, I must know about it.
   The Queen, like a woman, is perhaps ashamed
   To think of my low origin. But I
   Am a child of Luck, I can not be dishonored.   160
   Luck is my mother; the passing months, my brothers,
   Have seen me rich and poor.
                                 If this is so,
   How could I wish that I were someone else?
   How could I not be glad to know my birth?

ODE 3

Strophe

CHORUS. If ever the coming time were known
   To my heart's pondering,
   Kithairon, now by Heaven I see the torches
   At the festival of the next full moon
   And see the dance, and hear the choir sing   5
   A grace to your gentle shade:
   Mountain where Oedipus was found,
   O mountain guard of a noble race!
   May the god[27] who heals us lend his aid,
   And let that glory come to pass   10
   For our king's cradling-ground.

Antistrophe

   Of the nymphs that flower beyond the years,
   Who bore you, royal child,
   To Pan[28] of the hills or the timberline Apollo,
   Cold in delight where the upland clears,   15
   Or Hermes[29] for whom Kyllene's[30] heights are piled?
   Or flushed as evening cloud,

---

[27]Apollo

[28]God of nature, shepherds, and fertility; associated with lechery, and often represented as half-man, half-goat.

[29]Messenger of the gods.

[30]Mountain that was birthplace of Hermes.

Great Dionysos,[31] roamer of mountains,
He—was it he who found you there,
And caught you up in his own proud   *20*
Arms from the sweet god-ravisher
Who laughed by the Muses'[32] fountains?

SCENE 4

OEDIPUS. Sirs: though I do not know the man,
I think I see him coming, this shepherd we want:
He is old, like our friend here, and the men
Bringing him seem to be servants of my house.
But you can tell, if you have ever seen him.   *5*

(*Enter Shepherd escorted by Servants.*)

CHORAGOS. I know him, he was Laios' man. You can trust him.
OEDIPUS. Tell me first, you from Corinth: is this the shepherd
        We were discussing?
MESSENGER.   This is the very man.
OEDIPUS (*to Shepherd*). Come here. No, look at me.
        You must answer
        Everything I ask.—You belonged to Laios?   *10*
SHEPHERD. Yes: born his slave, brought up in his house.
OEDIPUS. Tell me: what kind of work did you do for him?
SHEPHERD. I was a shepherd of his, most of my life.
OEDIPUS. Where mainly did you go for pasturage?
SHEPHERD. Sometimes Kithairon, sometimes the hills near-by.   *15*
OEDIPUS. Do you remember ever seeing this man out there?
SHEPHERD. What would he be doing there? This man?
OEDIPUS. This man standing here. Have you ever seen him before?
SHEPHERD. At least, not to my recollection.
MESSENGER. And that is not strange, my lord. But I'll refresh   *20*
        His memory: he must remember when we two
        Spent three whole seasons together, March to September,
        On Kithairon or thereabouts. He had two flocks;
        I had one. Each autumn I'd drive mine home
        And he would go back with his to Laios' sheepfold.—   *25*
        Is this not true, just as I have described it?

---

[31]Another name for Bacchus.

[32]Group of sister goddesses, patrons of poetry, music, art, and sciences.

SHEPHERD. True, yes; but it was all so long ago.
MESSENGER. Well, then: do you remember, back in those days,
    That you gave me a baby boy to bring up as my own?
SHEPHERD. What if I did? What are you trying to say?   *30*
MESSENGER. King Oedipus was once that little child.
SHEPHERD. Damn you, hold your tongue!
OEDIPUS.   No more of that!
    It is your tongue needs watching, not this man's.
SHEPHERD. My king, my master, what is it I have done wrong?
OEDIPUS. You have not answered his question about the boy.   *35*
SHEPHERD. He does not know . . . He is only making trouble . . .
OEDIPUS. Come, speak plainly, or it will go hard with you.
SHEPHERD. In God's name, do not torture an old man!
OEDIPUS. Come here, one of you; bind his arms behind him.
SHEPHERD. Unhappy king! What more do you wish to learn?   *40*
OEDIPUS. Did you give this man the child he speaks of?
SHEPHERD.   I did.
    And I would to God I had died that very day.
OEDIPUS. You will die now unless you speak the truth.
SHEPHERD. Yet if I speak the truth, I am worse than dead.
OEDIPUS (*to Attendant*). He intends to draw it out, apparently—   *45*
SHEPHERD. No! I have told you already that I gave him the boy.
OEDIPUS. Where did you get him? From your house?
    From somewhere else?
SHEPHERD. Not from mine, no. A man gave him to me.
OEDIPUS. Is that man here? Whose house did he belong to?
SHEPHERD. For God's love, my king, do not ask me any more!   *50*
OEDIPUS. You are a dead man if I have to ask you again.
SHEPHERD. Then . . . Then the child was from the palace of Laios.
OEDIPUS. A slave child? or a child of his own line?
SHEPHERD. Ah, I am on the brink of dreadful speech!
OEDIPUS. And I of dreadful hearing. Yet I must hear.   *55*
SHEPHERD. If you must be told, then . . .
                     They said it was Laios' child;
    But it is your wife who can tell you about that.
OEDIPUS. My wife—Did she give it to you?
SHEPHERD.   My lord, she did.
OEDIPUS. Do you know why?
SHEPHERD.   I was told to get rid of it.
OEDIPUS. Oh heartless mother!
SHEPHERD.   But in dread of prophecies . . .   *60*

OEDIPUS. Tell me.

SHEPHERD.   It was said that the boy would kill his own father.

OEDIPUS. Then why did you give him over to this old man?

SHEPHERD. I pitied the baby, my king,
    And I thought that this man would take him far away
    To his own country.

                                        He saved him—but for what a fate!   65
    For if you are what this man says you are,
    No man living is more wretched than Oedipus.

OEDIPUS. Ah God!
    It was true!

                                        All the prophecies!
                                                —Now,
    O Light, may I look on you for the last time!   70
    I, Oedipus,
    Oedipus, damned in his birth, in his marriage damned,
    Damned in the blood he shed with his own hand!

(*He rushes into the palace.*)

ODE 4

Strophe 1

CHORUS. Alas for the seed of men.
    What measure shall I give these generations
    That breathe on the void and are void
    And exist and do not exist?
    Who bears more weight of joy   5
    Than mass of sunlight shifting in images,
    Or who shall make his thought stay on
    That down time drifts away?
    Your splendor is all fallen.
    O naked brow of wrath and tears,   10
    O change of Oedipus!
    I who saw your days call no man blest—
    Your great days like ghosts gone.

Antistrophe 1

That mind was a strong bow.
    Deep, how deep you drew it then, hard archer,   15
    At a dim fearful range,

And brought dear glory down!
You overcame the stranger[33]—
The virgin with her hooking lion claws—
And though death sang, stood like a tower   20
To make pale Thebes take heart.
Fortress against our sorrow!
True king, giver of laws,
Majestic Oedipus!
No prince in Thebes had ever such renown,   25
No prince won such grace of power.

Strophe 2

And now of all men ever known
Most pitiful is this man's story:
His fortunes are most changed; his state
Fallen to a low slave's   30
Ground under bitter fate.
O Oedipus, most royal one!
The great door[34] that expelled you to the light
Gave at night—ah, gave night to your glory:
As to the father, to the fathering son.   35
All understood too late.
How could that queen whom Laios won,
The garden that he harrowed at his height,
Be silent when that act was done?

Antistrophe 2

But all eyes fail before time's eye,   40
All actions come to justice there.
Though never willed, though far down the deep past,
Your bed, your dread sirings,
Are brought to book at last.
Child by Laios doomed to die,   45
Then doomed to lose that fortunate little death,
Would God you never took breath in this air
That with my wailing lips I take to cry:

[33]The Sphinx

[34]Iokasate's womb

For I weep the world's outcast.
I was blind, and now I can tell why:
Asleep, for you had given ease of breath
To Thebes, while the false years went by.   *50*

EXODOS[35]

Enter, from the palace, Second Messenger.

SECOND MESSENGER. Elders of Thebes, most honored in this land,
  What horrors are yours to see and hear, what weight
  Of sorrow to be endured, if, true to your birth,
  You venerate the line of Labdakos!
  I think neither Istros nor Phasis, those great rivers,   *5*
  Could purify this place of all the evil
  It shelters now, or soon must bring to light—
  Evil not done unconsciously, but willed.

  The greatest griefs are those we cause ourselves.
CHORAGOS. Surely, friend, we have grief enough already;   *10*
  What new sorrow do you mean?
SECOND MESSENGER.   The queen is dead.
CHORAGOS. O miserable queen! But at whose hand?
SECOND MESSENGER.   Her own.
  The full horror of what happened you can not know,
  For you did not see it; but I, who did, will tell you
  As clearly as I can how she met her death.   *15*

  When she had left us,
  In passionate silence, passing through the court,
  She ran to her apartment in the house,
  Her hair clutched by the fingers of both hands.
  She closed the doors behind her; then, by that bed
  Where long ago the fatal son was conceived—   *20*
  That son who should bring about his father's death—
  We heard her call upon Laios, dead so many years,
  And heard her wail for the double fruit of her marriage,
  A husband by her husband, children by her child.   *25*

---

[35]Final scene

Exactly how she died I do not know:
For Oedipus burst in moaning and would not let us
Keep vigil to the end: it was by him
As he stormed about the room that our eyes were caught.
From one to another of us he went, begging a sword,   30
Hunting the wife who was not his wife, the mother
Whose womb had carried his own children and himself.
I do not know: it was none of us aided him,
But surely one of the gods was in control!
For with a dreadful cry   35
He hurled his weight, as though wrenched out of himself,
At the twin doors: the bolts gave, and he rushed in.
And there we saw her hanging, her body swaying
From the cruel cord she had noosed about her neck.
A great sob broke from him, heartbreaking to hear,   40
As he loosed the rope and lowered her to the ground.

I would blot out from my mind what happened next!
For the king ripped from her gown the golden brooches
That were her ornament, and raised them, and plunged them
    down
Straight into his own eyeballs, crying, "No more,   45
No more shall you look on the misery about me,
The horrors of my own doing! Too long you have known
The faces of those whom I should never have seen,
Too long been blind to those for whom I was searching!
From this hour, go in darkness!" And as he spoke,   50
He struck at his eyes—not once, but many times;
And the blood spattered his beard,
Bursting from his ruined sockets like red hail.
So from the unhappiness of two this evil has sprung,
A curse on the man and woman alike. The old   55
Happiness of the house of Labdakos
Was happiness enough: where is it today?
It is all wailing and ruin, disgrace, death—all
The misery of mankind that has a name—
And it is wholly and for ever theirs.   60
CHORAGOS. Is he in agony still? Is there no rest for him?
SECOND MESSENGER. He is calling for someone to open the doors
    wide
        So that all the children of Kadmos may look upon
        His father's murderer, his mother's—no,

I can not say it!

And then he will leave Thebes,   65
Self-exiled, in order that the curse
Which he himself pronounced may depart from the house.
He is weak, and there is none to lead him,
So terrible is his suffering.

But you will see:
Look, the doors are opening; in a moment   70
You will see a thing that would crush a heart of stone.

(*The central door is opened; Oedipus, blinded, is led in.*)

CHORAGOS. Dreadful indeed for men to see.
Never have my own eyes
Looked on a sight so full of fear.

Oedipus!   75
What madness came upon you, what demon
Leaped on your life with heavier
Punishment than a mortal man can bear?
No: I can not even
Look at you, poor ruined one.   80
And I would speak, question, ponder,
If I were able. No.
You make me shudder.
OEDIPUS. God. God.
Is there a sorrow greater?   85
Where shall I find harbor in this world?
My voice is hurled far on a dark wind.
What has God done to me?
CHORAGOS. Too terrible to think of, or to see.

Strophe 1

OEDIPUS. O cloud of night,   90
Never to be turned away: night coming on,
I can not tell how: night like a shroud!
My fair winds brought me here.

O God. Again
The pain of the spikes where I had sight,
The flooding pain   95
Of memory, never to be gouged out.

CHORAGOS. This is not strange.
      You suffer it all twice over, remorse in pain,
      Pain in remorse.

Antistrophe 1

OEDIPUS. Ah dear friend   *100*
      Are you faithful even yet, you alone?
      Are you still standing near me, will you stay here,
      Patient, to care for the blind?
                                             The blind man!
      Yet even blind I know who it is attends me,
      By the voice's tone—   *105*
      Though my new darkness hide the comforter.
CHORAGOS. Oh fearful act!
      What god was it drove you to rake black
      Night across your eyes?

Strophe 2

OEDIPUS. Apollo. Apollo. Dear   *110*
      Children, the god was Apollo.
      He brought my sick, sick fate upon me.
      But the blinding hand was my own!
      How could I bear to see
      When all my sight was horror everywhere?   *115*
CHORAGOS. Everywhere; that is true.
OEDIPUS. And now what is left?
      Images? Love? A greeting even,
      Sweet to the senses? Is there anything?
      Ah, no, friends: lead me away.   *120*
      Lead me away from Thebes.
                                    Lead the great wreck
      And hell of Oedipus, whom the gods hate.
CHORAGOS. Your misery, you are not blind to that.
      Would God you had never found it out!

Antistrophe 2

OEDIPUS. Death take the man who unbound   *125*
      My feet on that hillside
      And delivered me from death to life! What life?

If only I had died,
This weight of monstrous doom
Could not have dragged me and my darlings down.   *130*
CHORAGOS. I would have wished the same.
OEDIPUS. Oh never to have come here
    With my father's blood upon me! Never
    To have been the man they call his mother's husband!
    Oh accurst! Oh child of evil,   *135*
    To have entered that wretched bed—the selfsame one!
    More primal than sin itself, this fell to me.
CHORAGOS. I do not know what words to offer you.
    You were better dead than alive and blind.
OEDIPUS. Do not counsel me any more. This punishment   *140*
    That I have laid upon myself is just.
    If I had eyes,
    I do not know how I could bear the sight
    Of my father, when I came to the house of Death,
    Or my mother: for I have sinned against them both   *145*
    So vilely that I could not make my peace
    By strangling my own life.
                                Or do you think my children,
    Born as they were born, would be sweet to my eyes?
    Ah never, never! Nor this town with its high walls,
    Nor the holy images of the gods.
                                        For I, *150*
    Thrice miserable!—Oedipus, noblest of all the line
    Of Kadmos, have condemned myself to enjoy
    These things no more, by my own malediction
    Expelling that man whom the gods declared
    To be a defilement in the house of Laios.   *155*
    After exposing the rankness of my own guilt,
    How could I look men frankly in the eyes?
    No, I swear it,
    If I could have stifled my hearing at its source,
    I would have done it and made all this body   *160*
    A tight cell of misery, blank to light and sound:
    So I should have been safe in my dark mind
    Beyond external evil.
                                Ah Kithairon!
    Why did you shelter me? When I was cast upon you,
    Why did I not die? Then I should never   *165*
    Have shown the world my execrable birth.

Ah Polybos! Corinth, city that I believed
The ancient seat of my ancestors: how fair
I seemed, your child! And all the while this evil
Was cancerous within me!

                                    For I am sick   *170*
In my own being, sick in my origin.
O three roads, dark ravine, woodland and way
Where three roads met; you, drinking my father's blood,
My own blood, spilled by my own hand: can you remember
The unspeakable things I did there, and the things   *175*
I went on from there to do?

                           O marriage, marriage!
The act that engendered me, and again the act
Performed by the son in the same bed—

                              Ah, the net
Of incest, mingling fathers, brothers, sons,
With brides, wives, mothers: the last evil   *180*
That can be known by men: no tongue can say
How evil!

                No. For the love of God, conceal me
Somewhere far from Thebes; or kill me; or hurl me
Into the sea, away from men's eyes for ever.

Come, lead me. You need nor fear to touch me.   *185*
Of all men, I alone can bear this guilt.

(*Enter Kreon.*)

CHORAGOS. Kreon is here now. As to what you ask,
    He may decide the course to take. He only
    Is left to protect the city in your place.
OEDIPUS. Alas, how can I speak to him? What right have I   *190*
    To beg his courtesy whom I have deeply wronged?
KREON. I have not come to mock you, Oedipus,
    Or to reproach you, either.
    (*To Attendants.*)—   You, standing there:
    If you have lost all respect for man's dignity,
    At least respect the flame of Lord Helios:[36]   *195*
    Do not allow this pollution to show itself
    Openly here, an affront to the earth

---

[36]Helios: sun god.

And Heaven's rain and the light of day. No, take him
Into the house as quickly as you can.
For it is proper   200
That only the close kindred see his grief.
OEDIPUS. I pray you in God's name, since your courtesy
Ignores my dark expectation, visiting
With mercy this man of all men most execrable:
Give me what I ask—for your good, not for mine.   205
KREON. And what is it that you turn to me begging for?
OEDIPUS. Drive me out of this country as quickly as may be
To a place where no human voice can ever greet me.
KREON. I should have done that before now—only,
God's will had not been wholly revealed to me.   210
OEDIPUS. But his command is plain: the parricide
Must be destroyed. I am that evil man.
KREON. That is the sense of it, yes; but as things are,
We had best discover clearly what is to be done.
OEDIPUS. You would learn more about a man like me?   215
KREON. You are ready now to listen to the god.
OEDIPUS. I will listen. But it is to you
That I must turn for help. I beg you, hear me.

The woman is there—
Give her whatever funeral you think proper: 220
She is your sister.
                            —But let me go, Kreon!
Let me purge my father's Thebes of the pollution
Of my living here, and go out to the wild hills,
To Kithairon, that has won such fame with me,
The tomb my mother and father appointed for me,   225
And let me die there, as they willed I should.
And yet I know
Death will not ever come to me through sickness
Or in any natural way: I have been preserved
For some unthinkable fate. But let that be.   230

As for my sons, you need not care for them.
They are men, they will find some way to live.
But my poor daughters, who have shared my table,
Who never before have been parted from their father—
Take care of them, Kreon; do this for me.   235

And will you let me touch them with my hands
A last time, and let us weep together?
Be kind, my lord,
Great prince, be kind!
       Could I but touch them,
They would be mine again, as when I had my eyes.   *240*

(*Enter Antigone and Ismene, attended.*)

Ah, God!
Is it my dearest children I hear weeping?
Has Kreon pitied me and sent my daughters?
KREON. Yes, Oedipus: I knew that they were dear to you
 In the old days, and know you must love them still.   *245*
OEDIPUS. May God bless you for this—and be a friendlier
 Guardian to you than he has been to me!

Children, where are you?
Come quickly to my hands: they are your brother's—
Hands that have brought your father's once clear eyes   *250*
To this way of seeing—
        Ah dearest ones,
I had neither sight nor knowledge then, your father
By the woman who was the source of his own life!
And I weep for you—having no strength to see you—,
I weep for you when I think of the bitterness   *255*
That men will visit upon you all your lives.
What homes, what festivals can you attend
Without being forced to depart again in tears?
And when you come to marriageable age,
Where is the man, my daughters, who would dare   *260*
Risk the bane that lies on all my children?
Is there any evil wanting? Your father killed
His father; sowed the womb of her who bore him;
Engendered you at the fount of his own existence!
That is what they will say of you.

        Then, whom *265*
Can you ever marry? There are no bridegrooms for you,
And your lives must wither away in sterile dreaming.

O Kreon, son of Menoikeus!
You are the only father my daughters have,

Since we, their parents, are both of us gone for ever. *270*
They are your own blood: you will not let them
Fall into beggary and loneliness;
You will keep them from the miseries that are mine!
Take pity on them; see, they are only children,
Friendless except for you. Promise me this, *275*
Great prince, and give me your hand in token of it.

(*Kreon clasps his right hand.*)

    Children:
I could say much, if you could understand me,
But as it is, I have only this prayer for you:
Live where you can, be as happy as you can— *280*
Happier, please God, than God has made your father.
KREON. Enough. You have wept enough. Now go within.
OEDIPUS. I must, but it is hard.
KREON.   Time eases all things.
OEDIPUS. You know my mind, then?
KREON.   Say what you desire.
OEDIPUS. Send me from Thebes!
KREON.   God grant that I may! *285*
OEDIPUS. But since God hates me . . .
KREON.   No, he will grant your wish.
OEDIPUS. You promise?
KREON. I can not speak beyond my knowledge.
OEDIPUS. Then lead me in.
KREON. Come now, and leave your children.
OEDIPUS. No! Do not take them from me!
KREON.   Think no longer
That you are in command here, but rather think *290*
How, when you were, you served your own destruction.

(*Exeunt into the house all but the Chorus; the Choragos chants directly to the audience.*)

CHORAGOS. Men of Thebes: look upon Oedipus.
This is the king who solved the famous riddle
And towered up, most powerful of men.
No mortal eyes but looked on him with envy, *295*
Yet in the end ruin swept over him.

Let every man in mankind's frailty
Consider his last day; and let none
Presume on his good fortune until he find
Life, at his death, a memory without pain. *300*

[C. 430 B.C.E.]

QUESTIONS

SOPHOCLES, *Oedipus Rex*

1. Describe the background and current situation that the Prologue of *Oedipus Rex* establishes for the audience.

2. Find instances in the play that foreshadow the Shepherd's disclosures. Why is Oedipus so impervious to these suggestions of his guilt?

3. What is Oedipus's fate as decreed by Apollo? What does Oedipus do in an attempt to avoid this fate? Do you think that he could have prevented his tragic downfall, or do you think it was inevitable? Support your claim with evidence from the text.

4. Why is Teiresias reluctant to announce the truth to Oedipus and the Theban citizens?

5. Trace the images of blindness and sight throughout the play. What purpose do these many references serve in the play? Are they instances of dramatic irony?

6. How are the gods characterized in *Oedipus Rex*? Do they seem unfairly cruel? Why do you think Sophocles depicts them as he does?

7. The Chorus provides entertainment and variety through song and movement, but what is its narrative function? For instance, what do they single out as Oedipus's great flaw?

8. Paraphrase one strophe or antistrophe provided by the Chorus in order to ascertain its literal meaning.

9. At the conclusion of the play, what does Oedipus tell his daughters, Antigone and Ismene? What does he fear for them? Why do you think he turns to them at the end of the play—and why are they silent?

10. *Oedipus Rex* presents its audiences with shocking events, such as incest and self-mutilation, which unfold in an unfamiliar time and place. Yet this play, since its premiere, captivates audiences. Why does this tragedy speak to contemporary audiences? Support your claim with evidence from the text, citing examples of adept characterization, plot construction, or theme.

11. In "On the Nature and Elements of a Tragedy" in *Poetics*, the Greek philosopher Aristotle describes catharsis as a response to tragedy that is characterized by the playgoer's feelings of pity and fear. He also celebrates the facility of *Oedipus Rex* in eliciting this response from its audiences. Look closely at one scene from the play and describe how its language (metaphors or other figures of speech), its characterization, or its plot progression serves to inspire catharsis.

William Shakespeare
[1564–1616]

WILLIAM SHAKESPEARE *was born in Stratford-upon-Avon, the son of a glove-maker and wool dealer. Though his father, John, held some status in the city, at some point the family lost its position and thus, though his eldest son William attended Stratford Grammar School and may have had hopes of attending university, he did not. When Shakespeare was eighteen years old, he married Anne Hathaway and had three children before his twenty-first birthday. By the early 1590s he was established in London as an actor and a playwright, as well as the part-owner and manager of a theater company. He was a prolific writer, having written (or, in a couple of cases, co-written) at the time of his death thirty-eight plays and several volumes of poetry—*The Sonnets *(1609),* Venus and Adonis *(1593), and* The Rape of Lucrece *(1593).*

Perhaps the most pored-over of all authors, Shakespeare fascinates in part because of the lack of detail known about his life. However, a good deal is discernable about the social milieu surrounding his life and work. By the time Shakespeare emerged as an actor and a playwright in the theater scene in London of the early 1590s, he must have spent some time as an apprentice actor, and tried his hand at playwriting. Theater-going at that time spanned all social classes. His earliest plays draw heavily on classical sources and models, suggesting something about his early education. Playwriting at that time was probably considered more a professional skill than an art. When theaters were shut down because of the plague (1592–1593), he wrote his narrative poems, probably dedicated to the Earl of Southampton, a patron. When Shakespeare retired to Stratford-upon-Avon, he had seen to the publication of the poems, though not his plays. Plays at that time were written for a fee, with the rights retained by production companies. Shakespeare owned a share of the theater company, which had Lord Chamberlain as its patron and was under the royal sponsorship of King James. The company built the Globe Theater, where many of the plays were produced. He was buried in the same parish church where he was baptized. Not until seven years after his death were most of the plays collected and published by two of his partners.

The sonnets have a special place in the Shakespeare oeuvre. They are still considered models of the form, and are part of a vibrant sonnet-writing tradition in the Renaissance. The kind of sonnet Shakespeare—and other Renaissance writers such as Sir Thomas Wyatt, Henry Howard, Earl of Surrey, Edmund Spenser, and Sir Philip Sidney—wrote is often called the Elizabethan or Shakespearean sonnet. Differing from the Italian or Petrarchan sonnet, the

Elizabethan sonnet was organized in quatrains, with a concluding couplet. (The Petrarchan sonnet had an octave and a sestet.) Typically, the quatrains created an argument of examples, with each set of four lines offering an instance or amplification of the poem's central idea.

🔯 🔯 🔯

Hamlet, Prince of Denmark

WILLIAM SHAKESPEARE

DRAMATIS PERSONAE

GHOST OF HAMLET, the former King of Denmark
CLAUDIUS, King of Denmark, the former King's brother
GERTRUDE, Queen of Denmark, widow of the former King and now wife of Claudius
HAMLET, Prince of Denmark, son of the late King and of Gertrude

POLONIUS councillor to the King
LAERTES, his son
OPHELIA, his daughter
REYNALDO, his servant

HORATIO, Hamlet's friend and fellow student

VOLTIMAND,
CORNELIUS,
ROSENCRANTZ,
GUILDENSTERN, } members of the Danish court
OSRIC,
A GENTLEMAN,
A LORD,

BERNARDO,
FRANCISCO, } Officers and soldiers on watch
MARCELLUS,

FORTINBRAS, Prince of Norway
CAPTAIN, In his army

Reprinted from *The Complete Works of Shakespeare*, edited by David Bevington, (2004), by permission of Pearson Education.

THREE OR FOUR PLAYERS, taking the roles of PROLOGUE, PLAYER
KING, PLAYER QUEEN, and LUCIANUS
TWO MESSENGERS
FIRST SAILOR
TWO CLOWNS, a gravedigger and his companion
PRIEST
FIRST AMBASSADOR, from England

Lords, Soldiers, Attendants, Guards, other Players,
Followers of Laertes, other Sailors, another Ambassador or Ambassadors from England

SCENE: *Denmark*

1.1

(*Enter* BERNARDO *and* FRANCISCO, *two sentinels,*
[meeting].)

BERNARDO.   Who's there?
FRANCISCO.
Nay, answer me. Stand and unfold yourself.   *2*
BERNARDO.   Long live the King!
FRANCISCO.   Bernardo?
BERNARDO.   He.
FRANCISCO.
You come most carefully upon your hour.
BERNARDO.
'Tis now struck twelve. Get thee to bed, Francisco.
FRANCISCO.
For this relief much thanks. 'Tis bitter cold,
And I am sick at heart.
BERNARDO.   Have you had quiet guard?
FRANCISCO.   Not a mouse stirring.
BERNARDO.   Well, good night.
If you do meet Horatio and Marcellus,
The rivals of my watch, bid them make haste.   *14*

1.1 Location: Elsinore castle. A guard platform.
2 me (Francisco emphasizes that **he** is the sentry currently on watch.) **unfold yourself** reveal your
identity. **14 rivals** partners

(*Enter* HORATIO *and* MARCELLUS.)

FRANCISCO.
 I think I hear them.—Stand, ho! Who is there?
HORATIO.   Friends to this ground.   16
MARCELLUS.   And liegemen to the Dane.   17
FRANCISCO.   Give you good night.   18
MARCELLUS.
 Oh, farewell, honest soldier. Who hath relieved you?
FRANCISCO.
 Bernardo hath my place. Give you good night.

(*Exit* FRANCISCO.)

MARCELLUS.   Holla! Bernardo!
BERNARDO.   Say, what, is Horatio there?
HORATIO.   A piece of him.
BERNARDO.
 Welcome, Horatio. Welcome, good Marcellus.
HORATIO.
 What, has this thing appeared again tonight?
BERNARDO.   I have seen nothing.
MARCELLUS.
 Horatio says 'tis but our fantasy,   27
 And will not let belief take hold of him
 Touching this dreaded sight twice seen of us.
 Therefore I have entreated him along   30
 With us to watch the minutes of this night,   31
 That if again this apparition come
 He may approve our eyes and speak to it.   33
HORATIO.
 Tush, tush, 'twill not appear.
BERNARDO.   Sit down awhile And let us once again assail your ears,
 That are so fortified against our story,
 What we have two nights seen.
HORATIO.   Well, sit we down, And let us hear Bernardo speak of this.
BERNARDO.   Last night of all,   39
 When yond same star that's westward from the pole   40
 Had made his course t'illume that part of heaven   41

---

16 ground country, land **17 liegemen to the Dane** men sworn to serve the Danish king. **18 Give** May God give **27 fantasy** imagination **30 along** to come along **31 watch** keep watch during **33 approve** corroborate **39 Last . . . all** i.e., This *very* last night. (Emphatic.) **40 pole** polestar, north star **41 his** its. **t'illume** to illuminate

Where now it burns, Marcellus and myself,
The bell then beating one—

(*Enter* GHOST.)

MARCELLUS.
Peace, break thee off! Look where it comes again!
BERNARDO.
In the same figure like the King that's dead.
MARCELLUS
Thou art a scholar. Speak to it, Horatio.   46
BERNARDO.
Looks 'a not like the King? Mark it, Horatio.   47
HORATIO.
Most like. It harrows me with fear and wonder.
BERNARDO.
It would be spoke to.
MARCELLUS.   Speak to it, Horatio.   49
HORATIO.
What art thou that usurp'st this time of night,   50
Together with that fair and warlike form
In which the majesty of buried Denmark   52
Did sometimes march? By heaven, I charge thee, speak!   53
MARCELLUS.
It is offended.
BERNARDO.   See, it stalks away.
HORATIO.
Stay! Speak, speak! I charge thee, speak!

(*Exit* GHOST.)

MARCELLUS.   'Tis gone and will not answer.
BERNARDO.
How now, Horatio? You tremble and look pale.
Is not this something more than fantasy?
What think you on't?   59
HORATIO.
Before my God, I might not this believe
Without the sensible and true avouch   61

---

46 scholar one learned enough to know how to question a ghost properly. **47 'a** he **49 It . . . to** (It was commonly believed that a ghost could not speak until spoken to.) **50 usurp'st** wrongfully takes over **52 buried Denmark** the buried King of Denmark **53 sometimes** formerly **59 on't** of it **61 sensible** confirmed by the senses. **avouch** warrant, evidence

Of mine own eyes.
MARCELLUS.   Is it not like the King?
HORATIO.   As thou art to thyself.
　　Such was the very armor he had on
　　When he the ambitious Norway combated.　　　　　　65
　　So frowned he once when, in an angry parle,　　　　66
　　He smote the sledded Polacks on the ice.　　　　　 67
　　'Tis strange.
MARCELLUS.
　　Thus twice before, and jump at this dead hour,　　　69
　　With martial stalk hath he gone by our watch.　　　 70
HORATIO.
　　In what particular thought to work I know not,　　　71
　　But in the gross and scope of mine opinion　　　　 72
　　This bodes some strange eruption to our state.
MARCELLUS.
　　Good now, sit down, and tell me, he that knows,　　74
　　Why this same strict and most observant watch
　　So nightly toils the subject of the land,　　　　　 76
　　And why such daily cast of brazen cannon　　　　　77
　　And foreign mart for implements of war,　　　　　 78
　　Why such impress of shipwrights, whose sore task　 79
　　Does not divide the Sunday from the week.
　　What might be toward, that this sweaty haste　　　 81
　　Doth make the night joint-laborer with the day?
　　Who is't that can inform me?
HORATIO.   That can I;
　　At least, the whisper goes so. Our last king,
　　Whose image even but now appeared to us,
　　Was, as you know, by Fortinbras of Norway,
　　Thereto pricked on by a most emulate pride,　　　 87
　　Dared to the combat; in which our valiant Hamlet—
　　For so this side of our known world esteemed him—　89
　　Did slay this Fortinbras; who by a sealed compact　 90

---

65 Norway King of Norway **66 parle** parley **67 sledded** traveling on sleds. **Polacks** Poles **69 jump** exactly **70 stalk** stride **71 to work** i.e., to collect my thoughts and try to understand this **72 gross and scope** general drift **74 Good now** (An expression denoting entreaty or expostulation.) **76 toils** causes to toil. **subject** subjects **77 cast** casting **78 mart** shopping **79 impress** impressment, conscription **81 toward** in preparation **87 Thereto . . .pride** (Refers to old Fortinbras, not the Danish King.) **pricked on** incited. **emulate** emulous, ambitious **89 this . . .world** i.e., all Europe, the Western world **90 sealed** certified, confirmed

Well ratified by law and heraldry   91
Did forfeit, with his life, all those his lands
Which he stood seized of, to the conqueror;   93
Against the which a moiety competent   94
Was gagèd by our king, which had returned   95
To the inheritance of Fortinbras   96
Had he been vanquisher, as, by the same cov'nant   97
And carriage of the article designed,   98
His fell to Hamlet. Now, sir, young Fortinbras,
Of unimprovèd mettle hot and full,   100
Hath in the skirts of Norway here and there   101
Sharked up a list of lawless resolutes   102
For food and diet to some enterprise   103
That hath a stomach in't, which is no other—   104
As it doth well appear unto our state—
But to recover of us, by strong hand
And terms compulsatory, those foresaid lands
So by his father lost. And this, I take it,
Is the main motive of our preparations,
The source of this our watch, and the chief head   110
Of this posthaste and rummage in the land.   111
BERNARDO.
I think it be no other but e'en so.
Well may it sort that this portentous figure   113
Comes armèd through our watch so like the King
That was and is the question of these wars.   115
HORATIO.
A mote it is to trouble the mind's eye.   116
In the most high and palmy state of Rome,   117
A little ere the mightiest Julius fell,   118
The graves stood tenantless, and the sheeted dead   119
Did squeak and gibber in the Roman streets;
As stars with trains of fire and dews of blood,   121

---

91 heraldry chivalry 93 seized possessed 94 Against the in return for. moiety competent corresponding portion 95 gagèd engaged, pledged. had returned would have passed 96 inheritance possession 97 cov'-nant i.e., the *sealed compact* of line 90 98 carriage...designed purport of the article referred to 100 unimprovèd mettle untried, undisciplined spirits 101 skirts outlying regions, outskirts 102–4 Sharked .. .in't rounded up (as a shark scoops up fish) a troop of lawless desperadoes to feed and supply an enterprise of considerable daring 110 head source 111 posthaste and rummage frenetic activity and bustle 113 Well ... sort That would explain why 115 question focus of contention 116 mote speck of dust 117 palmy flourishing 118 Julius Julius Caesar 119 sheeted shrouded 121 As (This abrupt transition suggests that matter is possibly omitted between lines 120 and 121.) trains trails

Disasters in the sun; and the moist star   122
Upon whose influence Neptune's empire stands   123
Was sick almost to doomsday with eclipse.   124
And even the like precurse of feared events,   125
As harbingers preceding still the fates   126
And prologue to the omen coming on,   127
Have heaven and earth together demonstrated
Unto our climatures and countrymen.   129

(*Enter* GHOST.)

But soft, behold! Lo, where it comes again!   130
I'll cross it, though it blast me. (*It spreads his arms.*) Stay,
    illusion!   131
If thou hast any sound or use of voice,
Speak to me!
If there be any good thing to be done
That may to thee do ease and grace to me,
Speak to me!
If thou art privy to thy country's fate,   137
Which, happily, foreknowing may avoid,   138
Oh, speak!
Or if thou hast uphoarded in thy life
Extorted treasure in the womb of earth,
For which, they say, you spirits oft walk in death,
Speak of it! (*The cock crows.*) Stay and speak!—Stop it, Marcellus.
MARCELLUS.
    Shall I strike at it with my partisan?   144
HORATIO.   Do, if it will not stand.   (*They strike at it.*)
BERNARDO.   'Tis here!   146
HORATIO.   'Tis here!   147

(*Exit* GHOST.)
MARCELLUS.   'Tis gone.

---

122 **Disasters** unfavorable signs or aspects. **moist star** i.e., moon, governing tides 123 **Neptune's** . . . **stands** the sea depends 124 **Was . . . eclipse** was eclipsed nearly to the cosmic darkness predicted for the second coming of Christ and the ending of the world. (See Matthew 24:29 and Revelation 6:12.) 125 **precurse** heralding, foreshadowing 126 **harbingers** forerunners. **still** always 127 **omen** calamitous event 129 **climatures** climes, regions 130 **soft** i.e., enough, break off 131 **cross** stand in its path, confront. **blast** wither, strike with a curse. 131 s.d. *his* its 137 **privy to** in on the secret of 138 **happily** haply, perchance 144 **partisan** long-handled spear 146–7 **'Tis Here! /'Tis here!** (Perhaps they attempt to strike at the Ghost, but are baffled by its seeming ability to be here and there and nowhere.)

We do it wrong, being so majestical,
To offer it the show of violence,
For it is as the air invulnerable,
And our vain blows malicious mockery.
BERNARDO.
    It was about to speak when the cock crew.
HORATIO.
    And then it started like a guilty thing
    Upon a fearful summons. I have heard
    The cock, that is the trumpet to the morn,   156
    Doth with his lofty and shrill-sounding throat
    Awake the god of day, and at his warning,
    Whether in sea or fire, in earth or air,
    Th'extravagant and erring spirit hies   160
    To his confine; and of the truth herein
    This present object made probation.   162
MARCELLUS.
    It faded on the crowing of the cock.
    Some say that ever 'gainst that season comes   164
    Wherein our Savior's birth is celebrated,
    This bird of dawning singeth all night long,
    And then, they say, no spirit dare stir abroad;
    The nights are wholesome, then no planets strike,   168
    No fairy takes, nor witch hath power to charm,   169
    So hallowed and so gracious is that time.   170
HORATIO.
    So have I heard and do in part believe it.
    But, look, the morn in russet mantle clad   172
    Walks o'er the dew of yon high eastward hill.
    Break we our watch up, and by my advice
    Let us impart what we have seen tonight
    Unto young Hamlet; for upon my life,
    This spirit, dumb to us, will speak to him.
    Do you consent we shall acquaint him with it,
    As needful in our loves, fitting our duty?
MARCELLUS.
    Let's do't, I pray, and I this morning know

---

156 trumpet trumpeter **160 extravagant and erring** wandering beyond bounds. (The words have similar meaning.) **hies** hastens **162 probation** proof **164 'gainst** just before **168 strike** destroy by evil influence **169 takes** bewitches. **charm** cast a spell, control by enchantment **170 gracious** full of grace **172 russet** reddish brown

Where we shall find him most conveniently.

(*Exeunt.*)

1.2

Flourish. Enter CLAUDIUS, *King of Denmark,* GERTRUDE *the Queen, [the] Council, as* POLONIUS *and his son* LAERTES, HAMLET, *cum aliis [including* VOLTIMAND *and* CORNELIUS].

KING.

Though yet of Hamlet our dear brother's death   1
The memory be green, and that it us befitted
To bear our hearts in grief and our whole kingdom
To be contracted in one brow of woe,
Yet so far hath discretion fought with nature
That we with wisest sorrow think on him
Together with remembrance of ourselves.
Therefore our sometime sister, now our queen,   8
Th'imperial jointress to this warlike state,   9
Have we, as 'twere with a defeated joy—
With an auspicious and a dropping eye,   11
With mirth in funeral and with dirge in marriage,
In equal scale weighing delight and dole—   13
Taken to wife. Nor have we herein barred
Your better wisdoms, which have freely gone
With this affair along. For all, our thanks.
Now follows that you know young Fortinbras,   17
Holding a weak supposal of our worth,   18
Or thinking by our late dear brother's death
Our state to be disjoint and out of frame,   20
Co-leaguèd with this dream of his advantage,   21
He hath not failed to pester us with message
Importing the surrender of those lands   23
Lost by his father, with all bonds of law,   24

1.2 Location: The castle.
0.2 as i.e., such as, including. 0.3 cum aliis with others 1 our my. (The royal "we"; also in the following lines.) 8 sometime former 9 jointress woman possessing property with her husband 11 With . . . eye with one eye smiling and the other weeping 13 dole grief 17 Now . . . know Next, you need to be informed that 18 weak supposal low estimate 20 disjoint . . . frame in a state of total disorder 21 Co-leaguèd . . . advantage joined to his illusory sense of having the advantage over us and to his vision of future success. 23 Importing having for its substance 24 with . . . law (See 1.1.91, "Well ratified by law and heraldry.")

To our most valiant brother. So much for him.
Now for ourself and for this time of meeting.
Thus much the business is: we have here writ
To Norway, uncle of young Fortinbras—
Who, impotent and bed-rid, scarcely hears   29
Of this his nephew's purpose—to suppress
His further gait herein, in that the levies,   31
The lists, and full proportions are all made   32
Out of his subject; and we here dispatch   33
You, good Cornelius, and you, Voltimand,
For bearers of this greeting to old Norway,
Giving to you no further personal power
To business with the King more than the scope
Of these dilated articles allow.   (*He gives a paper.*)   38
Farewell, and let your haste commend your duty.   39
CORNELIUS, VOLTIMAND.
    In that, and all things, will we show our duty.
KING.
    We doubt it nothing. Heartily farewell.   41

(*Exeunt* VOLTIMAND *and* CORNELIUS.)

And now, Laertes, what's the news with you?
You told us of some suit; what is't, Laertes?
You cannot speak of reason to the Dane   44
And lose your voice. What wouldst thou beg, Laertes,   45
That shall not be my offer, not thy asking?
The head is not more native to the heart,   47
The hand more instrumental to the mouth,   48
Than is the throne of Denmark to thy father.
What wouldst thou have, Laertes?
LAERTES.   My dread lord,
Your leave and favor to return to France,   51
From whence though willingly I came to Denmark
To show my duty in your coronation,
Yet now I must confess, that duty done,
My thoughts and wishes bend again toward France

---

29 impotent helpless   **31 His** i.e., Fortinbras'.   **gait** proceeding   **31–3 in that … subject** since the levying of troops and supplies is drawn entirely from the King of Norway's own subjects.   **38 dilated** set out at length   **39 let … duty** let your swift obeying of orders, rather than mere words, express your dutifulness.   **41 nothing** not at all   **44 the Dane** the Danish king   **45 lose your voice** waste your speech   **47 native** closely connected, related   **48 instrumental** serviceable   **51 leave and favor** kind permission

And bow them to your gracious leave and pardon. 56
KING.
Have you your father's leave? What says Polonius?
POLONIUS.
H'ath, my lord, wrung from me my slow leave 58
By laborsome petition, and at last
Upon his will I sealed my hard consent. 60
I do beseech you, give him leave to go.
KING.
Take thy fair hour, Laertes. Time be thine, 62
And thy best graces spend it at thy will. 63
But now, my cousin Hamlet, and my son— 64
HAMLET.
A little more than kin, and less than kind. 65
KING.
How is it that the clouds still hang on you?
HAMLET.
Not so, my lord. I am too much in the sun. 67
QUEEN.
Good Hamlet, cast thy nighted color off, 68
And let thine eye look like a friend on Denmark. 69
Do not forever with thy vailèd lids 70
Seek for thy noble father in the dust.
Thou know'st 'tis common, all that lives must die, 72
Passing through nature to eternity.
HAMLET.
Ay, madam, it is common.
QUEEN. If it be,
Why seems it so particular with thee? 75
HAMLET.
Seems, madam? Nay, it is. I know not "seems."

---

56 bow ... pardon entreatingly make a deep bow, asking your permission to depart. **58 H'ath** He has **60 sealed** (as if sealing a legal document). **hard** reluctant **62 Take thy fair hour** Enjoy your time of youth **63 And ... will** and may your time be spent in exercising your best qualities. **64 cousin** any kin not of the immediate family **65 A little ... kind** Too close a blood relation, and yet we are less than kinsmen in that our relationship lacks affection and is indeed unnatural. (Hamlet plays on *kind* as [1] kindly [2] belonging to nature, suggesting that Claudius is not the same kind of being as the rest of humanity. The line is often delivered as an aside, though it need not be.) **67 the sun** i.e., the sunshine of the King's royal favor. (With pun on *son*.) **68 nighted color** (1) mourning garments of black (2) dark melancholy **69 Denmark** the King of Denmark. **70 vailèd lids** lowered eyes **72 common** of universal occurrence. (But Hamlet plays on the sense of "vulgar" in line 74.). **75 particular** personal

'Tis not alone my inky cloak, good mother,
Nor customary suits of solemn black,   *78*
Nor windy suspiration of forced breath,   *79*
No, nor the fruitful river in the eye,   *80*
Nor the dejected havior of the visage,   *81*
Together with all forms, moods, shapes of grief,   *82*
That can denote me truly. These indeed seem,
For they are actions that a man might play.
But I have that within which passes show;
These but the trappings and the suits of woe.
KING.
'Tis sweet and commendable in your nature, Hamlet,
To give these mourning duties to your father.
But you must know your father lost a father,
That father lost, lost his, and the survivor bound
In filial obligation for some term
To do obsequious sorrow. But to persevere   *92*
In obstinate condolement is a course   *93*
Of impious stubbornness. 'Tis unmanly grief.
It shows a will most incorrect to heaven,
A heart unfortified, a mind impatient,   *96*
An understanding simple and unschooled.   *97*
For what we know must be and is as common
As any the most vulgar thing to sense,   *99*
Why should we in our peevish opposition
Take it to heart? Fie, 'tis a fault to heaven,
A fault against the dead, a fault to nature,
To reason most absurd, whose common theme
Is death of fathers, and who still hath cried,   *104*
From the first corpse till he that died today,   *105*
"This must be so." We pray you, throw to earth
This unprevailing woe and think of us   *107*
As of a father; for let the world take note,
You are the most immediate to our throne,   *109*
And with no less nobility of love
Than that which dearest father bears his son

---

78 customary customary to mourning   **79 suspiration** sighing   **80 fruitful** abundant   **81 havior** expression   **82 moods** outward expression of feeling   **92 obsequious** suited to obsequies or funerals   **93 condolement** sorrowing   **96 unfortified** i.e., against adversity   **97 simple** ignorant   **99 As... sense** as the most ordinary experience   **104 still** always   **105 the first corpse** (Abel's)   **107 unprevailing** unavailing, useless   **109 most immediate** next in succession

Do I impart toward you. For your intent 112
In going back to school in Wittenberg, 113
It is most retrograde to our desire, 114
And we beseech you bend you to remain 115
Here in the cheer and comfort of our eye,
Our chiefest courtier, cousin, and our son.

QUEEN.
Let not thy mother lose her prayers, Hamlet.
I pray thee, stay with us, go not to Wittenberg.

HAMLET.
I shall in all my best obey you, madam. 120

KING.
Why, 'tis a loving and a fair reply.
Be as ourself in Denmark. Madam, come.
This gentle and unforced accord of Hamlet
Sits smiling to my heart, in grace whereof 124
No jocund health that Denmark drinks today 125
But the great cannon to the clouds shall tell,
And the King's rouse the heaven shall bruit again, 127
Respeaking earthly thunder. Come away. 128

(*Flourish. Exeunt all but* HAMLET.)

HAMLET.
Oh, that this too too sullied flesh would melt, 129
Thaw, and resolve itself into a dew!
Or that the Everlasting had not fixed
His canon 'gainst self-slaughter! Oh, God, God, 132
How weary, stale, flat, and unprofitable
Seem to me all the uses of this world!
Fie on't, ah fie! 'Tis an unweeded garden
That grows to seed. Things rank and gross in nature
Possess it merely. That it should come to this! 137
But two months dead—nay, not so much, not two.

---

112 **impart toward** liberally bestow on.   **For** As for   113 **to school** i.e., to your studies.
Wittenberg famous German university founded in 1502   114 **retrograde** contrary   115 **bend you**
incline yourself   120 **in all my best** to the best of my ability   124 **to** i.e., at.   **grace** thanksgiving
125 **jocund** merry   127 **rouse** drinking of a draft of liquor.   **bruit again** loudly echo   128 **thunder**
i.e., of trumpet and kettledrum, sounded when the King drinks; see 1.4.8–12.   129 **sullied** defiled.
(The early quartos read "sallied"; the Folio, "solid.")   132 **canon** law   137 **merely** completely

So excellent a king, that was to this   *139*
Hyperion to a satyr, so loving to my mother   *140*
That he might not beteem the winds of heaven   *141*
Visit her face too roughly. Heaven and earth,
Must I remember? Why, she would hang on him
As if increase of appetite had grown
By what it fed on, and yet within a month—
Let me not think on't; frailty, thy name is woman!—
A little month, or ere those shoes were old   *147*
With which she followed my poor father's body,
Like Niobe, all tears, why she, even she—   *149*
Oh, God, a beast, that wants discourse of reason,   *150*
Would have mourned longer—married with my uncle,
My father's brother, but no more like my father
Than I to Hercules. Within a month,
Ere yet the salt of most unrighteous tears
Had left the flushing in her gallèd eyes,   *155*
She married. Oh, most wicked speed, to post   *156*
With such dexterity to incestuous sheets!   *157*
It is not, nor it cannot come to good.
But break, my heart, for I must hold my tongue.

(*Enter* HORATIO, MARCELLUS, *and* BERNARDO.)

HORATIO.
    Hail to Your Lordship!
HAMLET.   I am glad to see you well.
    Horatio!—or I do forget myself.
HORATIO.
    The same, my lord, and your poor servant ever.
HAMLET.
    Sir, my good friend; I'll change that name with you.   *163*
    And what make you from Wittenberg, Horatio?—   *164*
    Marcellus.

---

139 **to** in comparison to   140 **Hyperion** Titan sun-god, father of Helios.   **satyr** a lecherous creature of classical mythology, half-human but with a goat's legs, tail, ears, and horns   141 **beteem**
allow   147 **or ere** even before   149 **Niobes** Tantalus's daughter, Queen of Thebes, who boasted that
she had more sons and daughters than Leto; for this, Apollo and Artemis, children of Leto, slew her
fourteen children. She was turned by Zeus into a stone that continually dropped tears.   150 **wants ..**
. reason lacks the faculty of reason   155 **gallèd** irritated, inflamed   156 **post** hasten   157 **incestu-**
ous (In Shakespeare's day, the marriage of a man like Claudius to his deceased brother's wife was
considered incestuous.)   163 **change that name** i.e., give and receive reciprocally the name of "friend"
rather than talk of "servant." Or Hamlet may be saying, "No, I am *your* servant."   164 **make you**
from are you doing away from

MARCELLUS.   My good lord.
HAMLET.
  I am very glad to see you. (*To* BERNARDO.) Good even, sir.—
  But what in faith make you from Wittenberg?
HORATIO.
  A truant disposition, good my lord.
HAMLET.
  I would not hear your enemy say so,
  Nor shall you do my ear that violence
  To make it truster of your own report   *171*
  Against yourself. I know you are no truant.
  But what is your affair in Elsinore?
  We'll teach you to drink deep ere you depart.
HORATIO.
  My lord, I came to see your father's funeral.
HAMLET.
  I prithee, do not mock me, fellow student;
  I think it was to see my mother's wedding.
HORATIO.
  Indeed, my lord, it followed hard upon.   *179*
HAMLET.
  Thrift, thrift, Horatio! The funeral baked meats   *180*
  Did coldly furnish forth the marriage tables.   *181*
  Would I had met my dearest foe in heaven   *182*
  Or ever I had seen that day, Horatio!   *183*
  My father!—Methinks I see my father.
HORATIO.
  Where, my lord?
HAMLET.   In my mind's eye, Horatio.
HORATIO.
  I saw him once. 'A was a goodly king.   *186*
HAMLET.
  'A was a man. Take him for all in all,
  I shall not look upon his like again.
HORATIO.
  My lord, I think I saw him yesternight.
HAMLET.   Saw? Who?
HORATIO.   My lord, the King your father.

---

171 **To . . . of** to make it trust   179 **hard** close   180 **baked meats** meat pies   181 **coldly** i.e., as cold leftovers   182 **dearest** closest (and therefore deadliest)   183 **Or ever** ere, before   186 **'A** He

HAMLET.   The King my father?

HORATIO.

Season your admiration for a while   193

With an attent ear till I may deliver,   194

Upon the witness of these gentlemen,

This marvel to you.

HAMLET.   For God's love, let me hear!

HORATIO.

Two nights together had these gentlemen,

Marcellus and Bernardo, on their watch,

In the dead waste and middle of the night,   199

Been thus encountered. A figure like your father,

Armèd at point exactly, cap-à-pie,   201

Appears before them, and with solemn march

Goes slow and stately by them. Thrice he walked

By their oppressed and fear-surprisèd eyes

Within his truncheon's length, whilst they, distilled   205

Almost to jelly with the act of fear,   206

Stand dumb and speak not to him. This to me

In dreadful secrecy impart they did,   208

And I with them the third night kept the watch,

Where, as they had delivered, both in time,

Form of the thing, each word made true and good,

The apparition comes. I knew your father;

These hands are not more like.

HAMLET.   But where was this?

MARCELLUS.

My lord, upon the platform where we watch.

HAMLET.

Did you not speak to it?

HORATIO.   My lord, I did,

But answer made it none. Yet once methought

It lifted up it head and did address   217

Itself to motion, like as it would speak;   218

But even then the morning cock crew loud,   219

And at the sound it shrunk in haste away

---

193 **Season your admiration** Moderate your astonishment   194 **attent** attentive   199 **dead waste** desolate stillness   201 **at point** correctly in every detail.   **cap-à-pie** from head to foot   205 **truncheon** officer's staff.   **distilled** dissolved   206 **act** action, operation   208 **dreadful** full of dread   217 **it** its   217–18 **did . . . speak** prepared to move as though it was about to speak   219 **even then** at that very instant

And vanished from our sight.

HAMLET.   'Tis very strange.

HORATIO.

As I do live, my honored lord, 'tis true,
And we did think it writ down in our duty
To let you know of it.

HAMLET.

Indeed, indeed, sirs. But this troubles me.
Hold you the watch tonight?

ALL.   We do, my lord.

HAMLET.   Armed, say you?

ALL.   Armed, my lord.

HAMLET.   From top to toe?

ALL.   My lord, from head to foot.

HAMLET.   Then saw you not his face?

HORATIO.

Oh, yes, my lord, he wore his beaver up.   *232*

HAMLET.   What looked he, frowningly?   *233*

HORATIO.

A countenance more in sorrow than in anger.

HAMLET.   Pale or red?

HORATIO.   Nay, very pale.

HAMLET.   And fixed his eyes upon you?

HORATIO.   Most constantly.

HAMLET.   I would I had been there.

HORATIO.   It would have much amazed you.

HAMLET.   Very like, very like. Stayed it long?

HORATIO.

While one with moderate haste might tell a hundred.   *242*

MARCELLUS, BERNARDO.   Longer, longer.

HORATIO.   Not when I saw't.

HAMLET.   His beard was grizzled—no?

HORATIO.

It was, as I have seen it in his life,
A sable silvered.

HAMLET.   I will watch tonight.
Perchance 'twill walk again.

HORATIO.   I warr'nt it will.

---

232 **beaver** visor on the helmet   233 **What** How   242 **tell** count

HAMLET.
> If it assume my noble father's person,
> I'll speak to it though hell itself should gape
> And bid me hold my peace. I pray you all,
> If you have hitherto concealed this sight,
> Let it be tenable in your silence still,   *253*
> And whatsomever else shall hap tonight,
> Give it an understanding but no tongue.
> I will requite your loves. So, fare you well.
> Upon the platform twixt eleven and twelve
> I'll visit you.

ALL.   Our duty to Your Honor.

HAMLET.
> Your loves, as mine to you. Farewell.   *259*

(*Exeunt [all but* HAMLET*].*)

> My father's spirit in arms! All is not well.
> I doubt some foul play. Would the night were come!   *261*
> Till then sit still, my soul. Foul deeds will rise,
> Though all the earth o'erwhelm them, to men's eyes.

Exit.

1.3

Enter LAERTES *and* OPHELIA, *his sister.*

LAERTES.
> My necessaries are embarked. Farewell.
> And, sister, as the winds give benefit
> And convoy is assistant, do not sleep   *3*
> But let me hear from you.

OPHELIA.   Do you doubt that?

LAERTES.
> For Hamlet, and the trifling of his favor,   *5*
> Hold it a fashion and a toy in blood,   *6*
> A violet in the youth of primy nature,   *7*
> Forward, not permanent, sweet, not lasting,   *8*

---

253 tenable held   **259 Your loves** i.e., Say "Your loves" to me, not just your "duty."   **261 doubt** suspect

1.3. Location: Polonius's chambers.
3 convoy is assistant means of conveyance are available   **5 For** As for   **6 toy in blood** passing amorous fancy   **7 primy** in its prime, springtime   **8 Forward** precocious

The perfume and suppliance of a minute— 9
No more.
OPHELIA. No more but so?
LAERTES. Think it no more.
For nature crescent does not grow alone 11
In thews and bulk, but as this temple waxes 12
The inward service of the mind and soul
Grows wide withal. Perhaps he loves you now, 14
And now no soil nor cautel doth besmirch 15
The virtue of his will; but you must fear, 16
His greatness weighed, his will is not his own. 17
For he himself is subject to his birth.
He may not, as unvalued persons do,
Carve for himself, for on his choice depends 20
The safety and health of this whole state,
And therefore must his choice be circumscribed
Unto the voice and yielding of that body 23
Whereof he is the head. Then if he says he loves you,
It fits your wisdom so far to believe it
As he in his particular act and place 26
May give his saying deed, which is no further
Than the main voice of Denmark goes withal. 28
Then weigh what loss your honor may sustain
If with too credent ear you list his songs, 30
Or lose your heart, or your chaste treasure open
To his unmastered importunity. 32
Fear it, Ophelia, fear it, my dear sister,
And keep you in the rear of your affection, 34
Out of the shot and danger of desire.
The chariest maid is prodigal enough 36
If she unmask her beauty to the moon. 37
Virtue itself scapes not calumnious strokes.

---

9 suppliance pastime, something to fill the time **11–14 For nature ... withal** For nature, as it ripens, does not grow only in physical strength, but as the body matures the inner qualities of mind and soul grow along with it. (Laertes warns Ophelia that the mature Hamlet may not cling to his youthful interests.) **15 soil nor cautel** blemish nor deceit **16 The ... will** the purity of his desire **17 His greatness weighed** taking into account his high fortune **20 Carve** i.e., choose **23 voice and yielding** assent, approval **26 in ... place** in his particular restricted circumstances **28 main voice** general assent. **withal** along with. **30 credent** credulous. **list** listen to **32 unmastered** uncontrolled **34 keep ... affection** don't advance as far as your affection might lead you. (A military metaphor.) **36 chariest** most scrupulously modest **37 If she unmask** if she does no more than show her beauty. **moon** (Symbol of chastity.)

The canker galls the infants of the spring 39
Too oft before their buttons be disclosed, 40
And in the morn and liquid dew of youth 41
Contagious blastments are most imminent. 42
Be wary then; best safety lies in fear.
Youth to itself rebels, though none else near. 44

OPHELIA.

I shall the effect of this good lesson keep
As watchman to my heart. But, good my brother,
Do not, as some ungracious pastors do, 47
Show me the steep and thorny way to heaven,
Whiles like a puffed and reckless libertine 49
Himself the primrose path of dalliance treads,
And recks not his own rede.

(*Enter* POLONIUS.)

LAERTES.   Oh, fear me not. 51
I stay too long. But here my father comes.
A double blessing is a double grace; 53
Occasion smiles upon a second leave. 54

POLONIUS.

Yet here, Laertes? Aboard, aboard, for shame!
The wind sits in the shoulder of your sail,
And you are stayed for. There—my blessing with thee!
And these few precepts in thy memory
Look thou character. Give thy thoughts no tongue, 59
Nor any unproportioned thought his act. 60
Be thou familiar, but by no means vulgar. 61
Those friends thou hast, and their adoption tried, 62
Grapple them unto thy soul with hoops of steel,
But do not dull thy palm with entertainment 64
Of each new-hatched, unfledged courage. Beware 65

---

39 **canker galls** cankerworm destroys   40 **buttons be disclosed** buds be opened   41 **liquid dew** i.e., time when dew is fresh and bright   42 **blastments** blights   44 **Youth ... rebels** Youth yields to the rebellion of the flesh   47 **ungracious** ungodly   49 **puffed** bloated, or swollen with pride   51 **recks** heeds.   **rede** counsel.   **fear me not** don't worry on my account.   53–4 **A double ... leave** The goddess Occasion or Opportunity smiles on the happy circumstance of being able to say good-bye twice and thus receive a second blessing.   59 **Look thou character** see to it that you inscribe.   60 **unproportioned** badly calculated, intemperate.   **his** its   61 **familiar** sociable.   **vulgar** common.   62 **and ... tried** and their suitability to be your friends having been put to the test   64 **dull thy palm** i.e., shake hands so often as to make the gesture meaningless   65 **courage** swashbuckler.

Of entrance to a quarrel, but being in,
Bear't that th'opposèd may beware of thee. 67
Give every man thy ear, but few thy voice;
Take each man's censure, but reserve thy judgment. 69
Costly thy habit as thy purse can buy, 70
But not expressed in fancy; rich, not gaudy, 71
For the apparel oft proclaims the man,
And they in France of the best rank and station
Are of a most select and generous chief in that. 74
Neither a borrower nor a lender be,
For loan oft loses both itself and friend,
And borrowing dulleth edge of husbandry. 77
This above all: to thine own self be true,
And it must follow, as the night the day,
Thou canst not then be false to any man.
Farewell. My blessing season this in thee! 81
LAERTES.
Most humbly do I take my leave, my lord.
POLONIUS.
The time invests you. Go, your servants tend. 83
LAERTES.
Farewell, Ophelia, and remember well
What I have said to you.
OPHELIA. 'Tis in my memory locked,
And you yourself shall keep the key of it.
LAERTES. Farewell. (*Exit* LAERTES.)
POLONIUS.
What is't, Ophelia, he hath said to you?
OPHELIA.
So please you, something touching the Lord Hamlet.
POLONIUS. Marry, well bethought. 91
'Tis told me he hath very oft of late
Given private time to you, and you yourself
Have of your audience been most free and bounteous.
If it be so—as so 'tis put on me, 95

---

67 **Bear't that** manage it so that 69 **censure** opinion, judgment 70 **habit** clothing 71 **fancy** excessive ornament, decadent fashion 74 **Are … that** are of a most refined and well-bred preeminence in choosing what to wear. 77 **husbandry** thrift 81 **season** mature 83 **invests** besieges, presses upon. **tend** attend, wait. 91 **Marry** i.e., By the Virgin Mary. (A mild oath.) 95 **put on** impressed on, told to

And that in way of caution—I must tell you
You do not understand yourself so clearly
As it behooves my daughter and your honor. 98
What is between you? Give me up the truth.

OPHELIA.

He hath, my lord, of late made many tenders 100
Of his affection to me.

POLONIUS.

Affection? Pooh! You speak like a green girl,
Unsifted in such perilous circumstance. 103
Do you believe his tenders, as you call them?

OPHELIA.

I do not know, my lord, what I should think.

POLONIUS.

Marry, I will teach you. Think yourself a baby
That you have ta'en these tenders for true pay
Which are not sterling. Tender yourself more dearly, 108
Or—not to crack the wind of the poor phrase, 109
Running it thus—you'll tender me a fool. 110

OPHELIA.

My lord, he hath importuned me with love
In honorable fashion.

POLONIUS.

Ay, fashion you may call it. Go to, go to. 113

OPHELIA.

And hath given countenance to his speech, my lord, 114
With almost all the holy vows of heaven.

POLONIUS.

Ay, springes to catch woodcocks. I do know, 116
When the blood burns, how prodigal the soul 117
Lends the tongue vows. These blazes, daughter,
Giving more light than heat, extinct in both
Even in their promise as it is a-making, 120
You must not take for fire. From this time
Be something scanter of your maiden presence. 122

---

98 **behooves** befits   100 **tenders** offers   103 **Unsifted** i.e., untried   108 **sterling** legal currency.
Tender ... dearly (1) Bargain for your favors at a higher rate—i.e., hold out for marriage (2) Show
greater care of yourself   109 **crack the wind** i.e., run it until it is broken-winded   110 **tender ...
fool** (1) make a fool of me (2) present me with a *fool* or baby.   113 **fashion** mere form, pretense.
Go to (An expression of impatience.)   114 **countenance** credit, confirmation   116 **springes** snares.
woodcocks birds easily caught; here used to connote gullibility.   117 **prodigal** prodigally   120 **it**
i.e., the promise   122 **something** somewhat

Set your entreatments at a higher rate	*123*
Than a command to parle. For Lord Hamlet,	*124*
Believe so much in him that he is young,	*125*
And with a larger tether may he walk	
Than may be given you. In few, Ophelia,	*127*
Do not believe his vows, for they are brokers,	*128*
Not of that dye which their investments show,	*129*
But mere implorators of unholy suits,	*130*
Breathing like sanctified and pious bawds,	*131*
The better to beguile. This is for all:	*132*
I would not, in plain terms, from this time forth	
Have you so slander any moment leisure	*134*
As to give words or talk with the Lord Hamlet.	
Look to't, I charge you. Come your ways.	*136*

OPHELIA.   I shall obey, my lord.   (*Exeunt.*)

1.4

Enter HAMLET, HORATIO, *and* MARCELLUS.

HAMLET.
   The air bites shrewdly; it is very cold.   *1*
HORATIO.
   It is a nipping and an eager air.   *2*
HAMLET.
   What hour now?
HORATIO.   I think it lacks of twelve.   *3*
MARCELLUS.
   No, it is struck.
HORATIO.   Indeed? I heard it not.
   It then draws near the season   *5*
   Wherein the spirit held his wont to walk.   *6*
(*A flourish of trumpets, and two pieces go off [within].*)

123–4 **Set . . . parle** i.e., As defender of your chastity, negotiate for something better than a surrender simply because the besieger requests an interview.   124 **For** As for   125 **so . . . him** this much concerning him   127 **In few** Briefly   128 **brokers** go-betweens, procurers   129 **dye** color or sort. **investments** clothes. (The vows are not what they seem.)   130 **mere implorators** out-and-out solicitors   131 **Breathing** speaking   132 **for all** once for all, in sum   134 **slander** abuse, misuse. **moment** moment's   136 **Come your ways** Come along.

1.4 Location: The guard platform.
1 **shrewdly** keenly, sharply   2 **eager** biting   3 **lacks of** is just short of   5 **season** time   6 **held his wont** was accustomed.   6.1 *pieces* i.e., of ordnance, cannon

What does this mean, my lord?

HAMLET.

 The King doth wake tonight and takes his rouse,   8

 Keeps wassail, and the swagg'ring upspring reels;   9

 And as he drains his drafts of Rhenish down,   10

 The kettledrum and trumpet thus bray out

 The triumph of his pledge.

HORATIO. Is it a custom?   12

HAMLET. Ay, marry, is't,

 But to my mind, though I am native here

 And to the manner born, it is a custom   15

 More honored in the breach than the observance.   16

 This heavy-headed revel east and west   17

 Makes us traduced and taxed of other nations.   18

 They clepe us drunkards, and with swinish phrase   19

 Soil our addition; and indeed it takes   20

 From our achievements, though performed at height,   21

 The pith and marrow of our attribute.   22

 So, oft it chances in particular men,

 That for some vicious mole of nature in them,   24

 As in their birth—wherein they are not guilty,

 Since nature cannot choose his origin—   26

 By their o'ergrowth of some complexion,   27

 Oft breaking down the pales and forts of reason,   28

 Or by some habit that too much o'erleavens   29

 The form of plausive manners, that these men,   30

 Carrying, I say, the stamp of one defect,

 Being nature's livery or fortune's star,   32

---

8 wake stay awake and hold revel. **takes his rouse** carouses **9 Keeps . . . reels** carouses, and riotously dances a German dance called the upspring **10 Rhenish** Rhine wine **12 The triumph . . . pledge** the celebration of his offering a toast. **15 manner** custom (of drinking) **16 More . . . observance** better neglected than followed. **17 east and west** i.e., everywhere **18 taxed of** censured by **19 clepe** call. **with swinish phrase** i.e., by calling us swine **20 addition** reputation **21 at height** outstandingly **22 The pith . . . attribute** the most essential part of the esteem that should be attributed to us. **24 for . . . mole** on account of some natural defect in their constitutions. **26 his** its **27 their o'ergrowth . . . complexion** the excessive growth in individuals of some natural trait **28 pales** palings, fences (as of a fortification) **29–30 o'erleavens . . . manners** i.e., infects the way we should behave (much as bad yeast spoils the dough). *Plausive* means "pleasing." **32 Being . . . star** (that stamp of defect) being a sign identifying one as wearing the livery of, and hence being the servant to, nature (unfortunate inherited qualities) or fortune (mischance).

His virtues else, be they as pure as grace,   33
As infinite as man may undergo,   34
Shall in the general censure take corruption   35
From that particular fault. The dram of evil   36
Doth all the noble substance often dout   37
To his own scandal.

(*Enter* GHOST.)

HORATIO.   Look, my lord, it comes!   38
HAMLET.
Angels and ministers of grace defend us!   39
Be thou a spirit of health or goblin damned,   40
Bring with thee airs from heaven or blasts from hell,   41
Be thy intents wicked or charitable,   42
Thou com'st in such a questionable shape   43
That I will speak to thee. I'll call thee Hamlet,
King, father, royal Dane. Oh, answer me!
Let me not burst in ignorance, but tell
Why thy canonized bones, hearsèd in death,   47
Have burst their cerements; why the sepulcher   48
Wherein we saw thee quietly inurned   49
Hath oped his ponderous and marble jaws
To cast thee up again. What may this mean,
That thou, dead corpse, again in complete steel,   52
Revisits thus the glimpses of the moon,   53
Making night hideous, and we fools of nature   54
So horridly to shake our disposition   55
With thoughts beyond the reaches of our souls?
Say, why is this? Wherefore? What should we do?

(*The* GHOST *beckons* HAMLET.)

---

33 His virtues else i.e., the other qualities of *these men* (line 30)   **34 may undergo** can sustain   **35 in ... censure** in overall appraisal, in people's opinion generally   **36-8 The dram ... scandal** i.e., The small drop of evil blots out or works against the noble substance of the whole and brings it into disrepute. (To *dout* is to blot out. A famous crux.)   **39 ministers of grace** messengers of God   **40 Be. ..health** Whether you are a good angel   **41 Bring** whether you bring   **42 Be thy intents** whether your intentions are   **43 questionable** inviting question   **47 canonized** buried according to the canons of the church.   **hearsèd** coffined   **48 cerements** grave clothes   **49 inurned** entombed   **52 complete steel** full armor   **53 the glimpses ... moon** i.e., the sublunary world, all that is beneath the moon   **54 fools of nature** mere mortals, limited to natural knowledge and subject to nature   **55 So ... disposition** to distress our mental composure so violently

HORATIO.

It beckons you to go away with it,

As if it some impartment did desire   59

To you alone.

MARCELLUS.   Look with what courteous action

It wafts you to a more removèd ground.

But do not go with it.

HORATIO.   No, by no means.

HAMLET.

It will not speak. Then I will follow it.

HORATIO.

Do not, my lord!

HAMLET.   Why, what should be the fear?

I do not set my life at a pin's fee,   65

And for my soul, what can it do to that,   66

Being a thing immortal as itself?

It waves me forth again. I'll follow it.

HORATIO.

What if it tempt you toward the flood, my lord,   69

Or to the dreadful summit of the cliff

That beetles o'er his base into the sea,   71

And there assume some other horrible form

Which might deprive your sovereignty of reason   73

And draw you into madness? Think of it.

The very place puts toys of desperation,   75

Without more motive, into every brain

That looks so many fathoms to the sea

And hears it roar beneath.

HAMLET.

It wafts me still.—Go on, I'll follow thee.

MARCELLUS.

You shall not go, my lord.   (*They try to stop him.*)

HAMLET.   Hold off your hands!

HORATIO.

Be ruled. You shall not go.

---

59 **impartment** communication   65 **fee** value   66 **for** as for   69 **flood** sea   71 **beetles o'er** over-
hangs threateningly (like bushy eyebrows).   **his** its   73 **deprive . . . reason** take away the rule of reason over your mind   75 **toys of desperation** fancies of desperate acts, i.e., suicide

HAMLET.   My fate cries out,   *81*
   And makes each petty artery in this body   *82*
   As hardy as the Nemean lion's nerve.   *83*
   Still am I called. Unhand me, gentlemen.
   By heaven, I'll make a ghost of him that lets me!   *85*
   I say, away!—Go on, I'll follow thee.

(*Exeunt* GHOST *and* HAMLET.)

HORATIO.
   He waxes desperate with imagination.
MARCELLUS.
   Let's follow. 'Tis not fit thus to obey him.
HORATIO.
   Have after. To what issue will this come?   *89*
MARCELLUS.
   Something is rotten in the state of Denmark.
HORATIO.
   Heaven will direct it.   *91*
MARCELLUS.   Nay, let's follow him.   (*Exeunt.*)

1.5

(*Enter* GHOST *and* HAMLET.)

HAMLET.
   Whither wilt thou lead me? Speak. I'll go no further.
GHOST.
   Mark me.
HAMLET.   I will.
GHOST.   My hour is almost come,
   When I to sulf'rous and tormenting flames
   Must render up myself.
HAMLET.   Alas, poor ghost!
GHOST.
   Pity me not, but lend thy serious hearing
   To what I shall unfold.

---

81 **My fate cries out** My destiny summons me   82 **petty** weak.   **artery** blood vessel system through which the vital spirits were thought to have been conveyed.   83 **Nemean lion's nerve** as a sinew of the huge lion slain by Hercules as the first of his twelve labors.   85 **lets** hinders   89 **Have after** Let's go after him.   **issue** outcome
91 **it** i.e., the outcome

1.5 Location: The battlements of the castle.

HAMLET.　Speak. I am bound to hear.　　　　　　　　　　*7*
GHOST.
　　So art thou to revenge, when thou shalt hear.
HAMLET.　What?
GHOST.　I am thy father's spirit,
　　Doomed for a certain term to walk the night,
　　And for the day confined to fast in fires,　　　　　　*12*
　　Till the foul crimes done in my days of nature　　　*13*
　　Are burnt and purged away. But that I am forbid　*14*
　　To tell the secrets of my prison house,
　　I could a tale unfold whose lightest word
　　Would harrow up thy soul, freeze thy young blood,　*17*
　　Make thy two eyes like stars start from their spheres,　*18*
　　Thy knotted and combinèd locks to part,　　　　　*19*
　　And each particular hair to stand on end
　　Like quills upon the fretful porcupine.
　　But this eternal blazon must not be　　　　　　　　*22*
　　To ears of flesh and blood. List, list, oh, list!
　　If thou didst ever thy dear father love—
HAMLET.　Oh, God!
GHOST.
　　Revenge his foul and most unnatural murder.
HAMLET.　Murder?
GHOST.
　　Murder most foul, as in the best it is,　　　　　　*28*
　　But this most foul, strange, and unnatural.
HAMLET.
　　Haste me to know't, that I, with wings as swift
　　As meditation or the thoughts of love,
　　May sweep to my revenge.
GHOST.　I find thee apt;
　　And duller shouldst thou be than the fat weed　　*33*
　　That roots itself in ease on Lethe wharf,　　　　　*34*

---

7 **bound** (1) ready (2) obligated by duty and fate. (The Ghost, in line 8, answers in the second sense.)　12 **fast** do penance by fasting　13 **crimes** sins.　**of nature** as a mortal　14 **But that** Were it not that　17 **harrow up** lacerate, tear　18 **spheres** i.e., eye-sockets, here compared to the orbits or transparent revolving spheres in which, according to Ptolemaic astronomy, the heavenly bodies were fixed　19 **knotted ... locks** hair neatly arranged and confined　22 **eternal blazon** revelation of the secrets of eternity　28 **in the best** even at best　33 **shouldst thou be** you would have to be.　**fat** torpid, lethargic　34 **Lethe** the river of forgetfulness in Hades

Wouldst thou not stir in this. Now, Hamlet, hear.
'Tis given out that, sleeping in my orchard,   *36*
A serpent stung me. So the whole ear of Denmark
Is by a forgèd process of my death   *38*
Rankly abused. But know, thou noble youth,   *39*
The serpent that did sting thy father's life
Now wears his crown.
HAMLET.   Oh, my prophetic soul! My uncle!
GHOST.
Ay, that incestuous, that adulterate beast,   *43*
With witchcraft of his wit, with traitorous gifts—   *44*
Oh, wicked wit and gifts, that have the power
So to seduce!—won to his shameful lust
The will of my most seeming-virtuous queen.
Oh, Hamlet, what a falling off was there!
From me, whose love was of that dignity
That it went hand in hand even with the vow   *50*
I made to her in marriage, and to decline
Upon a wretch whose natural gifts were poor
To those of mine!   *53*
But virtue, as it never will be moved,   *54*
Though lewdness court it in a shape of heaven,   *55*
So lust, though to a radiant angel linked,
Will sate itself in a celestial bed   *57*
And prey on garbage.
But soft, methinks I scent the morning air.
Brief let me be. Sleeping within my orchard,
My custom always of the afternoon,
Upon my secure hour thy uncle stole,   *62*
With juice of cursèd hebona in a vial,   *63*
And in the porches of my ears did pour   *64*
The leprous distillment, whose effect   *65*
Holds such an enmity with blood of man

---

36 orchard garden   **38 forgèd process** falsified account   **39 abused** deceived   **43 adulterate** adulterous   **44 gifts** (1) talents (2) presents   **50 even with the vow** with the very vow   **53 To** compared with   **54 virtue, as it** just as virtue   **55 shape of heaven** heavenly form   **57 sate . . . bed** gratify its lustful appetite to the point of revulsion or ennui, even in a virtuously lawful marriage.   **62 secure hour** time of being free from worries   **63 hebona** a poison. (The word seems to be a form of *ebony,* though it is thought perhaps to be related to *henbane,* a poison, or to *ebenus,* "yew.")   **64 porches** gateways   **65 leprous distillment** distillation causing leprosylike disfigurement

That swift as quicksilver it courses through
The natural gates and alleys of the body,   *68*
And with a sudden vigor it doth posset   *69*
And curd, like eager droppings into milk,   *70*
The thin and wholesome blood. So did it mine,
And a most instant tetter barked about,   *72*
Most lazar-like, with vile and loathsome crust,   *73*
All my smooth body.
Thus was I, sleeping, by a brother's hand
Of life, of crown, of queen at once dispatched,   *76*
Cut off even in the blossoms of my sin,
Unhouseled, disappointed, unaneled,   *78*
No reck'ning made, but sent to my account   *79*
With all my imperfections on my head.
Oh, horrible! Oh, horrible, most horrible!
If thou hast nature in thee, bear it not.   *82*
Let not the royal bed of Denmark be
A couch for luxury and damnèd incest.   *84*
But, howsomever thou pursues this act,
Taint not thy mind nor let thy soul contrive
Against thy mother aught. Leave her to heaven
And to those thorns that in her bosom lodge,
To prick and sting her. Fare thee well at once.
The glowworm shows the matin to be near,   *90*
And 'gins to pale his uneffectual fire.   *91*
Adieu, adieu, adieu! Remember me.   (*Exit.*)
HAMLET.
O all you host of heaven! O earth! What else?
And shall I couple hell? Oh, fie! Hold, hold, my heart,   *94*
And you, my sinews, grow not instant old,   *95*
But bear me stiffly up. Remember thee?
Ay, thou poor ghost, whiles memory holds a seat
In this distracted globe. Remember thee?   *98*
Yea, from the table of my memory   *99*
I'll wipe away all trivial fond records,   *100*

---

68 gates entry ways   **69–70 posset . . . curd** coagulate and curdle   **70 eager** sour, acid   **72 tetter** eruption of scabs.   **barked** covered with a rough covering, like bark on a tree   **73 lazar-like** leper-like   **76 dispatched** suddenly deprived   **78 Unhouseled . . . unaneled** without having received the Sacrament or other last rites including confession, absolution, and the holy oil of extreme unction.   **79 reck'ning** settling of accounts   **82 nature** i.e., the promptings of a son   **84 luxury** lechery   **90 matin** morning   **91 his** its   **94 couple** add.   **Hold** Hold together   **95 instant** instantly   **98 globe** (1) head (2) world (3) Globe Theater.   **99 table** tablet, slate   **100 fond** foolish

All saws of books, all forms, all pressures past 101
That youth and observation copied there,
And thy commandment all alone shall live
Within the book and volume of my brain,
Unmixed with baser matter. Yes, by heaven!
Oh, most pernicious woman!
Oh, villain, villain, smiling, damnèd villain!
My tables—meet it is I set it down 108
That one may smile, and smile, and be a villain.
At least I am sure it may be so in Denmark.
So, uncle, there you are. Now to my word: 111
It is "Adieu, adieu! Remember me."
I have sworn't.

(*Enter* HORATIO *and* MARCELLUS.)

HORATIO.　My lord, my lord!
MARCELLUS.　Lord Hamlet!
HORATIO.　Heavens secure him! 116
HAMLET.　So be it.
MARCELLUS.　Hillo, ho, ho, my lord!
HAMLET.　Hillo, ho, ho, boy! Come, bird, come. 119
MARCELLUS.　How is't, my noble lord?
HORATIO.　What news, my lord?
HAMLET.　Oh, wonderful!
HORATIO.　Good my lord, tell it.
HAMLET.　No, you will reveal it.
HORATIO.　Not I, my lord, by heaven.
MARCELLUS.　Nor I, my lord
HAMLET.
　　How say you, then, would heart of man once think it? 127
　　But you'll be secret?
HORATIO, MARCELLUS.　Ay, by heaven, my lord.
HAMLET.
　　There's never a villain dwelling in all Denmark
　　But he's an arrant knave. 130

---

101 All ... past all wise sayings, all shapes or images imprinted on the tablets of my memory, all past impressions.　**108 My tables ... down** (Editors often specify that Hamlet makes a note in his writing tablet, but he may simply mean that he is making a mental observation of lasting impression.)　**111 there you are** i.e., there, I've noted that against you.　**116 secure him** keep him safe.　**119 Hillo ... come** (A falconer's call to a hawk in air. Hamlet mocks the hallooing as though it were a part of hawking.)　**127 once** ever　**130 But ... knave** (Hamlet jokingly gives a self-evident answer: every villain is a thoroughgoing knave.)

HORATIO.

There needs no ghost, my lord, come from the grave

To tell us this.

HAMLET.   Why, right, you are in the right.

And so, without more circumstance at all,   *133*

I hold it fit that we shake hands and part,

You as your business and desire shall point you—

For every man hath business and desire,

Such as it is—and for my own poor part,

Look you, I'll go pray.

HORATIO.

These are but wild and whirling words, my lord.

HAMLET.

I am sorry they offend you, heartily;

Yes, faith, heartily.

HORATIO.   There's no offense, my lord.

HAMLET.

Yes, by Saint Patrick, but there is, Horatio,   *142*

And much offense too. Touching this vision here,   *143*

It is an honest ghost, that let me tell you.   *144*

For your desire to know what is between us,

O'ermaster't as you may. And now, good friends,

As you are friends, scholars, and soldiers,

Give me one poor request.

HORATIO.   What is't, my lord? We will.

HAMLET.

Never make known what you have seen tonight.

HORATIO, MARCELLUS.   My lord, we will not.

HAMLET.   Nay, but swear't.

HORATIO.   In faith, my lord, not I.   *153*

MARCELLUS.   Nor I, my lord, in faith.

HAMLET.   Upon my sword.   (*He holds out his sword.*) *155*

MARCELLUS.   We have sworn, my lord, already.   *156*

HAMLET.   Indeed, upon my sword, indeed.

GHOST (*cries under the stage*).   Swear.

---

133 circumstance ceremony, elaboration   **142 Saint Patrick** the keeper of Purgatory   **143 offense** (Hamlet deliberately changes Horatio's "no offense taken" to "an offense against all decency.") **144 honest** genuine   **153 In faith . . . I** i.e., I swear not to tell what I have seen. (Horatio is not refusing to swear.)   **155 sword** i.e., the hilt in the form of a cross.   **156 We . . . already** i.e., We swore *in faith.*

HAMLET.

    Ha, ha, boy, say'st thou so? Art thou there, truepenny?   *159*

    Come on, you hear this fellow in the cellarage.

    Consent to swear.

HORATIO.   Propose the oath, my lord.

HAMLET.

    Never to speak of this that you have seen,

    Swear by my sword.

GHOST (*beneath*).   Swear.   (*They swear.*)   *164*

HAMLET.

    Hic et ubique? Then we'll shift our ground.   *165*

                      (*He moves to another spot.*)

    Come hither, gentlemen,

    And lay your hands again upon my sword.

    Swear by my sword

    Never to speak of this that you have heard.

GHOST (*beneath*).   Swear by his sword.   (*They swear.*)

HAMLET.

    Well said, old mole. Canst work i'th'earth so fast?

    A worthy pioneer!—Once more remove, good friends.   *172*

                      (*He moves again.*)

HORATIO.

    Oh, day and night, but this is wondrous strange!

HAMLET.

    And therefore as a stranger give it welcome.   *174*

    There are more things in heaven and earth, Horatio,

    Than are dreamt of in your philosophy.   *176*

    But come;

    Here, as before, never, so help you mercy,   *178*

    How strange or odd some'er I bear myself—

    As I perchance hereafter shall think meet

    To put an antic disposition on—   *181*

    That you, at such times seeing me, never shall,

    With arms encumbered thus, or this headshake,   *183*

    Or by pronouncing of some doubtful phrase

---

159 **truepenny** honest old fellow **164 s.d.** *They swear* (Seemingly they swear here, and at lines 170 and 190, as they lay their hands on Hamlet's sword. Triple oaths would have particular force; these three oaths deal with what they have seen, what they have heard, and what they promise about Hamlet's *antic disposition.*) **165** *Hic et ubique?* Here and everywhere? (Latin.) **172 pioneer** foot soldier assigned to dig tunnels and excavations. **174 as a stranger** i.e., needing your hospitality **176 your philosophy** this subject that is called "natural philosophy" or "science." (*Your* is not personal.) **178 so help you mercy** as you hope for God's mercy when you are judged. **181 antic** grotesque, strange **183 encumbered** folded

As "Well, we know," or "We could, an if we would," 185
Or "If we list to speak," or "There be, an if they
    might," 186
Or such ambiguous giving out, to note 187
That you know aught of me—this do swear, 188
So grace and mercy at your most need help you.
GHOST (*beneath*).   Swear.   (*They swear.*)
HAMLET.

Rest, rest, perturbèd spirit!—So, gentlemen,
With all my love I do commend me to you; 192
And what so poor a man as Hamlet is
May do t'express his love and friending to you, 194
God willing, shall not lack. Let us go in together, 195
And still your fingers on your lips, I pray. 196
The time is out of joint. Oh, cursèd spite 197
That ever I was born to set it right!

(*They wait for him to leave first.*)

Nay, come, let's go together.   (*Exeunt.*) 199

2.1

Enter old Polonius with his man REYNALDO.

POLONIUS.
Give him this money and these notes, Reynaldo.

(*He gives money and papers.*)

REYNALDO.   I will, my lord.
POLONIUS.
You shall do marvelous wisely, good Reynaldo, 3
Before you visit him, to make inquire 4
Of his behavior.
REYNALDO.   My lord, I did intend it.

---

185 **an if** if   186 **list** wished.   **There ... might** There are those who could talk if they were at liberty
to do so   187 **note** indicate   188 **aught** anything   192 **commend ... you** give you my best wishes
194 **friending** friendliness   195 **lack** be lacking   196 **still** always   197 **out of joint** in utter disorder
199 **let's go together** (Probably they wait for him to leave first, but he refuses this ceremoniousness.)

2.1 **Location: Polonius's chambers.**
3 **marvelous** marvelously   4 **inquire** inquiry

POLONIUS.
Marry, well said, very well said. Look you, sir,
Inquire me first what Danskers are in Paris,   7
And how, and who, what means, and where they
        keep,   8
What company, at what expense; and finding
By this encompassment and drift of question   10
That they do know my son, come you more nearer   11
Than your particular demands will touch it.   12
Take you, as 'twere, some distant knowledge of him,   13
As thus, "I know his father and his friends,
And in part him." Do you mark this, Reynaldo?
REYNALDO.   Ay, very well, my lord.
POLONIUS.
"And in part him, but," you may say, "not well.
But if 't be he I mean, he's very wild,
Addicted so and so," and there put on him   19
What forgeries you please—marry, none so rank   20
As may dishonor him, take heed of that,
But, sir, such wanton, wild, and usual slips   22
As are companions noted and most known
To youth and liberty.
REYNALDO.   As gaming, my lord.
POLONIUS.   Ay, or drinking, fencing, swearing,
Quarreling, drabbing—you may go so far.   27
REYNALDO.   My lord, that would dishonor him.
POLONIUS.
Faith, no, as you may season it in the charge.   29
You must not put another scandal on him
That he is open to incontinency;   31
That's not my meaning. But breathe his faults so
        quaintly   32
That they may seem the taints of liberty,   33
The flash and outbreak of a fiery mind,
A savageness in unreclaimèd blood,   35
Of general assault.   36

---

7 Danskers Danes   **8 what means** what wealth (they have).   **keep** dwell   **10 encompassment . . .**
question roundabout way of questioning   **11-12 come . . . it** you will find out more this way than by
asking pointed questions (*particular demands*).   **13 Take you** Assume, pretend   **19 put on** impute
to   **20 forgeries** invented tales.   **rank** gross   **22 wanton** sportive, unrestrained   **27 drabbing**
whoring   **29 season** temper, soften   **31 incontinency** habitual sexual excess   **32 quaintly** artfully,
subtly   **33 taints of liberty** faults resulting from free living   **35-6 A savageness . . . assault** a wildness in untamed youth that assails all indiscriminately.

REYNALDO.   But, my good lord—
POLONIUS.   Wherefore should you do this?
REYNALDO.   Ay, my lord, I would know that.
POLONIUS.   Marry, sir, here's my drift,
    And I believe it is a fetch of warrant.   *41*
    You laying these slight sullies on my son,
    As 'twere a thing a little soiled wi'th' working,   *43*
    Mark you,
    Your party in converse, him you would sound,   *45*
    Having ever seen in the prenominate crimes   *46*
    The youth you breathe of guilty, be assured   *47*
    He closes with you in this consequence: *48*
    "Good sir," or so, or "friend," or "gentleman,"
    According to the phrase or the addition   *50*
    Of man and country.
REYNALDO.   Very good, my lord.
POLONIUS.   And then, sir, does 'a this—'a does—what
    was I about to say? By the Mass, I was about to say
    something. Where did I leave?
REYNALDO.   At "closes in the consequence."
POLONIUS.

    At "closes in the consequence," ay, marry.
    He closes thus: "I know the gentleman,
    I saw him yesterday," or "th'other day,"
    Or then, or then, with such or such, "and as you say,
    There was 'a gaming," "there o'ertook in 's rouse,"   *60*
    "There falling out at tennis," or perchance   *61*
    "I saw him enter such a house of sale,"
    Videlicet a brothel, or so forth. See you now,   *63*
    Your bait of falsehood takes this carp of truth;   *64*
    And thus do we of wisdom and of reach,   *65*
    With windlasses and with assays of bias,   *66*
    By indirections find directions out.   *67*

---

41 fetch of warrant legitimate trick.   **43 wi'th' working** in the process of being made, i.e., in everyday experience   **45 Your ... converse** the person you are conversing with.   **sound** sound out   **46 Having ever** if he has ever.   **prenominate crimes** aforenamed offenses   **47 breathe** speak   **48 closes ... consequence** takes you into his confidence as follows   **50 addition** title   **60 o'ertook in 's rouse** overcome by drink   **61 falling out** quarreling
63 Videlicet namely   **64 carp** a fish   **65 reach** capacity, ability   **66 windlasses** i.e., circuitous paths. (Literally, circuits made to head off the game in hunting.)   **assays of bias** attempts through indirection (like the curving path of the bowling ball, which is biased or weighted to one side)   **67 directions** i.e., the way things really are

So by my former lecture and advice 68
Shall you my son. You have me, have you not? 69
REYNALDO.
My lord, I have.
POLONIUS.   God b'wi'ye; fare ye well.
REYNALDO.   Good my lord.
POLONIUS.
Observe his inclination in yourself. 72
REYNALDO.   I shall, my lord.
POLONIUS.   And let him ply his music.
REYNALDO.   Well, my lord.
POLONIUS.
Farewell.   (*Exit* REYNALDO.)

(*Enter* OPHELIA.)

How now, Ophelia, what's the matter?
OPHELIA.
Oh, my lord, my lord, I have been so affrighted!
POLONIUS.   With what, i'th' name of God?
OPHELIA.
My lord, as I was sewing in my closet, 79
Lord Hamlet, with his doublet all unbraced, 80
No hat upon his head, his stockings fouled,
Ungartered, and down-gyvèd to his ankle, 82
Pale as his shirt, his knees knocking each other,
And with a look so piteous in purport 84
As if he had been loosèd out of hell
To speak of horrors—he comes before me.
POLONIUS.
Mad for thy love?
OPHELIA.   My lord, I do not know,
But truly I do fear it.
POLONIUS.   What said he?
OPHELIA.
He took me by the wrist and held me hard.
Then goes he to the length of all his arm,
And, with his other hand thus o'er his brow

---

68 former lecture just-ended set of instructions **69 have** understand **72 in yourself** in your own person (as well as by asking questions of others). **79 closet** private chamber **80 doublet** close-fitting jacket. **unbraced** unfastened **82 down-gyvèd** fallen to the ankles (like gyves or fetters) **84 in purport** in what it expressed

He falls to such perusal of my face
As 'a would draw it. Long stayed he so.   93
At last, a little shaking of mine arm
And thrice his head thus waving up and down,
He raised a sigh so piteous and profound
As it did seem to shatter all his bulk   97
And end his being. That done, he lets me go,
And with his head over his shoulder turned
He seemed to find his way without his eyes,
For out o' doors he went without their helps,
And to the last bended their light on me.

POLONIUS.
Come, go with me. I will go seek the King.
This is the very ecstasy of love,   104
Whose violent property fordoes itself   105
And leads the will to desperate undertakings
As oft as any passion under heaven
That does afflict our natures. I am sorry.
What, have you given him any hard words of late?

OPHELIA.
No, my good lord, but as you did command
I did repel his letters and denied
His access to me.

POLONIUS.   That hath made him mad.
I am sorry that with better heed and judgment
I had not quoted him. I feared he did but trifle   114
And meant to wrack thee. But beshrew my jealousy!   115
By heaven, it is as proper to our age   116
To cast beyond ourselves in our opinions   117
As it is common for the younger sort
To lack discretion. Come, go we to the King.
This must be known, which, being kept close, might
    move   120
More grief to hide than hate to utter love.   121

Come.   (*Exeunt.*)

---

93 **As** as if 97 **As** that. **bulk** body 104 **ecstasy** madness 105 **property fordoes** nature destroys 114
quoted observed 115 **wrack** ruin, seduce. **beshrew my jealousy!** a plague upon my suspicious
nature! 116 **proper ... age** characteristic of us (old) men 117 **cast beyond** overshoot, miscalculate.
(A metaphor from hunting.) 120 **known** made known (to the King). **close** secret 120-1 **might ...
love** i.e., might cause more grief (because of what Hamlet might do) by hiding the knowledge of
Hamlet's strange behavior to Ophelia than unpleasantness by telling it.

2.2

Flourish. Enter KING *and* QUEEN, ROSENCRANTZ, *and*
GUILDENSTERN (*with others*).

KING.
Welcome, dear Rosencrantz and Guildenstern.
Moreover that we much did long to see you,   2
The need we have to use you did provoke
Our hasty sending. Something have you heard
Of Hamlet's transformation—so call it,
Sith nor th'exterior nor the inward man   6
Resembles that it was. What it should be,   7
More than his father's death, that thus hath put him
So much from th'understanding of himself,
I cannot dream of. I entreat you both
That, being of so young days brought up with him,   11
And sith so neighbored to his youth and havior,   12
That you vouchsafe your rest here in our court   13
Some little time, so by your companies
To draw him on to pleasures, and to gather
So much as from occasion you may glean,   16
Whether aught to us unknown afflicts him thus
That, opened, lies within our remedy.   18
QUEEN.
Good gentlemen, he hath much talked of you,
And sure I am two men there is not living
To whom he more adheres. If it will please you
To show us so much gentry and good will   22
As to expend your time with us awhile
For the supply and profit of our hope,   24
Your visitation shall receive such thanks
As fits a kings's remembrance.   26

2.2 **Location: The castle.**

2 Moreover that Besides the fact that   **6 Sith nor** since neither   **7 that** what   **11–12 That . . . havior**
that, seeing as you were brought up with him from early youth (see 3.4.209, where Hamlet refers to
Rosencrantz and Guildenstern as "my two schoolfellows"), and since you have been intimately
acquainted with his youthful ways.   **13 vouchsafe your rest** consent to stay   **16 occasion** opportunity
18 opened being revealed   **22 gentry** courtesy   **24 supply . . . hope** aid and furtherance of what we
hope for   **26 As fits . . . remembrance** as would be a fitting gift of a king who rewards true service.

ROSENCRANTZ.   Both Your Majesties
  Might, by the sovereign power you have of us,   *27*
  Put your dread pleasures more into command   *28*
  Than to entreaty.
GUILDENSTERN.   But we both obey,
  And here give up ourselves in the full bent   *30*
  To lay our service freely at your feet,
  To be commanded.
KING.
  Thanks, Rosencrantz and gentle Guildenstern.
QUEEN.
  Thanks, Guildenstern and gentle Rosencrantz.
  And I beseech you instantly to visit
  My too much changèd son.—Go, some of you,
  And bring these gentlemen where Hamlet is.
GUILDENSTERN.
  Heavens make our presence and our practices   *38*
  Pleasant and helpful to him!
QUEEN.   Ay, amen!

(*Exeunt* ROSENCRANTZ *and* GUILDENSTERN, *with
some attendants.*)

(*Enter* POLONIUS.)

POLONIUS.
  Th'ambassadors from Norway, my good lord,
  Are joyfully returned.
KING.
  Thou still hast been the father of good news.   *42*
POLONIUS.
  Have I, my lord? I assure my good liege
  I hold my duty, as I hold my soul,
  Both to my God and to my gracious king;
  And I do think, or else this brain of mine
  Hunts not the trail of policy so sure   *47*
  As it hath used to do, that I have found

---

27 **of** over   28 **dread** inspiring awe   30 **in . . . bent** to the utmost degree of our capacity. (An archery metaphor.)   38 **practices** doings   42 **still** always   47 **policy** statecraft

The very cause of Hamlet's lunacy.

KING.

Oh, speak of that! That do I long to hear.

POLONIUS.

Give first admittance to th'ambassadors.

My news shall be the fruit to that great feast.   *52*

KING.

Thyself do grace to them and bring them in.   *53*

                      (*Exit* POLONIUS.)

He tells me, my dear Gertrude, he hath found

The head and source of all your son's distemper.

QUEEN.

I doubt it is no other but the main,   *56*

His father's death and our o'erhasty marriage.

(*Enter Ambassadors* VOLTIMAND *and* CORNELIUS, *with*
POLONIUS.)

KING.

Well, we shall sift him.—Welcome, my good friends!   *58*

Say, Voltimand, what from our brother Norway?   *59*

VOLTIMAND.

Most fair return of greetings and desires.   *60*

Upon our first, he sent out to suppress   *61*

His nephew's levies, which to him appeared

To be a preparation 'gainst the Polack,

But, better looked into, he truly found

It was against Your Highness. Whereat grieved

That so his sickness, age, and impotence   *66*

Was falsely borne in hand, sends out arrests   *67*

On Fortinbras, which he, in brief, obeys,

Receives rebuke from Norway, and in fine   *69*

Makes vow before his uncle never more

To give th'assay of arms against Your Majesty.   *71*

Whereon old Norway, overcome with joy,

Gives him three thousand crowns in annual fee

And his commission to employ those soldiers,

---

52 fruit dessert **53 grace** honor. (Punning on *grace* said before a *feast,* line 52.) **56 doubt** fear, suspect. **58 sift him** question Polonius (or Hamlet closely). **59 brother** fellow king **60 desires** good wishes. **61 Upon our first** At our first words on the business **66 impotence** weakness **67 borne in hand** deluded, taken advantage of. **arrests** orders to desist **69 in fine** in conclusion **71 give th'assay** make trial of strength, challenge

So levied as before, against the Polack,
With an entreaty, herein further shown,

(giving a paper)

That it might please you to give quiet pass
Through your dominions for this enterprise
On such regards of safety and allowance   *79*
As therein are set down.
KING.   It likes us well,   *80*
And at our more considered time we'll read,   *81*
Answer, and think upon this business.
Meantime we thank you for your well-took labor.
Go to your rest; at night we'll feast together.
Most welcome home!   *(Exeunt Ambassadors.)*
POLONIUS.   This business is well ended.
My liege, and madam, to expostulate   *86*
What majesty should be, what duty is,
Why day is day, night night, and time is time,
Were nothing but to waste night, day, and time.
Therefore, since brevity is the soul of wit,   *90*
And tediousness the limbs and outward flourishes,
I will be brief. Your noble son is mad.
Mad call I it, for, to define true madness,
What is't but to be nothing else but mad?
But let that go.
QUEEN.   More matter, with less art.
POLONIUS.
Madam, I swear I use no art at all.
That he's mad, 'tis true; 'tis true 'tis pity,
And pity 'tis 'tis true—a foolish figure,   *98*
But farewell it, for I will use no art.
Mad let us grant him, then, and now remains
That we find out the cause of this effect,
Or rather say, the cause of this defect,
For this effect defective comes by cause.   *103*
Thus it remains, and the remainder thus.
Perpend.   *105*
I have a daughter—have while she is mine—

---

79 **On ... allowance** i.e., with such considerations for the safety of Denmark and permission for Fortinbras.   80 **likes** pleases   81 **considered** suitable for deliberation   86 **expostulate** expound, inquire into   90 **wit** sense or judgment   98 **figure** figure of speech   103 **For ... cause** i.e., for this defective behavior, this madness, must have a cause.   105 **Perpend** Consider

Who, in her duty and obedience, mark,
Hath given me this. Now gather and surmise.   *108*
(*He reads the letter.*) "To the celestial and my soul's
idol, the most beautified Ophelia"—
That's an ill phrase, a vile phrase; "beautified" is a
vile phrase. But you shall hear. Thus:

(*He reads.*)

"In her excellent white bosom, these, etc."   *113*
QUEEN.   Came this from Hamlet to her?
POLONIUS.
Good madam, stay awhile, I will be faithful.   *115*

(*He reads.*)

"Doubt thou the stars are fire,
    Doubt that the sun doth move,
Doubt truth to be a liar,   *118*
    But never doubt I love.
O dear Ophelia, I am ill at these numbers. I have not   *120*
art to reckon my groans. But that I love thee best, O   *121*
most best, believe it. Adieu.
            Thine evermore, most dear lady, whilst this
                        machine is to him, Hamlet."   *124*
This in obedience hath my daughter shown me,
And, more above, hath his solicitings,   *126*
As they fell out by time, by means, and place,   *127*
All given to mine ear.
KING.   But how hath she   *128*
Received his love?
POLONIUS.   What do you think of me?
KING.
As of a man faithful and honorable.
POLONIUS.
I would fain prove so. But what might you think,   *131*
When I had seen this hot love on the wing—
As I perceived it, I must tell you that,

---

108 gather and surmise draw your own conclusions.   **113 "In . . . etc."** (The letter is poetically
addressed to her heart, where a letter would be kept by a young lady.)   **115 stay . . . faithful** i.e., hold
on, I will do as you wish.   **118 Doubt** suspect   **120 ill . . . numbers** unskilled at writing verses
121 reckon (1) count (2) number metrically, scan   **124 machine** i.e., body   **126–8 And . . . ear** and
moreover she has told me when, how, and where his solicitings of her occurred.   **131 fain** gladly

Before my daughter told me—what might you,
Or my dear Majesty your queen here, think,
If I had played the desk or table book,   136
Or given my heart a winking, mute and dumb,   137
Or looked upon this love with idle sight?   138
What might you think? No, I went round to work,   139
And my young mistress thus I did bespeak: 140
"Lord Hamlet is a prince out of thy star;   141
This must not be." And then I prescripts gave her,   142
That she should lock herself from his resort,
Admit no messengers, receive no tokens.
Which done, she took the fruits of my advice;
And he, repellèd—a short tale to make—
Fell into a sadness, then into a fast,
Thence to a watch, thence into a weakness,   148
Thence to a lightness, and by this declension   149
Into the madness wherein now he raves,
And all we mourn for.
KING (*to the Queen*). Do you think 'tis this?
QUEEN.   It may be, very like.
POLONIUS.
　Hath there been such a time—I would fain know
　　　that—
　That I have positively said "'Tis so,"
　When it proved otherwise?
KING.   Not that I know.
POLONIUS.
　Take this from this, if this be otherwise.   156
　If circumstances lead me, I will find
　Where truth is hid, though it were hid indeed
　Within the center.   159
KING.   How may we try it further?
POLONIUS.
　You know sometimes he walks four hours together

136–7 If . . . dumb if I had acted as go-between, passing love notes, or if I had refused to let my heart acknowledge what my eyes could see　**138 with idle sight** complacently or incomprehendingly.　**139 round** roundly, plainly　**140 bespeak** address　**141 out of thy star** above your sphere, position　**142 prescripts** orders　**148 watch** state of sleeplessness　**149 lightness** lightheadedness.　**declension** decline, deterioration. (With a pun on the grammatical sense.)　**156 Take this from this** (The actor probably gestures, indicating that he means his head from his shoulders, or his staff of office or chain from his hands or neck, or something similar.)　**159 center** center of the earth, traditionally an extraordinarily inaccessible place.　**try** test

Here in the lobby.

QUEEN.   So he does indeed.

POLONIUS.

    At such a time I'll loose my daughter to him.   *162*

    Be you and I behind an arras then.   *163*

    Mark the encounter. If he love her not

    And be not from his reason fall'n thereon,   *165*

    Let me be no assistant for a state,

    But keep a farm and carters.

KING.   We will try it.   *167*

(*Enter* HAMLET, *reading on a book.*)

QUEEN.

    But look where sadly the poor wretch comes reading.

POLONIUS.

    Away, I do beseech you both, away.

    I'll board him presently. Oh, give me leave.   *170*

(*Exeunt* KING *and* QUEEN, *with attendants.*)

    How does my good Lord Hamlet?

HAMLET.   Well, God-a-mercy.

POLONIUS.   Do you know me, my lord?

HAMLET.   Excellent well. You are a fishmonger.   *174*

POLONIUS.   Not I, my lord.

HAMLET.   Then I would you were so honest a man.

POLONIUS.   Honest, my lord?

HAMLET.   Ay, sir. To be honest, as this world goes, is to
    be one man picked out of ten thousand.

POLONIUS.   That's very true, my lord.

HAMLET.   For if the sun breed maggots in a dead dog,
    being a good kissing carrion—Have you a daughter?   *182*

POLONIUS.   I have, my lord.

HAMLET.   Let her not walk i'th' sun. Conception is a   *184*
    blessing, but as your daughter may conceive, friend,
    look to't.

---

162 loose (As one might release an animal that is being mated.)   **163 arras** hanging, tapestry   **165 thereon** on that account   **167 carters** wagon drivers.   **170 I'll . . . leave** I'll accost him at once. Please leave us alone; leave him to me.   **172 God-a-mercy** God have mercy, i.e., thank you.   **174 fishmonger** fish merchant.   **182 a good kissing carrion** i.e., a good piece of flesh for kissing, or for the sun to kiss   **184 i'th' sun** in public. (With additional implication of the sunshine of princely favors.)   **Conception** (1) Understanding (2) Pregnancy

POLONIUS (*aside*). How say you by that? Still harping
  on my daughter. Yet he knew me not at first; 'a said
  I was a fishmonger. 'A is far gone. And truly in my
  youth I suffered much extremity for love, very near
  this. I'll speak to him again.—What do you read,
  my lord?
HAMLET. Words, words, words.
POLONIUS. What is the matter, my lord?   194
HAMLET. Between who?
POLONIUS. I mean, the matter that you read, my lord.
HAMLET. Slanders, sir; for the satirical rogue says here
  that old men have gray beards, that their faces are wrin-
  kled, their eyes purging thick amber and plum-tree   199
  gum, and that they have a plentiful lack of wit, to-   200
  gether with most weak hams. All which, sir, though I
  most powerfully and potently believe, yet I hold it not
  honesty to have it thus set down, for yourself, sir, shall   203
  grow old as I am, if like a crab you could go backward.   204
POLONIUS (*aside*). Though this be madness, yet there is
  method in't.—Will you walk out of the air, my lord?   206
HAMLET. Into my grave.
POLONIUS. Indeed, that's out of the air. (*Aside*) How
  pregnant sometimes his replies are! A happiness that   209
  often madness hits on, which reason and sanity could
  not so prosperously be delivered of. I will leave him   211
  and suddenly contrive the means of meeting between   212
  him and my daughter.—My honorable lord, I will
  most humbly take my leave of you.
HAMLET. You cannot, sir, take from me anything that I
  will more willingly part withal—except my life, except   216
  my life, except my life.

(*Enter* GUILDENSTERN *and* ROSENCRANTZ.)

POLONIUS. Fare you well, my lord.
HAMLET. These tedious old fools!
POLONIUS. You go to seek the Lord Hamlet. There he is.

---

194 matter substance. (But Hamlet plays on the sense of "basis for a dispute.") **199 purging** dis-
charging. **amber** i.e., resin, like the resinous *plum-tree gum* **200 wit** understanding **203 honesty**
decency, decorum **204 old** as old **206 out of the air** (The open air was considered dangerous for
sick people.) **209 pregnant** quick-witted, full of meaning. **happiness** felicity of expression
211 prosperously successfully **212 suddenly** immediately **216 withal** with

ROSENCRANTZ (*to* POLONIUS). God save you, sir!

(*Exit* POLONIUS.)

GUILDENSTERN. My honored lord!

ROSENCRANTZ. My most dear lord!

HAMLET. My excellent good friends! How dost thou, Guildenstern? Ah, Rosencrantz! Good lads, how do you both?

ROSENCRANTZ.
As the indifferent children of the earth. 227

GUILDENSTERN.
Happy in that we are not overhappy.
On Fortune's cap we are not the very button.

HAMLET. Nor the soles of her shoe?

ROSENCRANTZ. Neither, my lord.

HAMLET. Then you live about her waist, or in the mid- 232
dle of her favors? 233

GUILDENSTERN. Faith, her privates we.

HAMLET. In the secret parts of Fortune? Oh, most true, 234
she is a strumpet. What news? 236

ROSENCRANTZ. None, my lord, but the world's grown honest.

HAMLET. Then is doomsday near. But your news is not true. Let me question more in particular. What have you, my good friends, deserved at the hands of Fortune that she sends you to prison hither?

GUILDENSTERN. Prison, my lord?

HAMLET. Denmark's a prison.

ROSENCRANTZ. Then is the world one.

HAMLET. A goodly one, in which there are many confines, wards, and dungeons, Denmark being one 247
o'th' worst.

ROSENCRANTZ. We think not so, my lord.

HAMLET. Why then 'tis none to you, for there is nothing either good or bad but thinking makes it so. To me it is a prison.

ROSENCRANTZ. Why then, your ambition makes it one. 'Tis too narrow for your mind.

---

227 **indifferent** ordinary, at neither extreme of fortune or misfortune   232–3 **the middle ... favors** i.e., her genitals.   234 **her privates we** (1) we dwell in her privates, her genitals, in the middle of her favors (2) we are her ordinary footsoldiers.   236 **strumpet** (Fortune was proverbially thought of as fickle.)   247 **confines** places of confinement

HAMLET.   Oh, God, I could be bounded in a nutshell and
count myself a king of infinite space, were it not that
I have bad dreams.
GUILDENSTERN.   Which dreams indeed are ambition, for
the very substance of the ambitious is merely the   *259*
shadow of a dream.
HAMLET.   A dream itself is but a shadow.
ROSENCRANTZ.   Truly, and I hold ambition of so airy
and light a quality that it is but a shadow's shadow.
HAMLET.   Then are our beggars bodies, and our mon   *264*
-archs and outstretched heroes the beggars' shadows.   *265*
Shall we to th' court? For, by my fay, I cannot reason.   *266*
ROSENCRANTZ, GUILDENSTERN.   We'll wait upon you.   *267*
HAMLET.   No such matter. I will not sort you with the   *268*
rest of my servants, for, to speak to you like an honest
man, I am most dreadfully attended. But, in the   *270*
beaten way of friendship, what make you at Elsinore?   *271*
ROSENCRANTZ.   To visit you, my lord, no other occasion.
HAMLET.   Beggar that I am, I am even poor in thanks;
but I thank you, and sure, dear friends, my thanks are
too dear a halfpenny. Were you not sent for? Is it your   *275*
own inclining? Is it a free visitation? Come, come, deal   *276*
justly with me. Come, come. Nay, speak.
GUILDENSTERN.   What should we say, my lord?
HAMLET.   Anything but to th' purpose. You were sent   *279*
for, and there is a kind of confession in your looks
which your modesties have not craft enough to color.   *281*
I know the good King and Queen have sent for you.
ROSENCRANTZ.   To what end, my lord?
HAMLET.   That you must teach me. But let me conjure   *284*
you, by the rights of our fellowship, by the consonancy   *285*

---

259 the very ... ambitious that seemingly very substantial thing that the ambitious pursue   **264–5 Then ... shadows** (Hamlet pursues their argument about ambition to its absurd extreme: if ambition is only a shadow of a shadow, then beggars (who are presumably without ambition) must be real, whereas monarchs and heroes are only their shadows—*outstretched* like elongated shadows, made to look bigger than they are.)   **266 fay** faith   **267 wait upon** accompany, attend. (But Hamlet uses the phrase in the sense of providing menial service.)   **268 sort** class, categorize   **270 dreadfully attended** waited upon in slovenly fashion.   **271 beaten way** familiar path, tried-and-true course. **make** do   **275 too dear a halfpenny** (1) too expensive at even a halfpenny, i.e., of little worth (2) too expensive *by* a halfpenny in return for worthless kindness.   **276 free** voluntary   **279 Anything but to th' purpose** Anything except a straightforward answer. (Said ironically.)   **281 color** disguise   **284 conjure** adjure, entreat   **285–6 the consonancy of our youth** our closeness in our younger days

of our youth, by the obligation of our ever-preserved	*286*
love, and by what more dear a better proposer	*287*
could charge you withal, be even and direct with me	*288*
whether you were sent for or no.	

ROSENCRANTZ (*aside to* GUILDENSTERN).   What say you?
HAMLET (*aside*).   Nay, then, I have an eye of you.—If   *291*
you love me, hold not off.   *292*
GUILDENSTERN.   My lord, we were sent for.
HAMLET.   I will tell you why; so shall my anticipation   *294*
prevent your discovery, and your secrecy to the King   *295*
and Queen molt no feather. I have of late—but   *296*
wherefore I know not—lost all my mirth, forgone all
custom of exercises; and indeed it goes so heavily with
my disposition that this goodly frame, the earth,
seems to me a sterile promontory; this most excellent
canopy, the air, look you, this brave o'erhanging   *301*
firmament, this majestical roof fretted with golden   *302*
fire, why, it appeareth nothing to me but a foul and
pestilent congregation of vapors. What a piece of work   *304*
is a man! How noble in reason, how infinite in faculties,
in form and moving how express and admirable, in   *306*
action how like an angel, in apprehension how like a   *307*
god! The beauty of the world, the paragon of animals!
And yet, to me, what is this quintessence of dust?   *309*
Man delights not me—no, nor woman neither,
though by your smiling you seem to say so.
ROSENCRANTZ.   My lord, there was no such stuff in my
thoughts.
HAMLET.   Why did you laugh, then, when I said man
delights not me?
ROSENCRANTZ.   To think, my lord, if you delight not in
man, what Lenten entertainment the players shall   *317*
receive from you. We coted them on the way, and   *318*
hither are they coming to offer you service.

---

287 **better** more skillful   288 **charge** urge.   **even** straight, honest   291 **of** on   292 **hold not off** don't hold back.   294–5 **so . . . discovery** in that way my saying it first will spare you from having to reveal the truth   296 **molt no feather** i.e., not diminish in the least.   301 **brave** splendid   302 **fretted** adorned (with fretwork, as in a vaulted ceiling)   304 **congregation** mass.   **piece of work** masterpiece   306 **express** well-framed, exact, expressive   307 **apprehension** power of comprehending   309 **quintessence** very essence. (Literally, the fifth essence beyond earth, water, air, and fire, supposed to be extractable from them.) 317 **Lenten entertainment** meager reception (appropriate to Lent)   318 **coted** overtook and passed by

HAMLET.　He that plays the king shall be welcome; His
　　Majesty shall have tribute of me. The adventurous　　　　*321*
　　knight shall use his foil and target, the lover shall not　　*322*
　　sigh gratis, the humorous man shall end his part in　　　*323*
　　peace, the clown shall make those laugh whose lungs　　*324*
　　are tickle o'th' sear, and the lady shall say her mind　　　*325*
　　freely, or the blank verse shall halt for't. What players　*326*
　　are they?
ROSENCRANTZ.　Even those you were wont to take such
　　delight in, the tragedians of the city.　　　　　　　　　　*329*
HAMLET.　How chances it they travel? Their residence,　　*330*
　　both in reputation and profit, was better both ways.
ROSENCRANTZ.　I think their inhibition comes by the　　　*332*
　　means of the late innovation.　　　　　　　　　　　　　　*333*
HAMLET.　Do they hold the same estimation they did
　　when I was in the city? Are they so followed?
ROSENCRANTZ.　No, indeed are they not.
HAMLET.　How comes it? Do they grow rusty?　　　　　　*337*
ROSENCRANTZ.　Nay, their endeavor keeps in the wonted　*338*
　　pace. But there is, sir, an aerie of children, little eyases,　*339*
　　that cry out on the top of question and are most tyran-　*340*
　　nically clapped for't. These are now the fashion, and　　*341*
　　so berattle the common stages—so they call them—　　*342*
　　that many wearing rapiers are afraid of goose quills　　*343*
　　and dare scarce come thither.
HAMLET.　What, are they children? Who maintains 'em?
　　How are they escotted? Will they pursue the quality no　*346*

---

321 tribute (1) applause (2) homage paid in money.　**of** from　**322 foil and target** sword and
shield　**323 gratis** for nothing.　**humorous man** eccentric character, dominated by one trait or
"humor"　**323–4 in peace** i.e., with full license　**325 tickle o'th' sear** hair trigger, ready to laugh easily. (A *sear* is part of a gun-lock.)　**326 halt** limp　**329 tragedians** actors　**330 residence** remaining
in their usual place, i.e., in the city　**332 inhibition** formal prohibition (from acting plays in the
city)　**333 late innovation** i.e., recent new fashion in satirical plays performed by boy actors in the
"private" theaters; or the Earl of Essex's abortive rebellion in 1601 against Elizabeth's government. (A
much debated passage of seemingly topical reference.)　**337 How … rusty?** Have they lost their pol-
ish, gone out of fashion? (This passage, through line 362, alludes to the rivalry between the children's
companies and the adult actors, given strong impetus by the reopening of the Children of the
Chapel at the Blackfriars Theater in late 1600.)　**338 keeps … wonted** continues in the usual　**339
aerie** nest.　**eyases** young hawks　**340 cry … question** speak shrilly, dominating the controversy (in
decrying the public theaters).　**340–1 tyrannically** vehemently　**342 berattle … stages** clamor
against the public theaters　**343 many wearing rapiers** i.e., many men of fashion, afraid to patronize
the common players for fear of being satirized by the poets writing for the boy actors.　**goose quills**
i.e., pens of satirists　**346 escotted** maintained.　**quality** (acting) profession　**346–7 no longer …
sing** i.e., only until their voices change.

longer than they can sing? Will they not say after- 347
wards, if they should grow themselves to common 348
players—as it is most like, if their means are no 349
better—their writers do them wrong to make them 350
exclaim against their own succession? 351
ROSENCRANTZ.   Faith, there has been much to-do on 352
both sides, and the nation holds it no sin to tar them to 353
controversy. There was for a while no money bid for 354
argument unless the poet and the player went to cuffs 355
in the question. 356
HAMLET.   Is't possible?
GUILDENSTERN.   Oh, there has been much throwing
about of brains.
HAMLET.   Do the boys carry it away? 360
ROSENCRANTZ.   Ay, that they do, my lord—Hercules 361
and his load too. 362
HAMLET.   It is not very strange; for my uncle is King of
Denmark, and those that would make mouths at him 364
while my father lived give twenty, forty, fifty, a
hundred ducats apiece for his picture in little. 'Sblood, 366
there is something in this more than natural, if philosophy could find it out.

(*A flourish of trumpets within.*)

GUILDENSTERN.   There are the players.
HAMLET.   Gentlemen, you are welcome to Elsinore. Your
hands, come then. Th'appurtenance of welcome is 371
fashion and ceremony. Let me comply with you in this 372
garb, lest my extent to the players, which, I tell you, 373
must show fairly outwards, should more appear like 374
entertainment than yours. You are welcome. But my 375

---

348 **common** regular, adult   349 **like** likely   349–50 **if . . . better** if they find no better way to support themselves   351 **succession** i.e., future careers.   352 **to-do** ado   353 **tar** incite (as in inciting
dogs to attack a chained bear)   354–6 **There . . . question** i.e., For a while, no money was offered by
the acting companies to playwrights for the plot to a play unless the satirical poets who wrote for the
boys and the adult actors came to blows in the play itself.   360 **carry it away** i.e., win the day.
361–2 **Hercules . . . load** (Thought to be an allusion to the sign of the Globe Theatre, which allegedly
was Hercules bearing the world on his shoulders.)   364 **mouths** faces   366 **ducats** gold coins.   **in
little** in miniature.   **'Sblood** By God's (Christ's) blood   371 **Th'appurtenance** The proper accompaniment   372 **comply** observe the formalities of courtesy   373 **garb** i.e., manner.   **my extent** that
which I extend, i.e., my polite behavior   374 **show fairly outwards** show every evidence of cordiality
375 **entertainment** a (warm) reception

uncle-father and aunt-mother are deceived.

GUILDENSTERN.   In what, my dear lord?

HAMLET.   I am but mad north-north-west. When the *378*
wind is southerly I know a hawk from a handsaw. *379*

(*Enter* POLONIUS.)

POLONIUS.   Well be with you, gentlemen!

HAMLET.   Hark you, Guildenstern, and you too; at each
ear a hearer. That great baby you see there is not yet
out of his swaddling clouts. *383*

ROSENCRANTZ.   Haply he is the second time come to *384*
them, for they say an old man is twice a child.

HAMLET.   I will prophesy he comes to tell me of the
players. Mark it.—You say right, sir, o' Monday *387*
morning, 'twas then indeed. *388*

POLONIUS.   My lord, I have news to tell you.

HAMLET.   My lord, I have news to tell you. When Roscius *390*
was an actor in Rome—

POLONIUS.   The actors are come hither, my lord.

HAMLET.   Buzz, buzz! *393*

POLONIUS.   Upon my honor—

HAMLET.   Then came each actor on his ass.

POLONIUS.   The best actors in the world, either for
tragedy, comedy, history, pastoral, pastoral-comical,
historical-pastoral, tragical-historical, tragical-comical-
historical-pastoral, scene individable, or poem unlim- *399*
ited. Seneca cannot be too heavy, nor Plautus too *400*
light. For the law of writ and the liberty, these are the *401*
only men.

HAMLET.   O Jephthah, judge of Israel, what a treasure *403*
hadst thou!

---

378 north-north-west just off true north, only partly.   **379 I ... handsaw** (Speaking in his mad guise, Hamlet perhaps suggests that he can tell true from false. A *handsaw* may be a *hernshaw* or heron. Still, a supposedly mad disposition might compare hawks and handsaws.)   **383 swaddling clouts** cloths in which to wrap a newborn baby.   **384 Haply** Perhaps **387–8 You say ... then indeed** (Said to impress upon Polonius the idea that Hamlet is in serious conversation with his friends.)   **390 Roscius** a famous Roman actor who died in 62 B.C.   **393 Buzz** (An interjection used to denote stale news.)   **399–400 scene ... unlimited** plays that are unclassifiable and all-inclusive. (An absurdly catchall conclusion to Polonius's pompous list of categories.)   **400 Seneca** writer of Latin tragedies. **Plautus** writer of Latin comedies   **401 law ... liberty** dramatic composition both according to the rules and disregarding the rules.   **these** i.e., the actors   **403 Jephthah ... Israel** (Jephthah had to sacrifice his daughter; see Judges 11. Hamlet goes on to quote from a ballad on the theme.)

POLONIUS.   What a treasure had he, my lord?
HAMLET.   Why,
"One fair daughter, and no more,
The which he lovèd passing well."   *408*
POLONIUS (*aside*).   Still on my daughter.
HAMLET.   Am I not i'th' right, old Jephthah?
POLONIUS.   If you call me Jephthah, my lord, I have a
daughter that I love passing well.
HAMLET.   Nay, that follows not.   *413*
POLONIUS.   What follows then, my lord?   *414*

HAMLET.   Why,
"As by lot, God wot,"   *416*
and then, you know,
"It came to pass, as most like it was"—   *418*
the first row of the pious chanson will show you more,   *419*
for look where my abridgement comes.   *420*

(*Enter the* PLAYERS.)

You are welcome, masters; welcome, all. I am glad to   *421*
see thee well. Welcome, good friends. Oh, old friend!
Why, thy face is valanced since I saw thee last. Com'st   *423*
thou to beard me in Denmark? What, my young lady   *424*
and mistress! By'r Lady, Your Ladyship is nearer to   *425*
heaven than when I saw you last, by the altitude of a   *426*
chopine. Pray God your voice, like a piece of uncur-   *427*
rent gold, be not cracked within the ring. Masters, you   *428*
are all welcome. We'll e'en to't like French falconers,   *429*
fly at anything we see. We'll have a speech straight.   *430*
Come, give us a taste of your quality. Come, a   *431*

---

408 passing surpassingly   **413 that follows not** i.e., just because you resemble Jephthah in having a
daughter does not logically prove that you love her.   **414 What . . . lord?** What does follow logically?
(But Hamlet, pretending madness, answers with a fragment of a ballad, as if Polonius had asked, "What
comes next?" See 419n.)   **416 lot** chance.   **wot** knows   **418 like** likely, probable   **419 the first . . .
more** the first stanza of this biblically based ballad will satisfy your stated desire to know *what follows*
(line 414).   **420 my abridgment** something that cuts short my conversation; also, a diversion   **421
masters** good sirs   **423 valanced** fringed (with a beard)   **424 beard** confront, challenge. (With obvious pun.)   **young lady** i.e., boy playing women's parts   **425 By'r Lady** By Our Lady   **425–6 nearer to
heaven** i.e., taller   **427 chopine** thick-soled shoe of Italian fashion.   **427–8 uncurrent** not passable
as lawful coinage   **428 cracked . . . ring** i.e., changed from adolescent to male voice, no longer suitable for women's roles. (Coins featured rings enclosing the sovereign's head; if the coin was suffi-
ciently clipped to invade within this ring, it was unfit for currency.)   **429 e'en to't** go at it   **430
straight** at once   **431 quality** professional skill

passerate speech.

FIRST PLAYER.   What speech, my good lord?

HAMLET.   I heard thee speak me a speech once, but it
was never acted, or if it was, not above once, for the
play, I remember, pleased not the million; 'twas cav-   *436*
iar to the general. But it was—as I received it, and   *437*
others, whose judgments in such matters cried in the   *438*
top of mine—an excellent play, well digested in the   *439*
scenes, set down with as much modesty as cunning. I   *440*
remember one said there were no sallets in the lines to   *441*
make the matter savory, nor no matter in the phrase
that might indict the author of affectation, but called it   *443*
an honest method, as wholesome as sweet, and by very
much more handsome than fine. One speech in't I   *445*
chiefly loved: 'twas Aeneas' tale to Dido, and there-
about of it especially when he speaks of Priam's   *447*
slaughter. If it live in your memory, begin at this line: *448*
let me see, let me see—

"The rugged Pyrrhus, like th' Hyrcanian beast"—   *450*
'Tis not so. It begins with Pyrrhus:

"The rugged Pyrrhus, he whose sable arms,   *452*
Black as his purpose, did the night resemble
When he lay couchèd in th' ominous horse,   *454*
Hath now this dread and black complexion
smeared
With heraldry more dismal. Head to foot   *456*
Now is he total gules, horridly tricked   *457*
With blood of fathers, mothers, daughters, sons,
Baked and impasted with the parching streets,   *459*

436–7 caviar to the general i.e., an expensive delicacy not generally palatable to uneducated tastes.
438–9 cried in the top of i.e., spoke with greater authority than   **439 digested** arranged, ordered
440 modesty moderation, restraint.   **cunning** skill.   **441 sallets** i.e., something savory, spicy impro-
prieties   **443 indict** convict   **445 handsome** well-proportioned.   **fine** elaborately ornamented,
showy.   **447–8 Priam's slaughter** the slaying of the ruler of Troy, when the Greeks finally took the
city   **450 Pyrrhus** a Greek hero in the Trojan War, also known as Neoptolemus, son of Achilles—
another avenging son.   **th' Hyrcanian beast** i.e., the tiger. (On the death of Priam, see Virgil, *Aeneid*,
2.506 ff.; compare the whole speech with Marlowe's *Dido Queen of Carthage*, 2.1.214 ff. On the
Hyrcanian tiger, see *Aeneid*, 4.366–7. Hyrcania is on the Caspian Sea.)   **452 rugged** shaggy, savage.
sable black (for reasons of camouflage during the episode of the Trojan horse).   **454 couchèd** concealed.   **ominous horse** fateful Trojan horse, by which the Greeks gained access to Troy.   **456 dismal** calamitous   **457 total gules** entirely red. (A heraldic term.)   **tricked** spotted and smeared.
(Heraldic.)   **459 Baked ... streets** roasted and encrusted, like a thick paste, by the parching heat of
the streets (because of the fires everywhere)

That lend a tyrannous and a damnèd light 460
To their lord's murder. Roasted in wrath and fire, 461
And thus o'ersizèd with coagulate gore, 462
With eyes like carbuncles, the hellish Pyrrhus 463
Old grandsire Priam seeks."
So proceed you.
POLONIUS. 'Fore God, my lord, well spoken, with good
accent and good discretion.
FIRST PLAYER. "Anon he finds him
Striking too short at Greeks. His antique sword, 469
Rebellious to his arm, lies where it falls,
Repugnant to command. Unequal matched, 471
Pyrrhus at Priam drives, in rage strikes wide,
But with the whiff and wind of his fell sword 473
Th'unnervèd father falls. Then senseless Ilium, 474
Seeming to feel this blow, with flaming top
Stoops to his base, and with a hideous crash 476
Takes prisoner Pyrrhus' ear. For, lo! His sword,
Which was declining on the milky head 478
Of reverend Priam, seemed i'th'air to stick.
So as a painted tyrant Pyrrhus stood, 480
And, like a neutral to his will and matter, 481
Did nothing.
But as we often see against some storm 483
A silence in the heavens, the rack stand still, 484
The bold winds speechless, and the orb below 485
As hush as death, anon the dreadful thunder
Doth rend the region, so, after Pyrrhus' pause, 487
A rousèd vengeance sets him new a-work,
And never did the Cyclops' hammers fall 489
On Mars's armor forged for proof eterne 490
With less remorse than Pyrrhus' bleeding sword 491
Now falls on Priam.
Out, out, thou strumpet Fortune! All you gods

---

460 **tyrannous** cruel 461 **their lord's** i.e., Priam's 462 **o'ersizèd** covered as with size or glue 463 **carbuncles** large fiery-red precious stones thought to emit their own light 469 **antique** ancient, long-used 471 **Repugnant** disobedient, resistant 473 **fell** cruel 474 **Th' unnervèd** the strengthless. **senseless Ilium** inanimate citadel of Troy 476 **his** its 478 **declining** descending. **milky** white-haired 480 **painted** motionless, as in a painting 481 **like . . . matter** i.e., as though suspended between his intention and its fulfillment 483 **against** just before 484 **rack** mass of clouds 485 **orb** globe, earth 487 **region** sky 489 **Cyclops** giant armor makers in the smithy of Vulcan 490 **proof** proven or tested resistance to assault 491 **remorse** pity

In general synod take away her power! 494
Break all the spokes and fellies from her wheel, 495
And bowl the round nave down the hill of heaven 496
As low as to the fiends!"
POLONIUS. This is too long.
HAMLET. It shall to the barber's with your beard.—Pri-
thee, say on. He's for a jig or a tale of bawdry, or he 500
sleeps. Say on; come to Hecuba. 501
FIRST PLAYER.
"But who, ah woe! had seen the mobled queen"— 502
HAMLET. "The mobled queen?"
POLONIUS. That's good. "Mobled queen" is good.
FIRST PLAYER.
"Run barefoot up and down, threat'ning the flames 505
With bisson rheum, a clout upon that head 506
Where late the diadem stood, and, for a robe, 507
About her lank and all o'erteemed loins 508
A blanket, in the alarm of fear caught up—
Who this had seen, with tongue in venom steeped,
'Gainst Fortune's state would treason have
    pronounced. 511
But if the gods themselves did see her then
When she saw Pyrrhus make malicious sport
In mincing with his sword her husband's limbs,
The instant burst of clamor that she made,
Unless things mortal move them not at all,
Would have made milch the burning eyes of heaven, 517
And passion in the gods." 518
POLONIUS. Look whe'er he has not turned his color and 519
has tears in 's eyes. Prithee, no more.
HAMLET. 'Tis well; I'll have thee speak out the rest of
this soon.—Good my lord, will you see the players well
bestowed? Do you hear, let them be well used, for they 523
are the abstract and brief chronicles of the time. After 524

---

494 synod assembly **495 fellies** pieces of wood forming the rim of a wheel **496 nave** hub. **hill of heaven** Mount Olympus **500 jig** comic song and dance often given at the end of a play **501 Hecuba** wife of Priam. **502 who . . . had** anyone who had. (Also in line 510.) **mobled** muffled **505 threat'ning the flames** i.e., weeping hard enough to dampen the flames **506 bisson rheum** blinding tears. **clout** cloth **507 late** lately **508 all o'erteemed** utterly worn out with bearing children **511 state** rule, managing. **pronounced** proclaimed. **517 milch** milky, moist with tears. **burning eyes of heaven** i.e., stars, heavenly bodies **518 passion** overpowering emotion **519 whe'er** whether **523 bestowed** lodged **524 abstract** summary account

your death you were better have a bad epitaph than
their ill report while you live.

POLONIUS.   My lord, I will use them according to their
desert.

HAMLET.   God's bodikin, man, much better. Use every   *529*
man after his desert, and who shall scape whipping?
Use them after your own honor and dignity. The less   *531*
they deserve, the more merit is in your bounty. Take
them in.

POLONIUS.   Come, sirs.   (*Exit.*)

HAMLET.   Follow him, friends. We'll hear a play tomor-
row. (*As they start to leave,* HAMLET *detains the* FIRST
PLAYER.) Dost thou hear me, old friend? Can you play
The Murder of Gonzago?

FIRST PLAYER.   Ay, my lord.

HAMLET.   We'll ha 't tomorrow night. You could, for a   *540*
need, study a speech of some dozen or sixteen lines   *541*
which I would set down and insert in't, could you not?

FIRST PLAYER.   Ay, my lord.

HAMLET.   Very well. Follow that lord, and look you mock
him not.   (*Exeunt players.*)
My good friends, I'll leave you till night. You are welcome to Elsinore.

ROSENCRANTZ.   Good my lord!
                    (*Exeunt* ROSENCRANTZ *and* GUILDENSTERN.)

HAMLET.
Ay, so, goodbye to you.—Now I am alone.
Oh, what a rogue and peasant slave am I!
Is it not monstrous that this player here,
But in a fiction, in a dream of passion,   *552*
Could force his soul so to his own conceit   *553*
That from her working all his visage wanned,   *554*
Tears in his eyes, distraction in his aspect,   *555*
A broken voice, and his whole function suiting   *556*
With forms to his conceit? And all for nothing!   *557*
For Hecuba!

---

529 God's bodikin By God's (Christ's) little body, *bodykin*. (Not to be confused with *bodkin*, "dagger.")   **531 after** according to   **540 ha 't** have it   **541 study** memorize   **552 But** merely   **553 force** .
. . **conceit** bring his innermost being so entirely into accord with his conception (of the role)
554 from her working as a result of, or in response to, his soul's activity.   **wanned** grew pale
555 aspect look, glance   **556–7 his whole . . . conceit** all his bodily powers responding with actions
to suit his thought.

What's Hecuba to him, or he to Hecuba,
That he should weep for her? What would he do
Had he the motive and the cue for passion
That I have? He would drown the stage with tears
And cleave the general ear with horrid speech,   563
Make mad the guilty and appall the free,   564
Confound the ignorant, and amaze indeed   565
The very faculties of eyes and ears. Yet I,
A dull and muddy-mettled rascal, peak   567
Like John-a-dreams, unpregnant of my cause,   568
And can say nothing—no, not for a king
Upon whose property and most dear life   570
A damned defeat was made. Am I a coward?   571
Who calls me villain? Breaks my pate across?   572
Plucks off my beard and blows it in my face?
Tweaks me by the nose? Gives me the lie i'th' throat   574
As deep as to the lungs? Who does me this?
Ha, 'swounds, I should take it; for it cannot be   576
But I am pigeon-livered and lack gall   577
To make oppression bitter, or ere this   578
I should ha' fatted all the region kites   579
With this slave's offal. Bloody, bawdy villain!   580
Remorseless, treacherous, lecherous, kindless villain!   581
Oh, vengeance!
Why, what an ass am I! This is most brave,   583
That I, the son of a dear father murdered,
Prompted to my revenge by heaven and hell,
Must like a whore unpack my heart with words
And fall a-cursing, like a very drab,   587
A scullion! Fie upon't, foh! About, my brains!   588
Hum, I have heard
That guilty creatures sitting at a play

---

563 **the general ear** everyone's ear. **horrid** horrible   564 **appall** (Literally, make pale.)   **free** innocent   565 **Confound the ignorant** i.e., dumbfound those who know nothing of the crime that has
been committed.   **amaze** stun   567 **muddy-mettled** dull-spirited   567–8 **peak ... cause** mope,
like a dreaming idler, not quickened by my cause   570 **property** person and function   571 **damned
defeat** damnable act of destruction   572 **pate** head   574 **Gives ... throat** Calls me an out-and-out
liar   576 **'swounds** by his (Christ's) wounds   577 **pigeon-livered** (The pigeon or dove was popular-
ly supposed to be mild because it secreted no gall.)   578 **To ... bitter** to make things bitter for
oppressors   579 **region kites** kites (birds of prey) of the air   580 **offal** entrails   581 **Remorseless**
Pitiless.   **kindless** unnatural   583 **brave** fine, admirable. (Said ironically.)   587 **drab** whore
588 **scullion** menial kitchen servant. (Apt to be foul-mouthed.)   **About** About it, to work

Have by the very cunning of the scene   *591*
Been struck so to the soul that presently   *592*
They have proclaimed their malefactions;
For murder, though it have no tongue, will speak
With most miraculous organ. I'll have these players
Play something like the murder of my father
Before mine uncle. I'll observe his looks;
I'll tent him to the quick. If 'a do blench,   *598*
I know my course. The spirit that I have seen
May be the devil, and the devil hath power
T'assume a pleasing shape; yea, and perhaps,
Out of my weakness and my melancholy,
As he is very potent with such spirits,   *603*
Abuses me to damn me. I'll have grounds   *604*
More relative than this. The play's the thing   *605*
Wherein I'll catch the conscience of the King.   (*Exit.*)

3.1

Enter KING, QUEEN, POLONIUS, OPHELIA,
ROSENCRANTZ, GUILDENSTERN, *lords.*

KING.
  And can you by no drift of conference   *1*
  Get from him why he puts on this confusion,
  Grating so harshly all his days of quiet
  With turbulent and dangerous lunacy?
ROSENCRANTZ.
  He does confess he feels himself distracted,
  But from what cause 'a will by no means speak.
GUILDENSTERN.
  Nor do we find him forward to be sounded,   *7*
  But with a crafty madness keeps aloof
  When we would bring him on to some confession
  Of his true state.
QUEEN.   Did he receive you well?

---

591 cunning art, skill.   **scene** dramatic presentation   **592 presently** at once   **598 tent** probe.   **the quick** the tender part of a wound, the core.   **blench** quail, flinch   **603 spirits** humors (of melancholy)   **604 Abuses** deludes   **605 relative** cogent, pertinent

3.1 Location: The castle.
1 drift of conference course of talk   **7 forward** willing.   **sounded** questioned

ROSENCRANTZ.   Most like a gentleman.
GUILDENSTERN.
    But with much forcing of his disposition.   12
ROSENCRANTZ.
    Niggard of question, but of our demands   13
    Most free in his reply.
QUEEN.   Did you assay him   14
    To any pastime?
ROSENCRANTZ.
    Madam, it so fell out that certain players
    We o'erraught on the way. Of these we told him,   17
    And there did seem in him a kind of joy
    To hear of it. They are here about the court,
    And, as I think, they have already order
    This night to play before him.
POLONIUS.   'Tis most true,
    And he beseeched me to entreat Your Majesties
    To hear and see the matter.
KING.
    With all my heart, and it doth much content me
    To hear him so inclined.
    Good gentlemen, give him a further edge   26
    And drive his purpose into these delights.
ROSENCRANTZ.
    We shall, my lord.

(*Exeunt* ROSENCRANTZ *and* GUILDENSTERN.)

KING.   Sweet Gertrude, leave us too,
    For we have closely sent for Hamlet hither,   29
    That he, as 'twere by accident, may here
    Affront Ophelia.   31
    Her father and myself, lawful espials,   32
    Will so bestow ourselves that seeing, unseen,
    We may of their encounter frankly judge,
    And gather by him, as he is behaved,
    If't be th'affliction of his love or no
    That thus he suffers for.

---

12 **disposition** inclination   13 **Niggard of question** Laconic.   **demands** questions   14 **assay** try to win   17 **o'erraught** overtook   26 **edge** incitement   29 **closely** privately   31 **Affront** confront, meet   32 **espials** spies

QUEEN.   I shall obey you.
And for your part, Ophelia, I do wish
That your good beauties be the happy cause
Of Hamlet's wildness. So shall I hope your virtues
Will bring him to his wonted way again,
To both your honors.
OPHELIA.   Madam, I wish it may.

(Exit QUEEN.*)*

POLONIUS.
Ophelia, walk you here.—Gracious, so please you,   *43*
We will bestow ourselves. (*To* OPHELIA) Read on this
   book,   (*giving her a book*) *44*
That show of such an exercise may color   *45*
   Your loneliness. We are oft to blame in this—   *46*
'Tis too much proved—that with devotion's visage   *47*
And pious action we do sugar o'er
The devil himself.
KING (*aside*).   Oh, 'tis too true!
How smart a lash that speech doth give my
   conscience!
The harlot's cheek, beautied with plast'ring art,
Is not more ugly to the thing that helps it   *53*
Than is my deed to my most painted word.   *54*
Oh, heavy burden!
POLONIUS.
I hear him coming. Let's withdraw, my lord.   *56*

(*The* KING *and* POLONIUS *withdraw.*)

(*Enter* HAMLET. OPHELIA *pretends to read a book.*)

HAMLET.
To be, or not to be, that is the question:
Whether 'tis nobler in the mind to suffer
The slings and arrows of outrageous fortune,
Or to take arms against a sea of troubles
And by opposing end them. To die, to sleep—

---

43 Gracious Your Grace (i.e., the King) **44 bestow** conceal   **45 exercise** religious exercise. (The book she reads is one of devotion.)   **color** give a plausible appearance to   **46 loneliness** being alone   **47 too much proved** too often shown to be true, too often practiced   **53 to . . . helps it** in comparison with the cosmetic that fashions the cheek's false beauty.   **54 painted word** deceptive utterances.   **56 withdraw** (The King and Polonius may retire behind an arras. The stage directions specify that they "enter" again near the end of the scene.)

No more—and by a sleep to say we end
The heartache and the thousand natural shocks
That flesh is heir to. 'Tis a consummation
Devoutly to be wished. To die, to sleep;
To sleep, perchance to dream. Ay, there's the rub,   66
For in that sleep of death what dreams may come,
When we have shuffled off this mortal coil,   68
Must give us pause. There's the respect   69
That makes calamity of so long life.   70
For who would bear the whips and scorns of time,
Th'oppressor's wrong, the proud man's contumely,   72
The pangs of disprized love, the law's delay,   73
The insolence of office, and the spurns   74
That patient merit of th'unworthy takes,   75
When he himself might his quietus make   76
With a bare bodkin? Who would fardels bear,   77
To grunt and sweat under a weary life,
But that the dread of something after death,
The undiscovered country from whose bourn   80
No traveler returns, puzzles the will,
And makes us rather bear those ills we have
Than fly to others that we know not of?
Thus conscience does make cowards of us all;
And thus the native hue of resolution   85
Is sicklied o'er with the pale cast of thought,   86
And enterprises of great pitch and moment   87
With this regard their currents turn awry   88
And lose the name of action.—Soft you now,   89
The fair Ophelia.—Nymph, in thy orisons   90
Be all my sins remembered.   91
OPHELIA.   Good my lord,
How does Your Honor for this many a day?

---

66 rub (Literally, an obstacle in the game of bowls.)   **68 shuffled** sloughed, cast.   **coil** turmoil
69 respect consideration   **70 of ... life** so long-lived, something we willingly endure for so long.
(Also suggesting that long life is itself a calamity.)   **72 contumely** insolent abuse   **73 disprized**
unvalued   **74 office** officialdom.   **spurns** insults   **75 of ... takes** receives from unworthy persons
76 quietus acquittance; here, death   **77 a bare bodkin** a mere dagger, unsheathed.   **fardels** burdens
80 bourn frontier, boundary   **85 native hue** natural color, complexion   **86 cast** tinge, shade of
color   **87 pitch** height (as of a falcon's flight).   **moment** importance   **88 regard** respect, consideration.   **currents** courses   **89 Soft you** i.e., Wait a minute, gently   **90-1 in ... remembered** i.e., pray
for me, sinner that I am.

HAMLET.
I humbly thank you; well, well, well.

OPHELIA.
My lord, I have remembrances of yours,
That I have longèd long to redeliver.
I pray you, now receive them.   (*She offers tokens.*)

HAMLET.
No, not I, I never gave you aught.

OPHELIA.
My honored lord, you know right well you did,
And with them words of so sweet breath composed
As made the things more rich. Their perfume lost,
Take these again, for to the noble mind
Rich gifts wax poor when givers prove unkind.
There, my lord.   (*She gives tokens.*)

HAMLET.   Ha, ha! Are you honest?   104

OPHELIA.   My lord?

HAMLET.   Are you fair?   106

OPHELIA.   What means Your Lordship?

HAMLET.   That if you be honest and fair, your honesty   108
should admit no discourse to your beauty.   109

OPHELIA.   Could beauty, my lord, have better commerce   110
than with honesty?

HAMLET.   Ay, truly, for the power of beauty will sooner
transform honesty from what it is to a bawd than the
force of honesty can translate beauty into his likeness.   114
This was sometime a paradox, but now the time gives   115
it proof. I did love you once.   116

OPHELIA.   Indeed, my lord, you made me believe so.

HAMLET.   You should not have believed me, for virtue   118
cannot so inoculate our old stock but we shall relish of   119
it. I loved you not.   120

OPHELIA.   I was the more deceived.

HAMLET.   Get thee to a nunnery. Why wouldst thou be a   122
breeder of sinners? I am myself indifferent honest, but   123
yet I could accuse me of such things that it were better

---

104 honest (1) truthful (2) chaste   **106 fair** (1) beautiful (2) just, honorable   **108 your honesty**
your chastity   **109 discourse to** familiar dealings with   **110 commerce** dealings, intercourse
114 his its   **115–16 This . . . proof** This was formerly an unfashionable view, but now the present
age confirms how true it is.   **118–20 virtue . . . of it** virtue cannot be grafted onto our sinful condition without our retaining some taste of the old stock.   **122 nunnery** convent. (With an awareness
that the word was also used derisively to denote a brothel.)   **123 indifferent honest** reasonably
virtuous

my mother had not borne me: I am very proud, revengeful, ambitious, with more offenses at my beck   *126* than I have thoughts to put them in, imagination to give them shape, or time to act them in. What should such fellows as I do crawling between earth and heaven? We are arrant knaves all; believe none of us. Go thy ways to a nunnery. Where's your father?

OPHELIA.   At home, my lord.

HAMLET.   Let the doors be shut upon him, that he may play the fool nowhere but in 's own house. Farewell.

OPHELIA.   Oh, help him, you sweet heavens!

HAMLET.   If thou dost marry, I'll give thee this plague for thy dowry: be thou as chaste as ice, as pure as snow, thou shalt not escape calumny. Get thee to a nunnery, farewell. Or, if thou wilt needs marry, marry a fool, for wise men know well enough what monsters you   *140* make of them. To a nunnery, go, and quickly too. Farewell.

OPHELIA.   Heavenly powers, restore him!

HAMLET.   I have heard of your paintings too, well   *144* enough. God hath given you one face, and you make yourselves another. You jig, you amble, and you   *146* lisp, you nickname God's creatures, and make your   *147* wantonness your ignorance. Go to, I'll no more on't;   *148* it hath made me mad. I say we will have no more marriage. Those that are married already—all but one—shall live. The rest shall keep as they are. To a nunnery, go.   (*Exit.*)

OPHELIA.

Oh, what a noble mind is here o'erthrown!
The courtier's, soldier's, scholar's, eye, tongue, sword,
Th'expectancy and rose of the fair state,   *155*
The glass of fashion and the mold of form,   *156*
Th'observed of all observers, quite, quite down!   *157*

---

126 beck command   **140 monsters** (An illusion to the horns of a cuckold.)   **you** i.e., you women
144 paintings use of cosmetics   **146–8 You jig ... ignorance** i.e., You prance about frivolously and speak with affected coynesss, you put new labels on God's creatures (by your use of cosmetics), and you excuse your affectations on the grounds of pretended ignorance.   **148 on't** of it
155 Th'expectancy and rose the hope and ornament   **156 The glass ... form** the mirror of true self-fashioning and the pattern of courtly behavior   **157 Th'observed ... observers** i.e., the center of attention and honor in the court

And I, of ladies most deject and wretched,
That sucked the honey of his music vows,   *159*
Now see that noble and most sovereign reason
Like sweet bells jangled out of tune and harsh,
That unmatched form and feature of blown youth   *162*
Blasted with ecstasy. Oh, woe is me,   *163*
T'have seen what I have seen, see what I see!

(*Enter* KING *and* POLONIUS.)

KING.
Love? His affections do not that way tend;   *165*
Nor what he spake, though it lacked form a little,
Was not like madness. There's something in his soul
O'er which his melancholy sits on brood,   *168*
And I do doubt the hatch and the disclose   *169*
Will be some danger; which for to prevent,
I have in quick determination
Thus set it down: he shall with speed to England   *172*
For the demand of our neglected tribute.
Haply the seas and countries different
With variable objects shall expel   *175*
This something-settled matter in his heart,   *176*
Whereon his brains still beating puts him thus   *177*
From fashion of himself. What think you on't?   *178*
POLONIUS.
It shall do well. But yet do I believe
The origin and commencement of his grief
Sprung from neglected love.—How now, Ophelia?
You need not tell us what Lord Hamlet said;
We heard it all.—My lord, do as you please,
But, if you hold it fit, after the play
Let his queen-mother all alone entreat him
To show his grief. Let her be round with him;   *186*
And I'll be placed, so please you, in the ear
Of all their conference. If she find him not,   *188*

---

159 **music** musical, sweetly uttered   162 **blown** blossoming   163 **Blasted with ecstasy** blighted
with madness.   165 **affections** emotions, feelings   168 **sits on brood** sits like a bird on a nest,
about to *hatch* mischief (line 169)   169 **doubt** suspect, fear.   **disclose** disclosure, hatching
172 **set it down** resolved   175 **variable objects** various sights and surroundings to divert him
176 **This something ... heart** the strange matter settled in his heart   177 **still** continually   178
From ... himself out of his natural manner   186 **round** blunt   188 **find him not** fails to discover
what is troubling him

To England send him, or confine him where
Your wisdom best shall think.

KING.　It shall be so.
Madness in great ones must not unwatched go.

(*Exeunt.*)

3.2

Enter HAMLET *and three of the* PLAYERS.

HAMLET.　Speak the speech, I pray you, as I pronounced
it to you, trippingly on the tongue. But if you mouth
it, as many of our players do, I had as lief the town crier 　　　*3*
spoke my lines. Nor do not saw the air too much with
your hand, thus, but use all gently; for in the very
torrent, tempest, and, as I may say, whirlwind of your
passion, you must acquire and beget a temperance
that may give it smoothness. Oh, it offends me to the
soul to hear a robustious periwig-pated fellow tear a 　　　*9*
passion to tatters, to very rags, to split the ears of the
groundlings, who for the most part are capable of 　　　*11*
nothing but inexplicable dumb shows and noise. I 　　　*12*
would have such a fellow whipped for o'erdoing Ter 　　　*13*
magant. It out-Herods Herod. Pray you, avoid it. 　　　*14*

FIRST PLAYER.　I warrant Your Honor.

HAMLET.　Be not too tame neither, but let your own
discretion be your tutor. Suit the action to the word,
the word to the action, with this special observance,
that you o'erstep not the modesty of nature. For 　　　*19*
anything so o'erdone is from the purpose of playing, 　　　*20*
whose end, both at the first and now, was and is to
hold as 'twere the mirror up to nature, to show virtue
her feature, scorn her own image, and the very age 　　　*23*

3.2 Location: The castle.
3 our players players nowadays.　I had as lief I would just as soon　9 robustious violent, boister-
ous.　periwig-pated wearing a wig　11 groundlings spectators who paid least and stood in the
yard of the theater.　capable of able to understand　12 dumb shows and noise noisy spectacle
(rather than thoughtful drama)　13–14 Termagant a supposed deity of the Mohammedans, not
found in any English medieval play but elsewhere portrayed as violent and blustering.　14 Herod
Herod of Jewry. (A character in *The Slaughter of the Innocents* and other cycle plays. The part was
played with great noise and fury.)　19 modesty restraint, moderation　20 from contrary to
23 scorn i.e., something foolish and deserving of scorn　23–4 and the ... pressure and the present
state of affairs its likeness as seen in an impression, such as wax.

and body of the time his form and pressure. Now this 24
overdone or come tardy off, though it makes the 25
unskillful laugh, cannot but make the judicious grieve, 26
the censure of the which one must in your allowance 27
o'erweigh a whole theater of others. Oh, there be players that I have seen play, and heard others praise, and
that highly, not to speak it profanely, that, neither 30
having th'accent of Christians nor the gait of Chris- 31
tian, pagan, nor man, have so strutted and bellowed 32
that I have thought some of nature's journeymen had 33
made men and not made them well, they imitated
humanity so abominably. 35
FIRST PLAYER. I hope we have reformed that indifferently 36
with us, sir.
HAMLET. Oh, reform it altogether. And let those that play
your clowns speak no more than is set down for them;
for there be of them that will themselves laugh, to set 40
on some quantity of barren spectators to laugh too, 41
though in the meantime some necessary question of
the play be then to be considered. That's villainous,
and shows a most pitiful ambition in the fool that uses
it. Go make you ready. (*Exeunt* PLAYERS.)

(*Enter* POLONIUS, GUILDENSTERN, *and* ROSENCRANTZ.)

How now, my lord, will the King hear this piece of
work?
POLONIUS. And the Queen too, and that presently. 48
HAMLET. Bid the players make haste. (*Exit* POLONIUS.)
Will you two help to hasten them?
ROSENCRANTZ.
Ay, my lord. (*Exeunt they two.*)
HAMLET. What ho, Horatio!

(*Enter* HORATIO.)

---

25 **come tardy off** falling short 25–6 **the unskillful** those lacking in judgment 27 **the censure . . .
one** the judgment of even one of whom. **your allowance** your scale of values 30 **not . . . profanely** (Hamlet anticipates his idea in lines 33–4 that some men were not made by God at all.)
31-2 **Christians** i.e., ordinary decent folk 32 **nor man** i.e., nor any human being at all 33 **journeymen** common workmen 35 **abominably** (Shakespeare's usual spelling, "abhominably," suggests
a literal though etymologically incorrect meaning, "removed from human nature.") 36 **indifferently** tolerably 40 **of them** some among them 41 **barren** i.e., of wit 48 **presently** at once

HORATIO.   Here, sweet lord, at your service.
HAMLET.
 Horatio, thou art e'en as just a man
 As e'er my conversation coped withal.   *54*
HORATIO.
 Oh, my dear lord—
HAMLET.   Nay, do not think I flatter,
 For what advancement may I hope from thee
 That no revenue hast but thy good spirits
 To feed and clothe thee? Why should the poor be
  flattered?
 No, let the candied tongue lick absurd pomp,   *59*
 And crook the pregnant hinges of the knee   *60*
 Where thrift may follow fawning. Dost thou hear?   *61*
 Since my dear soul was mistress of her choice
 And could of men distinguish her election,   *63*
 Sh' hath sealed thee for herself, for thou hast been *64*
 As one, in suffering all, that suffers nothing,
 A man that Fortune's buffets and rewards
 Hast ta'en with equal thanks; and blest are those
 Whose blood and judgment are so well commeddled *68*
 That they are not a pipe for Fortune's finger
 To sound what stop she please. Give me that man   *70*
 That is not passion's slave, and I will wear him
 In my heart's core, ay, in my heart of heart,
 As I do thee.—Something too much of this.—
 There is a play tonight before the King.
 One scene of it comes near the circumstance
 Which I have told thee of my father's death.
 I prithee, when thou see'st that act afoot,
 Even with the very comment of thy soul   *78*
 Observe my uncle. If his occulted guilt   *79*
 Do not itself unkennel in one speech,   *80*
 It is a damnèd ghost that we have seen,
 And my imaginations are as foul

---

54 my . . . withal my dealings encountered.   59 candied sugared, flattering   60 pregnant compliant
61 thrift profit   63 could . . . election could make distinguishing choices among persons   64 sealed
thee (Literally, as one would seal a legal document to mark possession.)   68 blood passion.
commeddled commingled   70 stop hole in a wind instrument for controlling the sound   78 very . . .
soul your most penetrating observation and consideration   79 occulted hidden   80 unkennel (As
one would say of a fox driven from its lair.)

As Vulcan's stithy. Give him heedful note,   *83*
For I mine eyes will rivet to his face,
And after we will both our judgments join
In censure of his seeming.
HORATIO.   Well, my lord.   *86*
If 'a steal aught the whilst this play is playing   *87*
And scape detecting, I will pay the theft.

(*Flourish. Enter trumpets and kettledrums,* KING,
QUEEN, POLONIUS, OPHELIA, ROSENCRANTZ,
GUILDENSTERN, *and other lords, with guards
carrying torches.*)

HAMLET.   They are coming to the play. I must be idle.   *89*
Get you a place.   (*The* KING, QUEEN, *and courtiers sit.*)
KING.   How fares our cousin Hamlet?   *91*
HAMLET.   Excellent, i'faith, of the chameleon's dish: I eat *92*
the air, promise-crammed. You cannot feed capons so.   *93*
KING.   I have nothing with this answer, Hamlet. These   *94*
words are not mine.   *95*
HAMLET.   No, nor mine now. (*To* POLONIUS) My lord, you   *96*
played once i'th'university, you say?
POLONIUS.   That did I, my lord, and was accounted a
good actor.
HAMLET.   What did you enact?
POLONIUS.   I did enact Julius Caesar. I was killed i'th'   *101*
Capitol; Brutus killed me.   *102*
HAMLET.   It was a brute part of him to kill so capital a   *103*
calf there.—Be the players ready?   *104*
ROSENCRANTZ.   Ay, my lord. They stay upon your   *105*
patience.
QUEEN.   Come hither, my dear Hamlet, sit by me.

---

83 Vulcan's stithy the smithy, the place of stiths (anvils) of the Roman god of fire and metalworking.
86 censure of his seeming judgment of his appearance or behavior.   **87 If 'a steal aught** If he gets
away with anything   **89 idle** (1) unoccupied (2) mad.   **91 cousin** i.e., close relative   **92 chameleon's
dish** (Chameleons were supposed to feed on air. Hamlet deliberately misinterprets the King's *fares* as
"feeds." By his phrase *eat the air* he also plays on the idea of feeding himself with the promise of succession, of being the *heir*.)   **93 capons** roosters castrated and *crammed* with feed to make them suc-
culent.   **94 have ... with** make nothing of, or gain nothing from   **95 are not mine** do not respond to
what I asked.   **96 nor mine now** (Once spoken, words are proverbially no longer the speaker's own—
and hence should be uttered warily.)   **101–2 i'th' Capitol** (where Caesar was assassinated, according
to *Julius Caesar*, 3.1, but see 1.3.126n in that play)   **103 brute** (The Latin meaning of *brutus*, "stu-
pid," was often used punningly with the name Brutus.)   **part** (1) deed (2) role   **104 calf** fool
105 stay upon await

HAMLET.   No, good mother, here's metal more attractive.   *108*
POLONIUS (*to the* KING).   Oho, do you mark that?
HAMLET.   Lady, shall I lie in your lap?   *110*

(*Lying down at* OPHELIA's *feet.*)

OPHELIA.   No, my lord.
HAMLET.   I mean, my head upon your lap?
OPHELIA.   Ay, my lord.
HAMLET.   Do you think I meant country matters?   *114*
OPHELIA.   I think nothing, my lord.
HAMLET.   That's a fair thought to lie between maids'
  legs.
OPHELIA.   What is, my lord?
HAMLET.   Nothing.   *119*
OPHELIA.   You are merry, my lord.
HAMLET.   Who, I?
OPHELIA.   Ay, my lord.
HAMLET.   Oh, God, your only jig maker. What should a   *123*
  man do but be merry? For look you how cheerfully my
  mother looks, and my father died within 's two hours.   *125*
OPHELIA.   Nay, 'tis twice two months, my lord.
HAMLET.   So long? Nay then, let the devil wear black, for
  I'll have a suit of sables. O heavens! Die two months   *128*
  ago, and not forgotten yet? Then there's hope a great
  man's memory may outlive his life half a year. But, by'r
  Lady, 'a must build churches, then, or else shall 'a
  suffer not thinking on, with the hobbyhorse, whose   *132*
  epitaph is "For oh, for oh, the hobbyhorse is forgot."   *133*

(*The trumpets sound. Dumb show follows.*)

---

108 metal substance that is *attractive*, i.e., magnetic, but with suggestion also of *mettle*, "disposition".
110 Lady ... lap? Onstage, Hamlet often lies at Ophelia's feet, but he could instead offer to do this and
continue to stand.   114 country matters sexual intercourse. (With a bawdy pun on the first syllable
of *country*.)   119 Nothing The figure zero or naught, suggesting the female sexual anatomy. (*Thing*
not infrequently has a bawdy connotation of male or female anatomy, and the reference here could
be male.)   123 only jig maker very best composer of jigs, i.e., pointless merriment. (Hamlet replies
sardonically to Ophelia's observation that he is merry by saying, "If you're looking for someone who
is really merry, you've come to the right person.")   125 within 's within this (i.e., these)   128 suit
of sables garments trimmed with the dark fur of the sable and hence suited for a person in mourning.   132 suffer ... on undergo oblivion   133 "For ... forgot" (Verse of a song occurring also in
Love's Labor's Lost, 3.1.27–8. The hobbyhorse was a character made up to resemble a horse and rider,
appearing in the morris dance and such May-game sports. This song laments the disappearance of
such customs under pressure from the Puritans.)

(*Enter a* KING *and a* QUEEN, *very lovingly; the*
QUEEN *embracing him, and he her. She kneels,*
and makes show of protestation unto him. He
takes her up, and declines his head upon her neck.
He lies him down upon a bank of flowers. She,
seeing him asleep, leaves him. Anon comes in
another man, takes off his crown, kisses it, pours
poison in the sleeper's ears, and leaves him. The
QUEEN *returns, finds the* KING *dead, makes*
passionate action. The POISONER *with some three or*
four come in again, seem to condole with her. The
dead body is carried away. The POISONER *woos*
the QUEEN *with gifts; she seems harsh awhile, but in*
the end accepts love.)

(*Exeunt* PLAYERS.)

OPHELIA.   What means this, my lord?
HAMLET.   Marry, this' miching mallico; it means mis-   135
   chief.
OPHELIA.   Belike this show imports the argument of the   137
   play.

(*Enter* PROLOGUE.)

HAMLET.   We shall know by this fellow. The players can-
   not keep counsel; they'll tell all.   140
OPHELIA.   Will 'a tell us what this show meant?
HAMLET.   Ay, or any show that you will show him. Be   142
   not you ashamed to show, he'll not shame to tell you   143
   what it means.
OPHELIA.   You are naught, you are naught. I'll mark the   145
   play.
PROLOGUE.
   For us, and for our tragedy,
   Here stooping to your clemency,   148
   We beg your hearing patiently.   (*Exit.*)
HAMLET.   Is this a prologue, or the posy of a ring?   150

133.12 *condole with* offer sympathy to   135 **this' miching mallico** this is sneaking mischief
137 **Belike** Probably.   **argument** plot   140 **counsel** secret   142–3 **Be not you** Provided you are not
145 **naught** indecent. (Ophelia is reacting to Hamlet's pointed remarks about not being ashamed to
show all.)   148 **stooping** bowing   150 **posy ... ring** brief motto in verse inscribed in a ring.

OPHELIA. 'Tis brief, my lord.

HAMLET. As woman's love.

(*Enter two* PLAYERS *as* KING *and* QUEEN.)

PLAYER KING.

Full thirty times hath Phoebus' cart gone round   153
Neptune's salt wash and Tellus' orbèd ground,   154
And thirty dozen moons with borrowed sheen   155
About the world have times twelve thirties been,
Since love our hearts and Hymen did our hands   157
Unite commutual in most sacred bands.   158

PLAYER QUEEN.

So many journeys may the sun and moon
Make us again count o'er ere love be done!
But, woe is me, you are so sick of late,
So far from cheer and from your former state,
That I distrust you. Yet, though I distrust,   163
Discomfort you, my lord, it nothing must.   164
For women's fear and love hold quantity;   165
In neither aught, or in extremity.   166
Now, what my love is, proof hath made you know,   167
And as my love is sized, my fear is so.
Where love is great, the littlest doubts are fear;   169
Where little fears grow great, great love grows there.

PLAYER KING.

Faith, I must leave thee, love, and shortly too;
My operant powers their functions leave to do.   172
And thou shalt live in this fair world behind,   173
Honored, beloved; and haply one as kind
For husband shalt thou—

PLAYER QUEEN. Oh, confound the rest!

Such love must needs be treason in my breast.
In second husband let me be accurst!

---

153 **Phoebus' cart** the sun-god's chariot, making its yearly cycle 154 **salt** wash the sea. **Tellus** goddess of the earth, of the *orbèd* ground 155 **borrowed** i.e., reflected 157 **Hymen** god of matrimony 158 **commutual** mutually. **bands** bonds. 163 **distrust** am anxious about 164 **Discomfort ... must** it must not distress you at all. 165 **hold quantity** keep proportion with one another 166 **In ... extremity** (women feel) either no anxiety if they do not love or extreme anxiety if they do love. 167 **proof** experience 169 **the littlest** even the littlest 172 **My ... to do** my vital functions are shutting down. 173 **behind** after I have gone

None wed the second but who killed the first.   *178*
HAMLET.   Wormwood, wormwood.   *179*
PLAYER QUEEN.
   The instances that second marriage move   *180*
   Are base respects of thrift, but none of love.   *181*
   A second time I kill my husband dead
   When second husband kisses me in bed.
PLAYER KING.
   I do believe you think what now you speak,
   But what we do determine oft we break.
   Purpose is but the slave to memory,   *186*
   Of violent birth, but poor validity,   *187*
   Which now, like fruit unripe, sticks on the tree,   *188*
   But fall unshaken when they mellow be.
   Most necessary 'tis that we forget   *190*
   To pay ourselves what to ourselves is debt.   *191*
   What to ourselves in passion we propose,
   The passion ending, doth the purpose lose.
   The violence of either grief or joy
   Their own enactures with themselves destroy.   *195*
   Where joy most revels, grief doth most lament;   *196*
   Grief joys, joy grieves, on slender accident.   *197*
   This world is not for aye, nor 'tis not strange   *198*
   That even our loves should with our fortunes change;
   For 'tis a question left us yet to prove,
   Whether love lead fortune, or else fortune love.
   The great man down, you mark his favorite flies;   *202*
   The poor advanced makes friends of enemies.   *203*
   And hitherto doth love on fortune tend;   *204*
   For who not needs shall never lack a friend,   *205*

---

178 None (1) Let no woman; or (2) No woman does.   **but who** except the one who   **179
Wormwood** i.e., How bitter. (Literally, a bitter-tasting plant.)   **180 instances** motives.   **move** moti-
vate   **181 base ... thrift** ignoble considerations of material prosperity   **186 Purpose ... memory**
Our good intentions are subject to forgetfulness   **187 validity** strength, durability   **188 Which** i.e.,
purpose   **190–1 Most ... debt** It's inevitable that in time we forget the obligations we have imposed
on ourselves.   **195 enactures** fulfillments   **196–7 Where ... accident** The capacity for extreme joy
and grief go together, and often one extreme is instantly changed into its opposite on the slightest
provocation.   **198 aye** ever   **202 down** fallen in fortune   **203 The poor ... enemies** when one of
humble station is promoted, you see his enemies suddenly becoming his friends.   **204 hitherto** up
to this point in the argument, or, to this extent.   **tend** attend   **205 who not needs** he who is not in
need (of wealth)

And who in want a hollow friend doth try 206
Directly seasons him his enemy. 207
But, orderly to end where I begun,
Our wills and fates do so contrary run 209
That our devices still are overthrown; 210
Our thoughts are ours, their ends none of our own. 211
So think thou wilt no second husband wed,
But die thy thoughts when thy first lord is dead.

PLAYER QUEEN.
Nor earth to me give food, nor heaven light, 214
Sport and repose lock from me day and night, 215
To desperation turn my trust and hope,
An anchor's cheer in prison be my scope! 217
Each opposite that blanks the face of joy 218
Meet what I would have well and it destroy! 219
Both here and hence pursue me lasting strife 220
If, once a widow, ever I be wife!

HAMLET.   If she should break it now!

PLAYER KING.
'Tis deeply sworn. Sweet, leave me here awhile;
My spirits grow dull, and fain I would beguile 224
The tedious day with sleep.

PLAYER QUEEN.   Sleep rock thy brain,
And never come mischance between us twain!

(*He sleeps. Exit* PLAYER QUEEN.)

HAMLET.   Madam, how like you this play?
QUEEN.   The lady doth protest too much, methinks. 228
HAMLET.   Oh, but she'll keep her word.
KING.   Have you heard the argument? Is there no 230
offense in't?
HAMLET.   No, no, they do but jest, poison in jest. No of- 232

---

206 **who in want** he who, being in need. **try** test (his generosity)   207 **seasons him** ripens him into   209 **Our ... run** what we want and what we get go so contrarily   210 **devices** intentions. **still** continually   211 **ends** results   214 **Nor** Let neither   215 **Sport ... night** may day deny me its pastimes and night its repose   217 **anchor's cheer** anchorite's or hermit's fare. **my scope** the extent of my happiness.   218–19 **Each ... destroy!** May every adverse thing that causes the face of joy to turn pale meet and destroy everything that I desire to see prosper!   220 **hence** in the life hereafter 224 **spirits** vital spirits   228 **doth ... much** makes too many promises and protestations   230 **argument** plot.   232 **jest** make believe.

fense i'th' world. 233

KING. What do you call the play?

HAMLET. The Mousetrap. Marry, how? Tropically. 235
This play is the image of a murder done in Vienna.
Gonzago is the Duke's name, his wife, Baptista. You 237
shall see anon. 'Tis a knavish piece of work, but what
of that? Your Majesty, and we that have free souls, it 239
touches us not. Let the galled jade wince, our withers 240
are unwrung. 241

(*Enter* LUCIANUS.)

This is one Lucianus, nephew to the King.

OPHELIA. You are as good as a chorus, my lord. 243

HAMLET. I could interpret between you and your love, 244
if I could see the puppets dallying. 245

OPHELIA. You are keen, my lord, you are keen. 246

HAMLET. It would cost you a groaning to take off mine
edge.

OPHELIA. Still better, and worse. 249

HAMLET. So you mis-take your husbands.—Begin, mur- 250
derer; leave thy damnable faces and begin. Come, the
croaking raven doth bellow for revenge.

LUCIANUS.

Thoughts black, hands apt, drugs fit, and time
agreeing,
Confederate season, else no creature seeing, 254
Thou mixture rank, of midnight weeds collected,

232–3 **offense** crime, injury. (Hamlet playfully alters the King's use of the word in line 231 to mean "cause for objection.") 235 **Tropically** Figuratively. (The First Quarto reading, "trapically," suggests a pun on *trap* in *Mousetrap.*) 237 **Duke's** i.e., King's. (An inconsistency that may be due to Shakespeare's possible acquaintance with a historical incident, the alleged murder of the Duke of Urbino by Luigi Gonzaga in 1538.) 239 **free** guiltless 240 **galled jade** horse whose hide is rubbed by saddle or harness. **withers** the part between the horse's shoulder blades 241 **unwrung** not rubbed sore. 243 **chorus** (In many Elizabethan plays, the forthcoming action was explained by an actor known as the "chorus"; at a puppet show, the actor who spoke the dialogue was known as an "interpreter," as indicated by the lines following.) 244 **interpret** (1) ventriloquize the dialogue, as in puppet show (2) act as pander. 245 **puppets dallying** (With suggestion of sexual play, continued in *keen*, "sexually aroused," *groaning*, "moaning in pregnancy," and *edge*, "sexual desire" or "impetuosity.") 246 **keen** sharp, bitter 249 **Still . . . worse** More keen, always *bettering* what other people say with witty wordplay, but at the same time more offensive. 250 **So** Even thus (in marriage). **mis-take** take falseheartedly and cheat on. (The marriage vows say "for better, for worse.") 254 **Confederate . . . seeing** the time and occasion conspiring (to assist me), and also no one seeing me.

With Hecate's ban thrice blasted, thrice infected,   *256*
Thy natural magic and dire property   *257*
On wholesome life usurp immediately.

(*He pours the poison into the sleeper's ear.*)

HAMLET. 'A poisons him i'th' garden for his estate. His   *259*
name's Gonzago. The story is extant, and written in
very choice Italian. You shall see anon how the
murderer gets the love of Gonzago's wife.

                                           (CLAUDIUS *rises.*)

OPHELIA. The King rises.
HAMLET. What, frighted with false fire?   *264*
QUEEN. How fares my lord?
POLONIUS. Give o'er the play.
KING. Give me some light. Away!
POLONIUS. Lights, lights, lights!

(*Exeunt all but* HAMLET *and* HORATIO.)

HAMLET.
  "Why, let the strucken deer go weep,   *269*
    The hart ungallèd play.   *270*
  For some must watch, while some must sleep;   *271*
    Thus runs the world away."   *272*
  Would not this, sir, and a forest of feathers—if the   *273*
  rest of my fortunes turn Turk with me—with two   *274*
  Provincial roses on my razed shoes, get me a fellow-   *275*
  ship in a cry of players?   *276*
HORATIO. Half a share.
HAMLET. A whole one, I.
  "For thou dost know, O Damon dear,   *279*

---

256 **Hecate's ban** the curse of Hecate, the goddess of witchcraft   257 **dire property** baleful quality
259 **estate** i.e., the kingship.   **His** i.e., the King's   264 **false fire** the blank discharge of a gun loaded
with powder but no shot.   269–72 **Why . . . away** (Perhaps from an old ballad, with allusion to the
popular belief that a wounded deer retires to weep and die; compare with *As You Like It*, 2.1.33–66.)
270 **ungallèd** unafflicted   271 **watch** remain awake   272 **Thus . . . away** Thus the world goes.
273 **this** i.e., this success with the play I have just presented.   **feathers** (Allusion to the plumes that
Elizabethan actors were fond of wearing.)   274 **turn Turk with** turn renegade against, go back on
275 **Provincial roses** rosettes of ribbon, named for roses grown in a part of France.   **razed** with
ornamental slashing   275–6 **fellowship . . . players** partnership in a theatrical company.   276 **cry**
pack (of hounds, etc.)   279 **Damon** the friend of Pythias, as Horatio is friend of Hamlet; or, a traditional pastoral name

This realm dismantled was   *280*
Of Jove himself, and now reigns here   *281*
    A very, very—pajock."   *282*
HORATIO.   You might have rhymed.
HAMLET.   Oh, good Horatio, I'll take the ghost's word for
   a thousand pound. Didst perceive?
HORATIO.   Very well, my lord.
HAMLET.   Upon the talk of the poisoning?
HORATIO.   I did very well note him.

(*Enter* ROSENCRANTZ *and* GUILDENSTERN.)

HAMLET.   Aha! Come, some music! Come, the re-
   corders.
     "For if the King like not the comedy,
     Why then, belike, he likes it not, perdy."   *292*
   Come, some music.
GUILDENSTERN.   Good my lord, vouchsafe me a word
   with you.
HAMLET.   Sir, a whole history.
GUILDENSTERN.   The King, sir—
HAMLET.   Ay, sir, what of him?
GUILDENSTERN.   Is in his retirement marvelous dis-   *299*
   tempered.   *300*
HAMLET.   With drink, sir?
GUILDENSTERN.   No, my lord, with choler.   *302*
HAMLET.   Your wisdom should show itself more richer
   to signify this to the doctor, for for me to put him to his
   purgation would perhaps plunge him into more   *305*
   choler.
GUILDENSTERN.   Good my lord, put your discourse into
   some frame and start not so wildly from my affair.   *308*
HAMLET.   I am tame, sir. Pronounce.

280–2 This realm ... pajock i.e., Jove, representing divine authority and justice, has abandoned this realm to its own devices, leaving in his stead only a peacock or vain pretender to virtue (though the rhyme-word expected in place of *pajock or* "peacock" suggests that the realm is now ruled over by an "ass"). **280 dismantled** stripped, divested **292 perdy** (A corruption of the French *par dieu,* "by God.") **299 retirement** withdrawal to his chambers **299–300 distempered** out of humor. (But Hamlet deliberately plays on the wider application to any illness of mind or body, as in lines 335–6, especially to drunkenness.) **302 choler** anger. (But Hamlet takes the word in its more basic humoral sense of "bilious disorder.") **305 purgation** (Hamlet hints at something going beyond medical treatment to bloodletting and the extraction of confession.) **308 frame** order. **start** shy or jump away (like a horse; the opposite of *tame* in line 309)

GUILDENSTERN.   The Queen, your mother, in most great
   affliction of spirit, hath sent me to you.
HAMLET.   You are welcome.
GUILDENSTERN.   Nay, good my lord, this courtesy is not
   of the right breed. If it shall please you to make me a   314
   wholesome answer, I will do your mother's command-
   ment; if not, your pardon and my return shall be the   316
   end of my business.
HAMLET.   Sir, I cannot.
ROSENCRANTZ.   What, my lord?
HAMLET.   Make you a wholesome answer; my wit's diseased. But, sir, such answer as I can make, you shall
   command, or rather, as you say, my mother. Therefore
   no more, but to the matter. My mother, you say—
ROSENCRANTZ.   Then thus she says: your behavior hath
   struck her into amazement and admiration.   325
HAMLET.   Oh, wonderful son, that can so 'stonish a mother!
   But is there no sequel at the heels of this mother's ad-
   miration? Impart.
ROSENCRANTZ.   She desires to speak with you in her
   closet ere you go to bed.   330
HAMLET.   We shall obey, were she ten times our mother.
   Have you any further trade with us?
ROSENCRANTZ.   My lord, you once did love me.
HAMLET.   And do still, by these pickers and stealers.   334
ROSENCRANTZ.   Good my lord, what is your cause of
   distemper? You do surely bar the door upon your own
   liberty if you deny your griefs to your friend.   337
HAMLET.   Sir, I lack advancement.
ROSENCRANTZ.   How can that be, when you have the
   voice of the King himself for your succession in
   Denmark?
HAMLET.   Ay, sir, but "While the grass grows"—the   342
   proverb is something musty.   343

---

314 **breed** (1) kind (2) breeding, manners.   316 **pardon** permission to depart   325 **admiration**
bewilderment.   330 **closet** private chamber   334 **pickers and stealers** i.e., hands. (So called from
the catechism, "to keep my hands from picking and stealing.")   337 **liberty** i.e., being freed from
distemper, line 336; but perhaps with a veiled threat as well.   **deny** refuse to share   342 **"While...
grows"** (The rest of the proverb is "the silly horse starves"; Hamlet implies that his hopes of succession
are distant in time at best.)   343 **something** somewhat

(*Enter the* PLAYERS *with recorders.*)

Oh, the recorders. Let me see one. (He takes a recorder.)
To withdraw with you: why do you go about to recover   *345*
the wind of me, as if you would drive me into a toil?   *346*
GUILDENSTERN.   Oh, my lord, if my duty be too bold, my   *347*
love is too unmannerly.   *348*
HAMLET.   I do not well understand that. Will you play   *349*
upon this pipe?
GUILDENSTERN.   My lord, I cannot.
HAMLET.   I pray you.
GUILDENSTERN.   Believe me, I cannot.
HAMLET.   I do beseech you.
GUILDENSTERN.   I know no touch of it, my lord.
HAMLET.   It is as easy as lying. Govern these ventages   *356*
with your fingers and thumb, give it breath with your
mouth, and it will discourse most eloquent music.
Look you, these are the stops.
GUILDENSTERN.   But these cannot I command to any
utterance of harmony. I have not the skill.
HAMLET.   Why, look you now, how unworthy a thing
you make of me! You would play upon me, you would
seem to know my stops, you would pluck out the heart
of my mystery, you would sound me from my lowest   *365*
note to the top of my compass, and there is much   *366*
music, excellent voice, in this little organ, yet cannot   *367*
you make it speak. 'Sblood, do you think I am easier
to be played on than a pipe? Call me what instrument
you will, though you can fret me, you cannot play   *370*
upon me.

(*Enter* POLONIUS.)

God bless you, sir!
POLONIUS.   My lord, the Queen would speak with you,

343.1 **Players** actors   345 **withdraw** speak privately   345–6 **recover the wind** get to the windward side
(thus allowing the game to scent the hunter and thereby be driven in the opposite direction into the
toil or net)   346 **toil** snare   347–8 **if … unmannerly** if I am using an unmannerly boldness, it is my
love that occasions it.   349 **I … that** i.e., I don't understand how genuine love can be unmannerly.
356 **ventages** finger-holes or *stops* (line 359) of the recorder   365 **sound** (1) fathom (2) produce sound
in   366 **compass** range (of voice)   367 **organ** musical instrument   370 **fret** irritate. (With a quibble
on the *frets* or ridges on the fingerboard of some stringed instruments to regulate the fingering.)

and presently.   *374*

HAMLET. Do you see yonder cloud that's almost in
    shape of a camel?

POLONIUS. By th' Mass and 'tis, like a camel indeed.

HAMLET. Methinks it is like a weasel.

POLONIUS. It is backed like a weasel.

HAMLET. Or like a whale.

POLONIUS. Very like a whale.

HAMLET. Then I will come to my mother by and by.
    (*Aside*) They fool me to the top of my bent.—I will   *383*
    come by and by.

POLONIUS. I will say so.   (*Exit.*)

HAMLET. "By and by" is easily said. Leave me, friends.

(*Exeunt all but* HAMLET.)

    'Tis now the very witching time of night,   *387*
    When churchyards yawn and hell itself breathes out
    Contagion to this world. Now could I drink hot
        blood
    And do such bitter business as the day
    Would quake to look on. Soft, now to my mother.
    O heart, lose not thy nature! Let not ever   *392*
    The soul of Nero enter this firm bosom.   *393*
    Let me be cruel, not unnatural;
    I will speak daggers to her, but use none.
    My tongue and soul in this be hypocrites:
    How in my words somever she be shent,   *397*
    To give them seals never my soul consent!   (*Exit.*) *398*

3.3

Enter KING, ROSENCRANTZ, *and* GUILDENSTERN.

3.3. Location: The castle.
374 presently at once.   383 They fool ... bent They humor my odd behavior to the limit of my ability or endurance. (Literally, the extent to which a bow may be bent.)   387 witching time time when spells are cast and evil is abroad   392 nature natural feeling   393 Nero (This infamous Roman emperor put to death his mother, Agrippina, who had murdered her husband, Claudius.) 397–8 How ... consent! however much she is to be rebuked by my words, may my soul never consent to ratify those words with deeds of violence!

KING.

I like him not, nor stands it safe with us   *1*
To let his madness range. Therefore prepare you.
I your commission will forthwith dispatch,   *3*
And he to England shall along with you.
The terms of our estate may not endure   *5*
Hazard so near 's as doth hourly grow
Out of his brows.   *7*

GUILDENSTERN.   We will ourselves provide.
Most holy and religious fear it is   *8*
To keep those many many bodies safe
That live and feed upon Your Majesty.

ROSENCRANTZ.

The single and peculiar life is bound   *11*
With all the strength and armor of the mind
To keep itself from noyance, but much more   *13*
That spirit upon whose weal depends and rests   *14*
The lives of many. The cess of majesty   *15*
Dies not alone, but like a gulf doth draw   *16*
What's near it with it; or it is a massy wheel   *17*
Fixed on the summit of the highest mount,
To whose huge spokes ten thousand lesser things
Are mortised and adjoined, which, when it falls,   *20*
Each small annexment, petty consequence,   *21*
Attends the boist'rous ruin. Never alone   *22*
Did the King sigh, but with a general groan.

KING.

Arm you, I pray you, to this speedy voyage,   *24*
For we will fetters put about this fear,
Which now goes too free-footed.

ROSENCRANTZ.   We will haste us.

(*Exeunt gentlemen* ROSENCRANTZ *and* GUILDENSTERN.)

---

1 **him** i.e., his behavior   3 **dispatch** prepare, cause to be drawn up   5 **terms of our estate** circumstances of my royal position   7 **Out ... brows** i.e., from his brain, in the form of plots and threats.
We ... provide We'll put ourselves in readiness.   8 **religious fear** sacred concern   11 **single and peculiar** individual and private   13 **noyance** harm   14 **weal** well-being   15 **cess** decease, cessation
16 **gulf** whirlpool   17 **massy** massive   20 **mortised** fastened (as with a fitted joint).   **when it falls** i.e., when it descends, like the wheel of Fortune, bringing a king down with it   21 **Each ... consequence** i.e., every hanger-on and unimportant person or thing connected with the King   22 **Attends** participates in   24 **Arm** Provide, prepare

(*Enter* POLONIUS.)

POLONIUS.
My lord, he's going to his mother's closet.
Behind the arras I'll convey myself   *28*
To hear the process. I'll warrant she'll tax him home,   *29*
And, as you said—and wisely was it said—
'Tis meet that some more audience than a mother,   *31*
Since nature makes them partial, should o'erhear
The speech of vantage. Fare you well, my liege.   *33*
I'll call upon you ere you go to bed
And tell you what I know.
KING.   Thanks, dear my lord.

                                        (*Exit* POLONIUS.)
Oh, my offense is rank! It smells to heaven.
It hath the primal eldest curse upon't,   *37*
A brother's murder. Pray can I not,
Though inclination be as sharp as will;   *39*
My stronger guilt defeats my strong intent,
And like a man to double business bound   *41*
I stand in pause where I shall first begin,
And both neglect. What if this cursèd hand
Were thicker than itself with brother's blood,
Is there not rain enough in the sweet heavens
To wash it white as snow? Whereto serves mercy   *46*
But to confront the visage of offense?   *47*
And what's in prayer but this twofold force,
To be forestallèd ere we come to fall,   *49*
Or pardoned being down? Then I'll look up.
My fault is past. But oh, what form of prayer
Can serve my turn? "Forgive me my foul murder"?
That cannot be, since I am still possessed
Of those effects for which I did the murder:
My crown, mine own ambition, and my queen.

---

28 arras screen of tapestry placed around the walls of household apartments. (On the Elizabethan stage, the arras was presumably over a door or aperture in the tiring-house facade.)   **29 process** proceedings.   **tax him home** reprove him severely   **31 meet** fitting   **33 of vantage** from an advantageous place, or, in addition.   **37 the primal eldest curse** the curse of Cain, the first murderer; he killed his brother Abel   **39 Though ... will** though my desire is as strong as my determination   **41 bound** (1) destined (2) obliged. (The King wants to repent and still enjoy what he has gained.)   **46–7 Whereto ... offense?** What function does mercy serve other than to meet sin face to face?   **49 forestallèd** prevented (from sinning)

May one be pardoned and retain th'offense?   56
In the corrupted currents of this world   57
Offense's gilded hand may shove by justice,   58
And oft 'tis seen the wicked prize itself   59
Buys out the law. But 'tis not so above.
There is no shuffling, there the action lies   61
In his true nature, and we ourselves compelled,   62
Even to the teeth and forehead of our faults,   63
To give in evidence. What then? What rests?   64
Try what repentance can. What can it not?
Yet what can it, when one cannot repent?
O wretched state, O bosom black as death,
O limèd soul that, struggling to be free,   68
Art more engaged! Help, angels! Make assay.   69
Bow, stubborn knees, and heart with strings of steel,
Be soft as sinews of the newborn babe!
All may be well.   (*He kneels.*)

(*Enter* HAMLET.)

HAMLET.
Now might I do it pat, now 'a is a-praying;   73
And now I'll do't. (*He draws his sword.*) And so 'a goes to heaven,
And so am I revenged. That would be scanned: 75
A villain kills my father, and for that,
I, his sole son, do this same villain send
To heaven.
Why, this is hire and salary, not revenge.
'A took my father grossly, full of bread,   80
With all his crimes broad blown, as flush as May;   81
And how his audit stands who knows save heaven?   82
But in our circumstance and course of thought   83

---

56 th'offense the thing for which one offended   57 currents courses of events   58 gilded hand hand offering gold as a bribe.   shove by thrust aside   59 wicked prize prize won by wickedness
61 There...lies There in heaven can be no evasion, there the deed lies exposed to view   62 his its
63 to the teeth and forehead face to face, concealing nothing   64 give in provide.   rests remains.
68 limèd caught as with birdlime, a sticky substance used to ensnare birds   69 engaged entangled.
assay trial. (Said to himself, or to the angels to try him.)   73 pat opportunely   75 would be
scanned needs to be looked into, or, would be interpreted as follows   80 grossly, full of bread i.e.,
enjoying his worldly pleasures rather than fasting. (See Ezekiel 16:49.)   81 crimes broad blown sins
in full bloom.   flush vigorous   82 audit account.   save except for   83 in...thought as we see it
from our mortal perspective.

'Tis heavy with him. And am I then revenged,
To take him in the purging of his soul,
When he is fit and seasoned for his passage?   *86*
No!
Up, sword, and know thou a more horrid hent.   *88*

(*He puts up his sword.*)

When he is drunk asleep, or in his rage,   *89*
Or in th'incestuous pleasure of his bed,
At game, a-swearing, or about some act   *91*
That has no relish of salvation in't—   *92*
Then trip him, that his heels may kick at heaven,
And that his soul may be as damned and black
As hell, whereto it goes. My mother stays.   *95*
This physic but prolongs thy sickly days.   *96*
                      (*Exit.*)

KING.
My words fly up, my thoughts remain below.
Words without thoughts never to heaven go.   (*Exit.*)

3.4

Enter QUEEN GERTRUDE *and* POLONIUS.

POLONIUS.
'A will come straight. Look you lay home to him.   *1*
Tell him his pranks have been too broad to bear with,   *2*
And that Your Grace hath screened and stood   *4*
   between
Much heat and him. I'll silence me even here.
Pray you, be round with him.   *5*
HAMLET (*within*).   Mother, mother, mother!
QUEEN.   I'll warrant you, fear me not.
Withdraw, I hear him coming.

---

86 **seasoned** matured, readied   88 **know ... hent** await to be grasped by me on a more horrid occasion. (*Hent* means "act of seizing.")   89 **drunk ... rage** dead drunk, or in a fit of sexual passion   91 **game** gambling   92 **relish** trace, savor   95 **stays** awaits (me).   96 **physic** purging (by prayer), or, Hamlet's postponement of the killing

3.4. Location: The Queen's private chamber.
1 **lay home** reprove him soundly   2 **broad** unrestrained   4 **Much heat** i.e., the King's anger.
I'll silence me I'll quietly conceal myself. (Ironic, since it is his crying out at line 24 that leads to his death. Some editors emend *silence* to "sconce." The First Quarto's reading, "shroud," is attractive.)
5 **round** blunt

(POLONIUS *hides behind the arras.*)

(*Enter* HAMLET.)

HAMLET.   Now, mother, what's the matter?
QUEEN.
  Hamlet, thou hast thy father much offended.   *10*
HAMLET.
  Mother, you have my father much offended.
QUEEN.
  Come, come, you answer with an idle tongue.   *12*
HAMLET.
  Go, go, you question with a wicked tongue.
QUEEN.
  Why, how now, Hamlet?
HAMLET.   What's the matter now?
QUEEN.
  Have you forgot me?   *15*
HAMLET.   No, by the rood, not so:
  You are the Queen, your husband's brother's wife,
  And—would it were not so!—you are my mother.
QUEEN.
  Nay, then, I'll set those to you that can speak.   *18*
HAMLET.
  Come, come, and sit you down; you shall not budge.
  You go not till I set you up a glass
  Where you may see the inmost part of you.
QUEEN.
  What wilt thou do? Thou wilt not murder me?
  Help, ho!
POLONIUS (*behind the arras*).   What ho! Help!
HAMLET (*drawing*).
  How now? A rat? Dead for a ducat, dead!   *25*

(*He thrusts his rapier through the arras.*)

POLONIUS (*behind the arras*).
  Oh, I am slain!   (*He falls and dies.*)
QUEEN.   Oh, me, what hast thou done?

---

10 **thy father** i.e., your stepfather, Claudius   12 **idle** foolish   15 **forgot me** i.e., forgotten that I am
your mother.   **rood** cross of Christ   18 **speak** i.e., speak to someone so rude.   25 **Dead for a ducat**
i.e., I bet a ducat he's dead; or, a ducat is his life's fee.

HAMLET.   Nay, I know not. Is it the King?
QUEEN.
    Oh, what a rash and bloody deed is this!
HAMLET.
    A bloody deed—almost as bad, good mother,
    As kill a king, and marry with his brother.
QUEEN.
    As kill a king!
HAMLET.   Ay, lady, it was my word.

(*He parts the arras and discovers* POLONIUS.)

    Thou wretched, rash, intruding fool, farewell!
    I took thee for thy better. Take thy fortune.
    Thou find'st to be too busy is some danger.—   34
    Leave wringing of your hands. Peace, sit you down,
    And let me wring your heart, for so I shall,
    If it be made of penetrable stuff,
    If damnèd custom have not brazed it so   38
    That it be proof and bulwark against sense.   39
QUEEN.
    What have I done, that thou dar'st wag thy tongue
    In noise so rude against me?
HAMLET.   Such an act
    That blurs the grace and blush of modesty,
    Calls virtue hypocrite, takes off the rose
    From the fair forehead of an innocent love
    And sets a blister there, makes marriage vows   45
    As false as dicers' oaths. Oh, such a deed
    As from the body of contraction plucks   47
    The very soul, and sweet religion makes   48
    A rhapsody of words. Heaven's face does glow   49
    O'er this solidity and compound mass
    With tristful visage, as against the doom,
    Is thought-sick at the act.   52
QUEEN.   Ay me, what act,

---

34 **busy** nosey   38 **damnèd custom** habitual wickedness.   **brazed** brazened, hardened   39 **proof** impenetrable, like *proof* or tested armor.   **sense** feeling.   45 **sets a blister** i.e., brands as a harlot   47 **contraction** the marriage contract   48 **sweet religion makes** i.e., makes marriage vows   49 **rhapsody** senseless string   49–52 **Heaven's . . . act** Heaven's face blushes at this solid world compounded of the various elements, with sorrowful face as though the day of doom were near, and is sick with horror at the deed (i.e., Gertrude's marriage).

That roars so loud and thunders in the index?   *53*
HAMLET (*showing her two likenesses*).
Look here upon this picture, and on this,
The counterfeit presentment of two brothers.   *55*
See what a grace was seated on this brow:
Hyperion's curls, the front of Jove himself,   *57*
An eye like Mars to threaten and command,   *58*
A station like the herald Mercury   *59*
New-lighted on a heaven-kissing hill—   *60*
A combination and a form indeed
Where every god did seem to set his seal   *62*
To give the world assurance of a man.
This was your husband. Look you now what follows:
Here is your husband, like a mildewed ear,   *65*
Blasting his wholesome brother. Have you eyes?   *66*
Could you on this fair mountain leave to feed   *67*
And batten on this moor? Ha, have you eyes?   *68*
You cannot call it love, for at your age
The heyday in the blood is tame, it's humble,   *70*
And waits upon the judgment, and what judgment
Would step from this to this? Sense, sure, you have,   *72*
Else could you not have motion, but sure that sense
Is apoplexed, for madness would not err,   *74*
Nor sense to ecstasy was ne'er so thralled,   *75*
But it reserved some quantity of choice   *76*
To serve in such a difference. What devil was't   *77*
That thus hath cozened you at hoodman-blind?   *78*
Eyes without feeling, feeling without sight,
Ears without hands or eyes, smelling sans all,   *80*
Or but a sickly part of one true sense
Could not so mope. O shame, where is thy blush?   *82*

---

53 index table of contents, prelude or preface. **55 counterfeit presentment** representation in portraiture **57 Hyperion's** the sun-god's. **front** brow **58 Mars** god of war **59 station** manner of standing. **Mercury** winged messenger of the gods **60 New-lighted** newly alighted. **heaven-kissing** reaching to the sky **62 set his seal** i.e., affix his approval **65 ear** i.e., of grain **66 Blasting** blighting **67 leave** cease **68 batten** gorge. **moor** barren or marshy ground. (Suggesting also "dark-skinned.") **70 The heyday . . . blood** (The blood was thought to be the source of sexual desire.) **72 Sense** Perception through the five senses (the functions of the middle or sensible soul) **74 apoplexed** paralyzed. **err** so err **75–7 Nor . . . difference** nor could your physical senses ever have been so enthralled to *ecstasy* or lunacy that they could not distinguish to some degree between Hamlet Senior and Claudius. **78 cozened** cheated. **hoodman-blind** blindman's buff. (In this game, says Hamlet, the devil must have pushed Claudius toward Gertrude while she was blindfolded.) **80 sans** without **82 mope** be dazed, act aimlessly.

Rebellious hell,
If thou canst mutine in a matron's bones,   *84*
To flaming youth let virtue be as wax   *85*
And melt in her own fire. Proclaim no shame   *86*
When the compulsive ardor gives the charge,   *87*
Since frost itself as actively doth burn,   *88*
And reason panders will.   *89*

QUEEN.   Oh, Hamlet, speak no more!
Thou turn'st mine eyes into my very soul,
And there I see such black and grainèd spots   *92*
As will not leave their tinct.   *93*

HAMLET.   Nay, but to live
In the rank sweat of an enseamèd bed,   *94*
Stewed in corruption, honeying and making love   *95*
Over the nasty sty!   *96*

QUEEN.   Oh, speak to me no more!
These words like daggers enter in my ears.
No more, sweet Hamlet!

HAMLET.   A murderer and a villain,
A slave that is not twentieth part the tithe   *100*
Of your precedent lord, a vice of kings,   *101*
A cutpurse of the empire and the rule,
That from a shelf the precious diadem stole
And put it in his pocket!

QUEEN.   No more!   *105*

(*Enter* GHOST, *in his nightgown.*)

HAMLET.   A king of shreds and patches—   *106*
Save me, and hover o'er me with your wings,
You heavenly guards! What would your gracious
    figure?

---

84 mutine mutiny **85–6 To ... fire** when it comes to sexually passionate youth, let virtue melt like a candle or stick of sealing wax held over a candle flame. (There's no point in hoping for self-restraint among young people when matronly women set such a bad example.) **86–9 Proclaim ... will** Call it no shameful business when the compelling ardor of youth delivers the attack, i.e., commits lechery, since the *frost* of advanced age burns with as active a fire of lust and reason perverts itself by fomenting lust rather than restraining it. **92 grainèd** ingrained, indelible **93 leave their tinct** surrender their dark stain. **94 enseamèd** saturated in the grease and filth of passionate lovemaking **95 Stewed** soaked, bathed. (With a suggestion of "stew," brothel.) **96 Over ... sty** (Like barnyard animals.) **100 tithe** tenth part **101 precedent lord** former husband. **vice** (From the morality plays, a model of iniquity and a buffoon.) **105.1 *nightgown*** a robe for indoor wear **106 A king ... patches** i.e., a king whose splendor is all sham; a clown or fool dressed in motley

QUEEN.   Alas, he's mad!

HAMLET.

Do you not come your tardy son to chide,

That, lapsed in time and passion, lets go by   *111*

Th'important acting of your dread command?   *112*

Oh, say!

GHOST.

Do not forget. This visitation

Is but to whet thy almost blunted purpose.   *115*

But look, amazement on thy mother sits.   *116*

Oh, step between her and her fighting soul!

Conceit in weakest bodies strongest works.   *118*

Speak to her, Hamlet.

HAMLET.   How is it with you, lady?

QUEEN.   Alas, how is't with you,

That you do bend your eye on vacancy,

And with th'incorporal air do hold discourse?   *122*

Forth at your eyes your spirits wildly peep,

And, as the sleeping soldiers in th'alarm,   *124*

Your bedded hair, like life in excrements,   *125*

Start up and stand on end. O gentle son,

Upon the heat and flame of thy distemper   *127*

Sprinkle cool patience. Whereon do you look?

HAMLET.

On him, on him! Look you how pale he glares!

His form and cause conjoined, preaching to stones,   *130*

Would make them capable.—Do not look upon me,   *131*

Lest with this piteous action you convert   *132*

My stern effects. Then what I have to do   *133*

Will want true color—tears perchance for blood.   *134*

QUEEN.   To whom do you speak this?

HAMLET.   Do you see nothing there?

---

111 lapsed ... passion having let time and passion slip away   **112 Th'important** the importunate, urgent   **115 whet** sharpen   **116 amazement** distraction   **118 Conceit** Imagination   **122 th'incorporal** the immaterial   **124 as ... th'alarm** like soldiers called out of sleep by an alarum   **125 bedded** laid flat.   **like life in excrements** i.e., as though hair, an outgrowth of the body, had a life of its own. (Hair was thought to be lifeless because it lacks sensation, and so its standing on end would be unnatural and ominous.)   **127 distemper** disorder   **130 His ... conjoined** His appearance joined to his cause for speaking   **131 capable** capable of feeling, receptive.   **132–3 convert ... effects** divert me from my stern duty.   **134 want ... blood** lack plausibility so that (with a play on the normal sense of *color*) I shall shed colorless tears instead of blood.

QUEEN.

Nothing at all, yet all that is I see.

HAMLET.   Nor did you nothing hear?

QUEEN.   No, nothing but ourselves.

HAMLET.

Why, look you there, look how it steals away!

My father, in his habit as he lived!   *141*

Look where he goes even now out at the portal!

(*Exit* GHOST.)

QUEEN.

This is the very coinage of your brain.   *143*

This bodiless creation ecstasy   *144*

Is very cunning in.   *145*

HAMLET.   Ecstasy?

My pulse as yours doth temperately keep time,

And makes as healthful music. It is not madness

That I have uttered. Bring me to the test,

And I the matter will reword, which madness   *150*

Would gambol from. Mother, for love of grace,   *151*

Lay not that flattering unction to your soul   *152*

That not your trespass but my madness speaks.

It will but skin and film the ulcerous place,   *154*

Whiles rank corruption, mining all within,   *155*

Infects unseen. Confess yourself to heaven,

Repent what's past, avoid what is to come,

And do not spread the compost on the weeds   *158*

To make them ranker. Forgive me this my virtue;   *159*

For in the fatness of these pursy times   *160*

Virtue itself of vice must pardon beg,

Yea, curb and woo for leave to do him good.   *162*

QUEEN.

Oh, Hamlet, thou hast cleft my heart in twain.

HAMLET.

Oh, throw away the worser part of it,

And live the purer with the other half.

---

141 habit clothes.   **as** as when   143 **very** mere   144–5 **This . . . in** Madness is skillful in creating this kind of hallucination.   150 **reword** repeat word for word   151 **gambol** skip away   152 **unction** ointment   154 **skin** grow a skin over   155 **mining** working under the surface   158 **compost** manure   159 **this my virtue** my virtuous talk in reproving you   160 **fatness** grossness.   **pursy** flabby, out of shape   162 **curb** bow, bend the knee.   **leave** permission

Good night. But go not to my uncle's bed;
Assume a virtue, if you have it not.
That monster, custom, who all sense doth eat,   *168*
Of habits devil, is angel yet in this,   *169*
That to the use of actions fair and good
He likewise gives a frock or livery   *171*
That aptly is put on. Refrain tonight,   *172*
And that shall lend a kind of easiness
To the next abstinence; the next more easy;
For use almost can change the stamp of nature,   *175*
And either . . . the devil, or throw him out   *176*
With wondrous potency. Once more, good night;
And when you are desirous to be blest,   *178*
I'll blessing beg of you. For this same lord,   *179*

(*pointing to* POLONIUS)

I do repent; but heaven hath pleased it so
To punish me with this, and this with me,   *181*
That I must be their scourge and minister.   *182*
I will bestow him, and will answer well   *183*
The death I gave him. So, again, good night.
I must be cruel only to be kind.
This bad begins, and worse remains behind.   *186*
One word more, good lady.
QUEEN.   What shall I do?
HAMLET.
Not this by no means that I bid you do:
Let the bloat king tempt you again to bed,   *189*
Pinch wanton on your cheek, call you his mouse,   *190*
And let him, for a pair of reechy kisses,   *191*

---

168 who . . . eat which consumes and overwhelms the physical senses   **169 Of habits devil** devil-like in prompting evil habits   **171 livery** an outer appearance, a customary garb (and hence a predisposition easily assumed in time of stress)   **172 aptly** readily   **175 use** habit.   **the stamp of nature** our inborn traits   **176 And either** (A defective line, often emended by inserting the word "master" after *either*, following the Third Quarto and early editors, or some other word such as "shame," "lodge," "curb," or "house.")   **178–9 when . . . you** i.e., when you are ready to be penitent and seek God's blessing, I will ask your blessing as a dutiful son should.   **181 To punish . . . with me** to seek retribution from me for killing Polonius, and from him through my means   **182 their scourge and minister** i.e., agent of heavenly retribution.   **183 bestow** stow, dispose of.   **answer** account or pay for   **186 This** i.e., The killing of Polonius.   **behind** to come.   **189 bloat** bloated   **190 Pinch wanton** i.e., leave his love pinches on your cheeks, branding you as wanton   **191 reechy** dirty, filthy

Or paddling in your neck with his damned fingers,   192
Make you to ravel all this matter out   193
That I essentially am not in madness,
But mad in craft. 'Twere good you let him know,   195
For who that's but a queen, fair, sober, wise,
Would from a paddock, from a bat, a gib,   197
Such dear concernings hide? Who would do so?   198
No, in despite of sense and secrecy,   199
Unpeg the basket on the house's top,   200
Let the birds fly, and like the famous ape,   201
To try conclusions, in the basket creep   202
And break your own neck down.   203
QUEEN.
Be thou assured, if words be made of breath,
And breath of life, I have no life to breathe
What thou hast said to me.
HAMLET.
I must to England. You know that?
QUEEN.   Alack,
I had forgot. 'Tis so concluded on.
HAMLET.
There's letters sealed, and my two schoolfellows,
Whom I will trust as I will adders fanged,
They bear the mandate; they must sweep my way   211
And marshal me to knavery. Let it work.   212
For 'tis the sport to have the engineer   213
Hoist with his own petard, and 't shall go hard   214
But I will delve one yard below their mines   215
And blow them at the moon. Oh, 'tis most sweet

---

192 **paddling** fingering amorously   193 **ravel . . . out** unravel, disclose   195 **in craft** by cunning. **good** (Said sarcastically; also the following eight lines.)   197 **paddock** toad.   **gib** tomcat   198 **dear concernings** important affairs   199 **sense and secrecy** secrecy that common sense requires   200 **Unpeg the basket** open the cage, i.e., let out the secret   201 **famous ape** (In a story now lost.)   202 **try conclusions** test the outcome (in which the ape apparently enters a cage from which birds have been released and then tries to fly out of the cage as they have done, falling to its death)   203 **down** in the fall.   211–12 **sweep . . . knavery** sweep a path before me and conduct me to some *knavery* or treachery prepared for me.   212 **work** proceed.   213 **engineer** maker of *engines* of war   214 **Hoist with** blown up by.   **petard** an explosive used to blow in a door or make a breach   214–15 **'t shall . . . will** unless luck is against me, I will   215 **mines** tunnels used in warfare to undermine the enemy's emplacements; Hamlet will countermine by going under their mines

When in one line two crafts directly meet.   *217*
This man shall set me packing.   *218*
I'll lug the guts into the neighbor room.
Mother, good night indeed. This counselor
Is now most still, most secret, and most grave,
Who was in life a foolish prating knave.—
Come, sir, to draw toward an end with you.—   *223*
Good night, mother.

(*Exeunt separately,* HAMLET *dragging in* POLONIUS.)

4.1

Enter KING *and* QUEEN, *with* ROSENCRANTZ *and*
GUILDENSTERN.

KING.
There's matter in these sighs, these profound heaves.   *1*
You must translate; 'tis fit we understand them.
Where is your son?
QUEEN.
Bestow this place on us a little while.

(*Exeunt* ROSENCRANTZ *and* GUILDENSTERN.)

Ah, mine own lord, what have I seen tonight!
KING.
What, Gertrude? How does Hamlet?
QUEEN.
Mad as the sea and wind when both contend
Which is the mightier. In his lawless fit,

---

217 in one line i.e., mines and countermines on a collision course, or the countermines directly below the mines. **crafts** acts of guile, plots **218 set me packing** set me to making schemes, and set me to lugging (him), and, also, send me off in a hurry. **223 draw . . . end** finish up. (With a pun on *draw*, "pull.")

4.1 Location: The castle.
0.1 Enter . . . Queen (Some editors argue that Gertrude does not in fact exit at the end of 3.4 and that the scene is continuous here. It is true that the Folio ends 3.4 with "*Exit Hamlet tugging in Polonius*," not naming Gertrude, and opens 4.1 with "*Enter King*." Yet the Second Quarto concludes 3.4 with a simple "*Exit*," which often stands ambiguously for a single exit or an exeunt in early modern texts, and then starts 4.1 with "*Enter King, and Queene, with Rosencraus and Guyldensterne*." The King's opening lines in 4.1 suggest that he has had time, during a brief intervening pause, to become aware of Gertrude's highly wrought emotional state. In line 35, the King refers to Gertrude's *closet* as though it were elsewhere. The differences between the Second Quarto and the Folio offer an alternative staging. In either case, 4.1 follows swiftly upon 3.4.) **1 matter** significance. **heaves** heavy sighs.

Behind the arras hearing something stir,
Whips out his rapier, cries, "A rat, a rat!"
And in this brainish apprehension kills   11
The unseen good old man.   12
KING.   Oh, heavy deed!
It had been so with us, had we been there.   13
His liberty is full of threats to all—
To you yourself, to us, to everyone.
Alas, how shall this bloody deed be answered?   16
It will be laid to us, whose providence   17
Should have kept short, restrained, and out of haunt   18
This mad young man. But so much was our love,
We would not understand what was most fit,
But, like the owner of a foul disease,
To keep it from divulging, let it feed   22
Even on the pith of life. Where is he gone?
QUEEN.
To draw apart the body he hath killed,
O'er whom his very madness, like some ore   25
Among a mineral of metals base,   26
Shows itself pure: 'a weeps for what is done.
KING.   Oh, Gertrude, come away!
The sun no sooner shall the mountains touch
But we will ship him hence, and this vile deed
We must with all our majesty and skill
Both countenance and excuse.—Ho, Guildenstern!   32

(*Enter* ROSENCRANTZ *and* GUILDENSTERN.)

Friends both, go join you with some further aid.
Hamlet in madness hath Polonius slain,
And from his mother's closet hath he dragged him.
Go seek him out, speak fair, and bring the body   36
Into the chapel. I pray you, haste in this.

(*Exeunt* ROSENCRANTZ *and* GUILDENSTERN.)

Come, Gertrude, we'll call up our wisest friends

---

11 brainish apprehension frenzied misapprehension   **12 heavy** grievous   **13 us** i.e., me. (The royal "we"; also in line 15.)   **16 answered** explained   **17 providence** foresight   **18 short** i.e., on a short tether.   **out of haunt** secluded   **22 from divulging** from becoming publicly known   **25 ore** vein of gold   **26 mineral** mine   **32 countenance** put the best face on   **36 fair** gently, courteously

And let them know both what we mean to do
And what's untimely done   40
Whose whisper o'er the world's diameter,   41
As level as the cannon to his blank,   42
Transports his poisoned shot, may miss our name
And hit the woundless air. Oh, come away!   44
My soul is full of discord and dismay.   (*Exeunt.*)

4.2

Enter HAMLET.

HAMLET.   Safely stowed.
ROSENCRANTZ, GUILDENSTERN *(within)*. Hamlet! Lord
    Hamlet!
HAMLET.   But soft, what noise? Who calls on Hamlet? Oh,
    here they come.

(*Enter* ROSENCRANTZ *and* GUILDENSTERN.)

ROSENCRANTZ.
    What have you done, my lord, with the dead body?
HAMLET.
    Compounded it with dust, whereto 'tis kin.
ROSENCRANTZ.
    Tell us where 'tis, that we may take it thence
    And bear it to the chapel.
HAMLET.   Do not believe it.
ROSENCRANTZ.   Believe what?
HAMLET.   That I can keep your counsel and not mine   12
    own. Besides, to be demanded of a sponge, what rep-   13
    lication should be made by the son of a king?   14
ROSENCRANTZ.   Take you me for a sponge, my lord?
HAMLET.   Ay, sir, that soaks up the King's countenance,   16

---

40 And . . . done (A defective line; conjectures as to the missing words include "So, haply, slander" [Capell and others]; "For, haply, slander" [Theobald and others]; and "So envious slander" [Jenkins].)   41 diameter extent from side to side   42 As level with as direct aim.   his blank its target at point-blank range   44 woundless invulnerable

4.2 Location: The castle.
12–13 That . . . own i.e., Don't expect me to do as you bid me and not follow my own counsel.
13 demanded of questioned by   13–14 replication reply

his rewards, his authorities. But such officers do the 17
King best service in the end. He keeps them, like an
ape, an apple, in the corner of his jaw, first mouthed
to be last swallowed. When he needs what you have
gleaned, it is but squeezing you, and, sponge, you
shall be dry again.

ROSENCRANTZ.   I understand you not, my lord.

HAMLET.   I am glad of it. A knavish speech sleeps in a 24
foolish ear.

ROSENCRANTZ.   My lord, you must tell us where the
body is and go with us to the King.

HAMLET.   The body is with the King, but the King is not 28
with the body. The King is a thing— 29

GUILDENSTERN.   A thing, my lord?

HAMLET.   Of nothing. Bring me to him. Hide fox, and all 31
after!   (*Exeunt, running.*) 32

4.3

Enter KING, *and two or three.*

KING.
I have sent to seek him, and to find the body.
How dangerous is it that this man goes loose!
Yet must not we put the strong law on him.
He's loved of the distracted multitude, 4
Who like not in their judgment, but their eyes, 5
And where 'tis so, th'offender's scourge is weighed, 6
But never the offense. To bear all smooth and even, 7
This sudden sending him away must seem

---

16 **countenance** favor   17 **authorities** delegated power, influence   24 **sleeps in** has no meaning to
28–9 **The...body** (Perhaps alludes to the legal commonplace of "the king's two bodies," which drew
a distinction between the sacred office of kingship and the particular mortal who possessed it at any
given time. Hence, although Claudius's body is necessarily a part of him, true kingship is not contained in it. Similarly, Claudius will have Polonius's body when it is found, but there is no kingship
in this business either.)   31 **Of nothing** (1) of no account (2) lacking the essence of kingship, as in
lines 28–9 and note.   31–2 **Hide...after** (An old signal cry in the game of hide-and-seek, suggesting that Hamlet now runs away from them.)

4.3. Location: The castle.
4 **of** by.   **distracted** fickle, unstable   5 **Who...eyes** who choose not by judgment but by appearance   6–7 **th'offender's...offense** i.e., the populace often takes umbrage at the severity of a punishment without taking into account the gravity of the crime.   7 **To...even** To manage the business in an unprovocative way

Deliberate pause. Diseases desperate grown   9
By desperate appliance are relieved,   10
Or not at all.

(*Enter* ROSENCRANTZ, GUILDENSTERN,
and all the rest.)

How now, what hath befall'n?
ROSENCRANTZ.
Where the dead body is bestowed, my lord,
We cannot get from him.
KING. But where is he?
ROSENCRANTZ.
Without, my lord; guarded, to know your pleasure.   14
KING.
Bring him before us.
ROSENCRANTZ (*calling*). Ho! Bring in the lord.

(*They enter with* HAMLET.)

KING. Now, Hamlet, where's Polonius?
HAMLET. At supper.
KING. At supper? Where?
HAMLET. Not where he eats, but where 'a is eaten. A
certain convocation of politic worms are e'en at him.   20
Your worm is your only emperor for diet. We fat all   21
creatures else to fat us, and we fat ourselves for maggots. Your fat king and your lean beggar is but
variable service—two dishes, but to one table. That's   24
the end.
KING. Alas, alas!
HAMLET. A man may fish with the worm that hath eat   27
of a king, and eat of the fish that hath fed of that
worm.
KING. What dost thou mean by this?
HAMLET. Nothing but to show you how a king may go
a progress through the guts of a beggar.   32

---

9 **Deliberate pause** carefully considered action   10 **appliance** remedies   14 **Without** Outside
20 **politic worms** crafty worms (suited to a master spy like Polonius).   **e'en** even now   21 **Your**
worm Your average worm. (Compare *your fat king and your lean beggar* in line 23.)   **diet** food, eating. (With a punning reference to the Diet of Worms, a famous *convocation* held in 1521.)
24 **service** food served at table. (Worms feed on kings and beggars alike.)   27 **eat** eaten.
(Pronounced *et.*)   32 **progress** royal journey of state

KING.   Where is Polonius?

HAMLET.   In heaven. Send thither to see. If your messenger find him not there, seek him i'th'other place yourself. But if indeed you find him not within this month,
you shall nose him as you go up the stairs into the   *37*
lobby.

KING (*to some attendants*).   Go seek him there.

HAMLET.   'A will stay till you come.   (*Exeunt attendants.*)

KING.

Hamlet, this deed, for thine especial safety—
Which we do tender, as we dearly grieve   *42*
For that which thou hast done—must send thee hence
With fiery quickness. Therefore prepare thyself.
The bark is ready, and the wind at help,   *45*
Th'associates tend, and everything is bent   *46*
For England.

HAMLET.   For England!

KING.   Ay, Hamlet.

HAMLET.   Good.

KING.

So is it, if thou knew'st our purposes.

HAMLET..   I see a cherub that sees them. But come, for   *52*
England! Farewell, dear mother.

KING.   Thy loving father, Hamlet.

HAMLET.   My mother. Father and mother is man and
wife, man and wife is one flesh, and so, my mother.
Come, for England!   (*Exit.*)

KING.

Follow him at foot; tempt him with speed aboard.   *58*
Delay it not. I'll have him hence tonight.
Away! For everything is sealed and done
That else leans on th'affair. Pray you, make haste.   *61*

(*Exeunt all but the* KING.)

And, England, if my love thou hold'st at aught—   *62*
As my great power thereof may give thee sense,   *63*

---

37 nose smell   **42 tender** regard, hold dear.   **dearly** intensely   **45 bark** sailing vessel   **46 tend**
wait.   **bent** in readiness   **52 cherub** (Cherubim are angels of knowledge. Hamlet hints that both he
and heaven are onto Claudius's tricks.)   **58 at foot** close behind, at heel   **61 leans on** bears upon, is
related to   **62 England** i.e., King of England.   **at aught** at any value   **63 As . . . sense** for so my
great power may give you a just appreciation of the importance of valuing my love

Since yet thy cicatrice looks raw and red   64
After the Danish sword, and thy free awe   65
Pays homage to us—thou mayst not coldly set   66
Our sovereign process, which imports at full,   67
By letters congruing to that effect,   68
The present death of Hamlet. Do it, England,   69
For like the hectic in my blood he rages,   70
And thou must cure me. Till I know 'tis done,
Howe'er my haps, my joys were ne'er begun.   (*Exit.*) 72

4.4

Enter FORTINBRAS *with his army over the stage.*

FORTINBRAS.
   Go, Captain, from me greet the Danish king.
   Tell him that by his license Fortinbras   2
   Craves the conveyance of a promised march   3
   Over his kingdom. You know the rendezvous.
   If that His Majesty would aught with us,
   We shall express our duty in his eye;   6
   And let him know so.
CAPTAIN.   I will do't, my lord.
FORTINBRAS.   Go softly on.   9

(*Exeunt all but the* CAPTAIN.)

(*Enter* HAMLET, ROSENCRANTZ, GUILDENSTERN, *etc.*)

HAMLET.   Good sir, whose powers are these?   10
CAPTAIN.   They are of Norway, sir.
HAMLET.   How purposed, sir, I pray you?
CAPTAIN.   Against some part of Poland.
HAMLET.   Who commands them, sir?

---

64 cicatrice scar **65 free awe** unconstrained show of respect **66 coldly set** regard with indifference
67 process command. **imports at full** conveys specific directions for **68 congruing** agreeing **69 present** immediate **70 hectic** persistent fever **72 Howe'er . . . begun** whatever else happens, I cannot begin to be happy.

4.4 Location: The coast of Denmark.
2 license permission **3 conveyance** unhindered passage **6 We . . . eye** I will come pay my respects in person **9 softly** slowly, circumspectly **10 powers** forces

CAPTAIN.

    The nephew to old Norway, Fortinbras.

HAMLET.

    Goes it against the main of Poland, sir,   16

    Or for some frontier?

CAPTAIN.

    Truly to speak, and with no addition,   18

    We go to gain a little patch of ground

    That hath in it no profit but the name.

    To pay five ducats, five, I would not farm it;   21

    Nor will it yield to Norway or the Pole

    A ranker rate, should it be sold in fee.   23

HAMLET.

    Why, then the Polack never will defend it.

CAPTAIN.

    Yes, it is already garrisoned.

HAMLET.

    Two thousand souls and twenty thousand ducats

    Will not debate the question of this straw.   27

    This is th'impostume of much wealth and peace,   28

    That inward breaks, and shows no cause without   29

    Why the man dies. I humbly thank you, sir.

CAPTAIN.

    God b'wi'you, sir.   (*Exit.*)

ROSENCRANTZ.   Will't please you go, my lord?

HAMLET.

    I'll be with you straight. Go a little before.

(*Exeunt all except* HAMLET.)

    How all occasions do inform against me   33

    And spur my dull revenge! What is a man,

    If his chief good and market of his time   35

    Be but to sleep and feed? A beast, no more.

    Sure he that made us with such large discourse,   37

    Looking before and after, gave us not   38

    That capability and godlike reason

---

16 **main** main part   18 **addition** exaggeration   21 **To pay** i.e., For a yearly rental of.   **farm it** take a lease of it   23 **ranker** higher.   **in fee** fee simple, outright.   27 **debate . . . straw** argue about this trifling matter.   28 **th'impostume** the abscess   29 **inward breaks** festers within.   **without** externally   33 **inform against** denounce; take shape against   35 **market of** profit of   37 **discourse** power of reasoning   38 **Looking before and after** able to review past events and anticipate the future

To fust in us unused. Now, whether it be   *40*
Bestial oblivion, or some craven scruple   *41*
Of thinking too precisely on th'event—   *42*
A thought which, quartered, hath but one part
   wisdom
And ever three parts coward—I do not know
Why yet I live to say "This thing's to do,"
Sith I have cause, and will, and strength, and means   *46*
To do't. Examples gross as earth exhort me: *47*
Witness this army of such mass and charge,   *48*
Led by a delicate and tender prince,   *49*
Whose spirit with divine ambition puffed
Makes mouths at the invisible event,   *51*
Exposing what is mortal and unsure
To all that fortune, death, and danger dare,   *53*
Even for an eggshell. Rightly to be great   *54*
Is not to stir without great argument,   *55*
But greatly to find quarrel in a straw   *56*
When honor's at the stake. How stand I, then,   *57*
That have a father killed, a mother stained,
Excitements of my reason and my blood,   *59*
And let all sleep, while to my shame I see
The imminent death of twenty thousand men
That for a fantasy and trick of fame   *62*
Go to their graves like beds, fight for a plot   *63*
Whereon the numbers cannot try the cause,   *64*
Which is not tomb enough and continent   *65*
To hide the slain? Oh, from this time forth
My thoughts be bloody or be nothing worth!   (*Exit.*)

---

40 fust grow moldy   **41 oblivion** forgetfulness.   **craven** cowardly   **42 precisely** scrupulously. **th'event** the outcome   **46 Sith** since   **47 gross** obvious   **48 charge** expense   **49 delicate and tender** of fine and youthful qualities   **51 Makes mouths** makes scornful faces.   **invisible event** unforeseeable outcome   **53 dare** could do (to him)   **54–7 Rightly ... stake** True greatness is not a matter of being moved to action solely by a great cause; rather, it is to respond greatly to an apparently trivial cause when honor is at the stake.   **59 blood** (The supposed seat of the passions.)   **62 fantasy** fanciful caprice, illusion.   **trick** trifle, deceit   **63 plot** plot of ground   **64 Whereon ... cause** on which there is insufficient room for the soldiers needed to fight for it.   **65 continent** receptacle, container

4.5

Enter HORATIO, QUEEN GERTRUDE, *and a* GENTLEMAN.

QUEEN.
    I will not speak with her.
GENTLEMAN.   She is importunate,
    Indeed distract. Her mood will needs be pitied.   *2*
QUEEN.   What would she have?
GENTLEMAN.
    She speaks much of her father, says she hears
    There's tricks i'th' world, and hems, and beats her   *5*
        heart,
    Spurns enviously at straws, speaks things in doubt   *6*
    That carry but half sense. Her speech is nothing,
    Yet the unshapèd use of it doth move   *8*
    The hearers to collection; they yawn at it,   *9*
    And botch the words up fit to their own thoughts,   *10*
    Which, as her winks and nods and gestures yield   *11*
        them,
    Indeed would make one think there might be thought,   *12*
    Though nothing sure, yet much unhappily.   *13*
HORATIO.
    'Twere good she were spoken with, for she may strew
    Dangerous conjectures in ill-breeding minds.   *15*
QUEEN.   Let her come in.   (*Exit* GENTLEMAN.)
    (*Aside*) To my sick soul, as sin's true nature is,
    Each toy seems prologue to some great amiss.   *18*
    So full of artless jealousy is guilt,   *19*
    It spills itself in fearing to be spilt.   *20*

(*Enter* OPHELIA, *distracted.*)

4.5 Location: The castle.
2 distract out of her mind   **5 tricks** deceptions.   **hems** clears her throat, makes "hmm" sounds.
heart i.e., breast   **6 Spurns ... straws** kicks spitefully, takes offense at trifles.   **in doubt** of obscure
meaning   **8 unshapèd use** incoherent manner   **9 collection** inference, a guess at some sort of meaning.   **yawn** gape, wonder; grasp. (The Folio reading, "aim," is possible.)   **10 botch** patch   **11**
Which which words.   **yield** deliver, represent   **12–13 there might ... unhappily** that a great deal
could be guessed at of a most unfortunate nature, even if one couldn't be at all sure.   **15 ill-breed-**
ing prone to suspect the worst and to make mischief   **18 toy** trifle.   **amiss** calamity.   **19–20 So ...**
spilt Guilt is so burdened with conscience and guileless fear of detection that it reveals itself through
apprehension of disaster.   **20.1 *Enter Ophelia*** (In the First Quarto, Ophelia enters, "*playing on a
lute, and her hair down, singing.*")

OPHELIA.
Where is the beauteous majesty of Denmark?
QUEEN.   How now, Ophelia?
OPHELIA *(she sings)*.
"How should I your true love know
From another one?
By his cockle hat and staff,   *25*
And his sandal shoon."   *26*
QUEEN.   Alas, sweet lady, what imports this song?
OPHELIA.   Say you? Nay, pray you, mark.
"He is dead and gone, lady,   *(Song.)*
He is dead and gone;
At his head a grass-green turf,
At his heels a stone."
Oho!   *33*
QUEEN.   Nay, but Ophelia—
OPHELIA.   Pray you, mark.
(Sings) "White his shroud as the mountain snow"—

(Enter KING.*)*

QUEEN.   Alas, look here, my lord.
OPHELIA.
"Larded with sweet flowers;   *(Song.)* *38*
Which bewept to the ground did not go
With true-love showers."   *40*
KING.   How do you, pretty lady?
OPHELIA.   Well, God 'ild you! They say the owl was a   *42*
baker's daughter. Lord, we know what we are, but
know not what we may be. God be at your table!
KING.   Conceit upon her father.   *45*
OPHELIA.   Pray let's have no words of this; but when
they ask you what it means, say you this:
"Tomorrow is Saint Valentine's day,   *(Song.)*
All in the morning betime,   *49*
And I a maid at your window,

---

25 cockle hat hat with cockleshell stuck in it as a sign that the wearer had been a pilgrim to the
shrine of Saint James of Compostella in Spain.   **26 shoon** shoes.   **33 Oho!** (Perhaps a sigh.)
38 Larded strewn, bedecked   **40 showers** i.e., tears   **42 God 'ild** God yield or reward.   **owl** (Refers
to a legend about a baker's daughter who was turned into an owl for being ungenerous when Jesus
begged a loaf of bread.)   **45 Conceit** Fancy, brooding   **49 betime** early

To be your Valentine.
Then up he rose, and donned his clothes,
    And dupped the chamber door,   *53*
Let in the maid, that out a maid
    Never departed more."

KING.   Pretty Ophelia—

OPHELIA.   Indeed, la, without an oath, I'll make an end
on't:

    (*Sings*)   "By Gis and by Saint Charity,   *59*
        Alack, and fie for shame!
    Young men will do't, if they come to't;
        By Cock, they are to blame.   *62*
    Quoth she, 'Before you tumbled me,
        You promised me to wed.'"

He answers:

    "'So would I ha' done, by yonder sun,
    An thou hadst not come to my bed.'"   *67*

KING.   How long hath she been thus?

OPHELIA.   I hope all will be well. We must be patient,
but I cannot choose but weep to think they would lay
him i'th' cold ground. My brother shall know of it.
And so I thank you for your good counsel. Come, my
coach! Good night, ladies, good night, sweet ladies,
good night, good night.   (*Exit.*)

KING (*to* HORATIO).
    Follow her close. Give her good watch, I pray you.

(*Exit* HORATIO.)

    Oh, this is the poison of deep grief; it springs
    All from her father's death—and now behold!
    Oh, Gertrude, Gertrude,
    When sorrows come, they come not single spies,   *79*
    But in battalions. First, her father slain;
    Next, your son gone, and he most violent author
    Of his own just remove; the people muddied,   *82*
    Thick and unwholesome in their thoughts and
        whispers

---

53 dupped did up, opened   **59 Gis** Jesus   **62 Cock** (A perversion of "God" in oaths; here also with
a quibble on the slang word for penis.)   **67 An** if   **79 spies** scouts sent in advance of the main force
82 remove removal.   **muddied** stirred up, confused

For good Polonius' death—and we have done but
    greenly, 84
In hugger-mugger to inter him; poor Ophelia 85
Divided from herself and her fair judgment,
Without the which we are pictures or mere beasts;
Last, and as much containing as all these, 88
Her brother is in secret come from France,
Feeds on this wonder, keeps himself in clouds, 90
And wants not buzzers to infect his ear 91
With pestilent speeches of his father's death,
Wherein necessity, of matter beggared, 93
Will nothing stick our person to arraign 94
In ear and ear. Oh, my dear Gertrude, this, 95
Like to a murd'ring piece, in many places 96
Gives me superfluous death.   *(A noise within.)* 97
QUEEN.   Alack, what noise is this?
KING.   Attend! 99
    Where is my Switzers? Let them guard the door. 100

(Enter a MESSENGER.*)*

    What is the matter?
MESSENGER.   Save yourself, my lord!
    The ocean, overpeering of his list, 102
    Eats not the flats with more impetuous haste 103
    Than young Laertes, in a riotous head, 104
    O'erbears your officers. The rabble call him lord,
    And, as the world were now but to begin, 106
    Antiquity forgot, custom not known, 107
    The ratifiers and props of every word, 108
    They cry, "Choose we! Laertes shall be king!"
    Caps, hands, and tongues applaud it to the clouds, 110

---

84 greenly foolishly   **85 hugger-mugger** secret haste   **88 as much containing** as full of serious matter   **90 Feeds . . . clouds** feeds his resentment on this whole shocking turn of events, keeps himself aloof and mysterious.   **91 wants** lacks. **buzzers** gossipers, informers   **93 necessity** i.e., the need to invent some plausible explanation. **of matter beggared** unprovided with facts   **94–5 Will . . . ear** will not hesitate to accuse my (royal) person in everybody's ears.   **96 murd'ring piece** cannon loaded so as to scatter its shot   **97 Gives . . . death** kills me over and over.   **99 Attend!** Guard me!   **100 Switzers** Swiss guards, mercenaries   **102 overpeering of his list** overflowing its shore, boundary   **103 flats** i.e., flatlands near shore. **impetuous** violent (perhaps also with the meaning of *impiteous* ["impitious," Q2], "pitiless")   **104 riotous head** insurrectionary advance   **106–8 And . . . word** and, as if the world were to be started all over afresh, utterly setting aside all ancient traditional customs that should confirm and underprop our every word and promise.   **110 Caps** (The caps are thrown in the air.)

"Laertes shall be king, Laertes king!"
QUEEN.
How cheerfully on the false trail they cry!

(*A noise within.*)
Oh, this is counter, you false Danish dogs!   *113*

(*Enter* LAERTES *with others.*)

KING.   The doors are broke.
LAERTES.
Where is this King?—Sirs, stand you all without.
ALL.   No, let's come in.
LAERTES.   I pray you, give me leave.
ALL.   We will, we will.
LAERTES.   I thank you. Keep the door.   (*Exeunt followers.*)
Oh, thou vile king,
Give me my father!
QUEEN (*restraining him*).   Calmly, good Laertes.
LAERTES.
That drop of blood that's calm proclaims me bastard,
Cries cuckold to my father, brands the harlot
Even here between the chaste unsmirchèd brow   *123*
Of my true mother.
KING.   What is the cause, Laertes,
That thy rebellion looks so giantlike?   *125*
Let him go, Gertrude. Do not fear our person.   *126*
There's such divinity doth hedge a king   *127*
That treason can but peep to what it would,   *128*
Acts little of his will. Tell me, Laertes,   *129*
Why thou art thus incensed. Let him go, Gertrude.
Speak, man.
LAERTES.   Where is my father?
KING.   Dead.
QUEEN.
But not by him.
KING.   Let him demand his fill.

---

113 **counter** (A hunting term, meaning to follow the trail in a direction opposite to that which the game has taken.)   123 **between** amidst   125 **giantlike** (Recalling the rising of the giants of Greek mythology against Olympus.)   126 **fear our** fear for my   127 **hedge** protect, as with a surrounding barrier   128 **can ... would** can only peep furtively, as through a barrier, at what it would intend   129 **Acts ... will** (but) performs little of what it intends.

LAERTES.
How came he dead? I'll not be juggled with. 133
To hell, allegiance! Vows, to the blackest devil!
Conscience and grace, to the profoundest pit!
I dare damnation. To this point I stand, 136
That both the worlds I give to negligence, 137
Let come what comes, only I'll be revenged
Most throughly for my father. 139
KING. Who shall stay you?
LAERTES. My will, not all the world's. 141
And for my means, I'll husband them so well 142
They shall go far with little.
KING. Good Laertes,
If you desire to know the certainty
Of your dear father, is't writ in your revenge
That, swoopstake, you will draw both friend and foe, 146
Winner and loser?
LAERTES. None but his enemies.
KING. Will you know them, then?
LAERTES.
To his good friends thus wide I'll ope my arms,
And like the kind life-rendering pelican 151
Repast them with my blood. 152
KING. Why, now you speak
Like a good child and a true gentleman.
That I am guiltless of your father's death,
And am most sensibly in grief for it, 155
It shall as level to your judgment 'pear 156
As day does to your eye.   (*A noise within.*)
LAERTES.
How now, what noise is that?

(*Enter* OPHELIA.)

KING. Let her come in.

_____

133 **juggled with** cheated, deceived   136 **To ... stand** I am resolved in this   137 **both ... negligence** i.e., both this world and the next are of no consequence to me   139 **throughly** thoroughly   141 **My will ... world's** I'll stop (*stay*) when my will is accomplished, not for anyone else's.   142 **for** as for   146 **swoopstake** i.e., indiscriminately. (Literally, taking all stakes on the gambling table at once. *Draw* is also a gambling term, meaning "take from.")   151 **pelican** (Refers to the belief that the female pelican fed its young with its own blood.)   152 **Repast** feed   155 **sensibly** feelingly   156 **level** plain

LAERTES.
O heat, dry up my brains! Tears seven times salt
Burn out the sense and virtue of mine eye!   160
By heaven, thy madness shall be paid with weight   161
Till our scale turn the beam. O rose of May!   162
Dear maid, kind sister, sweet Ophelia!
O heavens, is't possible a young maid's wits
Should be as mortal as an old man's life?
Nature is fine in love, and where 'tis fine   166
It sends some precious instance of itself   167
After the thing it loves.   168
OPHELIA.
"They bore him barefaced on the bier,   *(Song.)*
    Hey non nonny, nonny, hey nonny,
And in his grave rained many a tear—"
Fare you well, my dove!
LAERTES.
Hadst thou thy wits and didst persuade revenge,
It could not move thus.
OPHELIA.   You must sing "A-down a-down," and you   175
"call him a-down-a." Oh, how the wheel becomes it! It 176
is the false steward that stole his master's daughter. 177
LAERTES.   This nothing's more than matter.   178
OPHELIA.   There's rosemary, that's for remembrance; 179
pray you, love, remember. And there is pansies; that's 180
for thoughts.
LAERTES.   A document in madness, thoughts and re-   182
membrance fitted.
OPHELIA.   There's fennel for you, and columbines.   184

---

160 **virtue** faculty, power   161 **paid with weight** repaid, avenged equally or more   162 **beam** cross-bar of a balance   166–8 **Nature . . . loves** Human nature is exquisitely sensitive in matters of love, and in cases of sudden loss it sends some precious part of itself after the lost object of that love. (In this case, Ophelia's sanity deserts her out of sorrow for her lost father and perhaps too out of her love for Hamlet.)   175–6 **You . . . a-down-a** (Ophelia assigns the singing of refrains, like her own "Hey non nonny," to others present.)   176 **wheel** spinning wheel as accompaniment to the song, or refrain.   177 **false steward** (The story is unknown.)   178 **This . . . matter** This seeming nonsense is more eloquent than sane utterance.   179 **rosemary** (Used as a symbol of remembrance both at weddings and at funerals.)   180 **pansies** (Emblems of love and courtship; perhaps from French *pensées,* "thoughts.")   182 **document** instruction, lesson   184 **There's fennel . . . columbines** (*Fennel* betokens flattery; *columbines,* unchastity or ingratitude. Throughout, Ophelia addresses her various listeners, giving one flower to one and another to another, perhaps with particular symbolic significance in each case.)

There's rue for you, and here's some for me; we may   *185*
call it herb of grace o' Sundays. You must wear your
rue with a difference. There's a daisy. I would give   *187*
you some violets, but they withered all when my   *188*
father died. They say 'a made a good end—
(*Sings*) "For bonny sweet Robin is all my joy."
LAERTES.
Thought and affliction, passion, hell itself,   *191*
She turns to favor and to prettiness.   *192*
OPHELIA.
"And will 'a not come again?   *(Song.)*
And will 'a not come again?
   No, no, he is dead.
   Go to thy deathbed,
He never will come again.
"His beard was as white as snow,
   All flaxen was his poll.   *199*
   He is gone, he is gone,
   And we cast away moan.
God ha' mercy on his soul!"
And of all Christian souls, I pray God. God b'wi'you.

(*Exit, followed by* GERTRUDE.)

LAERTES.   Do you see this, O God?
KING.
Laertes, I must commune with your grief,
Or you deny me right. Go but apart,
Make choice of whom your wisest friends you will,   *207*
And they shall hear and judge twixt you and me.
If by direct or by collateral hand   *209*
They find us touched, we will our kingdom give,   *210*
Our crown, our life, and all that we call ours
To you in satisfaction; but if not,
Be you content to lend your patience to us,

---

185 rue (Emblem of repentance—a signification that is evident in its popular name, *herb of grace*.)
187 with a difference (A device used in heraldry to distinguish one family from another on the coat
of arms, here suggesting that Ophelia and the others have different causes of sorrow and repentance;
perhaps with a play on *rue* in the sense of "ruth," "pity.")   **daisy** (Emblem of love's victims and of
faithlessness.)   **188 violets** (Emblems of faithfulness.)   **191 Thought** Melancholy.   **passion** suffering   **192 favor** grace, beauty   **199 poll** head   **207 whom** whichever of   **209 collateral hand** indi-
rect agency   **210 us touched** me implicated

And we shall jointly labor with your soul
To give it due content.
LAERTES.   Let this be so.
His means of death, his obscure funeral—
No trophy, sword, nor hatchment o'er his bones,   217
No noble rite, nor formal ostentation—   218
Cry to be heard, as 'twere from heaven to earth,
That I must call't in question.   220
KING.   So you shall,
And where th'offense is, let the great ax fall.
I pray you, go with me.   (*Exeunt.*)

4.6

Enter HORATIO *and others.*

HORATIO.
What are they that would speak with me?
GENTLEMAN.   Seafaring men, sir. They say they have
letters for you.   3
HORATIO.   Let them come in.   (*Exit* GENTLEMAN.)
I do not know from what part of the world
I should be greeted, if not from Lord Hamlet.

(*Enter* SAILORS.)

FIRST SAILOR.   God bless you, sir.
HORATIO.   Let him bless thee too.
FIRST SAILOR.   'A shall, sir, an't please him. There's a   9
letter for you, sir—it came from th'ambassador that   10
was bound for England—if your name be Horatio, as
I am let to know it is.   (*He gives a letter.*)
HORATIO (*reads*).   "Horatio, when thou shalt have over —   13
looked this, give these fellows some means to the King;   14
they have letters for him. Ere we were two days old at

---

217 **trophy** memorial.   **hatchment** tablet displaying the armorial bearings of a deceased person
218 **ostentation** ceremony   220 **That** so that.   **call't in question** demand an explanation.

4.6. Location: The castle.
3 **letters** a letter   9 **an't** if it   10 **th'ambassador** (Hamlet's ostensible role; see 3.2.172-3.)
13–14 **overlooked** looked over   14 **means** means of access

sea, a pirate of very warlike appointment gave us 16
chase. Finding ourselves too slow of sail, we put on a
compelled valor, and in the grapple I boarded them.
On the instant they got clear of our ship, so I alone
became their prisoner. They have dealt with me like
thieves of mercy, but they knew what they did: I am to 21
do a good turn for them. Let the King have the letters
I have sent, and repair thou to me with as much speed 23
as thou wouldest fly death. I have words to speak in
thine ear will make thee dumb, yet are they much too
light for the bore of the matter. These good fellows will 26
bring thee where I am. Rosencrantz and Guildenstern
hold their course for England. Of them I have much to
tell thee. Farewell.

    He that thou knowest thine, Hamlet."
Come, I will give you way for these your letters, 31
And do't the speedier that you may direct me
To him from whom you brought them.   (*Exeunt.*)

4.7

Enter KING *and* LAERTES.

KING.
    Now must your conscience my acquittance seal, 1
    And you must put me in your heart for friend,
    Sith you have heard, and with a knowing ear, 3
    That he which hath your noble father slain
    Pursued my life.
LAERTES.   It well appears. But tell me
    Why you proceeded not against these feats 6
    So crimeful and so capital in nature, 7
    As by your safety, greatness, wisdom, all things else,
    You mainly were stirred up. 9
KING.   Oh, for two special reasons,

---

16 **appointment** equipage   21 **thieves of mercy** merciful thieves
23 **repair** come   26 **bore** caliber, i.e., importance   31 **way** means of access

4.7. **Location: The castle.**
1 **my acquittance seal** confirm or acknowledge my innocence   3 **Sith** since   6 **feats** acts   7 **capital** punishable by death   9 **mainly** greatly

Which may to you perhaps seem much unsinewed,   *11*
But yet to me they're strong. The Queen his mother
Lives almost by his looks, and for myself—
My virtue or my plague, be it either which—
She is so conjunctive to my life and soul   *15*
That, as the star moves not but in his sphere,   *16*
I could not but by her. The other motive
Why to a public count I might not go   *18*
Is the great love the general gender bear him,   *19*
Who, dipping all his faults in their affection,
Work like the spring that turneth wood to stone,   *21*
Convert his gyves to graces, so that my arrows,   *22*
Too slightly timbered for so loud a wind,   *23*
Would have reverted to my bow again
But not where I had aimed them.
LAERTES.
And so have I a noble father lost,
A sister driven into desp'rate terms,   *27*
Whose worth, if praises may go back again,   *28*
Stood challenger on mount of all the age   *29*
For her perfections. But my revenge will come.
KING.
Break not your sleeps for that. You must not think
That we are made of stuff so flat and dull
That we can let our beard be shook with danger
And think it pastime. You shortly shall hear more.
I loved your father, and we love ourself;
And that, I hope, will teach you to imagine—

(*Enter a* MESSENGER *with letters.*)

How now? What news?
MESSENGER.   Letters, my lord, from Hamlet:
This to Your Majesty, this to the Queen.

---

11 **unsinewed** weak 15 **conjunctive** closely united. (An astronomical metaphor.) 16 **his** its.
sphere one of the hollow spheres in which, according to Ptolemaic astronomy, the planets were supposed to move 18 **count** account, reckoning, indictment 19 **general gender** common people
21 **Work** operate, act. **spring** i.e., a spring with such a concentration of lime that it coats a piece of
wood with limestone, in effect gilding and petrifying it 22 **gyves** fetters (which, gilded by the people's praise, would look like badges of honor) 23 **Too ... wind** with too light a shaft for so powerful a gust (of popular sentiment) 27 **terms** state, condition 28 **go back** recall what she was
29 **on mount** set up on high

(*He gives letters.*)

KING.   From Hamlet? Who brought them?
MESSENGER.
   Sailors, my lord, they say. I saw them not.
   They were given me by Claudio. He received them
   Of him that brought them.
KING.   Laertes, you shall hear them.—
   Leave us.   (*Exit* MESSENGER.)
   (*He reads.*) "High and mighty, you shall know I am set
   naked on your kingdom. Tomorrow shall I beg leave   *45*
   to see your kingly eyes, when I shall, first asking your
   pardon, thereunto recount the occasion of my sudden   *47*
   and more strange return. Hamlet."
   What should this mean? Are all the rest come back?
   Or is it some abuse, and no such thing?   *50*
LAERTES.
   Know you the hand?
KING.   'Tis Hamlet's character. "Naked!"   *51*
   And in a postscript here he says "alone."
   Can you devise me?   *53*
LAERTES.
   I am lost in it, my lord. But let him come.
   It warms the very sickness in my heart
   That I shall live and tell him to his teeth,
   "Thus didst thou."   *57*
KING.   If it be so, Laertes—
   As how should it be so? How otherwise?—   *58*
   Will you be ruled by me?
LAERTES.   Ay, my lord,
   So you will not o'errule me to a peace.   *60*
KING.
   To thine own peace. If he be now returned,
   As checking at his voyage, and that he means   *62*
   No more to undertake it, I will work him

---

45 naked destitute, unarmed, without following   **47 pardon** (for returning without authorization)
50 abuse deceit. **no such thing** not what the letter says. **51 character** handwriting. **53 devise** explain to **57 Thus didst thou** i.e., Here's for what you did to my father. **58 As ... otherwise?** how can this (Hamlet's return) be true? Yet how otherwise than true (since we have the evidence of his letter)? **60 So** provided that **62 checking at** i.e., turning aside from (like a falcon leaving the quarry to fly at a chance bird). **that** if

To an exploit, now ripe in my device,   64
Under the which he shall not choose but fall;
And for his death no wind of blame shall breathe,
But even his mother shall uncharge the practice   67
And call it accident.
LAERTES.   My lord, I will be ruled,
The rather if you could devise it so
That I might be the organ.   70
KING.   It falls right.
You have been talked of since your travel much,
And that in Hamlet's hearing, for a quality
Wherein they say you shine. Your sum of parts   73
Did not together pluck such envy from him
As did that one, and that, in my regard,
Of the unworthiest siege.   76
LAERTES.   What part is that, my lord?
KING.
A very ribbon in the cap of youth,
Yet needful too, for youth no less becomes   79
The light and careless livery that it wears
Than settled age his sables and his weeds   81
Importing health and graveness. Two months since   82
Here was a gentleman of Normandy.
I have seen myself, and served against, the French,
And they can well on horseback, but this gallant   85
Had witchcraft in't; he grew unto his seat,
And to such wondrous doing brought his horse
As had he been incorpsed and demi-natured   88
With the brave beast. So far he topped my thought   89
That I in forgery of shapes and tricks   90
Come short of what he did.
LAERTES.   A Norman was't?
KING.   A Norman.
LAERTES.
Upon my life, Lamord.

---

64 **device** devising, invention   67 **uncharge the practice** acquit the stratagem of being a plot
70 **organ** agent, instrument.   73 **Your ... parts** All your other virtues   76 **unworthiest siege** least
important rank.   79 **no less becomes** is no less adorned by   81–2 **his sables ... graveness** its rich
robes furred with sable and its garments denoting dignified well-being and seriousness.   85 **can well**
are skilled   88–9 **As ... beast** as if, centaurlike, he had been made into one body with the horse, possessing half its nature.   89 **topped** surpassed   90 **forgery** fabrication

KING. The very same.

LAERTES.

I know him well. He is the brooch indeed   94

And gem of all the nation.

KING. He made confession of you,

And gave you such a masterly report

For art and exercise in your defense,   98

And for your rapier most especial,

That he cried out 'twould be a sight indeed

If one could match you. Th'escrimers of their nation,   101

He swore, had neither motion, guard, nor eye

If you opposed them. Sir, this report of his

Did Hamlet so envenom with his envy

That he could nothing do but wish and beg

Your sudden coming o'er, to play with you.   106

Now, out of this—

LAERTES. What out of this, my lord?

KING.

Laertes, was your father dear to you?

Or are you like the painting of a sorrow,

A face without a heart?

LAERTES. Why ask you this?

KING.

Not that I think you did not love your father,

But that I know love is begun by time,   112

And that I see, in passages of proof,   113

Time qualifies the spark and fire of it.   114

There lives within the very flame of love

A kind of wick or snuff that will abate it,   116

And nothing is at a like goodness still,   117

For goodness, growing to a pleurisy,   118

Dies in his own too much. That we would do,   119

We should do when we would; for this "would"

    changes

---

94 **brooch** ornament   96 **confession** testimonial, admission of superiority   98 **For . . . defense** with respect to your skill and practice with your weapon   101 **Th'escrimers** The fencers   106 **sudden** immediate.   **play** fence   112 **begun by time** i.e., created by the right circumstance and hence subject to change   113 **passages of proof** actual well-attested instances   114 **qualifies** weakens, moderates   116 **snuff** the charred part of a candlewick   117 **nothing . . . still** nothing remains at a constant level of perfection   118 **pleurisy** excess, plethora. (Literally, a chest inflammation.)   119 **in . . . much** of its own excess.   **That** That which

And hath abatements and delays as many 121
As there are tongues, are hands, are accidents, 122
And then this "should" is like a spendthrift sigh, 123
That hurts by easing. But, to the quick o'th'ulcer: 124
Hamlet comes back. What would you undertake
To show yourself in deed your father's son
More than in words?

LAERTES.   To cut his throat i'th' church.

KING.

No place, indeed, should murder sanctuarize; 128
Revenge should have no bounds. But good Laertes,
Will you do this, keep close within your chamber. 130
Hamlet returned shall know you are come home.
We'll put on those shall praise your excellence 132
And set a double varnish on the fame
The Frenchman gave you, bring you in fine together, 134
And wager on your heads. He, being remiss, 135
Most generous, and free from all contriving, 136
Will not peruse the foils, so that with ease,
Or with a little shuffling, you may choose
A sword unbated, and in a pass of practice 139
Requite him for your father.

LAERTES.   I will do't,
And for that purpose I'll anoint my sword.
I bought an unction of a mountebank 142
So mortal that, but dip a knife in it,
Where it draws blood no cataplasm so rare, 144
Collected from all simples that have virtue 145
Under the moon, can save the thing from death 146
That is but scratched withal. I'll touch my point
With this contagion, that if I gall him slightly, 148

---

121 **abatements** diminutions   122 **As ... accidents** as there are tongues to dissuade, hands to pre-vent, and chance events to intervene   123 **spendthrift sigh** (An allusion to the belief that sighs draw blood from the heart.)   124 **hurts by easing** i.e., costs the heart blood and wastes precious opportu-nity even while it affords emotional relief.   **quick o'th'ulcer** i.e., heart of the matter 128 **sanctuarize** protect from punishment. (Alludes to the right of sanctuary with which certain religious places were invested.)   130 **Will you do this** if you wish to do this   132 **put on those shall** arrange for some to 134 **in fine** finally   135 **remiss** negligently unsuspicious   136 **generous** noble-minded   139 **unbat-ed** not blunted, having no button.   **pass of practice** treacherous thrust in an arranged bout.
142 **unction** ointment.   **mountebank** quack doctor   144 **cataplasm** plaster or poultice   145 **sim-ples** herbs.   **virtue** potency   146 **Under the moon** i.e., anywhere (with reference perhaps to the belief that herbs gathered at night had a special power).   148 **gall** graze, wound

It may be death.

KING.   Let's further think of this,
Weigh what convenience both of time and means
May fit us to our shape. If this should fail,   *151*
And that our drift look through our bad performance,   *152*
'Twere better not assayed. Therefore this project
Should have a back or second, that might hold
If this did blast in proof. Soft, let me see.   *155*
We'll make a solemn wager on your cunnings—   *156*
I ha 't!
When in your motion you are hot and dry—
As make your bouts more violent to that end—   *159*
And that he calls for drink, I'll have prepared him
A chalice for the nonce, whereon but sipping,   *161*
If he by chance escape your venomed stuck,   *162*
Our purpose may hold there. (*A cry within.*) But stay,
     what noise?

(*Enter* QUEEN.)

QUEEN.
One woe doth tread upon another's heel,
So fast they follow. Your sister's drowned, Laertes.
LAERTES.   Drowned! Oh, where?
QUEEN.
There is a willow grows askant the brook,   *167*
That shows his hoar leaves in the glassy stream;   *168*
Therewith fantastic garlands did she make
Of crowflowers, nettles, daisies, and long purples,   *170*
That liberal shepherds give a grosser name,   *171*
But our cold maids do dead men's fingers call them.   *172*
There on the pendent boughs her crownet weeds   *173*
Clamb'ring to hang, an envious sliver broke,   *174*
When down her weedy trophies and herself   *175*
Fell in the weeping brook. Her clothes spread wide,

---

151 shape part we propose to act.   **152 drift . . . performance** intention should be made visible by our bungling   **155 blast in proof** come to grief when put to the test.   **156 cunnings** respective skills   **159 As** i.e., and you should   **161 nonce** occasion   **162 stuck** thrust. (From *stoccado,* a fencing term.)   **167 askant** aslant   **168 hoar leaves** white or gray undersides of the leaves   **170 long purples** early purple orchids   **171 liberal** free-spoken.   **a grosser name** (The testicle-resembling tubers of the orchid, which also in some cases resemble *dead men's fingers,* have earned various slang names like "dogstones" and "cullions.")   **172 cold** chaste   **173 pendent** overhanging.   **crownet** made into a chaplet or coronet   **174 envious sliver** malicious branch   **175 weedy** i.e., of plants

And mermaidlike awhile they bore her up,
Which time she chanted snatches of old lauds,   *178*
As one incapable of her own distress,   *179*
Or like a creature native and endued   *180*
Unto that element. But long it could not be
Till that her garments, heavy with their drink,
Pulled the poor wretch from her melodious lay   *183*
To muddy death.

LAERTES.   Alas, then she is drowned?

QUEEN.   Drowned, drowned.

LAERTES.
Too much of water hast thou, poor Ophelia,
And therefore I forbid my tears. But yet
It is our trick; nature her custom holds,   *188*
Let shame say what it will. (*He weeps.*) When these   *189*
      are gone,
The woman will be out. Adieu, my lord.   *190*
I have a speech of fire that fain would blaze,
But that this folly douts it.   (*Exit.*) *192*

KING.   Let's follow, Gertrude.
How much I had to do to calm his rage!
Now fear I this will give it start again;
Therefore let's follow.   (*Exeunt.*)

5.1

Enter two CLOWNS, *with spades and mattocks.*

FIRST CLOWN.   Is she to be buried in Christian burial,
      when she willfully seeks her own salvation?   *2*
SECOND CLOWN.   I tell thee she is; therefore make her
      grave straight. The crowner hath sat on her, and finds   *4*
      it Christian burial.   *5*

---

178 **lauds** hymns   179 **incapable of** lacking capacity to apprehend   180 **endued** adapted by nature
183 **lay** ballad, song   188 **It is our trick** i.e., weeping is our natural way (when sad)   189–90 **When
... out** When my tears are all shed, the woman in me will be expended, satisfied.   192 **douts** extinguishes. (The Second Quarto reads "drownes.")

5.1 **Location: A churchyard.**
0.1 *Clowns* rustics   2 **salvation** (A blunder for "damnation," or perhaps a suggestion that Ophelia
was taking her own shortcut to heaven.)   4 **straight** straightway, immediately. (But with a pun on
strait, "narrow.")   **crowner** coroner.   **sat on her** conducted an inquest on her case   4–5 **finds it**
gives his official verdict that her means of death was consistent with

FIRST CLOWN.   How can that be, unless she drowned
  herself in her own defense?
SECOND CLOWN.   Why, 'tis found so.   8
FIRST CLOWN.   It must be *se offendendo*, it cannot be else.   9
  For here lies the point: if I drown myself wittingly,
  it argues an act, and an act hath three branches—it is
  to act, to do, and to perform. Argal, she drowned her-   12
  self wittingly.
SECOND CLOWN.   Nay, but hear you, goodman delve—   14
FIRST CLOWN.   Give me leave. Here lies the water; good.
  Here stands the man; good. If the man go to this
  water and drown himself, it is, will he, nill he, he   17
  goes, mark you that. But if the water come to him and
  drown him, he drowns not himself. Argal, he that is
  not guilty of his own death shortens not his own life.
SECOND CLOWN.   But is this law?
FIRST CLOWN.   Ay, marry, is't—crowner's quest law.   22
SECOND CLOWN.   Will you ha' the truth on't? If this had
  not been a gentlewoman, she should have been
  buried out o' Christian burial.
FIRST CLOWN.   Why, there thou say'st. And the more   26
  pity that great folk should have countenance in this   27
  world to drown or hang themselves, more than their
  even-Christian. Come, my spade. There is no ancient   29
  gentlemen but gardeners, ditchers, and grave makers.
  They hold up Adam's profession.   31
SECOND CLOWN.   Was he a gentleman?
FIRST CLOWN.   'A was the first that ever bore arms.   33
SECOND CLOWN.   Why, he had none.
FIRST CLOWN.   What, art a heathen? How dost thou
  understand the Scripture? The Scripture says Adam
  digged. Could he dig without arms? I'll put another   37
  question to thee. If thou answerest me not to the
  purpose, confess thyself—   39

---

8 found so determined so in the coroner's verdict.   **9 *se offendendo*** (A comic mistake for *se defend-
endo,* a term used in verdicts of self-defense.)   **12 Argal** (Corruption of *ergo,* "therefore.")
14 goodman (An honorific title often used with the name of a profession or craft.)   **17 will he, nill
he** whether he will or no, willy-nilly.   **22 quest** inquest   **26 there thou say'st** i.e., that's right.
27 countenance privilege   **29 even-Christian** fellow Christians.   **ancient** going back to ancient
times   **31 hold up** maintain   **33 bore arms** (To be entitled to bear a coat of arms would make
Adam a gentleman, but as one who bore a spade, our common ancestor was an ordinary delver in
the earth.)   **37 arms** i.e., the arms of the body.   **39 confess thyself** (The saying continues, "and be
hanged.")

SECOND CLOWN.   Go to.

FIRST CLOWN.   What is he that builds stronger than
either the mason, the shipwright, or the carpenter?

SECOND CLOWN.   The gallows maker, for that frame   *43*
outlives a thousand tenants.

FIRST CLOWN.   I like thy wit well, in good faith. The
gallows does well. But how does it well? It does well to   *46*
those that do ill. Now thou dost ill to say the gallows
is built stronger than the church. Argal, the gallows
may do well to thee. To't again, come.

SECOND CLOWN.   "Who builds stronger than a mason, a
shipwright, or a carpenter?"

FIRST CLOWN.   Ay, tell me that, and unyoke.   *52*

SECOND CLOWN.   Marry, now I can tell.

FIRST CLOWN.   To't.

SECOND CLOWN.   Mass, I cannot tell.   *55*

(*Enter* HAMLET *and* HORATIO *at a distance.*)

FIRST CLOWN.   Cudgel thy brains no more about it, for
your dull ass will not mend his pace with beating; and
when you are asked this question next, say "a grave
maker." The houses he makes lasts till doomsday. Go
get thee in and fetch me a stoup of liquor.   *60*

(*Exit* SECOND CLOWN. FIRST CLOWN *digs.*)

                                                            (*Song.*)
        "In youth, when I did love, did love,   *61*
            Methought it was very sweet,
        To contract—oh—the time for—a—my behove,   *63*
            Oh, methought there—a—was nothing—a—   *64*
            meet."

HAMLET.   Has this fellow no feeling of his business, 'a   *65*
sings in grave-making?

HORATIO.   Custom hath made it in him a property of   *67*
easiness.   *68*

---

43 frame (1) gallows (2) structure   **46 does well** (1) is an apt answer (2) does a good turn.   **52
unyoke** i.e., after this great effort, you may unharness the team of your wits.   **55 Mass** By the Mass
60 stoup two-quart measure   **61 In . . . love** (This and the two following stanzas, with nonsensical
variations, are from a poem attributed to Lord Vaux and printed in *Tottel's Miscellany*, 1557. The *oh*
and *a* [for "ah"] seemingly are the grunts of the digger.)   **63 To contract . . . behove** i.e., to shorten
the time for my own advantage. (Perhaps he means to *prolong* it.)   **64 meet** suitable, i.e., more suitable.   **65 'a** that he   **67–8 property of easiness** something he can do easily and indifferently.

HAMLET.   'Tis e'en so. The hand of little employment
    hath the daintier sense.   70
FIRST CLOWN.   (*Song.*)
    "But age with his stealing steps
      Hath clawed me in his clutch,
    And hath shipped me into the land,   73
      As if I had never been such."

(*He throws up a skull.*)

HAMLET.   That skull had a tongue in it and could sing
    once. How the knave jowls it to the ground, as if   76
    'twere Cain's jawbone, that did the first murder! This
    might be the pate of a politician, which this ass now   78
    o'erreaches, one that would circumvent God, might   79
    it not?
HORATIO.   It might, my lord.
HAMLET.   Or of a courtier, which could say, "Good
    morrow, sweet lord! How dost thou, sweet lord?"
    This might be my Lord Such-a-one, that praised my
    Lord Such-a-one's horse when 'a meant to beg it,
    might it not?
HORATIO.   Ay, my lord.
HAMLET.   Why, e'en so, and now my Lady Worm's,
    chapless, and knocked about the mazard with a sex-   89
    ton's spade. Here's fine revolution, an we had the trick   90
    to see't. Did these bones cost no more the breeding   91
    but to play at loggets with them? Mine ache to think   92
    on't.
FIRST CLOWN.   (*Song.*)
    "A pickax and a spade, a spade,
      For and a shrouding sheet;   95
    Oh, a pit of clay for to be made
      For such a guest is meet."

(*He throws up another skull.*)

---

70 daintier sense more delicate sense of feeling.   **73 into the land** i.e., toward my grave (?) (But note the lack of rhyme in *steps, land.*)   **76 jowls** dashes. (With a pun on *jowl,* "jawbone.")
78 politician schemer, plotter   **79 o'erreaches** circumvents, gets the better of   **89 chapless** having no lower jaw.   **mazard** i.e., head. (Literally, a drinking vessel.)   **90 revolution** turn of Fortune's wheel, change.   **trick** knack   **91–2 cost ... but** involve so little expense and care in upbringing that we may   **92 loggets** a game in which pieces of hard wood shaped like Indian clubs or bowling pins are thrown to lie as near as possible to a stake   **95 For and** and moreover

HAMLET.   There's another. Why may not that be the skull
of a lawyer? Where be his quiddities now, his quilli-   99
ties, his cases, his tenures, and his tricks? Why does   100
he suffer this mad knave now to knock him about the
sconce with a dirty shovel, and will not tell him of his   102
action of battery? Hum, this fellow might be in 's time   103
a great buyer of land, with his statutes, his recogni-   104
zances, his fines, his double vouchers, his recoveries.   105
Is this the fine of his fines and the recovery of his   106
recoveries, to have his fine pate full of fine dirt? Will   107
his vouchers vouch him no more of his purchases, and   108
double ones too, than the length and breadth of a   109
pair of indentures? The very conveyances of his lands   110
will scarcely lie in this box, and must th'inheritor   111
himself have no more, ha?
HORATIO.   Not a jot more, my lord.
HAMLET.   Is not parchment made of sheepskins?
HORATIO.   Ay, my lord, and of calves' skins too.
HAMLET.   They are sheep and calves which seek out as-   116
surance in that. I will speak to this fellow.—Whose   117
grave's this, sirrah?   118
FIRST CLOWN.   Mine, sir.
(*Sings*) "Oh, pit of clay for to be made
For such a guest is meet."
HAMLET.   I think it be thine, indeed, for thou liest in't.
FIRST CLOWN.   You lie out on't, sir, and therefore 'tis
not yours. For my part, I do not lie in't, yet it is mine.
HAMLET.   Thou dost lie in't, to be in't and say it is

99–100 his quiddities ... quillities his subtleties, his legal niceties   **100 tenures** the holding of a
piece of property or office, or the conditions or period of such holding   **102 sconce** head
103 action of battery lawsuit about physical assault.   **104 his statutes** his legal documents acknowl-
edging obligation of a debt   **104–5 recognizances** bonds undertaking to repay debts   **105 fines**
procedures for converting entailed estates into "fee simple" or freehold.   **double vouchers** vouchers
signed by two signatories guaranteeing the legality of real estate titles.   **recoveries** suits to obtain the
authority of a court judgment for the holding of land.   **106–7 Is this ... dirt?** Is this the end of his
legal maneuvers and profitable land deals, to have the skull of his elegant head filled full of minutely
sifted dirt? (With multiple wordplay on *fine* and *fines*.)   **107–10 Will ... indentures?** Will his vouchers, even double ones, guarantee him no more land than is needed to bury him in, being no bigger
than the deed of conveyance? (An *indenture* is literally a legal document drawn up in duplicate on a
single sheet and then cut apart on a zigzag line so that each pair was uniquely matched.)   **111 box**
(1) deed box (2) coffin.   **th'inheritor** the acquirer, owner   **116–17 assurance in that** safety in legal
parchments.   **118 sirrah** (A term of address to inferiors.)

thine. 'Tis for the dead, not for the quick; therefore   *126*
thou liest.
FIRST CLOWN.   'Tis a quick lie, sir; 'twill away again
from me to you.
HAMLET.   What man dost thou dig it for?
FIRST CLOWN.   For no man, sir.
HAMLET.   What woman, then?
FIRST CLOWN.   For none, neither.
HAMLET.   Who is to be buried in't?
FIRST CLOWN.   One that was a woman, sir, but, rest her
soul, she's dead.
HAMLET.   How absolute the knave is! We must speak by   *137*
the card, or equivocation will undo us. By the Lord,   *138*
Horatio, this three years I have took note of it: the age   *139*
is grown so picked that the toe of the peasant comes so   *140*
near the heel of the courtier he galls his kibe.—How   *141*
long hast thou been grave maker?
FIRST CLOWN.   Of all the days i'th' year, I came to't that
day that our last king Hamlet overcame Fortinbras.
HAMLET.   How long is that since?
FIRST CLOWN.   Cannot you tell that? Every fool can tell
that. It was that very day that young Hamlet was
born—he that is mad and sent into England.
HAMLET.   Ay, marry, why was he sent into England?
FIRST CLOWN.   Why, because 'a was mad. 'A shall
recover his wits there, or if 'a do not, 'tis no great
matter there.
HAMLET.   Why?
FIRST CLOWN.   'Twill not be seen in him there. There the
men are as mad as he.
HAMLET.   How came he mad?
FIRST CLOWN.   Very strangely, they say.
HAMLET.   How strangely?
FIRST CLOWN.   Faith, e'en with losing his wits.
HAMLET.   Upon what ground?   *160*

---

126 quick living   137 absolute strict, precise   137–8 by the card i.e., with precision. (Literally, by
the mariner's compass-card, on which the points of the compass were marked.)   138 equivocation
ambiguity in the use of terms   139 took taken   139–41 the age . . . kibe i.e., the age has grown so
finical and mannered that the lower classes ape their social betters, chafing at their heels. (*Kibes* are
chilblains on the heels.)   160 ground cause. (But, in the next line, the gravedigger takes the word in
the sense of "land," "country.")

FIRST CLOWN.   Why, here in Denmark. I have been
  sexton here, man and boy, thirty years.
HAMLET.   How long will a man lie i'th'earth ere he rot?
FIRST CLOWN.   Faith, if 'a be not rotten before 'a die—as
  we have many pocky corpses nowadays, that will   165
  scarce hold the laying in—'a will last you some eight   166
  year or nine year. A tanner will last you nine year.
HAMLET.   Why he more than another?
FIRST CLOWN.   Why, sir, his hide is so tanned with his
  trade that 'a will keep out water a great while, and
  your water is a sore decayer of your whoreson dead   171
  body. (*He picks up a skull.*) Here's a skull now hath
  lien you i'th'earth three-and-twenty years.   173
HAMLET.   Whose was it?
FIRST CLOWN.   A whoreson mad fellow's it was. Whose
  do you think it was?
HAMLET.   Nay, I know not.
FIRST CLOWN.   A pestilence on him for a mad rogue! 'A
  poured a flagon of Rhenish on my head once. This   179
  same skull, sir, was, sir, Yorick's skull, the King's jester.
HAMLET.   This?
FIRST CLOWN.   E'en that.
HAMLET.   Let me see. (*He takes the skull.*) Alas, poor
  Yorick! I knew him, Horatio, a fellow of infinite jest, of
  most excellent fancy. He hath bore me on his back a   185
  thousand times, and now how abhorred in my
  imagination it is! My gorge rises at it. Here hung those   187
  lips that I have kissed I know not how oft. Where be
  your gibes now? Your gambols, your songs, your   189
  flashes of merriment that were wont to set the table on
  a roar? Not one now, to mock your own grinning?
  Quite chopfallen? Now get you to my lady's chamber   192
  and tell her, let her paint an inch thick, to this favor   193
  she must come. Make her laugh at that. Prithee,
  Horatio, tell me one thing.

---

165 **pocky** rotten, diseased. (Literally, with the pox, or syphilis.)   166 **hold the laying in** hold together long enough to be interred.   **last you** last. (*You* is used colloquially here and in the following
lines.)   171 **sore** keen, veritable.   **whoreson** (An expression of contemptuous familiarity.)   173 **lien**
you lain. (See the note at line 166.)   179 **Rhenish** Rhine wine   185 **bore** borne   187 **My gorge**
rises i.e., I feel nauseated   189 **gibes** taunts   192 **chopfallen** (1) lacking the lower jaw (2) dejected.
193 **favor** aspect, appearance

HORATIO.   What's that, my lord?

HAMLET.   Dost thou think Alexander looked o' this
fashion i'th'earth?

HORATIO.   E'en so.

HAMLET.   And smelt so? Pah! (*He throws down the skull.*)

HORATIO.   E'en so, my lord.

HAMLET.   To what base uses we may return, Horatio!
Why may not imagination trace the noble dust of
Alexander till 'a find it stopping a bunghole?   204

HORATIO.   'Twere to consider too curiously to consider   205
so.

HAMLET.   No, faith, not a jot, but to follow him thither
with modesty enough, and likelihood to lead it. As   208
thus: Alexander died, Alexander was buried, Alexander returneth to dust, the dust is earth, of earth we
make loam, and why of that loam whereto he was   211
converted might they not stop a beer barrel?
Imperious Caesar, dead and turned to clay,   213
Might stop a hole to keep the wind away.
Oh, that that earth which kept the world in awe
Should patch a wall t'expel the winter's flaw!   216

(*Enter* KING, QUEEN, LAERTES, *and the corpse of*
OPHELIA, *in procession, with* PRIEST, *lords, etc.*)

But soft, but soft awhile! Here comes the King,   217
The Queen, the courtiers. Who is this they follow?
And with such maimèd rites? This doth betoken   219
The corpse they follow did with desperate hand
Fordo it own life. 'Twas of some estate.   221
Couch we awhile and mark.   222

(*He and* HORATIO *conceal themselves.*
OPHELIA's *body is taken to the grave.*)

LAERTES.   What ceremony else?

---

204 bunghole hole for filling or emptying a cask.   **205 curiously** minutely   **208 with . . . lead it**
with moderation and plausibility.   **211 loam** a mixture of clay, straw, sand, etc. used to mold bricks,
or, in this case, bungs for a beer barrel.   **213 Imperious** Imperial   **216 flaw** gust of wind   **217 soft**
i.e., wait, be careful   **219 maimèd** mutilated, incomplete   **221 Fordo it** destroy its.   **estate** rank.
222 Couch we Let's hide, lie low

HAMLET (*to* HORATIO).
    That is Laertes, a very noble youth. Mark.
LAERTES.   What ceremony else?
PRIEST.
    Her obsequies have been as far enlarged
    As we have warranty. Her death was doubtful,   *227*
    And but that great command o'ersways the order   *228*
    She should in ground unsanctified been lodged   *229*
    Till the last trumpet. For charitable prayers,   *230*
    Shards, flints, and pebbles should be thrown on her. *231*
    Yet here she is allowed her virgin crants,   *232*
    Her maiden strewments, and the bringing home   *233*
    Of bell and burial.   *234*
LAERTES.
    Must there no more be done?
PRIEST.   No more be done.
    We should profane the service of the dead
    To sing a requiem and such rest to her   *237*
    As to peace-parted souls.   *238*
LAERTES.   Lay her i'th'earth,
    And from her fair and unpolluted flesh
    May violets spring! I tell thee, churlish priest,   *240*
    A ministering angel shall my sister be
    When thou liest howling.   *242*
HAMLET (*to* HORATIO).   What, the fair Ophelia!
QUEEN (*scattering flowers*).   Sweets to the sweet! Farewell.
    I hoped thou shouldst have been my Hamlet's wife.
    I thought thy bride-bed to have decked, sweet maid,
    And not t' have strewed thy grave.
LAERTES.   Oh, treble woe
    Fall ten times treble on that cursèd head
    Whose wicked deed thy most ingenious sense   *248*
    Deprived thee of! Hold off the earth awhile,
    Till I have caught her once more in mine arms.

---

227 **warranty** i.e., ecclesiastical authority   228 **order** (1) prescribed practice (2) religious order of clerics   229 **She should . . . lodged** she should have been buried in unsanctified ground   230 **For** In place of   231 **Shards** broken bits of pottery   232 **crants** garlands betokening maidenhood 233 **strewments** flowers strewn on a coffin   233–4 **bringing . . . burial** laying the body to rest, to the sound of the bell.   237 **such rest** i.e., to pray for such rest   238 **peace-parted souls** those who have died at peace with God.   240 **violets** (See 4.5.188 and note.)   242 **howling** i.e., in hell.   248 **ingenious sense** a mind that is quick, alert, of fine qualities

(*He leaps into the grave and embraces* OPHELIA.)

Now pile your dust upon the quick and dead,
Till of this flat a mountain you have made
T' o'ertop old Pelion or the skyish head   *253*
Of blue Olympus.
HAMLET (*coming forward*).   What is he whose grief
Bears such an emphasis, whose phrase of sorrow   *255*
Conjures the wandering stars and makes them stand   *256*
Like wonder-wounded hearers? This is I,   *257*
Hamlet the Dane.   *258*
LAERTES   (*grappling with him*).   The devil take thy soul!   *259*
HAMLET.   Thou pray'st not well.
I prithee, take thy fingers from my throat,
For though I am not splenitive and rash,   *262*
Yet have I in me something dangerous,
Which let thy wisdom fear. Hold off thy hand.
KING.   Pluck them asunder.
QUEEN.   Hamlet, Hamlet!
ALL.   Gentlemen!
HORATIO.   Good my lord, be quiet.

(HAMLET *and* LAERTES *are parted.*)

HAMLET.
Why, I will fight with him upon this theme
Until my eyelids will no longer wag.   *270*
QUEEN.   Oh, my son, what theme?
HAMLET.
I loved Ophelia. Forty thousand brothers
Could not with all their quantity of love
Make up my sum. What wilt thou do for her?
KING.   Oh, he is mad, Laertes.

---

253 Pelion a mountain in northern Thessaly; compare *Olympus* and *Ossa* in lines 254 and 286. (In their rebellion against the Olympian gods, the giants attempted to heap Ossa on Pelion in order to scale Olympus.) **255 emphasis** i.e., rhetorical and florid emphasis. (*Phrase* has a similar rhetorical connotation.)   **256 wandering stars** planets   **257 wonder-wounded** struck with amazement **258 the Dane** (This title normally signifies the King; see 1.1.17 and note.)   **259 s.d.** *grappling with him* The testimony of the First Quarto that "*Hamlet leaps in after Laertes*" and of the ballad "Elegy on Burbage," published in *Gentleman's Magazine* in 1825 ("Oft have I seen him leap into a grave") seem to indicate one way in which this fight was staged; however, the difficulty of fitting two contenders and Ophelia's body into a confined space (probably the trapdoor) suggests to many editors the alternative, that Laertes jumps out of the grave to attack Hamlet.)   **262 splenitive** quick-tempered   **270 wag** move. (A fluttering eyelid is a conventional sign that life has not yet gone.)

QUEEN.   For love of God, forbear him.   *276*
HAMLET.
   'Swounds, show me what thou'lt do.   *277*
   Woo't weep? Woo't fight? Woo't fast? Woo't tear   *278*
      thyself?
   Woo't drink up eisel? Eat a crocodile?   *279*
   I'll do't. Dost come here to whine?
   To outface me with leaping in her grave?
   Be buried quick with her, and so will I.   *282*
   And if thou prate of mountains, let them throw
   Millions of acres on us, till our ground,
   Singeing his pate against the burning zone,   *285*
   Make Ossa like a wart! Nay, an thou'lt mouth,   *286*
   I'll rant as well as thou.   *287*
QUEEN.   This is mere madness,
   And thus awhile the fit will work on him;
   Anon, as patient as the female dove
   When that her golden couplets are disclosed,   *290*
   His silence will sit drooping.
HAMLET.   Hear you, sir.
   What is the reason that you use me thus?
   I loved you ever. But it is no matter.
   Let Hercules himself do what he may,   *294*
   The cat will mew, and dog will have his day.   *295*

(*Exit* HAMLET.)

KING.
   I pray thee, good Horatio, wait upon him.

(*Exit* HORATIO.)

   (*To* LAERTES) Strengthen your patience in our last   *297*
      night's speech;

---

276 **forbear him** leave him alone.   277 **'Swounds** By His (Christ's) wounds   278 **Woo't** Wilt thou
279 **Woo't ... eisel?** Will you drink up a whole draft of vinegar? (An extremely self-punishing task as
a way of expressing grief.)   **crocodile** (Crocodiles were tough and dangerous, and were supposed to
shed crocodile tears.)   282 **quick** alive   285 **his pate** its head, i.e., top.   **burning zone** zone in the
celestial sphere containing the sun's orbit, between the tropics of Cancer and Capricorn   286 **Ossa**
(See 253n.)   **an thou'lt mouth** if you want to rant   287 **mere** utter   290 **golden couplets** two baby
pigeons, covered with yellow down.   **disclosed** hatched   294–5 **Let ... day** i.e., (1) Even Hercules
couldn't stop Laertes's theatrical rant (2) I, too, will have my turn; i.e., despite any blustering attempts
at interference, every person will sooner or later do what he or she must do.   297 **in** i.e., by recalling

We'll put the matter to the present push.— 298
Good Gertrude, set some watch over your son.—
This grave shall have a living monument. 300
An hour of quiet shortly shall we see; 301
Till then, in patience our proceeding be. (*Exeunt.*)

5.2

Enter HAMLET *and* HORATIO.

HAMLET.
So much for this, sir; now shall you see the other. 1
You do remember all the circumstance?
HORATIO. Remember it, my lord!
HAMLET.
Sir, in my heart there was a kind of fighting
That would not let me sleep. Methought I lay
Worse than the mutines in the bilboes. Rashly, 6
And praised be rashness for it—let us know 7
Our indiscretion sometime serves us well 8
When our deep plots do pall, and that should learn us 9
There's a divinity that shapes our ends,
Rough-hew them how we will— 11
HORATIO. That is most certain.
HAMLET. Up from my cabin,
My sea-gown scarfed about me, in the dark 13
Groped I to find out them, had my desire, 14
Fingered their packet, and in fine withdrew 15
To mine own room again, making so bold,
My fears forgetting manners, to unseal
Their grand commission; where I found, Horatio—
Ah, royal knavery!—an exact command,
Larded with many several sorts of reasons 20

---

298 **present push** immediate test.   300 **living** lasting. (For Laertes' private understanding, Claudius also hints that Hamlet's death will serve as such a monument.)   301 **hour of quiet** time free of conflict

5.2 **Location: The castle.**
1 **see the other** hear the other news. (See 4.6.24–6.)   6 **mutines** mutineers.   **bilboes** shackles.
Rashly On impulse. (This adverb goes with lines 12 ff.)   7 **know** acknowledge   8 **indiscretion** lack of foresight and judgment (not an indiscreet act)   9 **pall** fail, falter, go stale.   **learn** teach   11
Rough-hew shape roughly   13 **sea-gown** seaman's coat.   **scarfed** loosely wrapped   14 **them** i.e.,
Rosencrantz and Guildenstern   15 **Fingered** pilfered, pinched.   **in fine** finally, in conclusion   20
Larded garnished.   **several** different

Importing Denmark's health and England's too,   21
With, ho! such bugs and goblins in my life,   22
That on the supervise, no leisure bated,   23
No, not to stay the grinding of the ax,   24
My head should be struck off.
HORATIO.   Is't possible?
HAMLET *(giving a document.)*
Here's the commission. Read it at more leisure.
But wilt thou hear now how I did proceed?
HORATIO.   I beseech you.
HAMLET.
Being thus benetted round with villainies—
Ere I could make a prologue to my brains,   30
They had begun the play—I sat me down,   31
Devised a new commission, wrote it fair.   32
I once did hold it, as our statists do,   33
A baseness to write fair, and labored much   34
How to forget that learning, but, sir, now
It did me yeoman's service. Wilt thou know
Th'effect of what I wrote?
HORATIO.   Ay, good my lord.
HAMLET.
An earnest conjuration from the King,   38
As England was his faithful tributary,
As love between them like the palm might flourish,   40
As peace should still her wheaten garland wear   41
And stand a comma 'tween their amities,   42
And many suchlike "as"es of great charge,   43
That on the view and knowing of these contents,
Without debatement further more or less,
He should those bearers put to sudden death,
Not shriving time allowed.   47

---

21 **Importing** relating to   22 **With . . . life** i.e., with all sorts of warnings of imaginary dangers if I were allowed to continue living. (*Bugs* are bugbears, hobgoblins.)   23 **That . . . bated** that on the reading of this commission, no delay being allowed.   24 **stay** await   30–1 **Ere . . . play** before I could consciously turn my brain to the matter, it had started working on a plan.   32 **fair** in a clear hand. 33 **statists** politicians, men of public affairs   34 **A baseness** beneath my dignity   38 **conjuration** entreaty   40 **palm** (An image of health; see Psalm 92:12.)   41 **still** always.   **wheaten garland** (Symbolic of fruitful agriculture, of peace and plenty.)   42 **comma** (Indicating continuity, link.) 43 **"as"es** (1) the "whereases" of a formal document (2) asses.   **charge** (1) import (2) burden (appropriate to asses)   47 **shriving time** time for confession and absolution

HORATIO.   How was this sealed?
HAMLET.
Why, even in that was heaven ordinant.   *48*
I had my father's signet in my purse,   *49*
Which was the model of that Danish seal;   *50*
Folded the writ up in the form of th'other,   *51*
Subscribed it, gave't th'impression, placed it safely,   *52*
The changeling never known. Now, the next day   *53*
Was our sea fight, and what to this was sequent   *54*
Thou knowest already.
HORATIO.
So Guildenstern and Rosencrantz go to't.
HAMLET.
Why, man, they did make love to this employment.
They are not near my conscience. Their defeat   *58*
Does by their own insinuation grow.   *59*
'Tis dangerous when the baser nature comes   *60*
Between the pass and fell incensèd points   *61*
Of mighty opposites.   *62*
HORATIO.   Why, what a king is this!
HAMLET.
Does it not, think thee, stand me now upon—   *63*
He that hath killed my king and whored my mother,
Popped in between th'election and my hopes,   *65*
Thrown out his angle for my proper life,   *66*
And with such coz'nage—is't not perfect conscience   *67*
To quit him with this arm? And is't not to be damned   *68*
To let this canker of our nature come   *69*
In further evil?   *70*
HORATIO.
It must be shortly known to him from England
What is the issue of the business there.
HAMLET.
It will be short. The interim is mine,

---

48 ordinant directing   49 signet small seal   50 model replica   51 writ writing   52 Subscribed
signed (with forged signature).   impression i.e., with a wax seal   53 changeling i.e., substituted
letter. (Literally, a fairy child substituted for a human one.)   54 was sequent followed 58 defeat
destruction   59 insinuation intrusive intervention, sticking their noses in my business   60 baser of
lower social station   61 pass thrust.   fell fierce   62 opposites antagonists.   63 stand me now
upon become incumbent on me now   65 th'election (The Danish monarch was "elected" by a small
number of high-ranking electors.)   66 angle fishhook.   proper very   67 coz'nage trickery
68 quit requite, pay back   69 canker ulcer   69–70 come In grow into

And a man's life's no more than to say "one."   *74*
But I am very sorry, good Horatio,
That to Laertes I forgot myself,
For by the image of my cause I see
The portraiture of his. I'll court his favors.
But, sure, the bravery of his grief did put me   *79*
Into a tow'ring passion.
HORATIO.   Peace, who comes here?

(*Enter a Courtier,* OSRIC.)

OSRIC.   Your Lordship is right welcome back to Denmark.
HAMLET.   I humbly thank you, sir. (*To Horatio*) Dost
know this water fly?
HORATIO.   No, my good lord.
HAMLET.   Thy state is the more gracious, for 'tis a vice to
know him. He hath much land, and fertile. Let a beast   *86*
be lord of beasts, an his crib shall stand at the King's   *87*
mess. 'Tis a chuff, but, as I say, spacious in the   *88*
possession of dirt.
OSRIC.   Sweet lord, if Your Lordship were at leisure, I
should impart a thing to you from His Majesty.
HAMLET.   I will receive it, sir, with all diligence of spirit.
Put your bonnet to his right use; 'tis for the head.   *93*
OSRIC.   I thank Your Lordship, it is very hot.
HAMLET.   No, believe me, 'tis very cold. The wind is
northerly.
OSRIC.   It is indifferent cold, my lord, indeed.   *97*
HAMLET.   But yet methinks it is very sultry and hot for
my complexion.   *99*
OSRIC.   Exceedingly, my lord. It is very sultry, as
'twere—I cannot tell how. My lord, His Majesty bade
me signify to you that 'a has laid a great wager on your
head. Sir, this is the matter—
HAMLET.   I beseech you, remember.
(HAMLET *moves him to put on his hat.*)

---

74 a man's ... "one" one's whole life occupies such a short time, only as long as it takes to count to 1.   79 bravery bravado   86–8 Let ... mess i.e., If a man, no matter how beastlike, is as rich in livestock and possessions as Osric, he may eat at the King's table.   87 crib manger   88 chuff boor, churl. (The Second Quarto spelling, "chough," is a variant spelling that also suggests the meaning here of "chattering jackdaw.")   93 bonnet any kind of cap or hat.   his its   97 indifferent somewhat   99 complexion constitution

OSRIC.   Nay, good my lord; for my ease, in good faith.   *105*
Sir, here is newly come to court Laertes—believe me,
an absolute gentleman, full of most excellent differ-   *107*
ences, of very soft society and great showing. Indeed,   *108*
to speak feelingly of him, he is the card or calendar of   *109*
gentry, for you shall find in him the continent of what   *110*
part a gentleman would see.   *111*
HAMLET.   Sir, his definement suffers no perdition in   *112*
you, though I know to divide him inventorially would   *113*
dozy th'arithmetic of memory, and yet but yaw   *114*
neither in respect of his quick sail. But, in the verity of   *115*
extolment, I take him to be a soul of great article, and   *116*
his infusion of such dearth and rareness as, to make   *117*
true diction of him, his semblable is his mirror and   *118*
who else would trace him his umbrage, nothing   *119*
more.
OSRIC.   Your Lordship speaks most infallibly of him.
HAMLET.   The concernancy, sir? Why do we wrap the   *122*
gentleman in our more rawer breath?   *123*
OSRIC.   Sir?
HORATIO.   Is't not possible to understand in another   *125*
tongue? You will do't, sir, really.   *126*
HAMLET.   What imports the nomination of this gentle-   *127*
man?
OSRIC.   Of Laertes?
HORATIO (*to* HAMLET).   His purse is empty already; all 's

---

105 for my ease (A conventional reply declining the invitation to put the hat back on.)
107 absolute perfect   **107–8 differences** special qualities   **108 soft society** agreeable manners.
great showing distinguished appearance.   **109 feelingly** with just perception   **109–10 the card ...**
gentry the model or paradigm (literally, a chart or directory) of good breeding   **110–11 the conti-**
nent ... see one who contains in himself all the qualities a gentleman would like to see. (A *continent*
is that which contains.)   **112–15 his definement ... sail** the task of defining Laertes's excellences
suffers no diminution in your description of him, though I know that to enumerate all his graces
would stupify one's powers of memory, and even so could do no more than veer unsteadily off
course in a vain attempt to keep up with his rapid forward motion. (Hamlet mocks Osric by parody-
ing his jargon-filled speeches.)   **115–20 But ... more** But, in true praise of him, I take him to be a
person of remarkable value, and his essence of such rarity and excellence as, to speak truly of him,
none can compare with him other than his own mirror; anyone following in his footsteps can only
hope to be the shadow to his substance, nothing more.   **122 concernancy** import, relevance
123 rawer breath unrefined speech that can only come short in praising him.   **125–6 Is't ...**
tongue? i.e., Is it not possible for you, Osric, to understand and communicate in any other tongue
than the overblown rhetoric you have used? (Alternatively, Horatio could be asking Hamlet to speak
more plainly.)   **126 You will do't** i.e., You can if you try, or, you may well have to try (to speak
plainly).   **127 nomination** naming

golden words are spent.

HAMLET. Of him, sir.

OSRIC. I know you are not ignorant—

HAMLET. I would you did, sir. Yet in faith if you did, *134*
it would not much approve me. Well, sir? *135*

OSRIC. You are not ignorant of what excellence Laertes
is—

HAMLET. I dare not confess that, lest I should compare *138*
with him in excellence. But to know a man well were *139*
to know himself. *140*

OSRIC. I mean, sir, for his weapon; but in the imputation *141*
laid on him by them, in his meed he's unfellowed. *142*

HAMLET. What's his weapon?

OSRIC. Rapier and dagger.

HAMLET. That's two of his weapons—but well. *145*

OSRIC. The King, sir, hath wagered with him six Barbary
horses, against the which he has impawned, as I take *147*
it, six French rapiers and poniards, with their assigns, *148*
as girdle, hangers, and so. Three of the carriages, in *149*
faith, are very dear to fancy, very responsive to the *150*
hilts, most delicate carriages, and of very liberal con- *151*
ceit. *152*

HAMLET. What call you the carriages? *153*

HORATIO (*to* HAMLET). I knew you must be edified by
the margent ere you had done. *155*

OSRIC. The carriages, sir, are the hangers.

HAMLET. The phrase would be more germane to the
matter if we could carry a cannon by our sides; I would
it might be hangers till then. But, on: six Barbary horses

134–5 I would . . . approve me (Responding to Osric's incompleted sentence as though it were a complete statement, Hamlet says, with mock politeness, "I wish you did know me to be not ignorant [i.e., to be knowledgeable] about matters," and then turns this into an insult: "But if you did, your recommendation of me would be of little value in any case.") **138–40 I dare . . . himself** I dare not boast of knowing Laertes's excellence lest I seem to imply a comparable excellence in myself. Certainly, to know another person well, one must know oneself. **141–2 I mean . . . unfellowed** I mean his excellence with his rapier, not his general excellence; in the reputation he enjoys for use of his weapons, his merit is unequaled. **145 but well** but never mind **147 he** i.e., Laertes. **impawned** staked, wagered **148 poniards** daggers. **assigns** appurtenances **149 hangers** straps on the sword belt (*girdle*), from which the sword hung. **and so** and so on. **149–52 Three . . . conceit** Three of the hangers, truly, are very pleasing to the fancy, decoratively matched with the hilts, delicate in workmanship, and made with elaborate ingenuity. **153 What call you** What do you refer to when you say **155 margent** margin of a book, place for explanatory notes

against six French swords, their assigns, and three lib-
eral-conceited carriages; that's the French bet against
the Danish. Why is this impawned, as you call it?

OSRIC. The King, sir, hath laid, sir, that in a dozen   *163*
passes between yourself and him, he shall not exceed   *164*
you three hits. He hath laid on twelve for nine, and it
would come to immediate trial, if Your Lordship would
vouchsafe the answer.   *167*

HAMLET. How if I answer no?

OSRIC. I mean, my lord, the opposition of your person
in trial.

HAMLET. Sir, I will walk here in the hall. If it please His
Majesty, it is the breathing time of day with me. Let   *172*
the foils be brought, the gentleman willing, and the
King hold his purpose, I will win for him an I can; if
not, I will gain nothing but my shame and the odd
hits.

OSRIC. Shall I deliver you so?   *177*

HAMLET. To this effect, sir—after what flourish your
nature will.

OSRIC. I commend my duty to Your Lordship.   *180*

HAMLET. Yours, yours.   (*Exit* OSRIC.)
'A does well to commend it himself; there are no tongues
else for 's turn.   *183*

HORATIO. This lapwing runs away with the shell on his   *184*
head.

HAMLET. 'A did comply with his dug before 'a sucked   *186*
it. Thus has he—and many more of the same breed   *187*

---

163 laid wagered   **164 passes** bouts. (The odds of the betting are hard to explain. Possibly the King
bets that Hamlet will win at least five out of twelve, at which point Laertes raises the odds against
himself by betting he will win nine.)   **167 vouchsafe the answer** be so good as to accept the challenge. (Hamlet deliberately takes the phrase in its literal sense of replying.) **172 breathing time** exercise period.   **Let** i.e., If   **177 deliver you** report what you say   **180 commend** commit to your
favor. (A conventional salutation, but Hamlet wryly uses a more literal meaning, "recommend,"
"praise," in line 182.)   **183 for 's turn** for his purposes, i.e., to do it for him.   **184 lapwing** (A
proverbial type of youthful forwardness. Also, a bird that draws intruders away from its nest and was
thought to run about with its head in the shell when newly hatched; a seeming reference to Osric's
hat.)   **186 comply . . . dug** observe ceremonious formality toward his nurse's or mother's teat
187–93 Thus . . . are out Thus has he—and many like him of the sort our frivolous age dotes on—
acquired the trendy manner of speech of the time, and, out of habitual conversation with courtiers
of their own kind, have collected together a kind of frothy medley of current phrases, which enables
such gallants to hold their own among persons of the most select and well-sifted views; and yet do
but test them by merely blowing on them, and their bubbles burst.

that I know the drossy age dotes on—only got the 188
tune of the time, and, out of an habit of encounter, a 189
kind of yeasty collection, which carries them through 190
and through the most fanned and winnowed opin- 191
ions; and do but blow them to their trial, the bubbles 192
are out. 193

(*Enter a* LORD.)

LORD. My lord, His Majesty commended him to you by
    young Osric, who brings back to him that you attend
    him in the hall. He sends to know if your pleasure
    hold to play with Laertes, or that you will take longer 197
    time.
HAMLET. I am constant to my purposes; they follow the
    King's pleasure. If his fitness speaks, mine is ready; 200
    now or whensoever, provided I be so able as now.
LORD. The King and Queen and all are coming down.
HAMLET. In happy time. 203
LORD. The Queen desires you to use some gentle enter- 204
    tainment to Laertes before you fall to play. 205
HAMLET. She well instructs me.   (*Exit* LORD.)
HORATIO. You will lose, my lord.
HAMLET. I do not think so. Since he went into France, I
    have been in continual practice; I shall win at the odds.
    But thou wouldst not think how ill all's here about my
    heart; but it is no matter.
HORATIO. Nay, good my lord—
HAMLET. It is but foolery, but it is such a kind of gain- 213
    giving as would perhaps trouble a woman. 214
HORATIO. If your mind dislike anything, obey it. I will
    forestall their repair hither and say you are not fit. 216
HAMLET. Not a whit, we defy augury. There is special 217
    providence in the fall of a sparrow. If it be now, 'tis
    not to come; if it be not to come, it will be now; if it
    be not now; yet it will come. The readiness is all. Since 220
    no man of aught he leaves knows, what is't to leave 221

---

197 play fence.   **that if   200 If ... ready** If he declares his readiness, my convenience waits on his
203 In happy time (A phrase of courtesy indicating that the time is convenient.)   **204–5 entertainment** greeting   **213–14 gaingiving** misgiving   **216 repair** coming   **217 augury** the attempt to read
signs of future events in order to avoid predicted trouble.   **220–2 Since ... Let be** Since no one has
knowledge of what he is leaving behind, what does an early death matter after all? Enough; forbear.

betimes? Let be.   222

(A table prepared. Enter trumpets, drums, and officers with
cushions; KING, QUEEN, OSRIC, *and all the state; foils,*
daggers, and wine borne in; and LAERTES.)

KING.
   Come, Hamlet, come and take this hand from me.

(*The* KING *puts* LAERTES*'s hand into* HAMLET*'s.*)

HAMLET (*to* LAERTES).
   Give me your pardon, sir. I have done you wrong,
   But pardon't as you are a gentleman.
   This presence knows,   226
   And you must needs have heard, how I am punished   227
   With a sore distraction. What I have done
   That might your nature, honor, and exception   229
   Roughly awake, I here proclaim was madness.
   Was't Hamlet wronged Laertes? Never Hamlet.
   If Hamlet from himself be ta'en away,
   And when he's not himself does wrong Laertes,
   Then Hamlet does it not, Hamlet denies it.
   Who does it, then? His madness. If't be so,
   Hamlet is of the faction that is wronged;   236
   His madness is poor Hamlet's enemy.
   Sir, in this audience
   Let my disclaiming from a purposed evil
   Free me so far in your most generous thoughts
   That I have shot my arrow o'er the house
   And hurt my brother.
LAERTES.   I am satisfied in nature,   242
   Whose motive in this case should stir me most   243
   To my revenge. But in my terms of honor
   I stand aloof, and will no reconcilement
   Till by some elder masters of known honor
   I have a voice and precedent of peace   247
   To keep my name ungored. But till that time   248

222.1 *trumpets, drums* trumpeters, drummers   222.3 *all the state* the entire court   226 **presence**
royal assembly   227 **punished** afflicted   229 **exception** disapproval   236 **faction** party   242 **in**
nature i.e., as to my personal feelings   243 **motive** prompting   247 **voice** authoritative pronounce-
ment.   **of peace** for reconciliation   248 **name ungored** reputation unwounded.

I do receive your offered love like love,
And will not wrong it.
HAMLET.   I embrace it freely,
And will this brothers' wager frankly play.—   *251*
Give us the foils. Come on.
LAERTES.   Come, one for me.
HAMLET.
I'll be your foil, Laertes. In mine ignorance   *253*
Your skill shall, like a star i'th' darkest night,
Stick fiery off indeed.   *255*
LAERTES.   You mock me, sir.
HAMLET.   No, by this hand.
KING.
Give them the foils, young Osric. Cousin Hamlet,
You know the wager?
HAMLET.   Very well, my lord.
Your Grace has laid the odds o'th' weaker side.   *259*
KING.
I do not fear it; I have seen you both.
But since he is bettered, we have therefore odds.   *261*
LAERTES.
This is too heavy. Let me see another.

(*He exchanges his foil for another.*)

HAMLET.
This likes me well. These foils have all a length?   *263*

(*They prepare to fence.*)

OSRIC.   Ay, my good lord.
KING.
Set me the stoups of wine upon that table.
If Hamlet give the first or second hit,
Or quit in answer of the third exchange,   *267*
Let all the battlements their ordnance fire.
The King shall drink to Hamlet's better breath,   *269*

---

251 frankly without ill feeling or the burden of rancor   **253 foil** thin metal background which sets a jewel off. (With pun on the blunted rapier for fencing.)   **255 Stick fiery off** stand out brilliantly **259 laid . . . side** backed the weaker side.   **261 is bettered** is the odds-on favorite. (Laertes's handicap is the "three hits" specified in line 165.)   **263 likes** pleases   **267 Or . . . exchange** or draws even with Laertes by winning the third exchange.   **269 better breath** improved vigor

And in the cup an union shall he throw   *270*
Richer than that which four successive kings
In Denmark's crown have worn. Give me the cups,
And let the kettle to the trumpet speak,   *273*
The trumpet to the cannoneer without,
The cannons to the heavens, the heaven to earth,
"Now the King drinks to Hamlet." Come, begin.
                                             (*Trumpets the while.*)
    And you, the judges, bear a wary eye.
HAMLET.   Come on, sir.
LAERTES.   Come, my lord. (*They fence.* HAMLET *scores a hit.*)
HAMLET.   One.
LAERTES.   No.
HAMLET.   Judgment.
OSRIC.   A hit, a very palpable hit.

(*Drum, trumpets, and shot. Flourish.
A piece goes off.*)

LAERTES.   Well, again.
KING.
    Stay, give me drink. Hamlet, this pearl is thine.

(*He drinks, and throws a pearl in* HAMLET's *cup.*)

    Here's to thy health. Give him the cup.
HAMLET.
    I'll play this bout first. Set it by awhile.
    Come. (*They fence.*) Another hit; what say you?
LAERTES.   A touch, a touch, I do confess't.
KING.
    Our son shall win.
QUEEN.   He's fat and scant of breath.   *289*
    Here, Hamlet, take my napkin, rub thy brows.   *290*
    The Queen carouses to thy fortune, Hamlet.   *291*
HAMLET.   Good madam!
KING.   Gertrude, do not drink.
QUEEN.
    I will, my lord, I pray you pardon me.   (*She drinks.*)

---

270 **union** pearl. (So called, according to Pliny's *Natural History*, 9, because pearls are *unique*, never identical.)   273 **kettle** kettledrum   282.2 *A piece* A cannon   289 **fat** not physically fit, out of training   290 **napkin** handkerchief   291 **carouses** drinks a toast

KING (*aside*).

It is the poisoned cup. It is too late.

HAMLET.

I dare not drink yet, madam; by and by.

QUEEN.   Come, let me wipe thy face.

LAERTES (*aside to the* KING).

My lord, I'll hit him now.

KING.   I do not think't.

LAERTES (*aside*).

And yet it is almost against my conscience.

HAMLET.

Come, for the third, Laertes. You do but dally.

I pray you, pass with your best violence;   301

I am afeard you make a wanton of me.   302

LAERTES.   Say you so? Come on.   (*They fence.*)

OSRIC.   Nothing neither way.

LAERTES.

Have at you now!

(LAERTES *wounds* HAMLET; *then, in scuffling,*
they change rapiers, and HAMLET *wounds* LAERTES.)

KING.   Part them! They are incensed.

HAMLET.

Nay, come, again.   (*The* QUEEN *falls.*)

OSRIC.   Look to the Queen there, ho!

HORATIO.

They bleed on both sides. How is it, my lord?

OSRIC.   How is't, Laertes?

LAERTES.

Why, as a woodcock to mine own springe, Osric;   309

I am justly killed with mine own treachery.

HAMLET.

How does the Queen?

KING.   She swoons to see them bleed.

QUEEN.

No, no, the drink, the drink—Oh, my dear Hamlet—

---

301 pass thrust   **302 make ... me** i.e., treat me like a spoiled child, trifle with me.   **305.1–2** *in scuf-fling, they change rapiers* (This stage direction occurs in the Folio. According to a widespread stage tradition, Hamlet receives a scratch, realizes that Laertes's sword is unbated, and accordingly forces an exchange.)   **309 woodcock** a bird, a type of stupidity or as a decoy.   **springe** trap, snare

The drink, the drink! I am poisoned.   (*She dies.*)

HAMLET.

Oh, villainy! Ho, let the door be locked!

Treachery! Seek it out.   (LAERTES *falls. Exit* OSRIC.)

LAERTES.

It is here, Hamlet. Hamlet, thou art slain.

No med'cine in the world can do thee good;

In thee there is not half an hour's life.

The treacherous instrument is in thy hand,

Unbated and envenomed. The foul practice   *320*

Hath turned itself on me. Lo, here I lie,

Never to rise again. Thy mother's poisoned.

I can no more. The King, the King's to blame.

HAMLET.

The point envenomed too? Then, venom, to thy work.

    (*He stabs the* KING.)

ALL.   Treason! Treason!

KING.

Oh, yet defend me, friends! I am but hurt.

HAMLET (*forcing the* KING *to drink*).

Here, thou incestuous, murderous, damnèd Dane,

Drink off this potion. Is thy union here?   *328*

Follow my mother.   (*The* KING *dies.*)

LAERTES.   He is justly served.

It is a poison tempered by himself.   *330*

Exchange forgiveness with me, noble Hamlet.

Mine and my father's death come not upon thee,

Nor thine on me!   (*He dies.*)

HAMLET.

Heaven make thee free of it! I follow thee.

I am dead, Horatio. Wretched Queen, adieu!

You that look pale and tremble at this chance,   *336*

That are but mutes or audience to this act,   *337*

Had I but time—as this fell sergeant, Death,   *338*

Is strict in his arrest—oh, I could tell you—   *339*

But let it be. Horatio, I am dead;

---

320 Unbated not blunted with a button.   **practice** plot   **328 union** pearl. (See line 270; with grim puns on the word's other meanings: marriage, shared death.)   **330 tempered** mixed   **336 chance** mischance   **337 mutes** silent observers. (Literally, actors with nonspeaking parts.)   **338 fell sergeant** remorseless arresting officer   **339 strict** (1) severely just (2) unavoidable.   **arrest** (1) taking into custody (2) stopping my speech.

Thou livest. Report me and my cause aright
To the unsatisfied.

HORATIO.   Never believe it.
I am more an antique Roman than a Dane.   *343*
Here's yet some liquor left.

(*He attempts to drink from the poisoned cup.*
HAMLET *prevents him.*)

HAMLET.   As thou'rt a man,
Give me the cup! Let go! By heaven, I'll ha 't.
Oh, God, Horatio, what a wounded name,
Things standing thus unknown, shall I leave behind
    me!
If thou didst ever hold me in thy heart,
Absent thee from felicity awhile,
And in this harsh world draw thy breath in pain
To tell my story. A march afar off (*and a volley within*).
    What warlike noise is this?

(*Enter* OSRIC.)

OSRIC.
Young Fortinbras, with conquest come from Poland,
To th'ambassadors of England gives
This warlike volley.

HAMLET.   Oh, I die, Horatio!
The potent poison quite o'ercrows my spirit.   *355*
I cannot live to hear the news from England,
But I do prophesy th'election lights
On Fortinbras. He has my dying voice.   *358*
So tell him, with th'occurrents more and less   *359*
Which have solicited. The rest is silence.   (*He dies.*) *360*

HORATIO.
Now cracks a noble heart. Good night, sweet prince,
And flights of angels sing thee to thy rest!

                                        (*March within.*)
Why does the drum come hither?

---

343 **Roman** (Suicide was an honorable choice for many Romans as an alternative to a dishonorable
life.) 355 **o'ercrows** triumphs over (like the winner in a cockfight) 358 **voice** vote 359 **th'occurrents** the events, incidents 360 **solicited** moved, urged. (Hamlet doesn't finish saying what the
events have prompted—presumably, his acts of vengeance, or his reporting of those events to
Fortinbras.)

(*Enter* FORTINBRAS, *with the English* AMBASSADORS
with drum, colors, and attendants.)

FORTINBRAS.
  Where is this sight?
HORATIO.   What is it you would see?
  If aught of woe or wonder, cease your search.
FORTINBRAS.
  This quarry cries on havoc. O proud Death,   366
  What feast is toward in thine eternal cell,   367
  That thou so many princes at a shot
  So bloodily hast struck?
FIRST AMBASSADOR.   The sight is dismal,
  And our affairs from England come too late.
  The ears are senseless that should give us hearing,
  To tell him his commandment is fulfilled,
  That Rosencrantz and Guildenstern are dead.
  Where should we have our thanks?
HORATIO.   Not from his mouth,   374
  Had it th'ability of life to thank you.
  He never gave commandment for their death.
  But since, so jump upon this bloody question,   377
  You from the Polack wars and you from England
  Are here arrived, give order that these bodies
  High on a stage be placèd to the view,   380
  And let me speak to th' yet unknowing world
  How these things came about. So shall you hear
  Of carnal, bloody, and unnatural acts,
  Of accidental judgments, casual slaughters,   384
  Of deaths put on by cunning and forced cause,   385
  And, in this upshot, purposes mistook
  Fall'n on th'inventors' heads. All this can I
  Truly deliver.
FORTINBRAS.   Let us haste to hear it,
  And call the noblest to the audience.
  For me, with sorrow I embrace my fortune.
  I have some rights of memory in this kingdom,   391

---

366 This . . . havoc This heap of dead bodies loudly proclaims a general slaughter. **367 feast** i.e., Death feasting on those who have fallen. **toward** in preparation **374 his** Claudius's **377 so jump . . . question** so hard on the heels of this bloody business **380 stage** platform **384 judgments** retributions. **casual** occurring by chance **385 put on** instigated. **forced cause** contrivance **391 of memory** traditional, remembered, unforgotten

Which now to claim my vantage doth invite me.   392
HORATIO.
    Of that I shall have also cause to speak,
    And from his mouth whose voice will draw on more.   394
    But let this same be presently performed,   395
    Even while men's minds are wild, lest more
        mischance
    On plots and errors happen.
FORTINBRAS.   Let four captains   397
    Bear Hamlet, like a soldier, to the stage,
    For he was likely, had he been put on,   399
    To have proved most royal; and for his passage,   400
    The soldiers' music and the rite of war
    Speak loudly for him.   402
    Take up the bodies. Such a sight as this
    Becomes the field, but here shows much amiss.   404
    Go bid the soldiers shoot.

(*Exeunt, marching, bearing off the dead bodies;
a peal of ordnance is shot off.*)

---

392 **vantage** favorable opportunity   394 **voice . . . more** vote will influence still others.
395 **presently** immediately 397 **On** on top of   399 **put on** i.e., invested in royal office and so put to the test   400 **for his passage** to mark his passing 402 **Speak** (let them) speak   404 **Becomes the field** suits the field of battle

QUESTIONS

WILLIAM SHAKESPEARE, *Hamlet*

1. How does the very first line of *Hamlet* signal central themes and actions of the play?

2. Use the text to discuss whether the ghost of Hamlet Sr. is religiously neutral, Protestant, or Roman Catholic. Consider such words as "portent," "purgatory," and "hell"—as well as the symbolism of a cock crowing.

3. Look carefully at Prince Hamlet's advice to the professional players who visit Elsinore. Consider both his thoughts on "the purpose of playing" and his warning about clowns. Compare this to Shakespeare's own method of drama. Do *Hamlet* and Hamlet match up?

4. After seeing the ghost, Hamlet tells his friends he will pretend to be mad. Does he ever truly go mad? Defend your answer in the text.

5. Does Ophelia betray Hamlet when she cooperates with her father's plot to uncover the love that he thinks may cause the Prince's madness? Justify your answer using textual evidence.

6. Of what deeds can you *prove* Gertrude is guilty?

7. How old do you think Hamlet is? Why? In Act IV, how old does the play say Hamlet is? Why do the facts usually surprise people?

8. In a short paper, argue the case for Hamlet's guilt or innocence in causing the death of Polonius, and the deaths of Rosencrantz and Guildenstern.

9. Discuss in an essay the "right and wrong" of taking revenge as expressed in and by this play.

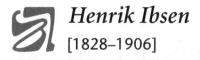

Henrik Ibsen
[1828–1906]

The playwright HENRIK IBSEN *was born into a provincial Norwegian family. As a young man, he studied medicine but soon began working as a stage manager at a local theater. While serving as the artistic director for the National Theater in Oslo, he wrote his first plays. Unfortunately, he met with little early success in his homeland. Consequently, he moved to Italy and to Germany, where he lived for twenty-seven years.*

During his early career, Ibsen wrote verse plays based on Norwegian myth and history, including Brand *(1866) and* Peer Gynt *(1867). He soon turned his attention to contemporary social problems and to dramatic realism. Dramatic realism endeavors to portray onstage an accurate representation of everyday life. These plays depict the details of contemporary existence through their dialogue, setting, and costumes; in doing so, they seek to produce the illusion of objectivity for their audiences. Created in opposition to the well-made play and to the popular melodrama, realism resisted the simple cause-and-effect plot structure and the sentimentality of those popular dramatic forms.*

Ibsen's three-act realist drama A Doll's House *(1879) addresses the "woman problem." As women became increasingly public and political during the nineteenth century, society grappled with the radical transformation of feminine roles—and with its consequent effects on the private sphere of the home.* A Doll's House *engages with these concerns by staging the marriage of Torvald and Nora Helmer in which the patronizing Torvald treats his wife Nora like a mindless child. This fictional marriage asked audiences to think critically about the oppressive roles to which women are confined. When Nora discovers her husband is a hypocrite, she leaves him, slamming the door in the final act of the play. Nineteenth century audiences, shocked by this conclusion, were challenged to speculate on Nora's fate. Audiences and readers are still intrigued by what happens to Nora once she leaves her home. (In a satirical sketch, the English comedy troupe Monty Python hypothesized that Nora walked out of the door . . . only to be met on the other side by a marching band, which promptly ran over her.)*

Like A Doll's House, *much of Ibsen's later work tackled social problems and the individuals affected by them. The plays—many of which continue to be produced regularly—include* An Enemy of the People *(1882);* The Wild Duck *(1884);* Hedda Gabler *(1890); and* The Master Builder *(1892). During the late nineteenth and early twentieth centuries, Ibsen's drama actively contributed to social debate. His critiques of society moved beyond the realm of the strictly artistic; they powerfully influenced society and politics. In fact, the term "Ibsenism" became a catchphrase for the critique of society, even as the playwright himself avoided politics. Notably, the content of these plays was frequently shocking and often bravely tackled subjects once taboo on the stage. For instance,* Ghosts *(1881) critiqued religious values and addressed frankly the issue of venereal disease.*

Ibsen has had a profound and enduring effect on modern drama. His contemporaries rapidly embraced his dramatic innovations, and his work was quickly translated and produced throughout Europe and the United States. He died in Norway in 1906.

A Doll's House

HENRIK IBSEN

DRAMATIS PERSONÆ

TORVALD HELMER.
NORA,   his wife.
DR. RANK.
MRS. LINDE.
NILS KROGSTAD.
THE HELMER'S THREE YOUNG CHILDREN.
ANNE,   their nurse.
A HOUSEMAID.
A PORTER.

SCENE

The action takes place in HELMER'S *house.*

ACT I

SCENE—*A room furnished comfortably and tastefully but not extravagantly. At the back a door to the right leads to the entrance hall; another to the left leads to* HELMER'S *study. Between the doors stands a piano. In the middle of the left-hand wall is a door and beyond a window. Near the window are a round table, armchairs and a small sofa. In the right-hand wall, at the farther end, another door; and on the same side, nearer the footlights, a stove, two easy chairs and a rocking chair; between the stove and the door a small table. Engravings on the walls; a cabinet with china and other small objects; a small bookcase with well-bound books. The floors are carpeted, and a fire burns in the stove. It is winter.*

A bell rings in the hall; shortly afterward the door is heard to open. Enter NORA, *humming a tune and in high spirits. She is in outdoor dress and carries a number of parcels; these she lays on the table to the right. She leaves the outer door open after her, and through it is seen a* PORTER *who is carrying a Christmas tree and a basket, which he gives to the* MAID *who has opened the door.*

NORA. Hide the Christmas tree carefully, Helen. Be sure the children do not see it till this evening, when it is dressed. (*To the* PORTER, *taking out her purse.*) How much?

POR. Sixpence.

NORA. There is a shilling. No, keep the change. (*The* PORTER *thanks her and goes out.* NORA *shuts the door. She is laughing to herself as she takes off her hat and coat. She takes a packet of macaroons from her pocket and eats one or two, then goes cautiously to her husband's door and listens.*) Yes, he is in. (*Still humming, she goes to the table on the right.*)

HEL. (*calls out from his room*). Is that my little lark twittering out there?

NORA (*busy opening some of the parcels*). Yes, it is!

HEL. Is it my little squirrel bustling about?

NORA. Yes!

HEL. When did my squirrel come home?

NORA. Just now. (*Puts the bag of macaroons into her pocket and wipes her mouth.*) Come in here, Torvald, and see what I have bought.

HEL. Don't disturb me. (*A little later he opens the door and looks into the room, pen in hand.*) Bought, did you say? All these things? Has my little spendthrift been wasting money again?

NORA. Yes, but, Torvald, this year we really can let ourselves go a little. This is the first Christmas that we have not needed to economize.

HEL. Still, you know, we can't spend money recklessly.

NORA. Yes, Torvald, we may be a wee bit more reckless now, mayn't we? Just a tiny wee bit! You are going to have a big salary and earn lots and lots of money.

HEL. Yes, after the new year; but then it will be a whole quarter before the salary is due.

NORA. Pooh! We can borrow till then.

HEL. Nora! (*Goes up to her and takes her playfully by the ear.*) The same little featherhead! Suppose, now, that I borrowed fifty pounds today and you spent it all in the Christmas week and then on New Year's Eve a slate fell on my head and killed me and——

NORA (*putting her hands over his mouth*). Oh! don't say such horrid things.

HEL. Still, suppose that happened,—what then?

NORA. If that were to happen, I don't suppose I should care whether I owed money or not.

HEL. Yes, but what about the people who had lent it?

NORA. They? Who would bother about them? I should not know who they were.

HEL. That is like a woman! But seriously, Nora, you know what I think about that. No debt, no borrowing. There can be no freedom or beauty about a home life that depends on borrowing and debt. We two have kept bravely on the straight road so far, and we will go on the same way for the short time longer that there need be any struggle.

NORA (*moving toward the stove*). As you please, Torvald.

HEL. (*following her*). Come, come, my little skylark must not droop her wings. What is this! Is my little squirrel out of temper? (*Taking out his purse.*) Nora, what do you think I have got here?

NORA (*turning round quickly*). Money!

HEL. There you are. (*Gives her some money.*) Do you think I don't know what a lot is wanted for housekeeping at Christmas time?

NORA (*counting*). Ten shillings—a pound—two pounds! Thank you, thank you, Torvald; that will keep me going for a long time.

HEL. Indeed it must.

NORA. Yes, yes, it will. But come here and let me show you what I have bought. And all so cheap! Look, here is a new suit for Ivar and a sword, and a horse and a trumpet for Bob, and a doll and dolly's bedstead for Emmy—they are very plain, but anyway she will soon break them in pieces. And here are dress lengths and handkerchiefs for the maids; old Anne ought really to have something better.

HEL. And what is in this parcel?

NORA (*crying out*). No, no! You mustn't see that till this evening.

HEL. Very well. But now tell me, you extravagant little person, what would you like for yourself?

NORA. For myself? Oh, I am sure I don't want anything.

HEL. Yes, but you must. Tell me something reasonable that you would particularly like to have.

NORA. No, I really can't think of anything—unless, Torvald——

HEL. Well?

NORA (*playing with his coat buttons and without raising her eyes to his*). If you really want to give me something, you might—you might——

HEL. Well, out with it!

NORA (*speaking quickly*). You might give me money, Torvald. Only just as much as you can afford; and then one of these days I will buy something with it.

HEL. But, Nora——

NORA. Oh, do! dear Torvald; please, please do! Then I will wrap it up in beautiful gilt paper and hang it on the Christmas tree. Wouldn't that be fun?

HEL. What are little people called that are always wasting money?

NORA. Spendthrifts—I know. Let us do as I suggest, Torvald, and then I shall have time to think what I am most in want of. That is a very sensible plan, isn't it?

HEL. (*smiling*). Indeed it is—that is to say, if you were really to save out of the money I give you and then really buy something for yourself. But if you spend it all on the housekeeping and any number of unnecessary things, then I merely have to pay up again.

NORA. Oh, but, Torvald——

HEL. You can't deny it, my dear little Nora. (*Puts his arm around her waist.*) It's a sweet little spendthrift, but she uses up a deal of money. One would hardly believe how expensive such little persons are!

NORA. It's a shame to say that. I do really save all I can.

HEL. (*laughing*). That's very true—all you can. But you can't save anything!

NORA (*smiling quietly and happily*). You haven't any idea how many expenses we skylarks and squirrels have, Torvald.

HEL. You are an odd little soul. Very like your father. You always find some new way of wheedling money out of me, and as soon as you have got it it seems to melt in your hands. You never know where it has gone. Still, one must take you as you are. It is in the blood; for indeed it is true that you can inherit these things, Nora.

NORA. Ah, I wish I had inherited many of Papa's qualities.

HEL. And I would not wish you to be anything but just what you are, my sweet little skylark. But, do you know, it strikes me that you are looking rather— what shall I say?—rather uneasy today.

NORA. Do I?

HEL. You do, really. Look straight at me.

NORA (*looks at him*). Well?

HEL. (*wagging his finger at her*). Hasn't Miss Sweet Tooth been breaking rules in town today?

NORA. No; what makes you think that?

HEL. Hasn't she paid a visit to the confectioner's?

NORA. No, I assure you, Torvald——

HEL. Not been nibbling sweets?

NORA. No, certainly not.

HEL. Not even taken a bite at a macaroon or two?

NORA. No, Torvald, I assure you, really——

HEL. There, there, of course I was only joking.

NORA (*going to the table on the right*). I should not think of going against your wishes.

HEL. No, I am sure of that; besides, you gave me your word. (*Going up to her.*) Keep your little Christmas secrets to yourself, my darling. They will all be revealed tonight when the Christmas tree is lit, no doubt.

NORA. Did you remember to invite Doctor Rank?

HEL. No. But there is no need; as a matter of course he will come to dinner with us. However, I will ask him when he comes in this morning. I have ordered some good wine. Nora, you can't think how I am looking forward to this evening.

NORA. So am I! And how the children will enjoy themselves, Torvald!

HEL. It is splendid to feel that one has a perfectly safe appointment and a big enough income. It's delightful to think of, isn't it?

NORA. It's wonderful!

HEL. Do you remember last Christmas? For a full three weeks before hand you shut yourself up every evening till long after midnight, making ornaments for the Christmas tree and all the other fine things that were to be a surprise to us. It was the dullest three weeks I ever spent!

NORA. I didn't find it dull.

HEL. (*smiling*). But there was precious little result, Nora.

NORA. Oh, you shouldn't tease me about that again. How could I help the cat's going in and tearing everything to pieces?

HEL. Of course you couldn't, poor little girl. You had the best of intentions to please us all, and that's the main thing. But it is a good thing that our hard times are over.

NORA. Yes, it is really wonderful.

HEL. This time I needn't sit here and be dull all alone and you needn't ruin your dear eyes and your pretty little hands——

NORA (*clapping her hands*). No, Torvald, I needn't any longer, need I! It's wonderfully lovely to hear you say so! (*Taking his arm.*) Now I will tell you how I have been thinking we ought to arrange things, Torvald. As soon as Christmas is over——(*A bell rings in the hall.*) There's the bell. (*She tidies the room a little.*) There's someone at the door. What a nuisance!

HEL. If it is a caller, remember I am not at home.

MAID (*in the doorway*). A lady to see you, ma'am—a stranger.

NORA. Ask her to come in.

MAID (*to* HELMER). The doctor came at the same time, sir.

HEL. Did he go straight into my room?

MAID. Yes sir.

(HELMER *goes into his room. The* MAID *ushers in* MRS. LINDE, *who is in traveling dress, and shuts the door.*)

MRS. L. (*in a dejected and timid voice*). How do you do, Nora?

NORA (*doubtfully*). How do you do——

MRS. L. You don't recognize me, I suppose.

NORA. No, I don't know—yes, to be sure, I seem to——(*Suddenly.*) Yes! Christine! Is it really you?

MRS. L. Yes, it is I.

NORA. Christine! To think of my not recognizing you! And yet how could I? (*In a gentle voice.*) How you have altered, Christine!

MRS. L. Yes, I have indeed. In nine, ten long years——

NORA. Is it so long since we met? I suppose it is. The last eight years have been a happy time for me, I can tell you. And so now you have come into the town and have taken this long journey in winter—that was plucky of you.

MRS. L. I arrived by steamer this morning.

NORA. To have some fun at Christmas time, of course. How delightful! We will have such fun together! But take off your things. You are not cold, I hope. (*Helps her.*) Now we will sit down by the stove and be cozy. No, take this armchair; I will sit here in the rocking chair. (*Takes her hands.*) Now you look like your old self again; it was only the first moment——You are a little paler, Christine, and perhaps a little thinner.

MRS. L. And much, much older, Nora.

NORA. Perhaps a little older; very, very little; certainly not much. (*Stops suddenly and speaks seriously*). What a thoughtless creature I am, chattering away like this. My poor, dear Christine, do forgive me.

MRS. L. What do you mean, Nora?

NORA (*gently*). Poor Christine, you are a widow.

MRS. L. Yes; it is three years ago now.

NORA. Yes, I knew; I saw it in the papers. I assure you, Christine, I meant ever so often to write to you at the time, but I always put it off and something always prevented me.

MRS. L. I quite understand, dear.

NORA. It was very bad of me, Christine. Poor thing, how you must have suffered. And he left you nothing?

MRS. L. No.

NORA. And no children?

MRS. L. No.

NORA. Nothing at all, then?

MRS. L. Not even any sorrow or grief to live upon.

NORA (*looking incredulously at her*). But, Christine, is that possible?

MRS. L. (*smiles sadly and strokes her hair*). It sometimes happens, Nora.

NORA. So you are quite alone. How dreadfully sad that must be. I have three lovely children. You can't see them just now, for they are out with their nurse. But now you must tell me all about it.

MRS. L. No, no; I want to hear about you.

NORA. No, you must begin. I mustn't be selfish today; today I must only think of your affairs. But there is one thing I must tell you. Do you know we have just had a great piece of good luck?

MRS. L. No, what is it?

NORA. Just fancy, my husband has been made manager of the bank!

MRS. L. Your husband? What good luck!

NORA. Yes, tremendous! A barrister's profession is such an uncertain thing, especially if he won't undertake unsavory cases; and naturally Torvald has never been willing to do that, and I quite agree with him. You may imagine how pleased we are! He is to take up his work in the bank at the new year, and then he will have a big salary and lots of commissions. For the future we can live quite differently—we can do just as we like. I feel so relieved and so happy, Christine! It will be splendid to have heaps of money and not need to have any anxiety, won't it?

MRS. L. Yes, anyhow I think it would be delightful to have what one needs.

NORA. No, not only what one needs but heaps and heaps of money.

MRS. L. (*smiling*). Nora, Nora, haven't you learned sense yet? In our schooldays you were a great spendthrift.

NORA (*laughing*). Yes, that is what Torvald says now. (*Wags her finger at her.*) But "Nora, Nora" is not so silly as you think. We have not been in a position for me to waste money. We have both had to work.

MRS. L. You too?

NORA. Yes; odds and ends, needlework, crochet work, embroidery and that kind of thing. (*Dropping her voice.*) And other things as well. You know Torvald left his office when we were married? There was no prospect of promotion there, and he had to try and earn more than before. But during the first year he overworked himself dreadfully. You see, he had to make money every way he could; and he worked early and late; but he couldn't stand it and fell dreadfully ill, and the doctors said it was necessary for him to go south.

MRS. L. You spent a whole year in Italy, didn't you?

NORA. Yes. It was no easy matter to get away, I can tell you. It was just after Ivar was born, but naturally we had to go. It was a wonderfully beautiful journey, and it saved Torvald's life. But it cost a tremendous lot of money, Christine.

MRS. L. So I should think.

NORA. It cost about two hundred and fifty pounds. That's a lot, isn't it?

MRS. L. Yes, and in emergencies like that it is lucky to have the money.

NORA. I ought to tell you that we had it from Papa.

MRS. L. Oh, I see. It was just about that time that he died, wasn't it?

NORA. Yes; and, just think of it, I couldn't go and nurse him. I was expecting little Ivar's birth every day and I had my poor sick Torvald to look after. My dear, kind father—I never saw him again, Christine. That was the saddest time I have known since our marriage.

MRS. L. I know how fond you were of him. And then you went off to Italy?

NORA. Yes; you see, we had money then, and the doctors insisted on our going, so we started a month later.

MRS. L. And your husband came back quite well?

NORA. As sound as a bell!

MRS. L. But—the doctor?

NORA. What doctor?

MRS. L. I thought your maid said the gentleman who arrived here just as I did was the doctor.

NORA. Yes, that was Doctor Rank, but he doesn't come here professionally. He is our greatest friend and comes in at least once every day. No, Torvald has not had an hour's illness since then, and our children are strong and healthy and so am I. (*Jumps up and claps her hands.*) Christine! Christine! It's good to be alive and happy! But how horrid of me; I am talking of nothing but my own affairs. (*Sits on a stool near her and rests her arms on her knees.*) You mustn't be angry with me. Tell me, is it really true that you did not love your husband? Why did you marry him?

MRS. L. My mother was alive then and was bedridden and helpless, and I had to provide for my two younger brothers; so I did not think I was justified in refusing his offer.

NORA. No, perhaps you were quite right. He was rich at that time, then?

MRS. L. I believe he was quite well off. But his business was a precarious one, and when he died it all went to pieces and there was nothing left.

NORA. And then?

MRS. L. Well, I had to turn my hand to anything I could find—first a small shop, then a small school and so on. The last three years have seemed like one long working day, with no rest. Now it is at an end, Nora. My poor mother needs me no more, for she is gone; and the boys do not need me either; they have got situations and can shift for themselves.

NORA. What a relief you must feel it.

MRS. L. No indeed; I only feel my life unspeakably empty. No one to live for any more. (*Gets up restlessly.*) That was why I could not stand the life in my little backwater any longer. I hope it may be easier here to find something which will busy me and occupy my thoughts. If only I could have the good luck to get some regular work—office work of some kind——

NORA. But, Christine, that is so frightfully tiring, and you look tired out now. You had far better go away to some watering place.

MRS. L. (*walking to the window*). I have no father to give me money for a journey, Nora.

NORA (*rising*). Oh, don't be angry with me.

MRS. L. (*going up to her*). It is you that must not be angry with me, dear. The worst of a position like mine is that it makes one so bitter. No one to work for and yet obliged to be always on the lookout for chances. One must live, and so one becomes selfish. When you told me of the happy turn your fortunes have taken—you will hardly believe it—I was delighted not so much on your account as on my own.

NORA. How do you mean? Oh, I understand. You mean that perhaps Torvald could get you something to do.

MRS. L. Yes, that was what I was thinking of.

NORA. He must, Christine. Just leave it to me; I will broach the subject very cleverly—I will think of something that will please him very much. It will make me so happy to be of some use to you.

MRS. L. How kind you are, Nora, to be so anxious to help me! It is doubly kind in you, for you know so little of the burdens and troubles of life.

NORA. I? I know so little of them?

MRS. L. (*smiling*). My dear! Small household cares and that sort of thing! You are a child, Nora.

NORA (*tosses her head and crosses the stage*). You ought not to be so superior.

MRS. L. No?

NORA. You are just like the others. They all think that I am incapable of anything really serious——

MRS. L. Come, come.

NORA. —that I have gone through nothing in this world of cares.

MRS. L. But, my dear Nora, you have just told me all your troubles.

NORA. Pooh!—those were trifles. (*Lowering her voice.*) I have not told you the important thing.

MRS. L. The important thing? What do you mean?

NORA. You look down upon me altogether, Christine—but you ought not to. You are proud, aren't you, of having worked so hard and so long for your mother?

MRS. L. Indeed, I don't look down on anyone. But it is true that I am both proud and glad to think that I was privileged to make the end of my mother's life almost free from care.

NORA. And you are proud to think of what you have done for your brothers.

MRS. L. I think I have the right to be.

NORA. I think so too. But now listen to this; I too have something to be proud and glad of.

MRS. L. I have no doubt you have. But what do you refer to?

NORA. Speak low. Suppose Torvald were to hear! He mustn't on any account—no one in the world must know, Christine, except you.

MRS. L. But what is it?

NORA. Come here. (*Pulls her down on the sofa beside her.*) Now I will show you that I too have something to be proud and glad of. It was I who saved Torvald's life.

MRS. L. "Saved"? How?

NORA. I told you about our trip to Italy. Torvald would never have recovered if he had not gone there.

MRS. L. Yes, but your father gave you the necessary funds.

NORA (*smiling*). Yes, that is what Torvald and the others think, but——

MRS. L. But——

NORA. Papa didn't give us a shilling. It was I who procured the money.

MRS. L. You? All that large sum?

NORA. Two hundred and fifty pounds. What do you think of that?

MRS. L. But, Nora, how could you possibly do it? Did you win a prize in the lottery?

NORA (*contemptuously*). In the lottery? There would have been no credit in that.

MRS. L. But where did you get it from, then?

NORA (*humming and smiling with an air of mystery*). Hm, hm! Aha!

MRS. L. Because you couldn't have borrowed it.

NORA. Couldn't I? Why not?

MRS. L. No, a wife cannot borrow without her husband's consent.

NORA (*tossing her head*). Oh, if it is a wife who has any head for business—a wife who has the wit to be a little bit clever——

MRS. L. I don't understand it at all, Nora.

NORA. There is no need you should. I never said I had borrowed the money. I may have got it some other way. (*Lies back on the sofa.*) Perhaps I got it from some other admirers. When anyone is as attractive as I am——

MRS. L. You are a mad creature.

NORA. Now you know you're full of curiosity, Christine.

MRS. L. Listen to me, Nora dear. Haven't you been a little bit imprudent?

NORA (*sits up straight*). Is it imprudent to save your husband's life?

MRS. L. It seems to me imprudent, without his knowledge, to——

NORA. But it was absolutely necessary that he should not know! My goodness, can't you understand that? It was necessary he should have no idea what a dangerous condition he was in. It was to me that the doctors came and said that his life was in danger and that the only thing to save him was to live in the south. Do you suppose I didn't try, first of all, to get what I wanted as if it were for myself? I told him how much I should love to travel abroad like other young wives; I tried tears and entreaties with him; I told him that he ought to remember the condition I was in and that he ought to be kind and indulgent to me; I even hinted that he might raise a loan. That nearly made him angry, Christine. He said I was thoughtless and that it was his duty as my husband not to indulge me in my whims and caprices—as I believe he called them. Very well, I thought, you must be saved—and that was how I came to devise a way out of the difficulty.

MRS. L. And did your husband never get to know from your father that the money had not come from him?

NORA. No, never. Papa died just at that time. I had meant to let him into the secret and beg him never to reveal it. But he was so ill then—alas, there never was any need to tell him.

MRS. L. And since then have you never told your secret to your husband?

NORA. Good heavens, no! How could you think so? A man who has such strong opinions about these things! And besides, how painful and humiliating it would be for Torvald, with his manly independence, to know that he owed me anything! It would upset our mutual relations altogether; our beautiful happy home would no longer be what it is now.

MRS. L. Do you mean never to tell him about it?

NORA (*meditatively and with a half-smile*). Yes—someday, perhaps, after many years, when I am no longer as nice looking as I am now. Don't laugh at me! I mean, of course, when Torvald is no longer as devoted to me as he is now; when my dancing and dressing-up and reciting have palled on him; then it may be a good thing to have something in reserve——(*Breaking off.*) What nonsense! That time will never come. Now what do you think of my great secret, Christine? Do you still think I am of no use? I can tell you, too, that this affair has caused me a lot of worry. It has been by no means easy for me to meet my engagements punctually. I may tell you that there is something that is called, in business, quarterly interest and another thing called payment in installments, and it is always so dreadfully difficult to manage them. I have had to save a little here and there, where I could, you understand. I have not been able to put aside much from my housekeeping money, for Torvald must have a good table. I couldn't let my children be shabbily dressed; I have felt obliged to use up all he gave me for them, the sweet little darlings!

MRS. L. So it has all had to come out of your own necessaries of life, poor Nora?

NORA. Of course. Besides, I was the one responsible for it. Whenever Torvald has given me money for new dresses and such things I have never spent more than half of it; I have always bought the simplest and cheapest things. Thank heaven any clothes look well on me, and so Torvald has never noticed it. But it was often very hard on me, Christine—because it is delightful to be really well dressed, isn't it?

MRS. L. Quite so.

NORA. Well, then I have found other ways of earning money. Last winter I was lucky enough to get a lot of copying to do, so I locked myself up and sat writing every evening until quite late at night. Many a time I was desperately tired, but all the same it was a tremendous pleasure to sit there working and earning money. It was like being a man.

MRS. L. How much have you been able to pay off in that way?

NORA. I can't tell you exactly. You see, it is very difficult to keep an account of a business matter of that kind. I only know that I have paid every penny that I could scrape together. Many a time I was at my wits' end. (*Smiles.*) Then I used to sit here and imagine that a rich old gentleman had fallen in love with me——

MRS. L. What! Who was it?

NORA. Be quiet!—that he had died and that when his will was opened it contained, written in big letters, the instruction: "The lovely Mrs. Nora Helmer is to have all I possess paid over to her at once in cash."

MRS. L. But, my dear Nora—who could the man be?

NORA. Good gracious, can't you understand? There was no old gentleman at all; it was only something that I used to sit here and imagine, when I couldn't think of any way of procuring money. But it's all the same now; the tiresome old person can stay where he is as far as I am concerned; I don't care about him or his will either, for I am free from care now. (*Jumps up.*) My goodness, it's delightful to think of, Christine! Free from care! To be able to be free from care, quite free from care; to be able to play and romp with the children; to be able to keep the house beautifully and have everything just as Torvald likes it! And, think of it, soon the spring will come and the big blue sky! Perhaps we shall be able to take a little trip—perhaps I shall see the sea again! Oh, it's a wonderful thing to be alive and be happy. (*A bell is heard in the hall.*)

MRS. L. (*rising*). There is the bell; perhaps I had better go.

NORA. No, don't go; no one will come in here; it is sure to be for Torvald.

SERVANT (*at the hall door*). Excuse me, ma'am—there is a gentleman to see the master, and as the doctor is with him——

NORA. Who is it?

KROG. (*at the door*). It is I, Mrs. Helmer. (MRS. LINDE *starts, trembles and turns to the window.*)

NORA (*takes a step toward him and speaks in a strained, low voice*). You? What is it? What do you want to see my husband about?

KROG. Bank business—in a way. I have a small post in the bank, and I hear your husband is to be our chief now.

NORA. Then it is——

KROG. Nothing but dry business matters, Mrs. Helmer; absolutely nothing else.

NORA. Be so good as to go into the study then. (*She bows indifferently to him and shuts the door into the hall, then comes back and makes up the fire in the stove.*)

MRS. L. Nora—who was that man?

NORA. A lawyer of the name of Krogstad.

MRS. L. Then it really was he.

NORA. Do you know the man?

MRS. L. I used to—many years ago. At one time he was a solicitor's clerk in our town.

NORA. Yes, he was.

MRS. L. He is greatly altered.

NORA. He made a very unhappy marriage.

MRS. L. He is a widower now, isn't he?

NORA. With several children. There now, it is burning up. (*Shuts the door of the stove and moves the rocking chair aside.*)

MRS. L. They say he carries on various kinds of business.

NORA. Really! Perhaps he does; I don't know anything about it. But don't let us think of business; it is so tiresome.

DR. RANK (*comes out of* HELMER'S *study. Before he shuts the door he calls to him*). No, my dear fellow, I won't disturb you; I would rather go in to your wife for a little while. (*Shuts the door and sees* MRS. LINDE.) I beg your pardon; I am afraid I am disturbing you too.

NORA. No, not at all. (*Introducing him.*) Doctor Rank, Mrs. Linde.

RANK. I have often heard Mrs. Linde's name mentioned here. I think I passed you on the stairs when I arrived, Mrs. Linde?

MRS. L. Yes, I go up very slowly; I can't manage stairs well.

RANK. Ah! Some slight internal weakness?

MRS. L. No, the fact is I have been overworking myself.

RANK. Nothing more than that? Then I suppose you have come to town to amuse yourself with our entertainments?

MRS. L. I have come to look for work.

RANK. Is that a good cure for overwork?

MRS. L. One must live, Doctor Rank.

RANK. Yes, the general opinion seems to be that it is necessary.

NORA. Look here, Doctor Rank—you know you want to live.

RANK. Certainly. However wretched I may feel, I want to prolong the agony as long as possible. All my patients are like that. And so are those who are morally diseased; one of them, and a bad case too, is at this very moment with Helmer——

MRS. L. (*sadly*). Ah!

NORA. Whom do you mean?

RANK. A lawyer of the name of Krogstad, a fellow you don't know at all. He suffers from a diseased moral character, Mrs. Helmer, but even he began talking of its being highly important that he should live.

NORA. Did he? What did he want to speak to Torvald about?

RANK. I have no idea; I only heard that it was something about the bank.

NORA. I didn't know this—what's his name?—Krogstad had anything to do with the bank.

RANK. Yes, he has some sort of appointment there. (*To* MRS. LINDE.) I don't know whether you find also in your part of the world that there are certain people who go zealously snuffing about to smell out moral corruption and, as soon as they have found some, put the person concerned into some lucrative position where they can keep their eye on him. Healthy natures are left out in the cold.

MRS. L. Still I think the sick are those who most need taking care of.

RANK (*shrugging his shoulders*). Yes, there you are. That is the sentiment that is turning society into a sick house.

(NORA, *who has been absorbed in her thoughts, breaks out into smothered laughter and claps her hands.*)

RANK. Why do you laugh at that? Have you any notion what society really is?

NORA. What do I care about tiresome society? I am laughing at something quite different, something extremely amusing. Tell me, Doctor Rank, are all the people who are employed in the bank dependent on Torvald now?

RANK. Is that what you find so extremely amusing?

NORA (*smiling and humming*). That's my affair! (*Walking about the room.*) It's perfectly glorious to think that we have—that Torvald has so much power over so many people. (*Takes the packet from her pocket.*) Doctor Rank, what do you say to a macaroon?

RANK. What, macaroons? I thought they were forbidden here.

NORA. Yes, but these are some Christine gave me.

MRS. L. What! I?

NORA. Oh well, don't be alarmed! You couldn't know that Torvald had forbidden them. I must tell you that he is afraid they will spoil my teeth. But, bah!—once in a way——That's so, isn't it, Doctor Rank? By your leave! (*Puts a macaroon into his mouth.*) You must have one too, Christine. And I shall have one, just a little one—or at most two. (*Walking about.*) I am tremendously happy. There is just one thing in the world now that I should dearly love to do.

RANK. Well, what is that?

NORA. It's something I should dearly love to say if Torvald could hear me.

RANK. Well, why can't you say it?

NORA. No, I daren't; it's so shocking.

MRS. L. Shocking?

RANK. Well, I should not advise you to say it. Still, with us you might. What is it you would so much like to say if Torvald could hear you?

NORA. I should just love to say—Well, I'm damned!

RANK. Are you mad?

MRS. L. Nora dear!

RANK. Say it, here he is!

NORA (*hiding the packet*). Hush! Hush! Hush!

(HELMER *comes out of his room with his coat over his arm and his hat in his hand.*)

NORA. Well, Torvald dear, have you got rid of him?

HEL. Yes, he has just gone.

NORA. Let me introduce you—this is Christine, who has come to town.

HEL. Christine? Excuse me, but I don't know——

NORA. Mrs. Linde, dear; Christine Linde.

HEL. Of course. A school friend of my wife's, I presume?

MRS. L. Yes, we have known each other since then.

NORA. And just think, she has taken a long journey in order to see you.

HEL. What do you mean?

MRS. L. No, really, I——

NORA. Christine is tremendously clever at bookkeeping, and she is frightfully anxious to work under some clever man, so as to perfect herself——

HEL. Very sensible, Mrs. Linde.

NORA. And when she heard you had been appointed manager of the bank— the news was telegraphed, you know—she traveled here as quick as she could. Torvald, I am sure you will be able to do something for Christine, for my sake, won't you?

HEL. Well, it is not altogether impossible. I presume you are a widow, Mrs. Linde?

MRS. L. Yes.

HEL. And have had some experience of bookkeeping?

MRS. L. Yes, a fair amount.

HEL. Ah well, it's very likely I may be able to find something for you.

NORA (*clapping her hands*). What did I tell you?

HEL. You have just come at a fortunate moment, Mrs. Linde.

MRS. L. How am I to thank you?

HEL. There is no need. (*Puts on his coat.*) But today you must excuse me——

RANK. Wait a minute; I will come with you. (*Brings his fur coat from the hall and warms it at the fire.*)

NORA. Don't be long away, Torvald dear.

HEL. About an hour, not more.

NORA. Are you going too, Christine?

MRS. L. (*putting on her cloak*). Yes, I must go and look for a room.

HEL. Oh well, then, we can walk down the street together.

NORA (*helping her*). What a pity it is we are so short of space here; I am afraid it is impossible for us——

MRS. L. Please don't think of it! Good-by, Nora dear, and many thanks.

NORA. Good-by for the present. Of course you will come back this evening. And you too, Doctor Rank. What do you say? If you are well enough? Oh, you must be! Wrap yourself up well. (*They go to the door all talking together. Children's voices are heard on the staircase.*)

NORA. There they are. There they are! (*She runs to open the door. The* NURSE *comes in with the children.*) Come in! Come in! (*Stoops and kisses them.*) Oh, you sweet blessings! Look at them, Christine! Aren't they darlings?

RANK. Don't let us stand here in the draught.

HEL. Come along, Mrs. Linde; the place will only be bearable for a mother now!

(RANK, HELMER *and* MRS. LINDE *go downstairs. The* NURSE *comes forward with the children;* NORA *shuts the hall door.*)

NORA. How fresh and well you look! Such red cheeks!—like apples and roses. (*The children all talk at once while she speaks to them.*) Have you had great fun? That's splendid! What, you pulled both Emmy and Bob along on the sledge? Both at once? That *was* good. You are a clever boy, Ivar. Let me take her for a little, Anne. My sweet little baby doll! (*Takes the baby from the* MAID *and dances it up and down.*) Yes, yes, Mother will dance with Bob too. What! Have you been snowballing? I wish I had been there too! No, no, I will take their things off, Anne; please let me do it, it is such fun. Go in now, you look half frozen. There is some hot coffee for you on the stove.

(*The* NURSE *goes into the room on the left.* NORA *takes off the children's things and throws them about while they all talk to her at once.*)

NORA. *Really!* Did a big dog run after you? But it didn't bite you? No, dogs don't bite nice little dolly children. You mustn't look at the parcels, Ivar. What are they? Ah, I daresay you would like to know. No, no—it's something nasty! Come, let us have a game! What shall we play at? Hide and seek? Yes, we'll play hide and seek. Bob shall hide first. Must I hide? Very well, I'll hide first. (*She and the children laugh and shout and romp in and out of the room; at last* NORA *hides under the table; the children rush in and look for her but do not see her; they hear her smothered laughter, run to the table, lift up the cloth and find her. Shouts of laughter. She crawls forward and pretends to frighten them. Fresh laughter. Meanwhile there has been a knock at the hall door but none of them has noticed it. The door is half opened and* KROGSTAD *appears. He waits a little; the game goes on.*)

KROG. Excuse me, Mrs. Helmer.

NORA (*with a stifled cry turns round and gets up onto her knees*). Ah! What do you want?

KROG. Excuse me, the outer door was ajar; I suppose someone forgot to shut it.

NORA (*rising*). My husband is out, Mr. Krogstad.

KROG. I know that.

NORA. What do you want here then?

KROG. A word with you.

NORA. With me? (*To the children, gently.*) Go in to Nurse. What? No, the strange man won't do Mother any harm. When he has gone we will have another game. (*She takes the children into the room on the left and shuts the door after them.*) You want to speak to me?

KROG. Yes, I do.

NORA. Today? It is not the first of the month yet.

KROG. No, it is Christmas Eve, and it will depend on yourself what sort of a Christmas you will spend.

NORA. What do you want? Today it is absolutely impossible for me——

KROG. We won't talk about that till later on. This is something different. I presume you can give me a moment?

NORA. Yes—yes, I can—although——

KROG. Good. I was in Olsen's Restaurant and saw your husband going down the street——

NORA. Yes?

KROG. With a lady.

NORA. What then?

KROG. May I make so bold as to ask if it was a Mrs. Linde?

NORA. It was.

KROG. Just arrived in town?

NORA. Yes, today.

KROG. She is a great friend of yours, isn't she?

NORA. She is. But I don't see——

KROG. I knew her too, once upon a time.

NORA. I am aware of that.

KROG. Are you? So you know all about it; I thought as much. Then I can ask you, without beating about the bush—is Mrs. Linde to have an appointment in the bank?

NORA. What right have you to question me, Mr. Krogstad? You, one of my husband's subordinates! But since you ask, you shall know. Yes, Mrs. Linde *is* to have an appointment. And it was I who pleaded her cause, Mr. Krogstad, let me tell you that.

KROG. I was right in what I thought then.

NORA (*walking up and down the stage*). Sometimes one has a tiny little bit of influence, I should hope. Because one is a woman it does not necessarily follow that——When anyone is in a subordinate position, Mr. Krogstad, they should really be careful to avoid offending anyone who—who——

KROG. Who has influence?

NORA. Exactly.

KROG. (*changing his tone*). Mrs. Helmer, you will be so good as to use your influence on my behalf.

NORA. What? What do you mean?

KROG. You will be so kind as to see that I am allowed to keep my subordinate position in the bank.

NORA. What do you mean by that? Who proposes to take your post away from you?

KROG. Oh, there is no necessity to keep up the pretense of ignorance. I can quite understand that your friend is not very anxious to expose herself to the chance of rubbing shoulders with me, and I quite understand, too, whom I have to thank for being turned off.

NORA. But I assure you——

KROG. Very likely; but, to come to the point, the time has come when I should advise you to use your influence to prevent that.

NORA. But, Mr. Krogstad, I *have* no influence.

KROG. Haven't you? I thought you said yourself just now——

NORA. Naturally I did not mean you to put that construction on it. I! What should make you think I have any influence of that kind with my husband?

KROG. Oh, I have known your husband from our student days. I don't suppose he is any more unassailable than other husbands.

NORA. If you speak slightingly of my husband, I shall turn you out of the house.

KROG. You are bold, Mrs. Helmer.

NORA. I am not afraid of you any longer. As soon as the New Year comes I shall in a very short time be free of the whole thing.

KROG. (*controlling himself*). Listen to me, Mrs. Helmer. If necessary, I am prepared to fight for my small post in the bank as if I were fighting for my life.

NORA. So it seems.

KROG. It is not only for the sake of the money; indeed, that weighs least with me in the matter. There is another reason—well, I may as well tell you. My position is this. I daresay you know, like everybody else, that once, many years ago, I was guilty of an indiscretion.

NORA. I think I have heard something of the kind.

KROG. The matter never came into court, but every way seemed to be closed to me after that. So I took to the business that you know of. I had to do something; and, honestly, I don't think I've been one of the worst. But now I must cut myself free from all that. My sons are growing up; for their sake I must try and win back as much respect as I can in the town. This post in the bank was like the first step up for me—and now your husband is going to kick me downstairs again into the mud.

NORA. But you must believe me, Mr. Krogstad; it is not in my power to help you at all.

KROG. Then it is because you haven't the will, but I have means to compel you.

NORA. You don't mean that you will tell my husband that I owe you money?

KROG. Hm! Suppose I were to tell him?

NORA. It would be perfectly infamous of you. (*Sobbing.*) To think of his learning my secret, which has been my joy and pride, in such an ugly, clumsy way—that he should learn it from you! And it would put me in a horribly disagreeable position.

KROG. Only disagreeable?

NORA (*impetuously*). Well, do it then!—and it will be the worse for you. My husband will see for himself what a blackguard you are, and you certainly won't keep your post then.

KROG. I asked you if it was only a disagreeable scene at home that you were afraid of?

NORA. If my husband does get to know of it, of course he will at once pay you what is still owing, and we shall have nothing more to do with you.

KROG. (*coming a step nearer*). Listen to me, Mrs. Helmer. Either you have a very bad memory or you know very little of business. I shall be obliged to remind you of a few details.

NORA. What do you mean?

KROG. When your husband was ill you came to me to borrow two hundred and fifty pounds.

NORA. I didn't know anyone else to go to.

KROG. I promised to get you that amount——

NORA. Yes, and you did so.

KROG. I promised to get you that amount on certain conditions. Your mind was so taken up with your husband's illness and you were so anxious to get the money for your journey that you seem to have paid no attention to the conditions of our bargain. Therefore it will not be amiss if I remind you of them. Now I promised to get the money on the security of a bond which I drew up.

NORA. Yes, and which I signed.

KROG. Good. But below your signature there were a few lines constituting your father a surety for the money; those lines your father should have signed.

NORA. Should? He did sign them.

KROG. I had left the date blank; that is to say your father should himself have inserted the date on which he signed the paper. Do you remember that?

NORA. Yes, I think I remember.

KROG. Then I gave you the bond to send by post to your father. Is that not so?

NORA. Yes.

KROG. And you naturally did so at once, because five or six days afterward you brought me the bond with your father's signature. And then I gave you the money.

NORA. Well, haven't I been paying it off regularly?

KROG. Fairly so, yes. But—to come back to the matter in hand—that must have been a very trying time for you, Mrs. Helmer?

NORA. It was, indeed.

KROG. Your father was very ill, wasn't he?

NORA. He was very near his end.

KROG. And died soon afterward?

NORA. Yes.

KROG. Tell me, Mrs. Helmer, can you by any chance remember what day your father died?—on what day of the month, I mean.

NORA. Papa died on the twenty-ninth of September.

KROG. That is correct; I have ascertained it for myself. And, as that is so, there is a discrepancy (*taking a paper from his pocket*) which I cannot account for.

NORA. What discrepancy? I don't know——

KROG. The discrepancy consists, Mrs. Helmer, in the fact that your father signed this bond three days after his death.

NORA. What do you mean? I don't understand.

KROG. Your father died on the twenty-ninth of September. But look here; your father has dated his signature the second of October. It is a discrepancy, isn't it? (NORA *is silent.*) Can you explain it to me? (NORA *is still silent.*) It is a remarkable thing, too, that the words "second of October," as well as the year, are not written in your father's handwriting but in one that I think I know. Well, of course it can be explained; your father may have forgotten to date his signature and someone else may have dated it haphazard before they knew of his death. There is no harm in that. It all depends on the signature of the name, and *that* is genuine, I suppose, Mrs. Helmer? It was your father himself who signed his name here?

NORA (*after a short pause, throws her head up and looks defiantly at him*). No, it was not. It was I that wrote Papa's name.

KROG. Are you aware that is a dangerous confession?

NORA. In what way? You shall have your money soon.

KROG. Let me ask you a question: why did you not send the paper to your father?

NORA. It was impossible; Papa was so ill. If I had asked him for his signature, I should have had to tell him what the money was to be used for; and when he was so ill himself I couldn't tell him that my husband's life was in danger—it was impossible.

KROG. It would have been better for you if you had given up your trip abroad.

NORA. No, that was impossible. That trip was to save my husband's life; I couldn't give that up.

KROG. But did it never occur to you that you were committing a fraud on me?

NORA. I couldn't take that into account; I didn't trouble myself about you at all. I couldn't bear you because you put so many heartless difficulties in my way although you knew what a dangerous condition my husband was in.

KROG. Mrs. Helmer, you evidently do not realize clearly what it is that you have been guilty of. But I can assure you that my one false step, which lost me all my reputation, was nothing more or nothing worse than what you have done.

NORA. You? Do you ask me to believe that you were brave enough to run a risk to save your wife's life?

KROG. The law cares nothing about motives.

NORA. Then it must be a very foolish law.

KROG. Foolish or not, it is the law by which you will be judged if I produce this paper in court.

NORA. I don't believe it. Is a daughter not to be allowed to spare her dying father anxiety and care? Is a wife not to be allowed to save her husband's life? I don't know much about law, but I am certain that there must be laws permitting such things as that. Have you no knowledge of such laws—you who are a lawyer? You must be a very poor lawyer, Mr. Krogstad.

KROG. Maybe. But matters of business—such business as you and I have had together—do you think I don't understand that? Very well. Do as you please. But let me tell you this—if I lose my position a second time, you shall lose yours with me. (*He bows and goes out through the hall.*)

NORA (*appears buried in thought for a short time, then tosses her head*). Nonsense! Trying to frighten me like that! I am not so silly as he thinks. (*Begins to busy herself putting the children's things in order.*) And yet—— No, it's impossible! I did it for love's sake.

THE CHILDREN (*in the doorway on the left*). Mother, the stranger man has gone out through the gate.

NORA. Yes, dears, I know. But don't tell anyone about the stranger man. Do you hear? Not even Papa.

CHILDREN. No, Mother; but will you come and play again?

NORA. No, no—not now.

CHILDREN. But, Mother, you promised us.

NORA. Yes, but I can't now. Run away in; I have such a lot to do. Run away in, my sweet little darlings. (*She gets them into the room by degrees and shuts the door on them, then sits down on the sofa, takes up a piece of needlework and sews a few stitches but soon stops.*) No! (*Throws down the work, gets up, goes to the hall door and calls out.*) Helen! bring the tree in. (*Goes to the table on the left, opens a drawer and stops again.*) No, no! It is quite impossible!

MAID (*coming in with the tree*). Where shall I put it, ma'am?

NORA. Here, in the middle of the floor.

MAID. Shall I get you anything else?

NORA. No, thank you. I have all I want.

(*Exit* MAID.)

NORA (*begins dressing the tree*). A candle here—and flowers here—— The horrible man! It's all nonsense—there's nothing wrong. The tree shall be splendid! I will do everything I can think of to please you, Torvald! I will sing for you, dance for you—— (HELMER *comes in with some papers under his arm.*) Oh, are you back already?

HEL. Yes. Has anyone been here?

NORA. Here? No.

HEL. That is strange. I saw Krogstad going out of the gate.

NORA. Did you? Oh yes, I forgot, Krogstad was here for a moment.

HEL. Nora, I can see from your manner that he has been here begging you to say a good word for him.

NORA. Yes.

HEL. And you were to appear to do it of your own accord; you were to conceal from me the fact of his having been here; didn't he beg that of you too?

NORA. Yes, Torvald, but——

HEL. Nora, Nora, and you would be a party to that sort of thing? To have any talk with a man like that and give him any sort of promise? And to tell me a lie into the bargain?

NORA. A lie?

HEL. Didn't you tell me no one had been here? (*Shakes his finger at her.*) My little songbird must never do that again. A songbird must have a clean beak to chirp with—no false notes! (*Puts his arm around her waist.*) That is so, isn't it? Yes, I am sure it is. (*Lets her go.*) We will say no more about it. (*Sits down by the stove.*) How warm and snug it is here! (*Turns over his papers.*)

NORA (*after a short pause during which she busies herself with the Christmas tree*). Torvald!

HEL. Yes.

NORA. I am looking forward tremendously to the fancy-dress ball at the Stenborgs' the day after tomorrow.

HEL. And I am tremendously curious to see what you are going to surprise me with.

NORA. It was very silly of me to want to do that.

HEL. What do you mean?

NORA. I can't hit upon anything that will do; everything I think of seems so silly and insignificant.

HEL. Does my little Nora acknowledge that at last?

NORA (*standing behind his chair with her arms on the back of it*). Are you very busy, Torvald?

HEL. Well——

NORA. What are all those papers?

HEL. Bank business.

NORA. Already?

HEL. I have got authority from the retiring manager to undertake the necessary changes in the staff and in the rearrangement of the work, and I must make use of the Christmas week for that, so as to have everything in order for the new year.

NORA. Then that was why this poor Krogstad——

HEL. Hm!

NORA (*leans against the back of his chair and strokes his hair*). If you hadn't been so busy, I should have asked you a tremendously big favor, Torvald.

HEL. What is that? Tell me.

NORA. There is no one has such good taste as you. And I do so want to look nice at the fancy-dress ball. Torvald, couldn't you take me in hand and decide what I shall go as and what sort of a dress I shall wear?

HEL. Aha! So my obstinate little woman is obliged to get someone to come to her rescue?

NORA. Yes, Torvald, I can't get along a bit without your help.

HEL. Very well, I will think it over; we shall manage to hit upon something.

NORA. That is nice of you. (*Goes to the Christmas tree. A short pause.*) How pretty the red flowers look! But tell me, was it really something very bad that this Krogstad was guilty of?

HEL. He forged someone's name. Have you any idea what that means?

NORA. Isn't it possible that he was driven to do it by necessity?

HEL. Yes; or, as in so many cases, by imprudence. I am not so heartless as to condemn a man altogether because of a single false step of that kind.

NORA. No, you wouldn't, would you, Torvald?

HEL. Many a man has been able to retrieve his character if he has openly confessed his fault and taken his punishment.

NORA. Punishment?

HEL. But Krogstad did nothing of that sort; he got himself out of it by a cunning trick, and that is why he has gone under altogether.

NORA. But do you think it would——

HEL. Just think how a guilty man like that has to lie and play the hypocrite with everyone, how he has to wear a mask in the presence of those near and dear to him, even before his own wife and children. And about the children—that is the most terrible part of it all, Nora.

NORA. How?

HEL. Because such an atmosphere of lies infects and poisons the whole life of a home. Each breath the children take in such a house is full of the germs of evil.

NORA (*coming nearer him*). Are you sure of that?

HEL. My dear, I have often seen it in the course of my life as a lawyer. Almost everyone who has gone to the bad early in life has had a deceitful mother.

NORA. Why do you only say—mother?

HEL. It seems most commonly to be the mother's influence, though naturally a bad father's would have the same result. Every lawyer is familiar with the fact. This Krogstad, now, has been persistently poisoning his own children with lies and dissimulation; that is why I say he has lost all moral character. (*Holds out his hands to her.*) That is why my sweet little Nora must promise me not to plead his cause. Give me your hand on it. Come, come, what is this? Give me your hand. There now, that's settled. I assure you it would be quite impossible for me to work with him; I literally feel physically ill when I am in the company of such people.

NORA (*takes her hand out of his and goes to the opposite side of the Christmas tree*). How hot it is in here, and I have such a lot to do.

HEL. (*getting up and putting his papers in order*). Yes, and I must try and read through some of these before dinner, and I must think about your costume too. And it is just possible I may have something ready in gold paper to hang up on the tree. (*Puts his hand on her head.*) My precious little singing bird! (*He goes into his room and shuts the door after him.*)

NORA (*after a pause, whispers*). No, no—it isn't true. It's impossible; it must be impossible.

(*The* NURSE *opens the door on the left.*)

NURSE. The little ones are begging so hard to be allowed to come in to Mamma.

NORA. No, no, no! Don't let them come in to me! You stay with them, Anne.

NURSE. Very well, ma'am. (*Shuts the door.*)

NORA (*pale with terror*). Deprave my little children? Poison my home? (*A short pause. Then she tosses her head.*) It's not true. It can't possibly be true.

ACT II

THE SAME SCENE—*The Christmas tree is in the corner by the piano, stripped of its ornaments and with burned-down candle ends on its disheveled branches.* NORA'S *cloak and hat are lying on the sofa. She is alone in the room, walking about uneasily. She stops by the sofa and takes up her cloak.*

NORA (*drops the cloak*). Someone is coming now. (*Goes to the door and listens.*) No—it is no one. Of course no one will come today, Christmas Day—nor tomorrow either. But perhaps—— (*Opens the door and looks out.*) No, nothing in the letter box; it is quite empty. (*Comes forward.*) What rubbish! Of course he can't be in earnest about it. Such a thing couldn't happen; it is impossible—I have three little children.

(*Enter the* NURSE *from the room on the left, carrying a big cardboard box.*)

NURSE. At last I have found the box with the fancy dress.

NORA. Thanks; put it on the table.

NURSE (*in doing so*). But it is very much in want of mending.

NORA. I should like to tear it into a hundred thousand pieces.

NURSE. What an idea! It can easily be put in order—just a little patience.

NORA. Yes, I will go and get Mrs. Linde to come and help me with it.

NURSE. What, out again? In this horrible weather? You will catch cold, ma'am, and make yourself ill.

NORA. Well, worse than that might happen. How are the children?

NURSE. The poor little souls are playing with their Christmas presents, but——

NORA. Do they ask much for me?

NURSE. You see, they are so accustomed to having their mamma with them.

NORA. Yes—but, Nurse, I shall not be able to be so much with them now as I was before.

NURSE. Oh well, young children easily get accustomed to anything.

NORA. Do you think so? Do you think they would forget their mother if she went away altogether?

NURSE. Good heavens!—went away altogether?

NORA. Nurse, I want you to tell me something I have often wondered about— how could you have the heart to put your own child out among strangers?

NURSE. I was obliged to if I wanted to be little Nora's nurse.

NORA. Yes, but how could you be willing to do it?

NURSE. What, when I was going to get such a good place by it? A poor girl who has got into trouble should be glad to. Besides, that wicked man did- n't do a single thing for me.

NORA. But I suppose your daughter has quite forgotten you.

NURSE. No, indeed she hasn't. She wrote to me when she was confirmed and when she was married.

NORA (*putting her arms round her neck*). Dear old Anne, you were a good mother to me when I was little.

NURSE. Little Nora, poor dear, had no other mother but me.

NORA. And if my little ones had no other mother, I am sure you would—— What nonsense I am talking! (*Opens the box.*) Go in to them. Now I must—— You will see tomorrow how charming I shall look.

NURSE. I am sure there will be no one at the ball so charming as you, ma'am. (*Goes into the room on the left.*)

NORA (*begins to unpack the box but soon pushes it away from her*). If only I dared go out. If only no one would come. If only I could be sure nothing would happen here in the meantime. Stuff and nonsense! No one will come. Only I mustn't think about it. I will brush my muff. What lovely, lovely gloves! Out of my thoughts, out of my thoughts! One, two, three, four, five, six—— (*Screams.*) Ah! there is someone coming. (*Makes a movement toward the door but stands irresolute.*)

(*Enter* MRS. LINDE *from the hall, where she has taken off her cloak and hat.*)

NORA. Oh, it's you, Christine. There is no one else out there, is there? How good of you to come!

MRS. L. I heard you were up asking for me.

NORA. Yes, I was passing by. As a matter of fact, it is something you could help me with. Let us sit down here on the sofa. Look here. Tomorrow evening there is to be a fancy-dress ball at the Stenborgs', who live above us, and Torvald wants me to go as a Neapolitan fishergirl and dance the tarantella that I learnt at Capri.

MRS. L. I see; you are going to keep up the character.

NORA. Yes, Torvald wants me to. Look, here is the dress; Torvald had it made for me there, but now it is all so torn, and I haven't any idea——

MRS. L. We will easily put that right. It is only some of the trimming come unsewn here and there. Needle and thread? Now then, that's all we want.

NORA. It *is* nice of you.

MRS. L. (*sewing*). So you are going to be dressed up tomorrow, Nora. I will tell you what—I shall come in for a moment and see you in your fine feathers. But I have completely forgotten to thank you for a delightful evening yesterday.

NORA (*gets up and crosses the stage*). Well, I don't think yesterday was as pleasant as usual. You ought to have come down to town a little earlier, Christine. Certainly Torvald does understand how to make a house dainty and attractive.

MRS. L. And so do you, it seems to me; you are not your father's daughter for nothing. But tell me, is Doctor Rank always as depressed as he was yesterday?

NORA. No; yesterday it was very noticeable. I must tell you that he suffers from a very dangerous disease. He has consumption of the spine, poor creature. His father was a horrible man who committed all sorts of excesses, and that is why his son was sickly from childhood, do you understand?

MRS. L. (*dropping her sewing*). But, my dearest Nora, how do you know anything about such things?

NORA (*walking about*). Pooh! When you have three children you get visits now and then from—from married women who know something of medical matters, and they talk about one thing and another.

MRS. L. (*goes on sewing. A short silence*). Does Doctor Rank come here every day?

NORA. Every day regularly. He is Torvald's most intimate friend and a friend of mine too. He is just like one of the family.

MRS. L. But tell me this—is he perfectly sincere? I mean, isn't he the kind of man that is very anxious to make himself agreeable?

NORA. Not in the least. What makes you think that?

MRS. L. When you introduced him to me yesterday he declared he had often heard my name mentioned in this house, but afterward I noticed that your husband hadn't the slightest idea who I was. So how could Doctor Rank——

NORA. That is quite right, Christine. Torvald is so absurdly fond of me that he wants me absolutely to himself, as he says. At first he used to seem almost jealous if I mentioned any of the dear folks at home, so naturally I gave up doing so. But I often talk about such things with Doctor Rank because he likes hearing about them.

MRS. L. Listen to me, Nora. You are still very like a child in many things, and I am older than you in many ways and have a little more experience. Let me tell you this—you ought to make an end of it with Doctor Rank.

NORA. What ought I to make an end of?

MRS. L. Of two things, I think. Yesterday you talked some nonsense about a rich admirer who was to leave you money——

NORA. An admirer who doesn't exist, unfortunately! But what then?

MRS. L. Is Doctor Rank a man of means?

NORA. Yes, he is.

MRS. L. And has no one to provide for?

NORA. No, no one; but——

MRS. L. And comes here every day?

NORA. Yes, I told you so.

MRS. L. But how can this well-bred man be so tactless?

NORA. I don't understand you at all.

MRS. L. Don't prevaricate, Nora. Do you suppose I don't guess who lent you the two hundred and fifty pounds?

NORA. Are you out of your senses? How can you think of such a thing! A friend of ours, who comes here every day! Do you realize what a horribly painful position that would be?

MRS. L. Then it really isn't he?

NORA. No, certainly not. It would never have entered into my head for a moment. Besides, he had no money to lend then; he came into his money afterward.

MRS. L. Well, I think that was lucky for you, my dear Nora.

NORA. No, it would never have come into my head to ask Doctor Rank. Although I am quite sure that if I had asked him——

MRS. L. But of course you won't.

NORA. Of course not. I have no reason to think it could possibly be necessary. But I am quite sure that if I told Doctor Rank——

MRS. L. Behind your husband's back?

NORA. I must make an end of it with the other one, and that will be behind his back too. I *must* make an end of it with him.

MRS. L. Yes, that is what I told you yesterday, but——

NORA (*walking up and down*). A man can put a thing like that straight much easier than a woman.

MRS. L. One's husband, yes.

NORA. Nonsense! (*Standing still.*) When you pay off a debt you get your bond back, don't you?

MRS. L. Yes, as a matter of course.

NORA. And can tear it into a hundred thousand pieces and burn it up—the nasty dirty paper!

MRS. L. (*looks hard at her, lays down her sewing and gets up slowly*). Nora, you are concealing something from me.

NORA. Do I look as if I were?

MRS. L. Something has happened to you since yesterday morning. Nora, what is it?

NORA (*going nearer to her*). Christine! (*Listens.*) Hush! There's Torvald come home. Do you mind going in to the children for the present? Torvald can't bear to see dressmaking going on. Let Anne help you.

MRS. L. (*gathering some of the things together*). Certainly—but I am not going away from here till we have had it out with one another. (*She goes into the room on the left as* HELMER *comes in from the hall.*)

NORA (*going up to* HELMER). I have wanted you so much, Torvald dear.

HEL. Was that the dressmaker?

NORA. No, it was Christine; she is helping me to put my dress in order. You will see I shall look quite smart.

HEL. Wasn't that a happy thought of mine, now?

NORA. Splendid! But don't you think it is nice of me, too, to do as you wish?

HEL. Nice?—because you do as your husband wishes? Well, well, you little rogue, I am sure you did not mean it in that way. But I am not going to disturb you; you will want to be trying on your dress, I expect.

NORA. I suppose you are going to work.

HEL. Yes. (*Shows her a bundle of papers.*) Look at that. I have just been in to the bank. (*Turns to go into his room.*)

NORA. Torvald.

HEL. Yes.

NORA. If your little squirrel were to ask you for something very, very prettily——

HEL. What then?

NORA. Would you do it?

HEL. I should like to hear what it is first.

NORA. Your squirrel would run about and do all her tricks if you would be nice and do what she wants.

HEL. Speak plainly.

NORA. Your skylark would chirp, chirp about in every room, with her song rising and falling——

HEL. Well, my skylark does that anyhow.

NORA. I would play the fairy and dance for you in the moonlight, Torvald.

HEL. Nora—you surely don't mean that request you made of me this morning?

NORA (*going near him*). Yes, Torvald, I beg you so earnestly——

HEL. Have you really the courage to open up that question again?

NORA. Yes, dear, you *must* do as I ask; you *must* let Krogstad keep his post in the bank.

HEL. My dear Nora, it is his post that I have arranged Mrs. Linde shall have.

NORA. Yes, you have been awfully kind about that, but you could just as well dismiss some other clerk instead of Krogstad.

HEL. This is simply incredible obstinacy! Because you chose to give him a thoughtless promise that you would speak for him I am expected to——

NORA. That isn't the reason, Torvald. It is for your own sake. This fellow writes in the most scurrilous newspapers; you have told me so yourself. He can do you an unspeakable amount of harm. I am frightened to death of him.

HEL. Ah, I understand; it is recollections of the past that scare you.

NORA. What do you mean?

HEL. Naturally you are thinking of your father.

NORA. Yes—yes, of course. Just recall to your mind what these malicious creatures wrote in the papers about Papa and how horribly they slandered him. I believe they would have procured his dismissal if the Department had not sent you over to inquire into it and if you had not been so kindly disposed and helpful to him.

HEL. My little Nora, there is an important difference between your father and me. Your father's reputation as a public official was not above suspicion. Mine is, and I hope it will continue to be so as long as I hold my office.

NORA. You never can tell what mischief these men may contrive. We ought to be so well off, so snug and happy here in our peaceful home, and have no cares—you and I and the children, Torvald! That is why I beg you so earnestly——

HEL. And it is just by interceding for him that you make it impossible for me to keep him. It is already known at the bank that I mean to dismiss Krogstad. Is it to get about now that the new manager has changed his mind at his wife's bidding?

NORA. And what if it did?

HEL. Of course!—if only this obstinate little person can get her way! Do you suppose I am going to make myself ridiculous before my whole staff, to let people think I am a man to be swayed by all sorts of outside influence? I should very soon feel the consequences of it, I can tell you! And besides, there is one thing that makes it quite impossible for me to have Krogstad in the bank as long as I am manager.

NORA. Whatever is that?

HEL. His moral failings I might perhaps have overlooked if necessary——

NORA. Yes, you could—couldn't you?

HEL. And I hear he is a good worker too. But I knew him when we were boys. It was one of those rash friendships that so often prove an incubus in afterlife. I may as well tell you plainly, we were once on very intimate terms with one another. But this tactless fellow lays no restraint on himself when other people are present. On the contrary, he thinks it gives him the right to adopt a familiar tone with me, and every minute it is "I say, Helmer, old fellow!" and that sort of thing. I assure you it is extremely painful for me. He would make my position in the bank intolerable.

NORA. Torvald, I don't believe you mean that.

HEL. Don't you? Why not?

NORA. Because it is such a narrow-minded way of looking at things.

HEL. What are you saying? Narrow-minded? Do you think I am narrow-minded?

NORA. No, just the opposite, dear—and it is exactly for that reason——

HEL. It's the same thing. You say my point of view is narrow-minded, so I must be so too. Narrow-minded! Very well—I must put an end to this. (*Goes to the hall door and calls.*) Helen!

NORA. What are you going to do?

HEL. (*looking among his papers*). Settle it. (*Enter* MAID.) Look here; take this letter and go downstairs with it at once. Find a messenger and tell him to deliver it and be quick. The address is on it, and here is the money.

MAID. Very well, sir. (*Exit with the letter.*)

HEL. (*putting his papers together*). Now then, little Miss Obstinate.

NORA (*breathlessly*). Torvald—what was that letter?

HEL. Krogstad's dismissal.

NORA. Call her back, Torvald! There is still time. Oh, Torvald, call her back!

Do it for my sake—for your own sake—for the children's sake! Do you hear me, Torvald? Call her back! You don't know what that letter can bring upon us.

HEL. It's too late.

NORA. Yes, it's too late.

HEL. My dear Nora, I can forgive the anxiety you are in, although really it is an insult to me. It is, indeed. Isn't it an insult to think that I should be afraid of a starving quill driver's vengeance? But I forgive you nevertheless, because it is such eloquent witness to your great love for me. (*Takes her in his arms.*) And that is as it should be, my own darling Nora. Come what will, you may be sure I shall have both courage and strength if they be needed. You will see I am man enough to take everything upon myself.

NORA (*in a horror-stricken voice*). What do you mean by that?

HEL. Everything, I say.

NORA (*recovering herself*). You will never have to do that.

HEL. That's right. Well, we will share it, Nora, as man and wife should. That is how it shall be. (*Caressing her.*) Are you content now? There! there!—not these frightened dove's eyes! The whole thing is only the wildest fancy! Now you must go and play through the tarantella and practice with your tambourine. I shall go into the inner office and shut the door, and I shall hear nothing; you can make as much noise as you please. (*Turns back at the door.*) And when Rank comes tell him where he will find me. (*Nods to her, takes his papers and goes into his room and shuts the door after him.*)

NORA (*bewildered with anxiety, stands as if rooted to the spot and whispers*). He was capable of doing it. He will do it. He will do it in spite of everything. No, not that! Never, never! Anything rather than that! Oh, for some help, some way out of it! (*The doorbell rings.*) Doctor Rank! Anything rather than that—anything, whatever it is! (*She puts her hands over her face, pulls herself together, goes to the door and opens it. RANK is standing without, hanging up his coat. During the following dialogue it begins to grow dark.*)

NORA. Good day, Doctor Rank. I knew your ring. But you mustn't go in to Torvald now; I think he is busy with something.

RANK. And you?

NORA (*brings him in and shuts the door after him*). Oh, you know very well I always have time for you.

RANK. Thank you. I shall make use of as much of it as I can.

NORA. What do you mean by that? As much of it as you can?

RANK. Well, does that alarm you?

NORA. It was such a strange way of putting it. Is anything likely to happen?

RANK. Nothing but what I have long been prepared for. But I certainly didn't expect it to happen so soon.

NORA (*gripping him by the arm*). What have you found out? Doctor Rank, you must tell me.

RANK (*sitting down by the stove*). It is all up with me. And it can't be helped.

NORA (*with a sigh of relief*). Is it about yourself?

RANK. Who else? It is no use lying to one's self. I am the most wretched of all my patients, Mrs. Helmer. Lately I have been taking stock of my internal economy. Bankrupt! Probably within a month I shall lie rotting in the churchyard.

NORA. What an ugly thing to say!

RANK. The thing itself is cursedly ugly, and the worst of it is that I shall have to face so much more that is ugly before that. I shall only make one more examination of myself; when I have done that I shall know pretty certainly when it will be that the horrors of dissolution will begin. There is something I want to tell you. Helmer's refined nature gives him an unconquerable disgust at everything that is ugly; I won't have him in my sickroom.

NORA. Oh, but, Doctor Rank——

RANK. I won't have him there. Not on any account. I bar my door to him. As soon as I am quite certain that the worst has come I shall send you my card with a black cross on it, and then you will know that the loathsome end has begun.

NORA. You are quite absurd today. And I wanted you so much to be in a really good humor.

RANK. With death stalking beside me? To have to pay this penalty for another man's sin! Is there any justice in that? And in every single family, in one way or another, some such inexorable retribution is being exacted.

NORA (*putting her hands over her ears*). Rubbish! Do talk of something cheerful.

RANK. Oh, it's a mere laughing matter; the whole thing. My poor innocent spine has to suffer for my father's youthful amusements.

NORA (*sitting at the table on the left*). I suppose you mean that he was too partial to asparagus and pâté de foie gras, don't you?

RANK. Yes, and to truffles.

NORA. Truffles, yes. And oysters too, I suppose?

RANK. Oysters, of course; that goes without saying.

NORA. And heaps of port and champagne. It is sad that all these nice things should take their revenge on our bones.

RANK. Especially that they should revenge themselves on the unlucky bones of those who have not had the satisfaction of enjoying them.

NORA. Yes, that's the saddest part of it all.

RANK (*with a searching look at her*). Hm!

NORA (*after a short pause*). Why did you smile?

RANK. No, it was you that laughed.

NORA. No, it was you that smiled, Doctor Rank!

RANK (*rising*). You are a greater rascal than I thought.

NORA. I am in a silly mood today.

RANK. So it seems.

NORA (*putting her hands on his shoulders*). Dear, dear Doctor Rank, death mustn't take you away from Torvald and me.

RANK. It is a loss you would easily recover from. Those who are gone are soon forgotten.

NORA (*looking at him anxiously*). Do you believe that?

RANK. People form new ties, and then——

NORA. Who will form new ties?

RANK. Both you and Helmer, when I am gone. You yourself are already on the highroad to it, I think. What did that Mrs. Linde want here last night?

NORA. Oho! You don't mean to say that you are jealous of poor Christine?

RANK. Yes, I am. She will be my successor in this house. When I am done for, this woman will——

NORA. Hush! Don't speak so loud. She is in that room.

RANK. Today again. There, you see.

NORA. She has only come to sew my dress for me. Bless my soul, how unreasonable you are! (*Sits down on the sofa.*) Be nice now, Doctor Rank, and tomorrow you will see how beautifully I shall dance, and you can imagine I am doing it all for you—and for Torvald too, of course. (*Takes various things out of the box.*) Doctor Rank, come and sit down here, and I will show you something.

RANK (*sitting down*). What is it?

NORA. Just look at those!

RANK. Silk stockings.

NORA. Flesh colored. Aren't they lovely? It is so dark here now, but tomorrow—— No, no, no! You must only look at the feet. Oh well, you may have leave to look at the legs too.

RANK. Hm!

NORA. Why are you looking so critical? Don't you think they will fit me?

RANK. I have no means of forming an opinion about that.

NORA (*looks at him for a moment*). For shame! (*Hits him lightly on the ear with the stockings.*) That's to punish you. (*Folds them up again.*)

RANK. And what other nice things am I to be allowed to see?

NORA. Not a single thing more, for being so naughty. (*She looks among the things, humming to herself.*)

RANK (*after a short silence*). When I am sitting here talking to you as intimately as this I cannot imagine for a moment what would have become of me if I had never come into this house.

NORA (*smiling*). I believe you do feel thoroughly at home with us.

RANK (*in a lower voice, looking straight in front of him*). And to be obliged to leave it all——

NORA. Nonsense, you are not going to leave it.

RANK (*as before*). And not be able to leave behind one the slightest token of one's gratitude, scarcely even a fleeting regret—nothing but an empty place which the firstcomer can fill as well as any other.

NORA. And if I asked you now for a—— No!

RANK. For what?

NORA. For a big proof of your friendship——

RANK. Yes, yes!

NORA. I mean a tremendously big favor——

RANK. Would you really make me so happy for once?

NORA. Ah, but you don't know what it is yet.

RANK. No—— but tell me.

NORA. I really can't, Doctor Rank. It is something out of all reason; it means advice and help and a favor——

RANK. The bigger a thing it is, the better. I can't conceive what it is you mean. Do tell me. Haven't I your confidence?

NORA. More than anyone else. I know you are my truest and best friend, and so I will tell you what it is. Well, Doctor Rank, it is something you must help me to prevent. You know how devotedly, how inexpressibly deeply Torvald loves me; he would never for a moment hesitate to give his life for me.

RANK (*leaning toward her*). Nora—do you think he is the only one——

NORA (*with a slight start*). The only one—— ?

RANK. The only one who would gladly give his life for your sake.

NORA (*sadly*). Is that it?

RANK. I was determined you should know it before I went away, and there will never be a better opportunity than this. Now you know it, Nora. And now you know, too, that you can trust me as you would trust no one else.

NORA (*rises deliberately and quietly*). Let me pass.

RANK (*makes room for her to pass him but sits still*). Nora!

NORA (*at the hall door*). Helen, bring in the lamp. (*Goes over to the stove.*) Dear Doctor Rank, that was really horrid of you.

RANK. To have loved you as much as anyone else does? Was that horrid?

NORA. No, but to go and tell me so. There was really no need——

RANK. What do you mean? Did you know? (MAID *enters with lamp, puts it down on the table and goes out.*) Nora—Mrs. Helmer—tell me, had you any idea of this?

NORA. Oh, how do I know whether I had or whether I hadn't? I really can't tell you. To think you could be so clumsy, Doctor Rank! We were getting on so nicely.

RANK. Well, at all events you know that you can command me body and soul. So won't you speak out?

NORA (*looking at him*). After what happened?

RANK. I beg you to let me know what it is.

NORA. I can't tell you anything now.

RANK. Yes, yes. You mustn't punish me in that way. Let me have permission to do for you whatever a man may do.

NORA. You can do nothing for me now. Besides, I really don't need any help at all. You will find that the whole thing is merely fancy on my part. It really is so—of course it is! (*Sits down in the rocking chair and looks at him with a smile.*) You are a nice sort of man, Doctor Rank! Don't you feel ashamed of yourself now the lamp has come?

RANK. Not a bit. But perhaps I had better go—forever?

NORA. No indeed, you shall not. Of course you must come here just as before. You know very well Torvald can't do without you.

RANK. Yes, but you?

NORA. Oh, I am always tremendously pleased when you come.

RANK. It is just that that put me on the wrong track. You are a riddle to me. I have often thought that you would almost as soon be in my company as in Helmer's.

NORA. Yes—you see, there are some people one loves best and others whom one would almost always rather have as companions.

RANK. Yes, there is something in that.

NORA. When I was at home of course I loved Papa best. But I always thought it tremendous fun if I could steal down into the maids' room, because they never moralized at all and talked to each other about such entertaining things.

RANK. I see—it is *their* place I have taken.

NORA (*jumping up and going to him*). Oh, dear, nice Doctor Rank, I never meant that at all. But surely you can understand that being with Torvald is a little like being with Papa——

(*Enter* MAID *from the hall.*)

MAID. If you please, ma'am. (*Whispers and hands her a card.*)

NORA (*glancing at the card*). Oh! (*Puts it in her pocket.*)

RANK. Is there anything wrong?

NORA. No, no, not in the least. It is only something—it is my new dress——

RANK. What? Your dress is lying there.

NORA. Oh yes, that one; but this is another. I ordered it. Torvald mustn't know about it.

RANK. Oho! Then that was the great secret.

NORA. Of course. Just go in to him; he is sitting in the inner room. Keep him as long as——

RANK. Make your mind easy; I won't let him escape. (*Goes into* HELMER'S *room.*)

NORA (*to the* MAID). And he is standing waiting in the kitchen?

MAID. Yes; he came up the back stairs.

NORA. But didn't you tell him no one was in?

MAID. Yes, but it was no good.

NORA. He won't go away?

MAID. No; he says he won't until he has seen you, ma'am.

NORA. Well, let him come in—but quietly. Helen, you mustn't say anything about it to anyone. It is a surprise for my husband.

MAID. Yes, ma'am, I quite understand. (*Exit.*)

NORA. This dreadful thing is going to happen! It will happen in spite of me! No, no, no, it can't happen—it shan't happen! (*She bolts the door of* HELMER'S *room. The* MAID *opens the hall door for* KROGSTAD *and shuts it after him. He is wearing a fur coat, high boots and a fur cap.*)

NORA (*advancing toward him*). Speak low—my husband is at home.

KROG. No matter about that.

NORA. What do you want of me?

KROG. An explanation of something.

NORA. Make haste then. What is it?

KROG. You know, I suppose, that I have got my dismissal.

NORA. I couldn't prevent it, Mr. Krogstad. I fought as hard as I could on your side, but it was no good.

KROG. Does your husband love you so little then? He knows what I can expose you to, and yet he ventures——

NORA. How can you suppose that he has any knowledge of the sort?

KROG. I didn't suppose so at all. It would not be the least like our dear Torvald Helmer to show so much courage——

NORA. Mr. Krogstad, a little respect for my husband, please.

KROG. Certainly—all the respect he deserves. But since you have kept the matter so carefully to yourself, I make bold to suppose that you have a little clearer idea than you had yesterday of what it actually is that you have done?

NORA. More than you could ever teach me.

KROG. Yes, such a bad lawyer as I am.

NORA. What is it you want of me?

KROG. Only to see how you were, Mrs. Helmer. I have been thinking about you all day long. A mere cashier, a quill driver, a—well, a man like me— even he has a little of what is called feeling, you know.

NORA. Show it then; think of my little children.

KROG. Have you and your husband thought of mine? But never mind about that. I only wanted to tell you that you need not take this matter too seriously. In the first place there will be no accusation made on my part.

NORA. No, of course not; I was sure of that.

KROG. The whole thing can be arranged amicably; there is no reason why anyone should know anything about it. It will remain a secret between us three.

NORA. My husband must never get to know anything about it.

KROG. How will you be able to prevent it? Am I to understand that you can pay the balance that is owing?

NORA. No, not just at present.

KROG. Or perhaps that you have some expedient for raising the money soon?

NORA. No expedient that I mean to make use of.

KROG. Well, in any case it would have been of no use to you now. If you stood there with ever so much money in your hand, I would never part with your bond.

NORA. Tell me what purpose you mean to put it to.

KROG. I shall only preserve it—keep it in my possession. No one who is not concerned in the matter shall have the slightest hint of it. So that if the thought of it has driven you to any desperate resolution——

NORA. It has.

KROG. If you had it in your mind to run away from your home——

NORA. I had.

KROG. Or even something worse——

NORA. How could you know that?

KROG. Give up the idea.

NORA. How did you know I had thought of *that*?

KROG. Most of us think of that at first. I did too—but I hadn't the courage.

NORA (*faintly*). No more than I.

KROG. (*in a tone of relief*). No, that's it, isn't it—you hadn't the courage either?

NORA. No, I haven't—I haven't.

KROG. Besides, it would have been a great piece of folly. Once the first storm at home is over—— I have a letter for your husband in my pocket.

NORA. Telling him everything?

KROG. In as lenient a manner as I possibly could.

NORA (*quickly*). He mustn't get the letter. Tear it up. I will find some means of getting money.

KROG. Excuse me, Mrs. Helmer, but I think I told you just now——

NORA. I am not speaking of what I owe you. Tell me what sum you are asking my husband for, and I will get the money.

KROG. I am not asking your husband for a penny.

NORA. What do you want then?

KROG. I will tell you. I want to rehabilitate myself, Mrs. Helmer; I want to get on, and in that your husband must help me. For the last year and a half I have not had a hand in anything dishonorable, and all that time I have been struggling in most restricted circumstances. I was content to work my way up step by step. Now I am turned out, and I am not going to be satisfied with merely being taken into favor again. I want to get on, I tell you. I want to get into the bank again, in a higher position. Your husband must make a place for me——

NORA. That he will never do!

KROG. He will; I know him; he dare not protest. And as soon as I am in there again with him then you will see! Within a year I shall be the manager's right hand. It will be Nils Krogstad and not Torvald Helmer who manages the bank.

NORA. That's a thing you will never see!

KROG. Do you mean that you will——

NORA. I have courage enough for it now.

KROG. Oh, you can't frighten me. A fine, spoilt lady like you——

NORA. You will see, you will see.

KROG. Under the ice, perhaps? Down into the cold, coal-black water? And then, in the spring, to float up to the surface, all horrible and unrecognizable, with your hair fallen out——

NORA. You can't frighten me.

KROG. Nor you me. People don't do such things, Mrs. Helmer. Besides, what use would it be? I should have him completely in my power all the same.

NORA. Afterward? When I am no longer——

KROG. Have you forgotten that it is I who have the keeping of your reputation? (NORA *stands speechlessly looking at him.*) Well, now, I have warned you. Do not do anything foolish. When Helmer has had my letter I shall expect a message from him. And be sure you remember that it is your husband himself who has forced me into such ways as this again. I will never forgive him for that. Good-by, Mrs. Helmer. (*Exit through the hall.*)

NORA (*goes to the hall door, opens it slightly and listens*). He is going. He is not putting the letter in the box. Oh no, no! that's impossible! (*Opens the door by degrees.*) What is that? He is standing outside. He is not going downstairs. Is he hesitating? Can he—— (*A letter drops in the box; then* KROGSTAD'S *footsteps are heard, till they die away as he goes downstairs.* NORA *utters a stifled cry and runs across the room to the table by the sofa. A short pause.*)

NORA. In the letter box. (*Steals across to the hall door.*) There it lies—Torvald, Torvald, there is no hope for us now!

(MRS. LINDE *comes in from the room on the left, carrying the dress.*)

MRS. L. There, I can't see anything more to mend now. Would you like to try it on?

NORA (*in a hoarse whisper*). Christine, come here.

MRS. L. (*throwing the dress down on the sofa*). What is the matter with you? You look so agitated!

NORA. Come here. Do you see that letter? There, look—you can see it through the glass in the letter box.

MRS. L. Yes, I see it.

NORA. That letter is from Krogstad.

MRS. L. Nora—it was Krogstad who lent you the money!

NORA. Yes, and now Torvald will know all about it.

MRS. L. Believe me, Nora, that's the best thing for both of you.

NORA. You don't know all. I forged a name.

MRS. L. Good heavens!

NORA. I only want to say this to you, Christine—you must be my witness.

MRS. L. Your witness? What do you mean? What am I to——

NORA. If I should go out of my mind—and it might easily happen——

MRS. L. Nora!

NORA. Or if anything else should happen to me—anything, for instance, that might prevent my being here——

MRS. L. Nora! Nora! you are quite out of your mind.

NORA. And if it should happen that there were someone who wanted to take all the responsibility, all the blame, you understand——

MRS. L. Yes, yes—but how can you suppose——

NORA. Then you must be my witness, that it is not true, Christine. I am not out of my mind at all; I am in my right senses now, and I tell you no one else has known anything about it; I, and I alone, did the whole thing. Remember that.

MRS. L. I will, indeed. But I don't understand all this.

NORA. How should you understand it? A wonderful thing is going to happen.

MRS. L. A wonderful thing?

NORA. Yes, a wonderful thing! But it is so terrible. Christine, it *mustn't* happen, not for all the world.

MRS. L. I will go at once and see Krogstad.

NORA. Don't go to him; he will do you some harm.

MRS. L. There was a time when he would gladly do anything for my sake.

NORA. He?

MRS. L. Where does he live?

NORA. How should I know? Yes—(*feeling in her pocket*)—here is his card. But the letter, the letter!

HEL. (*calls from his room, knocking at the door*). Nora!

NORA (*cries out anxiously*). Oh, what's that? What do you want?

HEL. Don't be so frightened. We are not coming in; you have locked the door. Are you trying on your dress?

NORA. Yes, that's it. I look so nice, Torvald.

MRS. L. (*who has read the card*). I see he lives at the corner here.

NORA. Yes, but it's no use. It is hopeless. The letter is lying there in the box.

MRS. L. And your husband keeps the key?

NORA. Yes, always.

MRS. L. Krogstad must ask for his letter back unread, he must find some pretense——

NORA. But it is just at this time that Torvald generally——

MRS. L. You must delay him. Go in to him in the meantime. I will come back as soon as I can. (*She goes out hurriedly through the hall door.*)

NORA (*goes to* HELMER'S *door, opens it and peeps in*). Torvald!

HEL. (*from the inner room*). Well? May I venture at last to come into my own room again? Come along, Rank, now you will see—— (*Halting in the doorway.*) But what is this?

NORA. What is what, dear?

HEL. Rank led me to expect a splendid transformation.

RANK (*in the doorway*). I understood so, but evidently I was mistaken.

NORA. Yes, nobody is to have the chance of admiring me in my dress until tomorrow.

HEL. But, my dear Nora, you look so worn out. Have you been practicing too much?

NORA. No, I have not practiced at all.

HEL. But you will need to——

NORA. Yes, indeed I shall, Torvald. But I can't get on a bit without you to help me; I have absolutely forgotten the whole thing.

HEL. Oh, we will soon work it up again.

NORA. Yes, help me, Torvald. Promise that you will! I am so nervous about it—all the people—— You must give yourself up to me entirely this evening. Not the tiniest bit of business—you mustn't even take a pen in your hand. Will you promise, Torvald dear?

HEL. I promise. This evening I will be wholly and absolutely at your service, you helpless little mortal. Ah, by the way, first of all I will just—— (*Goes toward the hall door.*)

NORA. What are you going to do there?

HEL. Only see if any letters have come.

NORA. No, no! Don't do that, Torvald!

HEL. Why not?

NORA. Torvald, please don't. There is nothing there.

HEL. Well, let me look. (*Turns to go to the letter box.* NORA, *at the piano, plays the first bars of the tarantella.* HELMER *stops in the doorway.*) Aha!

NORA. I can't dance tomorrow if I don't practice with you.

HEL. (*going up to her*). Are you really so afraid of it, dear?

NORA. Yes, so dreadfully afraid of it. Let me practice at once; there is time now, before we go to dinner. Sit down and play for me, Torvald dear; criticize me and correct me as you play.

HEL. With great pleasure, if you wish me to. (*Sits down at the piano.*)

NORA (*takes out of the box a tambourine and a long variegated shawl. She hastily drapes the shawl round her. Then she springs to the front of the stage and calls out*). Now play for me! I am going to dance!

(HELMER *plays and* NORA *dances.* RANK *stands by the piano behind* HELMER *and looks on.*)

HEL. (*as he plays*). Slower, slower!

NORA. I can't do it any other way.

HEL. Not so violently, Nora!

NORA. This is the way.

HEL. (*stops playing*). No, no—that is not a bit right.

NORA. (*laughing and swinging the tambourine*). Didn't I tell you so?

RANK. Let me play for her.

HEL. (*getting up*). Yes, do. I can correct her better then.

(RANK *sits down at the piano and plays.* NORA *dances more and more wildly.* HELMER *has taken up a position by the stove and during her dance gives her frequent instructions. She does not seem to hear him; her hair comes down and falls over her shoulders; she pays no attention to it but goes on dancing. Enter* MRS. LINDE.)

MRS. L. (*standing as if spellbound in the doorway*). Oh!

NORA (*as she dances*). Such fun, Christine!

HEL. My dear darling Nora, you are dancing as if your life depended on it.

NORA. So it does.

HEL. Stop, Rank this is sheer madness. Stop, I tell you! (RANK *stops playing, and* NORA *suddenly stands still.* HELMER *goes up to her.*) I could never have believed it. You have forgotten everything I taught you.

NORA. (*throwing away the tambourine*). There, you see.

HEL. You will want a lot of coaching.

NORA. Yes, you see how much I need it. You must coach me up to the last minute. Promise me that, Torvald!

HEL. You can depend on me.

NORA. You must not think of anything but me, either today or tomorrow; you mustn't open a single letter—not even open the letter box——

HEL. Ah, you are still afraid of that fellow——

NORA. Yes, indeed I am.

HEL. Nora, I can tell from your looks that there is a letter from him lying there.

NORA. I don't know; I think there is; but you must not read anything of that kind now. Nothing horrid must come between us till this is all over.

RANK (*whispers to* HELMER). You mustn't contradict her.

HEL. (*taking her in his arms*). The child shall have her way. But tomorrow night, after you have danced——

NORA. Then you will be free. (*The* MAID *appears in the doorway to the right.*)

MAID. Dinner is served, ma'am.

NORA. We will have champagne, Helen.

MAID. Very good, ma'am. (*Exit.*)

HEL. Hullo!—are we going to have a banquet?

NORA. Yes, a champagne banquet till the small hours. (*Calls out.*) And a few macaroons. Helen—lots, just for once!

HEL. Come, come, don't be so wild and nervous. Be my own little skylark, as you used.

NORA. Yes, dear, I will. But go in now, and you too, Doctor Rank, Christine, you must help me to do up my hair.

RANK. (*whispers to* HELMER *as they go out*). I suppose there is nothing—she is not expecting anything?

HEL. Far from it, my dear fellow; it is simply nothing more than this childish nervousness I was telling you of. (*They go into the right-hand room.*)

NORA. Well!

MRS. L. Gone out of town.

NORA. I could tell from your face.

MRS. L. He is coming home tomorrow evening. I wrote a note for him.

NORA. You should have let it alone; you must prevent nothing. After all, it is splendid to be waiting for a wonderful thing to happen.

MRS. L. What is it that you are waiting for?

NORA. Oh, you wouldn't understand. Go in to them, I will come in a moment. (MRS. LINDE goes into the dining room. NORA stands still for a little while, as if to compose herself. Then she looks at her watch.) Five o'clock. Seven hours till midnight; and then four-and-twenty hours till the next midnight. Then the tarantella will be over. Twenty-four and seven? Thirty-one hours to live.

HEL. (from the doorway on the right). Where's my little skylark?

NORA (going to him with her arms outstretched). Here she is!

ACT III

THE SAME SCENE—The table has been placed in the middle of the stage with chairs round it. A lamp is burning on the table. The door into the hall stands open. Dance music is heard in the room above. MRS. LINDE is sitting at the table idly turning over the leaves of a book; she tries to read but does not seem able to collect her thoughts. Every now and then she listens intently for a sound at the outer door.

MRS. L. (looking at her watch). Not yet—and the time is nearly up. If only he does not—— (Listens again.) Ah, there he is. (Goes into the hall and opens the outer door carefully. Light footsteps are heard on the stairs. She whispers.) Come in. There is no one here.

KROG. (in the doorway). I found a note from you at home. What does this mean?

MRS. L. It is absolutely necessary that I should have a talk with you.

KROG. Really? And it is absolutely necessary that it should be here?

MRS. L. It is impossible where I live; there is no private entrance to my rooms. Come in; we are quite alone. The maid is asleep, and the Helmers are at the dance upstairs.

KROG. (coming into the room). Are the Helmers really at a dance tonight?

MRS. L. Yes, why not?

KROG. Certainly—why not?

MRS. L. Now, Nils, let us have a talk.

KROG. Can we two have anything to talk about?

MRS. L. We have a great deal to talk about.

KROG. I shouldn't have thought so.

MRS. L. No, you have never properly understood me.

KROG. Was there anything else to understand except what was obvious to all the world—a heartless woman jilts a man when a more lucrative chance turns up?

MRS. L. Do you believe I am as absolutely heartless as all that? And do you believe it with a light heart?

KROG. Didn't you?

MRS. L. Nils, did you really think that?

KROG. If it were as you say, why did you write to me as you did at the time?

MRS. L. I could do nothing else. As I had to break with you, it was my duty also to put an end to all that you felt for me.

KROG. (*wringing his hands*). So that was it. And all this—only for the sake of money!

MRS. L. You mustn't forget that I had a helpless mother and two little brothers. We couldn't wait for you, Nils; your prospects seemed hopeless then.

KROG. That may be so, but you had no right to throw me over for anyone else's sake.

MRS. L. Indeed, I don't know. Many a time did I ask myself if I had the right to do it.

KROG. (*more gently*). When I lost you it was as if all the solid ground went from under my feet. Look at me now—I am a shipwrecked man clinging to a bit of wreckage.

MRS. L. But help may be near.

KROG. It *was* near, but then you came and stood in my way.

MRS. L. Unintentionally, Nils. It was only today that I learned it was your place I was going to take in the bank.

KROG. I believe you, if you say so. But now that you know it, are you not going to give it up to me?

MRS. L. No, because that would not benefit you in the least.

KROG. Oh, benefit, benefit—I would have done it whether or no.

MRS. L. I have learned to act prudently. Life and hard, bitter necessity have taught me that.

KROG. And life has taught me not to believe in fine speeches.

MRS. L. Then life has taught you something very reasonable. But deeds you must believe in.

KROG. What do you mean by that?

MRS. L. You said you were like a shipwrecked man clinging to some wreckage.

KROG. I had good reason to say so.

MRS. L. Well, I am like a shipwrecked woman clinging to some wreckage—no one to mourn for, no one to care for.

KROG. It was your own choice.

MRS. L. There was no other choice—then.

KROG. Well, what now?

MRS. L. Nils, how would it be if we two shipwrecked people could join forces?

KROG. What are you saying?

MRS. L. Two on the same piece of wreckage would stand a better chance than each on their own.

KROG. Christine!

MRS. L. What do you suppose brought me to town?

KROG. Do you mean that you gave me a thought?

MRS. L. I could not endure life without work. All my life, as long as I can remember, I have worked, and it has been my greatest and only pleasure. But now I am quite alone in the world—my life is so dreadfully empty and I feel so forsaken. There is not the least pleasure in working for one's self. Nils, give me someone and something to work for.

KROG. I don't trust that. It is nothing but a woman's overstrained sense of generosity that prompts you to make such an offer of yourself.

MRS. L. Have you ever noticed anything of the sort in me?

KROG. Could you really do it? Tell me—do you know all about my past life?

MRS. L. Yes.

KROG. And do you know what they think of me here?

MRS. L. You seemed to me to imply that with me you might have been quite another man.

KROG. I am certain of it.

MRS. L. Is it too late now?

KROG. Christine, are you saying this deliberately? Yes, I am sure you are. I see it in your face. Have you really the courage, then——

MRS. L. I want to be a mother to someone, and your children need a mother. We two need each other. Nils, I have faith in your real character—I can dare anything with you.

KROG. (grasps her hands). Thanks, thanks, Christine! Now I shall find a way to clear myself in the eyes of the world. Ah, but I forgot——

MRS. L. (listening). Hush! The tarantella! Go, go!

KROG. Why? What is it?

MRS. L. Do you hear them up there? When that is over we may expect them back.

KROG. Yes, yes—I will go. But it is all no use. Of course you are not aware what steps I have taken in the matter of the Helmers.

MRS. L. Yes, I know all about that.

KROG. And in spite of that have you the courage to——

MRS. L. I understand very well to what lengths a man like you might be driven by despair.

KROG. If I could only undo what I have done!

MRS. L. You cannot. Your letter is lying in the letter box now.

KROG. Are you sure of that?

MRS. L. Quite sure, but——

KROG. (*with a searching look at her*). Is that what it all means?—that you want to save your friend at any cost? Tell me frankly. Is that it?

MRS. L. Nils, a woman who has once sold herself for another's sake doesn't do it a second time.

KROG. I will ask for my letter back.

MRS. L. No, no.

KROG. Yes, of course I will. I will wait here till Helmer comes; I will tell him he must give me my letter back—that it only concerns my dismissal—that he is not to read it——

MRS. L. No, Nils, you must not recall your letter.

KROG. But, tell me, wasn't it for that very purpose that you asked me to meet you here?

MRS. L. In my first moment of fright it was. But twenty-four hours have elapsed since then, and in that time I have witnessed incredible things in this house. Helmer must know all about it. This unhappy secret must be disclosed; they must have a complete understanding between them, which is impossible with all this concealment and falsehood going on.

KROG. Very well, if you will take the responsibility. But there is one thing I can do in any case, and I shall do it at once.

MRS. L. (*listening*). You must be quick and go! The dance is over; we are not safe a moment longer.

KROG. I will wait for you below.

MRS. L. Yes, do. You must see me back to my door.

KROG. I have never had such an amazing piece of good fortune in my life! (*Goes out through the outer door. The door between the room and the hall remains open.*)

MRS. L. (*tidying up the room and laying her hat and cloak ready*). What a difference! What a difference! Someone to work for and live for—a home to bring comfort into. That I will do, indeed. I wish they would be quick and come. (*Listens.*) Ah, there they are now. I must put on my things. (*Takes up her hat and cloak. HELMER's and NORA's voices are heard outside; a key is turned, and HELMER brings NORA almost by force into the hall. She is in an Italian costume with a large black shawl round her; he is in evening dress and a black domino which is flying open.*)

NORA (*hanging back in the doorway and struggling with him*). No, no, no!—don't take me in. I want to go upstairs again; I don't want to leave so early.

HEL. But, my dearest Nora——

NORA. Please, Torvald dear—please, *please*—only an hour more.

HEL. Not a single minute, my sweet Nora. You know that was our agreement. Come along into the room; you are catching cold standing there. (*He brings her gently into the room in spite of her resistance.*)

MRS. L. Good evening.

NORA. Christine!

HEL. You here so late, Mrs. Linde?

MRS. L. Yes, you must excuse me; I was so anxious to see Nora in her dress.

NORA. Have you been sitting here waiting for me?

MRS. L. Yes; unfortunately I came too late—you had already gone upstairs— and I thought I couldn't go away again without having seen you.

HEL. (*taking off* NORA'S *shawl*). Yes, take a good look at her. I think she is worth looking at. Isn't she charming, Mrs. Linde?

MRS. L. Yes, indeed she is.

HEL. Doesn't she look remarkably pretty? Everyone thought so at the dance. But she is terribly self-willed, this sweet little person. What are we to do with her? You will hardly believe that I had almost to bring her away by force.

NORA. Torvald, you will repent not having let me stay, even if it were only for half an hour.

HEL. Listen to her, Mrs. Linde! She had danced her tarantella, and it had been a tremendous success, as it deserved—although possibly the performance was a trifle too realistic—a little more so, I mean, than was strictly compatible with the limitations of art. But never mind about that! The chief thing is, she had made a success—she had made a tremendous success. Do you think I was going to let her remain there after that and spoil the effect? No indeed! I took my charming little Capri maiden—my capricious little Capri maiden, I should say—on my arm, took one quick turn round the room, a curtsey on either side, and, as they say in novels, the beautiful apparition disappeared. An exit ought always to be effective, Mrs. Linde; but that is what I cannot make Nora understand. Pooh! this room is hot. (*Throws his domino on a chair and opens the door of his room.*) Hullo! it's all dark in here. Oh, of course—excuse me. (*He goes in and lights some candles.*)

NORA (*in a hurried and breathless whisper*). Well?

MRS. L. (*in a low voice*). I have had a talk with him.

NORA. Yes, and——

MRS. L. Nora, you must tell your husband all about it.

NORA (*in an expressionless voice*). I knew it.

MRS. L. You have nothing to be afraid of as far as Krogstad is concerned, but you must tell him.

NORA. I won't tell him.

MRS. L. Then the letter will.

NORA. Thank you, Christine. Now I know what I must do. Hush!

HEL. (*coming in again*). Well, Mrs. Linde, have you admired her?

MRS. L. Yes, and now I will say good night.

HEL. What, already? Is this yours, this knitting?

MRS. L. (*taking it*). Yes, thank you. I had very nearly forgotten it.

HEL. So you knit?

MRS. L. Of course.

HEL. Do you know, you ought to embroider.

MRS. L. Really? Why?

HEL. Yes, it's far more becoming. Let me show you. You hold the embroidery thus in your left hand and use the needle with the right—like this—with a long easy sweep. Do you see?

MRS. L. Yes, perhaps——

HEL. Yes, but in the case of knitting—that can never be anything but ungraceful; look here—the arms close together, the knitting needles going up and down—it has a sort of Chinese effect. . . . That was really excellent champagne they gave us.

MRS. L. Well—good night, Nora, and don't be self-willed any more.

HEL. That's right, Mrs. Linde.

MRS. L. Good night, Mr. Helmer.

HEL. (*accompanying her to the door*). Good night, good night. I hope you will get home all right. I should be very happy to—— But you haven't any great distance to go. Good night, good night. (*She goes out; he shuts the door after her and comes in again.*) Ah!—at last we have got rid of her. She is a frightful bore, that woman.

NORA. Aren't you very tired, Torvald?

HEL. No, not in the least.

NORA. Nor sleepy?

HEL. Not a bit. On the contrary I feel extraordinarily lively. And you?—you really look both tired and sleepy.

NORA. Yes, I am very tired. I want to go to sleep at once.

HEL. There, you see it was quite right of me not to let you stay there any longer.

NORA. Everything you do is quite right, Torvald.

HEL. (*kissing her on the forehead*). Now my little skylark is speaking reasonably. Did you notice what good spirits Rank was in this evening?

NORA. Really? Was he? I didn't speak to him at all.

HEL. And I very little, but I have not for a long time seen him in such good form. (*Looks for a while at her and then goes nearer to her.*) It is delightful to be at home by ourselves again, to be all alone with you—you fascinating, charming little darling!

NORA. Don't look at me like that, Torvald.

HEL. Why shouldn't I look at my dearest treasure?—at all the beauty that is mine, all my very own?

NORA (*going to the other side of the table*). You mustn't say things like that to me tonight.

HEL. (*following her*). You have still got the tarantella in your blood, I see. And it makes you more captivating than ever. Listen—the guests are beginning to go now. (*In a lower voice.*) Nora—soon the whole house will be quiet.

NORA. Yes, I hope so.

HEL. Yes, my own darling Nora. Do you know, when I am out at a party with you like this, why I speak so little to you, keep away from you and only send a stolen glance in your direction now and then?—do you know why I do that? It is because I make believe to myself that we are secretly in love and you are my secretly promised bride and that no one suspects there is anything between us.

NORA. Yes, yes—I know very well your thoughts are with me all the time.

HEL. And when we are leaving and I am putting the shawl over your beautiful young shoulders—on your lovely neck—then I imagine that you are my young bride and that we have just come from our wedding and I am bringing you, for the first time, into our home—to be alone with you for the first time—quite alone with my shy little darling! All this evening I have longed for nothing but you. When I watched the seductive figures of the tarantella my blood was on fire; I could endure it no longer, and that was why I brought you down so early——

NORA. Go away, Torvald! You must let me go. I won't——

HEL. What's that? You're joking, my little Nora! You won't—you won't? Am I not your husband? (*A knock is heard at the outer door.*)

NORA (*starting*). Did you hear——

HEL. (*going into the hall*). Who is it?

RANK (*outside*). It is I. May I come in for a moment?

HEL. (*in a fretful whisper*). Oh, what does he want now? (*Aloud.*) Wait a minute. (*Unlocks the door.*) Come, that's kind of you not to pass by our door.

RANK. I thought I heard your voice, and I felt as if I should like to look in. (*With a swift glance round.*) Ah yes!—these dear familiar rooms. You are very happy and cosy in here, you two.

HEL. It seems to me that you looked after yourself pretty well upstairs too.

RANK. Excellently. Why shouldn't I? Why shouldn't one enjoy everything in this world?—at any rate as much as one can and as long as one can. The wine was capital——

HEL. Especially the champagne.

RANK. So you noticed that too? It is almost incredible how much I managed to put away!

NORA. Torvald drank a great deal of champagne tonight too.

RANK. Did he?

NORA. Yes, and he is always in such good spirits afterward.

RANK. Well, why should one not enjoy a merry evening after a well-spent day?

HEL. Well-spent? I am afraid I can't take credit for that.

RANK (*clapping him on the back*). But I can, you know!

HEL. Exactly.

NORA. Doctor Rank, you must have been occupied with some scientific investigation today.

HEL. Just listen!—little Nora talking about scientific investigations!

NORA. And may I congratulate you on the result?

RANK. Indeed you may.

NORA. Was it favorable, then?

RANK. The best possible, for both doctor and patient—certainty.

NORA (*quickly and searchingly*). Certainty?

RANK. Absolute certainty. So wasn't I entitled to make a merry evening of it after that?

NORA. Yes, you certainly were, Doctor Rank.

HEL. I think so too, so long as you don't have to pay for it in the morning.

RANK. Oh well, one can't have anything in this life without paying for it.

NORA. Doctor Rank—are you fond of fancy-dress balls?

RANK. Yes, if there is a fine lot of pretty costumes.

NORA. Tell me—what shall we two wear at the next?

HEL. Little featherbrain!—are you thinking of the next already?

RANK. We two? Yes, I can tell you. You shall go as a good fairy——

HEL. Yes, but what do you suggest as an appropriate costume for that?

RANK. Let your wife go dressed just as she is in everyday life.

HEL. That was really very prettily turned. But can't you tell us what you will be?

RANK. Yes, my dear friend, I have quite made up my mind about that.

HEL. Well?

RANK. At the next fancy-dress ball I shall be invisible.

HEL. That's a good joke!

RANK. There is a big black hat—have you ever heard of hats that make you invisible? If you put one on, no one can see you.

HEL. (*suppressing a smile*). Yes, you are quite right.

RANK. But I am clean forgetting what I came for. Helmer, give me a cigar— one of the dark Havanas.

HEL. With the greatest pleasure. (*Offers him his case.*)

RANK (*takes a cigar and cuts off the end*). Thanks.

NORA (*striking a match*). Let me give you a light.

RANK. Thank you. (*She holds the match for him to light his cigar.*) And now good-by!

HEL. Good-by, good-by, dear old man!

NORA. Sleep well, Doctor Rank.

RANK. Thank you for that wish.

NORA. Wish me the same.

RANK. You? Well, if you want me to sleep well! And thanks for the light. (*He nods to them both and goes out.*)

HEL. (*in a subdued voice*). He has drunk more than he ought.

NORA (*absently*). Maybe. (HELMER *takes a bunch of keys out of his pocket and goes into the hall.*) Torvald! What are you going to do there?

HEL. Empty the letter box; it is quite full; there will be no room to put the newspaper in tomorrow morning.

NORA. Are you going to work tonight?

HEL. You know quite well I'm not. What is this? Someone has been at the lock.

NORA. At the lock?

HEL. Yes, someone has. What can it mean? I should never have thought the maid—— Here is a broken hairpin. Nora, it is one of yours.

NORA (*quickly*). Then it must have been the children.

HEL. Then you must get them out of those ways. There, at last I have got it open. (*Takes out the contents of the letter box and calls to the kitchen.*) Helen! Helen, put out the light over the front door. (*Goes back into the room and shuts the door into the hall. He holds out his hand full of letters.*) Look at that—look what a heap of them there are. (*Turning them over.*) What on earth is that?

NORA (*at the window*). The letter—— No! Torvald, no!

HEL. Two cards—of Rank's.

NORA. Of Doctor Rank's?

HEL. (*looking at them*). Doctor Rank. They were on the top. He must have put them in when he went out.

NORA. Is there anything written on them?

HEL. There is a black cross over the name. Look there—what an uncomfortable idea! It looks as if he were announcing his own death.

NORA. It is just what he is doing.

HEL. What? Do you know anything about it? Has he said anything to you?

NORA. Yes. He told me that when the cards came it would be his leave-taking from us. He means to shut himself up and die.

HEL. My poor old friend. Certainly I knew we should not have him very long with us. But so soon! And so he hides himself away like a wounded animal.

NORA. If it has to happen, it is best it should be without a word—don't you think so, Torvald?

HEL. (*walking up and down*). He had so grown into our lives. I can't think of him as having gone out of them. He, with his sufferings and his loneliness, was like a cloudy background to our sunlit happiness. Well, perhaps it is best so. For him, anyway. (*Standing still.*) And perhaps for us too, Nora. We two are thrown quite upon each other now. (*Puts his arms round her.*) My darling wife, I don't feel as if I could hold you tight enough. Do you know, Nora, I have often wished that you might be threatened by some great danger, so that I might risk my life's blood and everything for your sake.

NORA (*disengages herself and says firmly and decidedly*). Now you must read your letters, Torvald.

HEL. No, no; not tonight. I want to be with you, my darling wife.

NORA. With the thought of your friend's death——

HEL. You are right; it has affected us both. Something ugly has come between us—the thought of the horrors of death. We must try and rid our minds of that. Until then—we will each go to our own room.

NORA (*hanging on his neck*). Good night, Torvald—good night!

HEL. (*kissing her on the forehead*). Good night, my little singing bird. Sleep sound, Nora. Now I will read my letters through. (*He takes his letters and goes into his room, shutting the door after him.*)

NORA (*gropes distractedly about, seizes* HELMER'S *domino, throws it about her while she says in quick, hoarse, spasmodic whispers*). Never to see him again. Never! Never! (*Puts her shawl over her head.*) Never to see my children again either—never again. Never! Never! Ah! the icy black water—the unfathomable depths—if only it were over! He has got it now—now he is reading it. Good-by, Torvald and my children! (*She is about to rush out through the hall when* HELMER *opens his door hurriedly and stands with an open letter in his hand.*)

HEL. Nora!

NORA. Ah!

HEL. What is this? Do you know what is in this letter?

NORA. Yes, I know. Let me go! Let me get out!

HEL. (*holding her back*). Where are you going?

NORA (*trying to get free*). You shan't save me, Torvald!

HEL. (*reeling*). True? Is this true, that I read here? Horrible! No, no—it is impossible that it is true.

NORA. It is true. I have loved you above everything else in the world.

HEL. Oh, don't let us have any silly excuses.

NORA (*taking a step toward him*). Torvald!

HEL. Miserable creature—what have you done?

NORA. Let me go. You shall not suffer for my sake. You shall not take it upon yourself.

HEL. No tragedy airs, please. (*Locks the hall door.*) Here you shall stay and give me an explanation. Do you understand what you have done? Answer me! Do you understand what you have done?

NORA (*looks steadily at him and says with a growing look of coldness in her face*). Yes, now I am beginning to understand thoroughly.

HEL. (*walking about the room*). What a horrible awakening! All these eight years—she who was my joy and pride—a hypocrite, a liar—worse, worse—a criminal! The unutterable ugliness of it all! For shame! For shame! (NORA *is silent and looks steadily at him. He stops in front of her.*) I ought to have suspected that something of the sort would happen. I ought to have foreseen it. All your father's want of principle—be silent!—all your father's want of principle has come out in you. No religion, no morality, no sense of duty—— How I am punished for having winked at what he did! I did it for your sake, and this is how you repay me.

NORA. Yes, that's just it.

HEL. Now you have destroyed all my happiness. You have ruined all my future. It is horrible to think of! I am in the power of an unscrupulous man; he can do what he likes with me, ask anything he likes of me, give me any orders he pleases—I dare not refuse. And I must sink to such miserable depths because of a thoughtless woman!

NORA. When I am out of the way you will be free.

HEL. No fine speeches, please. Your father always had plenty of those ready too. What good would it be to me if you were out of the way, as you say? Not the slightest. He can make the affair known everywhere; and if he does, I may be falsely suspected of having been a party to your criminal action. Very likely people will think I was behind it all—that it was I who prompted you! And I have to thank you for all this—you whom I have cherished during the whole of our married life. Do you understand now what it is you have done for me?

NORA (*coldly and quietly*). Yes.

HEL. It is so incredible that I can't take it in. But we must come to some under-standing. Take off that shawl. Take it off, I tell you. I must try and appease him in some way or another. The matter must be hushed up at any cost. And as for you and me, it must appear as if everything between us were just as before—but naturally only in the eyes of the world. You will still remain in my house, that is a matter of course. But I shall not allow you to bring up the children; I dare not trust them to you. To think that I should be obliged to say so to one whom I have loved so dearly and whom I still—— No, that is all over. From this moment happiness is not the question; all that concerns us is to save the remains, the fragments, the appearance——

(*A ring is heard at the front-door bell.*)

HEL. (*with a start*). What is that? So late! Can the worst—can he—— Hide yourself, Nora. Say you are ill.

(NORA *stands motionless.* HELMER *goes and unlocks the hall door.*)

MAID (*half dressed, comes to the door*). A letter for the mistress.
HEL. Give it to me. (*Takes the letter and shuts the door.*) Yes, it is from him. You shall not have it; I will read it myself.
NORA. Yes, read it.
HEL. (*standing by the lamp*). I scarcely have the courage to do it. It may mean ruin for the both of us. No, I must know. (*Tears open the letter, runs his eye over a few lines, looks at a paper enclosed and gives a shout of joy.*) Nora! (*She looks at him questioningly.*) Nora! No, I must read it once again. Yes, it is true! I am saved! Nora, I am saved!
NORA. And I?
HEL. You too, of course; we are both saved, both you and I. Look, he sends you your bond back. He says he regrets and repents—that a happy change in his life—— Never mind what he says! We are saved, Nora! No one can do anything to you. Oh, Nora, Nora—— No, first I must destroy these hate-ful things. Let me see. (*Takes a look at the bond.*) No, no, I won't look at it. The whole thing shall be nothing but a bad dream to me. (*Tears up the bond and both letters, throws them all into the stove and watches them burn.*) There—now it doesn't exist any longer. He says that since Christmas Eve you—— These must have been three dreadful days for you, Nora.
NORA. I have fought a hard fight these three days.
HEL. And suffered agonies and seen no way out, but—— No, we won't call any of the horrors to mind. We will only shout with joy and keep saying, "It's all over! It's all over!" Listen to me, Nora. You don't seem to realize

that it is all over. What is this?—such a cold, set face! My poor little Nora, I quite understand; you don't feel as if you could believe that I have forgiven you. But it is true, Nora, I swear it; I have forgiven you everything. I know that what you did you did out of love for me.

NORA. That is true.

HEL. You have loved me as a wife ought to love her husband. Only you had not sufficient knowledge to judge of the means you used. But do you suppose you are any the less dear to me because you don't understand how to act on your own responsibility? No, no; only lean on me; I will advise and direct you. I should not be a man if this womanly helplessness did not just give you a double attractiveness in my eyes. You must not think any more about the hard things I said in my first moment of consternation, when I thought everything was going to overwhelm me. I have forgiven you, Nora; I swear to you I have forgiven you.

NORA. Thank you for your forgiveness. (*She goes out through the door to the right.*)

HEL. No, don't go. (*Looks in.*) What are you doing in there?

NORA (*from within*). Taking off my fancy dress.

HEL. (*standing at the open door*). Yes, do. Try and calm yourself and make your mind easy again, my frightened little singing bird. Be at rest and feel secure; I have broad wings to shelter you under. (*Walks up and down by the door.*) How warm and cosy our home is, Nora. Here is shelter for you; here I will protect you like a hunted dove that I have saved from a hawk's claws; I will bring peace to your poor beating heart. It will come, little by little, Nora, believe me. Tomorrow morning you will look upon it all quite differently; soon everything will be just as it was before. Very soon you won't need me to assure you that I have forgiven you; you will yourself feel the certainty that I have done so. Can you suppose I should ever think of such a thing as repudiating you or even reproaching you? You have no idea what a true man's heart is like, Nora. There is something so indescribably sweet and satisfying, to a man, in the knowledge that he has forgiven his wife—forgiven her freely and with all his heart. It seems as if that had made her, as it were, doubly his own; he has given her a new life, so to speak, and she has in a way become both wife and child to him. So you shall be for me after this, my little scared, helpless darling. Have no anxiety about anything, Nora; only be frank and open with me, and I will serve as will and conscience both to you—— What is this? Not gone to bed? Have you changed your things?

NORA (*in everyday dress*). Yes, Torvald, I have changed my things now.

HEL. But what for?—so late as this.

NORA. I shall not sleep tonight.

HEL. But, my dear Nora——

NORA (*looking at her watch*). It is not so very late. Sit down here, Torvald. You and I have much to say to one another. (*She sits down at one side of the table.*)

HEL. Nora—what is this?—this cold, set face?

NORA. Sit down. It will take some time; I have a lot to talk over with you.

HEL. (*sits down at the opposite side of the table*). You alarm me, Nora!—and I don't understand you.

NORA. No, that is just it. You don't understand me, and I have never understood you either—before tonight. No, you mustn't interrupt me. You must simply listen to what I say. Torvald, this is a settling of accounts.

HEL. What do you mean by that?

NORA (*after a short silence*). Isn't there one thing that strikes you as strange in our sitting here like this?

HEL. What is that?

NORA. We have been married now eight years. Does it not occur to you that this is the first time we two, you and I, husband and wife, have had a serious conversation?

HEL. What do you mean, serious?

NORA. In all these eight years—longer than that—from the very beginning of our acquaintance we have never exchanged a word on any serious subject.

HEL. Was it likely that I would be continually and forever telling you about worries that you could not help me to bear?

NORA. I am not speaking about business matters. I say that we have never sat down in earnest together to try and get at the bottom of anything.

HEL. But, dearest Nora, would it have been any good to you?

NORA. That is just it; you have never understood me. I have been greatly wronged, Torvald—first by Papa and then by you.

HEL. What! By us two—by us two who have loved you better than anyone else in the world?

NORA (*shaking her head*). You have never loved me. You have only thought it pleasant to be in love with me.

HEL. Nora, what do I hear you saying?

NORA. It is perfectly true, Torvald. When I was at home with Papa he told me his opinion about everything, and so I had the same opinions; and if I differed from him I concealed the fact, because he would not have liked it. He called me his doll child, and he played with me just as I used to play with my dolls. And when I came to live with you——

HEL. What sort of an expression is that to use about our marriage?

NORA (*undisturbed*). I mean that I was simply transferred from Papa's hands to yours. You arranged everything according to your own taste, and so I got the same tastes as you—or else I pretended to. I am really not quite sure which—I think sometimes the one and sometimes the other. When I look back on it it seems to me as if I have been living here like a poor woman—just from hand to mouth. I have existed merely to perform tricks for you, Torvald. But you would have it so. You and Papa have committed a great sin against me. It is your fault that I have made nothing of my life.

HEL. How unreasonable and how ungrateful you are, Nora! Have you not been happy here?

NORA. No, I have never been happy. I thought I was, but it has never really been so.

HEL. Not—not happy!

NORA. No, only merry. And you have always been so kind to me. But our home has been nothing but a playroom. I have been your doll wife, just as at home I was Papa's doll child; and here the children have been my dolls. I thought it great fun when you played with me, just as they thought it great fun when I played with them. That is what our marriage has been, Torvald.

HEL. There is some truth in what you say—exaggerated and strained as your view of it is. But for the future it shall be different. Playtime shall be over and lesson time shall begin.

NORA. Whose lessons? Mine or the children's?

HEL. Both yours and the children's, my darling Nora.

NORA. Alas, Torvald, you are not the man to educate me into being a proper wife for you.

HEL. And you can say that!

NORA. And I—how am I fitted to bring up the children?

HEL. Nora!

NORA. Didn't you say so yourself a little while ago—that you dare not trust me to bring them up?

HEL. In a moment of anger! Why do you pay any heed to that?

NORA. Indeed, you were perfectly right. I am not fit for the task. There is another task I must undertake first. I must try and educate myself—you are not the man to help me in that. I must do that for myself. And that is why I am going to leave you now.

HEL. (*springing up*). What do you say?

NORA. I must stand quite alone if I am to understand myself and everything about me. It is for that reason that I cannot remain with you any longer.

HEL. Nora, Nora!

NORA. I am going away from here now, at once. I am sure Christine will take me in for the night.

HEL. You are out of your mind! I won't allow it! I forbid you!

NORA. It is no use forbidding me anything any longer. I will take with me what belongs to myself. I will take nothing from you, either now or later.

HEL. What sort of madness is this?

NORA. Tomorrow I shall go home—I mean to my old home. It will be easiest for me to find something to do there.

HEL. You blind, foolish woman!

NORA. I must try and get some sense, Torvald.

HEL. To desert your home your husband and your children! And you don't consider what people will say!

NORA. I cannot consider that at all. I only know that it is necessary for me.

HEL. It's shocking. This is how you would neglect your most sacred duties.

NORA. What do you consider my most sacred duties?

HEL. Do I need to tell you that? Are they not your duties to your husband and your children?

NORA. I have other duties just as sacred.

HEL. That you have not. What duties could those be?

NORA. Duties to myself.

HEL. Before all else you are a wife and a mother.

NORA. I don't believe that any longer. I believe that before all else I am a reasonable human being just as you are—or, at all events, that I must try and become one. I know quite well, Torvald, that most people would think you right and that views of that kind are to be found in books; but I can no longer content myself with what most people say or with what is found in books. I must think over things for myself and get to understand them.

HEL. Can you understand your place in your own home? Have you not a reliable guide in such matters as that?—have you no religion?

NORA. I am afraid, Torvald, I do not exactly know what religion is.

HEL. What are you saying?

NORA. I know nothing but what the clergyman said when I went to be confirmed. He told us that religion was this and that and the other. When I am away from all this and am alone I will look into that matter too. I will see if what the clergyman said is true, or at all events if it is true for me.

HEL. This is unheard of in a girl of your age! But if religion cannot lead you aright, let me try and awaken your conscience. I suppose you have some moral sense? Or—answer me—am I to think you have none?

NORA. I assure you, Torvald, that is not an easy question to answer. I really don't know. The thing perplexes me altogether. I only know that you and I look at it in quite a different light. I am learning, too, that the law is quite another thing from what I supposed; but I find it impossible to convince myself that the law is right. According to it a woman has no right to spare her old dying father or to save her husband's life. I can't believe that.

HEL. You talk like a child. You don't understand the conditions of the world in which you live.

NORA. No, I don't. But now I am going to try. I am going to see if I can make out who is right, the world or I.

HEL. You are ill, Nora; you are delirious; I almost think you are out of your mind.

NORA. I have never felt my mind so clear and certain as tonight.

HEL. And is it with a clear and certain mind that you forsake your husband and your children?

NORA. Yes, it is.

HEL. Then there is only one possible explanation.

NORA. What is that?

HEL. You do not love me any more.

NORA. No, that is just it.

HEL. Nora!—and you can say that?

NORA. It gives me great pain, Torvald, for you have always been so kind to me, but I cannot help it. I do not love you any more.

HEL. (*regaining his composure*). Is that a clear and certain conviction too?

NORA. Yes, absolutely clear and certain. That is the reason why I will not stay here any longer.

HEL. And can you tell me what I have done to forfeit your love?

NORA. Yes, indeed I can. It was to-night, when the wonderful thing did not happen; then I saw you were not the man I had thought you.

HEL. Explain yourself better—I don't understand you.

NORA. I have waited so patiently for eight years; for, goodness knows, I knew very well that wonderful things don't happen every day. Then this horrible misfortune came upon me, and then I felt quite certain that the wonderful thing was going to happen at last. When Krogstad's letter was lying out there never for a moment did I imagine that you would consent to accept this man's conditions. I was so absolutely certain that you would say to him: Publish the thing to the whole world. And when that was done——

HEL. Yes, what then?—when I had exposed my wife to shame and disgrace?

NORA. When that was done I was so absolutely certain you would come forward and take everything upon yourself and say: I am the guilty one.

HEL. Nora!

NORA. You mean that I would never have accepted such a sacrifice on your part? No, of course not. But what would my assurances have been worth against yours? That was the wonderful thing which I hoped for and feared, and it was to prevent that that I wanted to kill myself.

HEL. I would gladly work night and day for you, Nora—bear sorrow and want for your sake. But no man would sacrifice his honor for the one he loves.

NORA. It is a thing hundreds of thousands of women have done.

HEL. Oh, you think and talk like a heedless child.

NORA. Maybe. But you neither think nor talk like the man I could bind myself to. As soon as your fear was over—and it was not fear for what threatened me but for what might happen to you—when the whole thing was past, as far as you were concerned it was exactly as if nothing at all had happened. Exactly as before, I was your little skylark, your doll, which you would in the future treat with doubly gentle care because it was so brittle and fragile. (*Getting up.*) Torvald—it was then it dawned upon me that for eight years I had been living here with a strange man and had borne him three children. Oh, I can't bear to think of it! I could tear myself into little bits!

HEL. (*sadly*). I see, I see. An abyss has opened between us—there is no denying it. But, Nora, would it not be possible to fill it up?

NORA. As I am now, I am no wife for you.

HEL. I have it in me to become a different man.

NORA. Perhaps—if your doll is taken away from you.

HEL. But to part!—to part from you! No, no, Nora; I can't understand that idea.

NORA (*going out to the right*). That makes it all the more certain that it must be done. (*She comes back with her cloak and hat and a small bag which she puts on a chair by the table.*)

HEL. Nora. Nora, not now! Wait till tomorrow.

NORA (*putting on her cloak*). I cannot spend the night in a strange man's room.

HEL. But can't we live here like brother and sister?

NORA (*putting on her hat*). You know very well that would not last long. (*Puts the shawl round her.*) Good-by, Torvald. I won't see the little ones. I know they are in better hands than mine. As I am now, I can be of no use to them.

HEL. But someday, Nora—someday?

NORA. How can I tell? I have no idea what is going to become of me.

HEL. But you are my wife, whatever becomes of you.

NORA. Listen, Torvald. I have heard that when a wife deserts her husband's house, as I am doing now, he is legally freed from all obligations toward her. In any case I set you free from all your obligations. You are not to feel yourself bound in the slightest way, any more than I shall. There must be perfect freedom on both sides. See, here is your ring back. Give me mine.

HEL. That too?

NORA. That too.

HEL. Here it is.

NORA. That's right. Now it is all over. I have put the keys here. The maids know all about everything in the house—better than I do. Tomorrow, after I have left her, Christine will come here and pack up my own things that I brought with me from home. I will have them sent after me.

HEL. All over! All over! Nora, shall you never think of me again?

NORA. I know I shall often think of you and the children and this house.

HEL. May I write to you, Nora?

NORA. No—never. You must not do that.

HEL. But at least let me send you——

NORA. Nothing—nothing.

HEL. Let me help you if you are in want.

NORA. No. I can receive nothing from a stranger.

HEL. Nora—can I never be anything more than a stranger to you?

NORA (*taking her bag*). Ah, Torvald, the most wonderful thing of all would have to happen.

HEL. Tell me what that would be!

NORA. Both you and I would have to be so changed that—— Oh, Torvald, I don't believe any longer in wonderful things happening.

HEL. But I will believe in it. Tell me. So changed that——

NORA. That our life together would be a real wedlock. Good-by. (*She goes out through the hall.*)

HEL. (*sinks down on a chair at the door and buries his face in his hands*). Nora! Nora! (*Looks round and rises.*) Empty! She is gone. (*A hope flashes across his mind.*) The most wonderful thing of all—— ?

(*The sound of a door shutting is heard from below.*)

[1879]

QUESTIONS

HENRIK IBSEN, *A Doll's House*

1. What is the significance of the play's title? Some translations title the play *A Doll House*, while others (including this one) label it *A Doll's House*. What difference in meaning does the possessive convey?

2. Realism is characterized frequently by its focus on the protagonist's struggle against social restrictions. Who is the protagonist of this play? Against what forces does the protagonist struggle? How does the protagonist develop over the course of the play?

3. Describe the setting of *A Doll's House*. What symbolic import does the drawing room convey, as opposed to a kitchen or bedroom? What does this setting tell us about the Helmers and their values?

4. *A Doll's House* regularly invokes symbols to convey meaning. Explain the function of one or more of the following: the Christmas tree, Nora's pet names, macaroons, the tarentella, the silk stockings.

5. What is the crisis of this play? Explain why you believe this moment to be the turning point of the plot.

6. Many of the characters in *A Doll's House* are paired and contrasted: Nora and Mrs. Linde; Nora and Krogstad; Nora and Rank; Torvald and Rank; Torvald and Krogstad; Krogstad and Mrs. Linde. Pick one of these pairs and describe how they are similar and how they differ.

7. At the end of the play, are you sympathetic to Nora? To Torvald? Using evidence from the text, explain how Ibsen encourages or undermines your affective connection to these characters.

8. What makes this play realistic? Think here of aspects of stagecraft, as well as of characterization, plot, and dialogue.

9. Find all of the instances in which money becomes a subject of discussion for the middle class characters of *A Doll's House*. What do we learn about the characters as the result of their perceptions of money—and its power? What statement, if any, is Ibsen making about middle class values? Does the function of money or the values associated with it differ for men and for women? How? Discuss the thematic function of money in *A Doll's House*.

10. In many ways, *A Doll's House* can be read as a feminist manifesto, one articulating a theme of advancing women's rights. Does the focus on

women's issues render this play obsolete? How does this play speak to contemporary audiences, or does it? Make a case for (or against) the contemporary relevance of *A Doll's House*.

Samuel Taylor Coleridge
[1772–1834]

Born in Ottery St. Mary, Devonshire, **SAMUEL TAYLOR COLERIDGE** *was the precocious son of the mild-mannered village vicar. The doting father died when Coleridge was nine, and the youth was sent off to school at Christ's Hospital. Both Coleridge's friend, Charles Lamb, and Coleridge himself recount those early years at school as lonely and sorrowful. Coleridge did in fact receive an excellent early education that led him to Jesus College, Cambridge, where he began as a good student but then lost focus, one time even running off with the Light Dragoons (a military outfit) using the pseudonyn, Silas Tomkyn Comberbacke. His friends had to buy him back from the outfit. Eventually he left Cambridge (1794) and joined poet Robert Southey in the strange adventure of setting up a utopian community in Pennsylvania. When this failed, he and Southey married sisters, Edith and Sarah Fricker. The chief claim to fame of these two women is being satirized in Lord Byron's* Don Juan. *Coleridge wandered off to meet the poet William Wordsworth and his sister, just after publishing his first book of poems,* Juvenile Poems *(1796). In 1797 he published two of his best poems,* The Rime of the Ancient Mariner *and* Christabel. The Rime *is one of the best-loved of all poems, but* Christabel *is more obscure, a poem about a hypnotic woman who turns into a serpent. The fragment breaks off leaving the reader entranced but unsatisfied. In 1798 he wrote his famous fragment poem* Kubla Khan *and published the* Lyrical Ballads *with Wordsworth. This work is considered the watershed moment in Romanticism. Before 1798 poets still are a part of an earlier era, but after the Preface lays out a sort of credo, theory, and definition for the Romantic poets, the writers move on within the collective constraints of that definition. The Wordsworth siblings and Coleridge then journeyed to Gottingen where Coleridge quickly learned German, read Kantian philosophy, and translated Friedrich Schiller's drama,* Wallenstein. *Soon he followed the Wordsworths back to England and joined them in the country life in Keswick. There he become addicted to opium and wrote two depressing works,* Dejection, an Ode *(1802) and* Youth and Age *(1828). Having licked his opium habit, he moved on to the lecture circuit and spoke widely about his theories of literature, especially creating a Romantic setting of Shakespeare's plays that still tends to dominate critical opinion. He was far better at talking about his ideas than he was at writing them down. He planned a work on theology and several longer poems, but no more were written, and in fact,* The Rime of the Ancient Mariner *is the only long poem Coleridge completed. He did however write two outstanding prose works, his* Biographia Literaria *(1817), in which he illuminates much about his relationship with Wordsworth, and* Table Talk, *conversations written down that are among the best of their kind.*

The Rime of the Ancient Mariner

Samuel Taylor Coleridge

Part I

It is an ancient Mariner,
And he stoppeth one of three.
`By thy long grey beard and glittering eye,
Now wherefore stopp'st thou me?

The bridegroom's doors are opened wide,
And I am next of kin;
The guests are met, the feast is set:
Mayst hear the merry din.'

He holds him with his skinny hand,
"There was a ship," quoth he.
`Hold off! unhand me, grey-beard loon!'
Eftsoons his hand dropped he.

He holds him with his glittering eye -
The Wedding-Guest stood still,
And listens like a three years' child:
The Mariner hath his will.

The Wedding-Guest sat on a stone:
He cannot choose but hear;
And thus spake on that ancient man,
The bright-eyed Mariner.

"The ship was cheered, the harbour cleared,
Merrily did we drop
Below the kirk, below the hill,
Below the lighthouse top.

The sun came up upon the left,
Out of the sea came he!

And he shone bright, and on the right
Went down into the sea.

Higher and higher every day,
Till over the mast at noon -"
The Wedding-Guest here beat his breast,
For he heard the loud bassoon.

The bride hath paced into the hall,
Red as a rose is she;
Nodding their heads before her goes
The merry minstrelsy.

The Wedding-Guest he beat his breast,
Yet he cannot choose but hear;
And thus spake on that ancient man,
The bright-eyed Mariner.

"And now the storm-blast came, and he
Was tyrannous and strong:
He struck with his o'ertaking wings,
And chased us south along.

With sloping masts and dipping prow,
As who pursued with yell and blow
Still treads the shadow of his foe,
And foward bends his head,
The ship drove fast, loud roared the blast,
And southward aye we fled.

And now there came both mist and snow,
And it grew wondrous cold:
And ice, mast-high, came floating by,
As green as emerald.

And through the drifts the snowy clifts
Did send a dismal sheen:
Nor shapes of men nor beasts we ken -
The ice was all between.

The ice was here, the ice was there,
The ice was all around:
It cracked and growled, and roared and howled,
Like noises in a swound!

At length did cross an Albatross,
Thorough the fog it came;
As it had been a Christian soul,
We hailed it in God's name.

It ate the food it ne'er had eat,
And round and round it flew.
The ice did split with a thunder-fit;
The helmsman steered us through!

And a good south wind sprung up behind;
The Albatross did follow,
And every day, for food or play,
Came to the mariner's hollo!

In mist or cloud, on mast or shroud,
It perched for vespers nine;
Whiles all the night, through fog-smoke white,
Glimmered the white moonshine."

`God save thee, ancient Mariner,
From the fiends that plague thee thus! -
Why look'st thou so?' -"With my crossbow
I shot the Albatross."

Part II

"The sun now rose upon the right:
Out of the sea came he,
Still hid in mist, and on the left
Went down into the sea.

And the good south wind still blew behind,
But no sweet bird did follow,
Nor any day for food or play
Came to the mariners' hollo!

And I had done a hellish thing,
And it would work 'em woe:
For all averred, I had killed the bird
That made the breeze to blow.
Ah wretch! said they, the bird to slay,
That made the breeze to blow!

Nor dim nor red, like God's own head,
The glorious sun uprist:
Then all averred, I had killed the bird
That brought the fog and mist.
'Twas right, said they, such birds to slay,
That bring the fog and mist.

The fair breeze blew, the white foam flew,
The furrow followed free;
We were the first that ever burst
Into that silent sea.

Down dropped the breeze, the sails dropped down,
'Twas sad as sad could be;
And we did speak only to break
The silence of the sea!

All in a hot and copper sky,
The bloody sun, at noon,
Right up above the mast did stand,
No bigger than the moon.

Day after day, day after day,
We stuck, nor breath nor motion;
As idle as a painted ship
Upon a painted ocean.

Water, water, every where,
And all the boards did shrink;
Water, water, every where,
Nor any drop to drink.

The very deep did rot: O Christ!
That ever this should be!
Yea, slimy things did crawl with legs
Upon the slimy sea.

About, about, in reel and rout
The death-fires danced at night;
The water, like a witch's oils,
Burnt green, and blue, and white.

And some in dreams assured were
Of the Spirit that plagued us so;
Nine fathom deep he had followed us
From the land of mist and snow.

And every tongue, through utter drought,
Was withered at the root;
We could not speak, no more than if
We had been choked with soot.

Ah! well-a-day! what evil looks
Had I from old and young!
Instead of the cross, the Albatross
About my neck was hung."

Part III

"There passed a weary time. Each throat
Was parched, and glazed each eye.
A weary time! a weary time!
How glazed each weary eye -
When looking westward, I beheld
A something in the sky.

At first it seemed a little speck,
And then it seemed a mist;
It moved and moved, and took at last
A certain shape, I wist.

A speck, a mist, a shape, I wist!
And still it neared and neared:
As if it dodged a water-sprite,
It plunged and tacked and veered.

With throats unslaked, with black lips baked,
We could nor laugh nor wail;
Through utter drought all dumb we stood!
I bit my arm, I sucked the blood,
And cried, A sail! a sail!

With throats unslaked, with black lips baked,
Agape they heard me call:
Gramercy! they for joy did grin,
And all at once their breath drew in,
As they were drinking all.

See! see! (I cried) she tacks no more!
Hither to work us weal;
Without a breeze, without a tide,
She steadies with upright keel!

The western wave was all a-flame,
The day was well nigh done!
Almost upon the western wave
Rested the broad bright sun;
When that strange shape drove suddenly
Betwixt us and the sun.

And straight the sun was flecked with bars,
(Heaven's Mother send us grace!)
As if through a dungeon-grate he peered
With broad and burning face.

Alas! (thought I, and my heart beat loud)
How fast she nears and nears!
Are those her sails that glance in the sun,
Like restless gossameres?

Are those her ribs through which the sun
Did peer, as through a grate?
And is that Woman all her crew?
Is that a Death? and are there two?
Is Death that Woman's mate?

Her lips were red, her looks were free,
Her locks were yellow as gold:
Her skin was as white as leprosy,
The Nightmare Life-in-Death was she,
Who thicks man's blood with cold.

The naked hulk alongside came,
And the twain were casting dice;
'The game is done! I've won! I've won!'
Quoth she, and whistles thrice.

The sun's rim dips; the stars rush out:
At one stride comes the dark;
With far-heard whisper o'er the sea,
Off shot the spectre-bark.

We listened and looked sideways up!
Fear at my heart, as at a cup,
My life-blood seemed to sip!
The stars were dim, and thick the night,
The steersman's face by his lamp gleamed white;
From the sails the dew did drip -
Till clomb above the eastern bar
The horned moon, with one bright star
Within the nether tip.

One after one, by the star-dogged moon,

Too quick for groan or sigh,
Each turned his face with a ghastly pang,
And cursed me with his eye.

Four times fifty living men,
(And I heard nor sigh nor groan)
With heavy thump, a lifeless lump,
They dropped down one by one.

The souls did from their bodies fly, -
They fled to bliss or woe!
And every soul it passed me by,
Like the whizz of my crossbow!"

Part IV

`I fear thee, ancient Mariner!
I fear thy skinny hand!
And thou art long, and lank, and brown,
As is the ribbed sea-sand.

I fear thee and thy glittering eye,
And thy skinny hand, so brown.' -
"Fear not, fear not, thou Wedding-Guest!
This body dropped not down.

Alone, alone, all, all alone,
Alone on a wide wide sea!
And never a saint took pity on
My soul in agony.

The many men, so beautiful!
And they all dead did lie;
And a thousand thousand slimy things
Lived on; and so did I.

I looked upon the rotting sea,
And drew my eyes away;

I looked upon the rotting deck,
And there the dead men lay.

I looked to heaven, and tried to pray;
But or ever a prayer had gusht,
A wicked whisper came and made
My heart as dry as dust.

I closed my lids, and kept them close,
And the balls like pulses beat;
Forthe sky and the sea, and the sea and the sky,
Lay like a load on my weary eye,
And the dead were at my feet.

The cold sweat melted from their limbs,
Nor rot nor reek did they:
The look with which they looked on me
Had never passed away.

An orphan's curse would drag to hell
A spirit from on high;
But oh! more horrible than that
Is the curse in a dead man's eye!
Seven days, seven nights, I saw that curse,
And yet I could not die.

The moving moon went up the sky,
And no where did abide:
Softly she was going up,
And a star or two beside -

Her beams bemocked the sultry main,
Like April hoar-frost spread;
But where the ship's huge shadow lay,
The charmed water burnt alway
A still and awful red.

Beyond the shadow of the ship
I watched the water-snakes:

They moved in tracks of shining white,
And when they reared, the elfish light
Fell off in hoary flakes.

Within the shadow of the ship
I watched their rich attire:
Blue, glossy green, and velvet black,
They coiled and swam; and every track
Was a flash of golden fire.

O happy living things! no tongue
Their beauty might declare:
A spring of love gushed from my heart,
And I blessed them unaware:
Sure my kind saint took pity on me,
And I blessed them unaware.

The selfsame moment I could pray;
And from my neck so free
The Albatross fell off, and sank
Like lead into the sea."

Part V

"Oh sleep! it is a gentle thing,
Beloved from pole to pole!
To Mary Queen the praise be given!
She sent the gentle sleep from heaven,
That slid into my soul.

The silly buckets on the deck,
That had so long remained,
I dreamt that they were filled with dew;
And when I awoke, it rained.

My lips were wet, my throat was cold,
My garments all were dank;
Sure I had drunken in my dreams,

And still my body drank.

I moved, and could not feel my limbs:
I was so light -almost
I thought that I had died in sleep,
And was a blessed ghost.

And soon I heard a roaring wind:
It did not come anear;
But with its sound it shook the sails,
That were so thin and sere.

The upper air burst into life!
And a hundred fire-flags sheen,
To and fro they were hurried about!
And to and fro, and in and out,
The wan stars danced between.

And the coming wind did roar more loud,
And the sails did sigh like sedge;
And the rain poured down from one black cloud;
The moon was at its edge.

The thick black cloud was cleft, and still
The moon was at its side:
Like waters shot from some high crag,
The lightning fell with never a jag,
A river steep and wide.

The loud wind never reached the ship,
Yet now the ship moved on!
Beneath the lightning and the moon
The dead men gave a groan.

They groaned, they stirred, they all uprose,
Nor spake, nor moved their eyes;
It had been strange, even in a dream,
To have seen those dead men rise.

The helmsman steered, the ship moved on;
Yet never a breeze up blew;
The mariners all 'gan work the ropes,
Where they were wont to do;
They raised their limbs like lifeless tools -
We were a ghastly crew.

The body of my brother's son
Stood by me, knee to knee:
The body and I pulled at one rope,
But he said nought to me."

`I fear thee, ancient Mariner!'
"Be calm, thou Wedding-Guest!
'Twas not those souls that fled in pain,
Which to their corses came again,
But a troop of spirits blest:

For when it dawned -they dropped their arms,
And clustered round the mast;
Sweet sounds rose slowly through their mouths,
And from their bodies passed.

Around, around, flew each sweet sound,
Then darted to the sun;
Slowly the sounds came back again,
Now mixed, now one by one.

Sometimes a-dropping from the sky
I heard the skylark sing;
Sometimes all little birds that are,
How they seemed to fill the sea and air
With their sweet jargoning!

And now 'twas like all instruments,
Now like a lonely flute;
And now it is an angel's song,
That makes the heavens be mute.

It ceased; yet still the sails made on
A pleasant noise till noon,
A noise like of a hidden brook
In the leafy month of June,
That to the sleeping woods all night
Singeth a quiet tune.

Till noon we quietly sailed on,
Yet never a breeze did breathe;
Slowly and smoothly went the ship,
Moved onward from beneath.

Under the keel nine fathom deep,
From the land of mist and snow,
The spirit slid: and it was he
That made the ship to go.
The sails at noon left off their tune,
And the ship stood still also.

The sun, right up above the mast,
Had fixed her to the ocean:
But in a minute she 'gan stir,
With a short uneasy motion -
Backwards and forwards half her length
With a short uneasy motion.

Then like a pawing horse let go,
She made a sudden bound:
It flung the blood into my head,
And I fell down in a swound.

How long in that same fit I lay,
I have not to declare;
But ere my living life returned,
I heard and in my soul discerned
Two voices in the air.

`Is it he?' quoth one, `Is this the man?
By him who died on cross,

With his cruel bow he laid full low
The harmless Albatross.

The spirit who bideth by himself
In the land of mist and snow,
He loved the bird that loved the man
Who shot him with his bow.'

The other was a softer voice,
As soft as honey-dew:
Quoth he, `The man hath penance done,
And penance more will do.'

Part VI

First Voice

But tell me, tell me! speak again,
Thy soft response renewing -
What makes that ship drive on so fast?
What is the ocean doing?

Second Voice

Still as a slave before his lord,
The ocean hath no blast;
His great bright eye most silently
Up to the moon is cast -

If he may know which way to go;
For she guides him smooth or grim.
See, brother, see! how graciously
She looketh down on him.

First Voice

But why drives on that ship so fast,
Without or wave or wind?

Second Voice

The air is cut away before,
And closes from behind.

Fly, brother, fly! more high, more high!
Or we shall be belated:
For slow and slow that ship will go,
When the Mariner's trance is abated.

"I woke, and we were sailing on
As in a gentle weather:
'Twas night, calm night, the moon was high;
The dead men stood together.

All stood together on the deck,
For a charnel-dungeon fitter:
All fixed on me their stony eyes,
That in the moon did glitter.

The pang, the curse, with which they died,
Had never passed away:
I could not draw my eyes from theirs,
Nor turn them up to pray.

And now this spell was snapped: once more
I viewed the ocean green,
And looked far forth, yet little saw
Of what had else been seen -

Like one that on a lonesome road
Doth walk in fear and dread,
And having once turned round walks on,
And turns no more his head;
Because he knows a frightful fiend
Doth close behind him tread.

But soon there breathed a wind on me,

Nor sound nor motion made:
Its path was not upon the sea,
In ripple or in shade.

It raised my hair, it fanned my cheek
Like a meadow-gale of spring -
It mingled strangely with my fears,
Yet it felt like a welcoming.

Swiftly, swiftly flew the ship,
Yet she sailed softly too:
Sweetly, sweetly blew the breeze -
On me alone it blew.

Oh! dream of joy! is this indeed
The lighthouse top I see?
Is this the hill? is this the kirk?
Is this mine own country?

We drifted o'er the harbour-bar,
And I with sobs did pray -
O let me be awake, my God!
Or let me sleep alway.

The harbour-bay was clear as glass,
So smoothly it was strewn!
And on the bay the moonlight lay,
And the shadow of the moon.

The rock shone bright, the kirk no less,
That stands above the rock:
The moonlight steeped in silentness
The steady weathercock.

And the bay was white with silent light,
Till rising from the same,
Full many shapes, that shadows were,
In crimson colours came.

A little distance from the prow
Those crimson shadows were:
I turned my eyes upon the deck -
Oh, Christ! what saw I there!

Each corse lay flat, lifeless and flat,
And, by the holy rood!
A man all light, a seraph-man,
On every corse there stood.

This seraph-band, each waved his hand:
It was a heavenly sight!
They stood as signals to the land,
Each one a lovely light;

This seraph-band, each waved his hand,
No voice did they impart -
No voice; but oh! the silence sank
Like music on my heart.

But soon I heard the dash of oars,
I heard the Pilot's cheer;
My head was turned perforce away,
And I saw a boat appear.

The Pilot and the Pilot's boy,
I heard them coming fast:
Dear Lord in heaven! it was a joy
The dead men could not blast.

I saw a third -I heard his voice:
It is the Hermit good!
He singeth loud his godly hymns
That he makes in the wood.
He'll shrieve my soul, he'll wash away
The Albatross's blood."

Part VII

"This Hermit good lives in that wood
Which slopes down to the sea.
How loudly his sweet voice he rears!
He loves to talk with marineers
That come from a far country.

He kneels at morn, and noon, and eve -
He hath a cushion plump:
It is the moss that wholly hides
The rotted old oak-stump.

The skiff-boat neared: I heard them talk,
`Why, this is strange, I trow!
Where are those lights so many and fair,
That signal made but now?'

`Strange, by my faith!' the Hermit said -
`And they answered not our cheer!
The planks looked warped! and see those sails,
How thin they are and sere!
I never saw aught like to them,
Unless perchance it were

Brown skeletons of leaves that lag
My forest-brook along;
When the ivy-tod is heavy with snow,
And the owlet whoops to the wolf below,
That eats the she-wolf's young.'

`Dear Lord! it hath a fiendish look -
(The Pilot made reply)
I am afeared' -`Push on, push on!'
Said the Hermit cheerily.

The boat came closer to the ship,
But I nor spake nor stirred;
The boat came close beneath the ship,
And straight a sound was heard.

Under the water it rumbled on,
Still louder and more dread:
It reached the ship, it split the bay;
The ship went down like lead.

Stunned by that loud and dreadful sound,
Which sky and ocean smote,
Like one that hath been seven days drowned
My body lay afloat;
But swift as dreams, myself I found
Within the Pilot's boat.

Upon the whirl where sank the ship
The boat spun round and round;
And all was still, save that the hill
Was telling of the sound.

I moved my lips -the Pilot shrieked
And fell down in a fit;
The holy Hermit raised his eyes,
And prayed where he did sit.

I took the oars: the Pilot's boy,
Who now doth crazy go,
Laughed loud and long, and all the while
His eyes went to and fro.
'Ha! ha!' quoth he, 'full plain I see,
The Devil knows how to row.'

And now, all in my own country,
I stood on the firm land!
The Hermit stepped forth from the boat,
And scarcely he could stand.

O shrieve me, shrieve me, holy man!
The Hermit crossed his brow.
'Say quick,' quoth he 'I bid thee say -
What manner of man art thou?'

Forthwith this frame of mine was wrenched
With a woeful agony,
Which forced me to begin my tale;
And then it left me free.

Since then, at an uncertain hour,
That agony returns;
And till my ghastly tale is told,
This heart within me burns.

I pass, like night, from land to land;
I have strange power of speech;
That moment that his face I see,
I know the man that must hear me:
To him my tale I teach.

What loud uproar bursts from that door!
The wedding-guests are there:
But in the garden-bower the bride
And bride-maids singing are;
And hark the little vesper bell,
Which biddeth me to prayer!

O Wedding-Guest! this soul hath been
Alone on a wide wide sea:
So lonely 'twas, that God himself
Scarce seemed there to be.

O sweeter than the marriage-feast,
'Tis sweeter far to me,
To walk together to the kirk
With a goodly company! -

To walk together to the kirk,
And all together pray,
While each to his great Father bends,
Old men, and babes, and loving friends,
And youths and maidens gay!

Farewell, farewell! but this I tell
To thee, thou Wedding-Guest!
He prayeth well, who loveth well
Both man and bird and beast.

He prayeth best, who loveth best
All things both great and small;
For the dear God who loveth us,
He made and loveth all."

The Mariner, whose eye is bright,
Whose beard with age is hoar,
Is gone; and now the Wedding-Guest
Turned from the bridegroom's door.

He went like one that hath been stunned,
And is of sense forlorn:
A sadder and a wiser man
He rose the morrow morn.

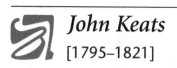
John Keats
[1795–1821]

JOHN KEATS'S *father kept a London livery stable—not a very auspicious beginning for the Romantic poet of the sublimely beautiful. His father died when he was nine, and when he was fifteen, he lost his mother to tuberculosis. His brother died of the same disease a few years later, and it took Keats, too, at age twenty-six. Tuberculosis was common in the early 1800s, and was especially prevelant among those who lived in London's smoggy interior. Despite these challenges, and his early death, Keats produced a large volume of memorable poetry.*

He attended school at Enfield, but in 1810 was apprenticed to a surgeon. The medical profession did not have the status that it has today, and this change was not a social improvement for the young Keats. Despite his removal from school, he read and fell in love with Edmund Spenser's Faerie Queen, *and even as he finished his apprenticeship and began work in a London hospital, his heart and imagination were with Spenser's world of elves and knights. He met all the Romantic writers, including Percy Byssche Shelley and Samuel Taylor Coleridge, and became friends with Leigh Hunt, editor of* The Examiner, *which published some of his early sonnets. Keats dedicated his first volume of poems to Hunt in 1817. His first long poem,* Endymion, *appeared in 1818, but his friendship with Hunt, who was on the outs with the London critics, drew criticism of the poem. Keats was hurt, but continued to write, despite Shelley's later argument in* Adonais *that the critics had killed Keats with their reviews. At the same time he fell hopelessly in love with Fanny Brawne, whose social position would not allow her to marry a stable-boy-turned-physician, whatever poetic talents he possessed. These losses seemed to fuel his poetic passion. In 1819, he published* The Eve of St. Agnes, *arguably the signature poem of the sensuous and fanciful wing of the Romantic movement. This poem tells the story of a young knight who brings beautiful food to his lady's chamber, and appears to her as if in a dream to persuade her to run away with him, which she does. His next two poems,* La Belle Dame sans Merci (The Beautiful Woman Without Mercy), *a poem about a witch, and* Lamia, *a poem about a woman who can become a snake, followed in 1820.* Isabella, *or* The Pot of Basil, *followed, a tale taken from Boccaccio's* Decameron *about a woman who plants her unfaithful lover's head in a pot of herbs. His last poem, the unfinished* Hyperion, *recounts a classical myth, and throughout the last years of his life, he wrote the sonnets that have become the jewels of the Romantic movement.*

La Belle Dame sans Merci. A Ballad

JOHN KEATS

The Beautiful Woman without Mercy

I

O what can ail thee, knight-at-arms,
    Alone and palely loitering?
The sedge has withered from the lake,
    And no birds sing.

II

O what can ail thee, knight-at-arms,   *5*
    So haggard and so woe-begone?
The squirrel's granary is full,
    And the harvest's done.

III

I see a lily on thy brow
    With anguish moist and fever-dew,   *10*
And on thy cheeks a fading rose
    Fast withereth too.

IV

I met a lady in the meads,
    Full beautiful—a faery's child,
Her hair was long, her foot was light,   *15*
    And her eyes were wild.

Composed in 1819 and first published in *Lamia, Isabella, The Eve of St. Agnes, and Other Poems* in 1820.

V

I made a garland for her head,
    And bracelets too, and fragrant zone;
She looked at me as she did love,
    And made sweet moan.   *20*

VI

I set her on my pacing steed,
    And nothing else saw all day long,
For sidelong would she bend, and sing
    A faery's song.

VII

She found me roots of relish sweet,   *25*
    And honey wild, and manna-dew,
And sure in language strange she said—
    'I love thee true'.

VIII

She took me to her elfin grot,
    And there she wept and sighed full sore,   *30*
And there I shut her wild wild eyes
    With kisses four.

IX

And there she lullèd me asleep
    And there I dreamed—Ah! woe betide!—
The latest dream I ever dreamt   *35*
    On the cold hill side.

X

I saw pale kings and princes too,
    Pale warriors, death-pale were they all;
They cried—'La Belle Dame sans Merci
    Thee hath in thrall!'   *40*

XI

I saw their starved lips in the gloam,
    With horrid warning gapèd wide,
And I awoke and found me here,
    On the cold hill's side.

XII

And this is why I sojourn here   *45*
    Alone and palely loitering,
Though the sedge is withered from the lake,
    And no birds sing.

[1819]

QUESTIONS

JOHN KEATS, *La Belle Dame sans Merci*. A Ballad

1. This poem tells of a medieval knight wandering in a barren field, where he meets a beautiful woman. What happens to him next? What does she give him? Where do they go?

2. What do the speakers in the knight's dream tell him? What happens when he wakes up? How does he feel?

3. This poem is more about feeling than about reason. What effect is the poem meant to have? Why do we sometimes like to feel wistful and nostalgic?

4. The story of the seductress who appears and leads young men off to her fairy den is an old one. What is the appeal this creature? What part of the inner psyche does she symbolize?

5. Ballads are sure to have unhappy endings, and this one is no exception. How does the ballad form tell the reader from the beginning that things are not going to turn out well? What would happen if you sang this ballad? Would it be more powerful?

6. The first and last verses are almost the same. How does this complete the song? How does it also tell the listener that this is not a singular event, and that this story has happened over and over again?

7. Think about an experience you've had meeting someone who was appealing but not very good for you. What is appealing about dangerous people? Write about your experience, and analyze your response.

8. The world of knights and adventures exists in the psyches of all Westerners. These images appear in modern cinema, and in video and computer games. Write about the influence of the world of kings and knights on the world we know today.